THE POWER OF TWO LANGUAGES

Literacy and Biliteracy for Spanish-Speaking Students

Josefina Villamil Tinajero and Alma Flor Ada, Editors

Macmillan/McGraw-Hill School Publishing Company
New York   Columbus

This book complements the Macmillan/McGraw-Hill Spanish and English Reading/Language Arts Programs, CUENTAMUNDOS and A NEW VIEW.

THIS BOOK IS DEDICATED TO

Howard Goodkin, for his sensitivity to the needs of students acquiring English, their parents, and teachers, and his commitment to the development of quality instructional materials.

My family: my husband, Roberto José, my daughters Gloria and Ana, and my sons Bert and Pat. With love for their understanding and support of everything that I do. *Josie V. Tinajero*

Jørgen, gratefully, for your understanding and support. *Alma Flor Ada*

ACKNOWLEDGEMENTS

The publisher gratefully acknowledges permission to reprint the following copyrighted material:

"Effective Transitioning Strategies: Are We Asking the Right Questions?" by Lilia Bartolomé reprinted from *Cultural Diversity and Second Language Learning* by B. MacLeod, ed. by permission of the State University of New York Press. © SUNY Press.

SCRAWLS (cartoon) reprinted by permission of NEA, Inc.

"We Speak in Many Tongues: Language Diversity and Multicultural Education" an article by Sonia Nieto from the book *Multicultural Education in the Twenty-First Century* edited by Carlos Díaz. Copyright © 1992, National Education Association. Reprinted by permission.

Cover Design: MKR Design, Inc.

Copyright © 1993 Macmillan/McGraw-Hill School Publishing Company

All rights reserved. No part of this book may be reproduced or transmitted in any form or by any means, electronic or mechanical, including photocopying, recording, or by any information storage and retrieval system, without permission in writing from the publisher.

Macmillan/McGraw-Hill School Division
10 Union Square East
New York, New York 10003

Printed in the United States of America
ISBN 0-02-178132-X
1 2 3 4 5 6 7 8 9 MAZ 99 98 97 96 95 94 93 92

Contents

INTRODUCTION 5

Part I: BILITERACY: A TRANSFORMATIVE PEDAGOGY

Empowerment through Biliteracy 9
  Jim Cummins

Literacy Instruction through Spanish:
Linguistic, Cultural, and Pedagogical Considerations 26
  Elly B. Pardo and Josefina Villamil Tinajero

We Speak in Many Tongues:
Language Diversity and Multicultural Education 37
  Sonia Nieto

Becoming Critical: Rethinking Literacy, Language, and Teaching ... 49
  Catherine E. Walsh

Making Our Whole-Language Bilingual Classrooms Also Liberatory ... 58
  Mary S. Poplin

Part II: DEVELOPING LITERACY

Listening to Children's Voices:
Opening the Door Through Fairy Tales 71
  Barbara Dube Moreno

Second Language Literacy and Immigrant Children:
The Inner World of the Immigrant Child 84
  Cristina Igoa

Cultural Integration of Children's Literature 100
  Elba Maldonado-Colón

Contemporary Trends in Children's Literature Written in
Spanish in Spain and Latin America 107
  Alma Flor Ada

Strategies for Working with Overage Students 117
  Carol Moran, Judy Stobbe, Josefina Villamil Tinajero, Ignacio Tinajero

Innovative Assessment in Traditional Settings 132
  JoAnn Canales

Part III: CREATING A CULTURE OF READING

Reading Begins in the Crib 145
    Eleanor Thonis

Teaching Language and Literacy in the Context of
Family and Community 152
    Ana Huerta-Macías and Elizabeth Quintero

Mother-Tongue Literacy as a Bridge Between
Home and School Cultures 158
    Alma Flor Ada

Helping Students Find Their Voice in Nonfiction Writing:
Team-Teaching Partnerships Between Distant Classes 164
    Dennis Sayers

Balancing the Tools of Technology with Our Own Humanity:
The Use of Technology in Building Partnerships and Communities 178
    Kristin Brown

The Principal's Role in Promoting Bilingual Literacy 199
    María Luisa González, Cynthia Risner-Schiller, and Elba-María Stell

Part IV: PROMOTING BILITERACY

Effective Transitioning Strategies:
Are We Asking the Right Questions? 209
    Lilia I. Bartolomé

Promoting Biliteracy:
Issues in Promoting English Literacy in Students Acquiring English ... 220
    Kathy Escamilla

Biliteracy From the Students' Points of View 234
    Toni Griego Jones

Cooperative Learning Strategies: Bilingual Classroom Applications ... 241
    Josefina Villamil Tinajero, Margarita E. Calderón, and Rachel Hertz-Lazarowitz

Enhancing the Skills of Emergent Writers Acquiring English 254
    Josefina Villamil Tinajero and Ana Huerta-Macías

Content Area Instruction for Students Acquiring English 264
    Carrol Moran

Developing Biliteracy in a Two-Way Immersion Program 276
    Jennifer Martinez and Julie A. Moore-O'Brien

Supporting and Encouraging Diversity: Literacy Learning for All ... 294
    Diane Lapp, James Flood, and Nancy Farnan

Introduction

The Power of Two Languages: Literacy and Biliteracy for Spanish-Speaking Students is written for and dedicated to all bilingual teachers and supervisors. We hope that the book will serve as a valuable resource in helping bilingual teachers build more meaningful learning experiences for their Spanish-speaking students. The defining theme of the readings, literacy and biliteracy for Spanish-speaking children, establishes the framework for the volume and integrates various papers, which are organized into four major sections: transformative pedagogy, developing literacy, creating a culture of reading, and instructional strategies for the development of biliteracy.

The first section of the book, Biliteracy: A Transformative Pedagogy, comprises a group of articles exploring literacy instruction. Linguistic, cultural, and pedagogical considerations of literacy instruction through Spanish and the constructs of transformative education are explored. Jim Cummins discusses the concept of empowerment through biliteracy and Mary Poplin examines how a whole-language classroom can become truly transformative.

The second section in the book, Developing Literacy, provides concrete children's literacy-learning experiences in which teachers have carefully listened to the voices of children.

Barbara Moreno discusses the depth of reflections of her second grade students as they learn to read through fairy tales. Cristina Igoa shares with us stories that only the children themselves could tell to point out how the inner world of the immigrant affects literacy.

The third section of this volume focuses on creating a culture of reading, in and out of school. Ana Huerta-Macías and Elizabeth Quintero recognize the importance of promoting literacy within the context of home and community. Dennis Sayers, one of the originators of Project ORILLAS, explores team-teaching partnerships that link classrooms located in the U.S. and abroad and provide opportunities for students to create and manipulate texts through technology. Kristin Brown, co-founder of ORILLAS, discusses how to create a balance between classroom technology and humanness.

Literacy is a powerful tool. Biliteracy can be twice as powerful. The last section of the book, Promoting Biliteracy, further explores the power of two languages and the techniques that can best support biliteracy. Authors featured in this section recognize that it is desirable for each child to achieve competence in the language of the society at large. Nonetheless, these authors argue that it is also an inalienable right for each child to retain his or her mother tongue, which will facilitate communication within the home and family.

In this last section, Jennifer Martínez and Julie Moore-O'Brien draw on their experience as initiators and developers of one of the most successful two-way bilingual immersion projects. Lilia Bartolomé invites the reader to reflect on whether we are asking the right questions to promote truly effective instruction. Toni Griego Jones makes us aware that literacy instruction must be grounded in a student's perspective if youngsters are to reap the full benefit of their classroom learning experiences.

In particular, we intend for this book to help teachers develop a broader knowledge base about the advantages of native language instruction in promoting full Spanish/English bilingualism and biliteracy. We also intend for teachers to share the contents of this book with their principals and supervisors as it is a useful reference for those who want to become better informed about bilingual education, its theory and practice. And most important, we hope that this book will help all who read it to reflect upon their vocations, as it did for one bilingual teacher in the El Paso area, Mr. Ignacio Tinajero, who wrote the following words to a song:

I Want to Make a Difference

I want to make a difference,
A difference in the life, a difference in the life of a child.
For I must remember what most of us forget,
That someone in our paths touched our lives.

When they come to me,
I must always see beyond the limits of my sight.
I must see a life and reach out with my heart,
In helping them become the most that they can be.

Helping them to reach a level of success
Is but one little part of my dream.
Helping them to be as happy as they can be,
To help the world become a place of peace and harmony.

Once I help them see, the beauty in their hearts
Their intellects will start to glow; and as they grow to be
Full of love and maturity, then and only then,
Will I have done my part.

It's difficult you say, for there is just no way
For me to make a dent in their lives.
You must remember when that someone in your path,
Shared their life with you
And made a difference in your life.

Josefina Villamil Tinajero and Alma Flor Ada

Part I

BILITERACY:
A TRANSFORMATIVE
PEDAGOGY

BILITERACY: A TRANSFORMATIVE PEDAGOGY

EMPOWERMENT through BILITERACY

Jim Cummins
*Ontario Institute for Studies in Education
Ontario, Canada*

For more than 15 years, educators, policymakers, and researchers in the United States have known how to create educational contexts that will develop fluent bilingual and biliteracy abilities among *all* American students, including those from both bilingual and monolingual English home backgrounds (see, for example, Lindholm & Aclan, 1991). However, only a tiny fraction of American schools even aspire to promote biliteracy. Most, in fact, are deliberately structured to minimize the possibility of biliteracy even among students who come to school already bilingual. Schools continue the tradition of eradicating students' bilingualism under the guise of helping them learn English.

For most educators it is not possible even to think of biliteracy as an educational option in view of the fact that schools appear to face an increasingly uphill battle in their efforts to develop literacy in just one language. Since the publication in 1983 of *A Nation at Risk* (National Commission on Excellence in Education, 1983), politicians and media commentators have regularly linked the declining international competitiveness of American industry with the failure of the educational system to deliver an adequate "product" to industry and business. There is a widespread perception that educational standards have been in decline for a number of years and, as a result, American business interests are placed in jeopardy in an increasingly competitive world economy. As expressed by *A Nation at Risk*: "Our once unchallenged preeminence in commerce, industry, science and technological innovations is being overtaken by competitors throughout the world" (1983, p. 1). In view of the documented low levels of "functional literacy" among the Latino/Latina population (e.g., Kirsch & Jungeblut, 1986) and their disproportionately high educational drop-out rates, development of adequate levels of literacy in English seems like a formidable task, let alone literacy in both English and Spanish.

The national concern about "functional illiteracy" and low levels of educational achievement has given rise to major efforts at school reform in most U.S. states. However, despite the fact that so-called "minorities" are strongly overrepresented among the low-achieving students, few of the prescriptions for school reform specifically address the causes of educational failure among such students (see, for example, Stedman, 1987). Even fewer contemplate bilingualism and biliteracy as part of the solution rather than as part of the problem.

I argue in this paper that biliteracy must become an essential component of educational reform efforts directed at underachieving Latino/Latina students. However, literacy or even biliteracy are insufficient as educational goals if they remain at the level of "functional literacy." The educational goals, and pedagogical processes to achieve those goals, must expand to include both *cultural* and *critical* literacies in addition to functional literacy. In other words, students must learn not only to "read the word" but also to "read the world" (Freire & Macedo, 1987). I argue that the public focus and apparent political commitment to improving the ability of students (and adults) to "read the word" represents a facade that obscures an underlying societal structure dedicated to preventing students from "reading the world." This reality implies that educators who strive to create educational contexts within which culturally diverse students develop a sense of empowerment, through acquisition of cultural and critical literacy, are of necessity challenging the societal power structure. By "power structure" I am referring to the division of status and resources in the society and also to the propaganda apparatus designed, in Chomsky's (1987) terms, to "manufacture consent." This propaganda apparatus is very much in evidence in the debate about bilingual education (Baker, 1992).

A further distinction relating to the societal power structure is useful to make at this point. Throughout the paper I distinguish between *coercive* and *collaborative* relations of power. Coercive relations of power refer to the exercise of power by a dominant group (or individual) to the detriment of a subordinated group (or individual). The assumption is that there is a fixed quantity of power that operates according to a balance effect; in other words, the more power one group has the less is left for other groups. Coercive relations of power have constituted the predominant mode of intergroup contact since the beginnings of human history at the level of both international and domestic relations.

Collaborative relations of power, on the other hand, operate on the assumption that power is not a fixed predetermined quantity but rather can be *generated* in interpersonal and intergroup relations, thereby becoming "additive" rather than "subtractive." In other words, participants are *empowered* through collaboration so that each is more affirmed in her or his identity and has a greater sense of efficacy to change her or his life or social situation. Thus, power is created in the relationship and shared among participants. In educational contexts, cooperative learning activities and sister class networks are documented examples of the academic and personal benefits that accrue when coercive relations of power shift to collaborative relations of power (e.g. DeVillar & Faltis, 1991; Sayers, 1991).

A fundamental argument of the present chapter is that the root causes of academic failure among subordinated group students are to be found in the fact that the interactions between educators and students reflect and reinforce the broader societal pattern of coercive relations of power between dominant and subordinated groups. Reversal of this pattern requires that educators resist and challenge the operation of coercive relations of power and actively seek to establish collaborative relations of power both in the school and in the broader society.

The next section focuses on the issue of biliteracy and examines the public debate on bilingual education in light of the research data, particularly the recent large-scale study of different program options carried out by Ramírez, Pasta, Yuen, Billings, and Ramey (1991). The goal is to demonstrate that biliteracy is a feasible educational outcome for all students and what requires explanation is the public discourse that vehemently denies this reality. I then shift from a focus on "biliteracy" to the broader issue of literacy itself. I suggest that not only are schools dedicated to reducing bilinguals to monolinguals, they are also structured to constrict the possibilities for students' identity formation and to control the scope of their ability to think, or in Freire's terms, to read the world. Finally, drawing on Ada's (1988a, 1988b) work, I suggest an alternative pedagogical orientation designed to promote critical biliteracy and student empowerment.

The Public Debate on Bilingual Education

THEORY UNDERLYING OPPOSITION TO BILINGUAL EDUCATION

Opponents of bilingual education have consistently attempted to attribute the low literacy levels of the Latino/Latina population, and their consequent low social mobility, to the attempts by "activist" educators to educate students in Spanish rather than in English (e.g., Chavez, 1991; Dunn, 1987; Porter, 1990). Bilingual education is thus seen as contributing not only to the impoverishment of Spanish speakers but also to the economic difficulties of the nation as a whole. Linda Chavez (1991) has presented a succinct account of this line of reasoning:

> Unlike previous groups of immigrants who were encouraged to learn English quickly, Hispanics today are officially urged to hold on to their native

BILITERACY: A TRANSFORMATIVE PEDAGOGY

language and culture. Public schools, which once stressed assimilation, now preach ethnic diversity. Nationally, about two-thirds of first-grade students from Spanish-speaking homes are taught to read in Spanish, and three-quarters are taught grammar and vocabulary in Spanish as well. Some students spend as little as 20 or 30 minutes a day being given English-language instruction while the rest of their lessons are taught in Spanish. In some school districts, Hispanic students spend from three to six years in bilingual programs....

Despite this dramatic change in school curricula, there is little evidence that Hispanic students are benefitting academically from being taught in Spanish. Even the most optimistic appraisals of bilingual programs show that Spanish-speaking students who are taught in Spanish are no more likely to keep up in math or social studies than similar children who are put into intensive English programs in which all their lessons are taught in English. Overall, Hispanics still lag significantly behind other students in academic achievement....

Like many social programs, bilingual education benefits primarily those who provide the services. Bilingual educators, unlike the clients they serve, are well educated, well organized, and politically effective. For more than 25 years, they have dominated public-policy debates on this issue, produced self-serving research and intimidated their opponents into silence....

Those who think they can ignore the problem had better begin looking at the nation's changing demographics. The Hispanic population is already growing at a rate five times as great as the rest of the population. Hispanics now make up more than 10% of school children, and their proportion is likely to increase dramatically in the next few decades. Today's Hispanic students will be tomorrow's workers. We simply cannot afford to have millions of such persons ill-prepared to function in the language of this nation. (p. 11A)

Chavez here presents a distorted picture of the proportion of time that Latino/Latina students are instructed in Spanish (studies suggest that only between 10 percent and 25 percent of instruction in the early grades is typically presented in students' primary language [L1] [Tikunoff, 1983; Wong Fillmore & Valadez, 1986]). She also ignores the large-scale Ramírez report (considered below) released about a year prior to her article that points to superior academic prospects for students who received the most intensive and sustained Spanish instruction throughout elementary school. This report clearly refutes her implication that intensive English programs result in better English academic performance than bilingual programs that instruct students in both Spanish and English. Also, to claim that bilingual education advocates have dominated public-policy debates ignores that fact that the vast majority of media articles on the topic have been strongly opposed to bilingual education (Cummins, 1981a).

In short, Chavez's account can only be described as a deliberately dishonest piece of propaganda (see Baker, 1992) designed to raise the alarm not only in regard to the growth of the Latino/Latina population but, more importantly, about the possibility that they might be less subject to control through the educational process if they are taught in Spanish rather than in English.

Other opponents of bilingual education (e.g., Imhoff, 1990; Porter, 1990) have provided more detail in regard to the theoretical basis of their opposition. Three major propositions, which are in principle testable, will be highlighted:

a. the claim that "time on task" is the major variable underlying language learning and hence immersion in English is the most effective means to ensure the learning of English;

b. the claim that under these conditions of immersion, language minority students will quickly (within 1–2 years) pick up sufficient English to survive academically without further special support; and

c. the claim that English immersion should start as early as possible in the student's school career since younger children are better language learners than older children.

Rosalie Pedalino Porter (1990) clearly articulates the first and third principles in stating:

> My personal experience and professional investigations together impel me to conclude that the two overriding conditions that promote the best learning of a second language are (1) starting at an early age, say at five, and (2) having as much exposure and carefully planned instruction in the language as possible. Effective time on task—the amount of time spent learning—is, as educators know, the single greatest predictor of educational achievement; this is at least as true, if not more so, for

low-socioeconomic-level, limited-English students. Children learn what they are taught, and if they are taught mainly in Spanish for several years, their Spanish-language skills will be far better than their English-language ones. (pp. 63–64)

Nathan Glazer (Glazer & Cummins, 1985) has articulated the second principle as follows:

> All our experience shows that the most extended and steady exposure to the spoken language is the best way of learning any language.... How long? It depends. But one year of intensive immersion seems to be enough to permit most children to transfer to [regular] English-language classes. (p. 48)

Many other examples of these positions could be cited based on both academic and media commentary (see Cummins, 1989). The opposition claims are in direct contrast to those made by academic advocates of bilingual education, as outlined below.

THEORY PROPOSED BY BILINGUAL EDUCATION ADVOCATES

It is important to highlight that most bilingual education theorists have distanced themselves from the popular conception of the rationale for bilingual programs, namely the "linguistic mismatch" hypothesis. This position suggests that a home-school language switch (or linguistic mismatch) inevitably leads to academic difficulties since children cannot learn through a language they do not understand. While this claim has been persuasive to many policymakers and educators (and underlies the quick-exit transitional focus of most U.S. bilingual education), it is seriously flawed.

Academic advocates of bilingual education have consistently rejected compensatory (or transitional) bilingual programs and argued for enrichment (or two-way) bilingual programs that promote biliteracy for both minority and majority language children (e.g., Fishman, 1976; Lambert, 1975; Swain, 1979). Three central psychoeducational principles, supported by empirical research, underlie this emphasis on enrichment or late-exit bilingual education:

a. continued development of both languages enhances children's educational and cognitive development (see Cummins, 1989; Lindholm & Zierlein, 1991);

b. literacy-related abilities are interdependent across languages such that knowledge and skills acquired in one language are potentially available in the other (Cummins, 1991; Verhoeven, 1991);

c. while conversational abilities may be acquired fairly rapidly in a second language, upwards of five years are usually required for second language learners to attain grade norms in academically-related aspects of the second language (Collier, 1987; Cummins, 1981b).

Together, these principles suggest that reinforcing children's conceptual base in their first language throughout elementary school (and beyond) will provide a foundation for long-term growth in English academic skills. The theory also suggests that we should not expect bilingual children to approach grade norms in English academic skills before the later grades of elementary school.

The extent to which the alternative positions on bilingual education are consistent with the findings of the Ramírez report (Ramírez, Pasta, Yuen et al., 1991) are considered in the next section.

CONSISTENCY OF ALTERNATIVE POSITIONS WITH THE FINDINGS OF THE RAMIREZ REPORT

The Ramírez study compared the academic progress of several thousand Latino/Latina elementary school children in three program types in different parts of the United States:

a. English "immersion," involving almost exclusive use of English throughout elementary school;

b. early-exit bilingual in which Spanish was used for about one-third of the time in kindergarten and first grade with a rapid phase-out thereafter; and

c. late-exit bilingual that used primarily Spanish instruction in kindergarten, with English used for about one-third of the time in grades 1 and 2, half the time in grade 3, and about 60 percent of the time thereafter.

One of the three late-exit programs in the study (site G) was an exception to this pattern in that students were abruptly transitioned into primarily English instruction at the end of grade 2. In other words, this "late-exit" program was similar in its implementation to early-exit. Students in the "immersion" and early-exit programs were followed from kindergarten through grade 3 while those in the late-exit program were followed in two cohorts (K–3 and 3–6).

BILITERACY: A TRANSFORMATIVE PEDAGOGY

It was possible to directly compare the progress of children in the English immersion and early-exit bilingual programs but only indirect comparisons were possible between these programs and the late-exit program because these latter programs were offered in different districts and schools from the former. The comparison of immersion and early-exit programs showed that by grade 3 students were performing at comparable levels in English language and reading skills as well as in mathematics. Students in each of these program types progress academically at about the same rate as students in the general population but the gap between their performance and that of the general population remains large. In other words, they tend not to fall further behind academically between first grade and third grade but neither do they bridge the gap in any significant way.

Contrary to the expectations of many policymakers, students in the "immersion strategy" program did not exit the program more quickly than students in the early-exit program. This suggests that immersion strategy programs are likely to be comparable in cost to bilingual programs.

While these results do not demonstrate the superiority of early-exit bilingual over English immersion, they clearly do refute the argument that there is a direct relation between the amount of time spent through English instruction and academic development in English. If the "time-on-task" notion were valid, the early-exit bilingual students should have performed at a considerably lower level than the English immersion students, which they did not.

The "time-on-task" notion suffers even further indignity from the late-exit bilingual program results. In contrast to students in the immersion and early-exit programs, the late-exit students in the two sites that continued primary language instruction for at least 40 percent of the time were catching up academically to students in the general population. This is despite the fact that these students received considerably less instruction in English than students in early-exit and immersion programs and proportionately more of their families came from the lowest income levels than was the case for students in the other two programs.

Differences were observed among the three late-exit sites with respect to mathematics, English language (i.e., skills such as punctuation, capitalization, etc.) and English reading; specifically, according to the report:

> As in mathematics and English language, it seems that those students in site E, who received the strongest opportunity to develop their primary language skills, realized a growth in their English reading skills that was greater than that of the norming population used in this study. If sustained, in time these students would be expected to catch up and approximate the average achievement level of this norming population. (Ramírez, Yuen & Ramey, 1991, p. 35)

By contrast, students in site G who were abruptly transitioned into almost all-English instruction in the early grades (in a similar fashion to early-exit students) seemed to lose ground in relation to the general population between grades 3 and 6 in mathematics, English language, and reading.

The report concludes that

> students who were provided with a substantial and consistent primary language development program learned mathematics, English language, and English reading skills as fast or faster than the norming population used in this study. As their growth in these academic skills is atypical of disadvantaged youth, it provides support for the efficacy of primary language development in facilitating the acquisition of English language skills. (p. 36)

These findings are entirely consistent with the results of other enrichment and two-way bilingual programs (e.g., Lindholm & Aclan, 1991) and show clearly that there is no direct relationship between the instructional time spent through the medium of a majority language and academic achievement in that language. If anything, the bulk of the evidence suggests an inverse relation between exposure to English instruction and English achievement for Latino/Latina students in the United States.

The Ramírez report data directly refute the three theoretical positions upon which the opposition to bilingual education is based. First, if the "task" is conceived as exposure to English, then there is an inverse relation between "time on task" and English academic development; second, students immersed in English do not pick up sufficient English to transfer to a regular program any more rapidly than those in bilingual programs; and third, early intensive exposure to English appears to be less effective than a more gradual introduction to English academic skills while students' L1 conceptual base and cultural identity are being reinforced.

By contrast, the data are consistent with the theoretical positions advocated by supporters of enrichment bilingual education. First, the emerging bilingualism and biliteracy of the late exit students is clearly not impeding their English academic development in any way; on the contrary, since these students appear to have the best academic prospects in English there may be some enhancement of language processing abilities, as suggested in other research; second, operation of the interdependence or academic transfer principle is evident in the fact that less time through the medium of English appears to result in more academic prospects in English; and third, consistent with the data suggesting that upwards of five years is required for language minority students to approach grade norms in English language arts, students in the late-exit bilingual programs only begin to close the gap between themselves and the norming group in the later grades of elementary school.

In summary, it is clear that programs that attempt to develop biliteracy through sustained L1 instruction throughout elementary school have better prospects for reversing the pattern of school failure for culturally-diverse students than programs that focus only on development of English literacy (see Crawford, 1989, and Cummins, 1989, for many other examples). I have suggested that the reasons for this are not only cognitive and academic in nature but relate also to the messages conveyed by the school to students about their cultural identity (Cummins, 1989; see also Ferdman, 1990).

The Ramírez report, however, suggests that other essential components required for students to develop a sense of empowerment are absent from all three program types. This is discussed in the next section.

BROADER EDUCATIONAL IMPLICATIONS OF THE RAMIREZ REPORT

One disturbing aspect of the findings of the Ramírez report is that the classroom environment in all three program types reflects transmission models of pedagogy, or what Paulo Freire (1983) has called a "banking education." As expressed in the report:

> Of major concern is that in over half of the interactions that teachers have with students, students do not produce any language as they are only listening or responding with non-verbal gestures or actions. ... Of equal concern is that when students do respond, typically they provide only simple information recall statements. Rather than being provided with the opportunity to generate original statements, students are asked to provide simple discrete close-ended or patterned (i.e., expected) responses. This pattern of teacher/student interaction not only limits a student's opportunity to create and manipulate language freely, but also limits the student's ability to engage in more complex learning (i.e., higher order thinking skills). In sum ... teachers in all three programs offer a passive language learning environment, limiting student opportunities to produce language and develop more complex language and thinking skills. (Ramírez, Yuen & Ramey, 1991, p. 8)

Efforts to reverse the pattern of Latino/Latina academic underachievement must examine not only the language of instruction but also the hidden curriculum being communicated to students through that instruction. While improving literacy levels has been a major goal of educational reform reports, few policymakers have asked the question: "What kinds of literacy and for what purposes?" This question has been answered by Sirotnik (1983), who points out that the typical American classroom contains

> a lot of teacher talk and a lot of student listening ... almost invariably closed and factual questions ... and predominantly total class instructional configurations around traditional activities—all in a virtually affectless environment. It is but a short inferential leap to suggest that we are implicitly teaching dependence upon authority, linear thinking, social apathy, passive involvement, and hands-off learning. (p. 29)

In other words, transmission models of pedagogy that predominate in programs for culturally diverse students aim to produce compliant consumers of information (and disinformation) rather than critical generators of knowledge; they also aim to produce passive individuals who accept current social conditions rather than act to transform patterns of social injustice.

The remainder of this article focuses on the development of literacy for empowerment. At this point it is sufficient to define empowerment as the collaborative creation of power whereby students and educators, through their interactions, develop a strong sense of personal and cultural identity and the critical thinking abilities to analyze their experience and take action to transform patterns of social injustice.

The Social Construction of Literacy

CRITERIA OF LITERACY

While different theorists have distinguished a variety of forms of literacy, for present purposes it is sufficient to distinguish *functional*, *cultural* and *critical* literacies (Williams & Snipper, 1990). Functional literacy implies a level of reading and writing that enables people to function adequately in society and, as such, is relative to changing societal demands.

Cultural literacy emphasizes the need for shared experiences and points of reference within an interpretive community in order to adequately comprehend texts. In contrast to functional literacy where the emphasis is on *skills*, cultural literacy focuses on particular content or knowledge that is basic to meaningful text interpretation in particular cultural contexts. For example, many recent immigrants may lack the "cultural literacy" to fully interpret typical situation-comedy programs on American television just as many middle-class white adults may lack the "cultural literacy" to interpret rap music.

Critical literacy, as expounded in Paulo Freire's work, focuses on the potential of written language as a tool that encourages people to analyze the division of power and resources in their society and work to transform discriminatory structures. For example, from the perspective of critical literacy, it is important to inquire who defines criteria of "adequacy" with respect to functional and cultural literacies and what social purposes are achieved by such definitions.

Most public policy reports in both Canada and the United States focus only on "functional literacy" and view it as a fixed inventory of skills operationally defined in terms of particular grade-level abilities in reading and writing. "Functional literacy" is viewed as though it were an autonomous, culturally neutral phenomenon that can be assessed outside of particular contexts of application.

Ferdman (1990) defines cultural identity as the behaviors, beliefs, values, and norms that a person considers to define himself or herself socially as a member of a particular cultural group and the value placed on those features in relation to those of other groups. Therefore, particular literacy behaviors that affirm the individual's sense of cultural identity will be acquired more easily and with more personal involvement than those that serve to deny or devalue his or her cultural identity.

The social construction process involved in defining functional and cultural literacies must be critically examined. What constitutes "adequate" functional literacy is determined by the dominant group in relation to the requirements of the system of production (i.e., the workplace). This is equally so today as it was at the time when it was illegal in the United States to teach slaves to read. From the perspective of the dominant group, critical literacy among workers or students is no more welcome today than it was in the era of slavery.

Similarly, the construct of "cultural literacy" cannot be isolated from historical and current intergroup power relations in particular societies. What constitutes valued knowledge or "cultural literacy" (in Hirsch's [1987] sense) in a particular society is socially constructed, and not surprisingly, the dominant group plays a greater role in the construction process than do subordinated groups. Hirsch's attempt to define "cultural literacy" is an attempt to further privilege the knowledge and values of the dominant group and to institutionalize the exclusion of subordinated group identities from the mainstream of economic and cultural life.

This analysis suggests that in the case of subordinated groups, literacy or educational reform programs that focus only on functional literacy (or in schools, standardized test performance) to the neglect of cultural and critical literacy are unlikely to succeed. The causes of educational underachievement and "illiteracy" among subordinated groups are rooted in the systematic devaluation of culture and denial of access to power and resources by the dominant group.

From this perspective it is possible to examine the ways in which the issues in the public debate on literacy have been framed to reinforce dominant group hegemony. I will consider the issues in this debate under three general categories: (a) the consequences for industry of alleged declining educational standards and literacy levels; (b) literacy instruction in school; and (c) literacy and subordinated group status.

THE PUBLIC DEBATES ON LITERACY

Worker Literacy, Education, and "Competitiveness" Many of the educational reform reports of the 1980s in the United States explicitly related the difficulties of American industry in competing against Asian countries to the inadequacies of the "human resources" that American industry had to draw on, specifically the low levels of worker "functional literacy." The low literacy of workers was, in turn, attributed to the failures of American schools to transmit basic literacy and numeracy skills in an organized and sequential way.

The recommendations of *A Nation at Risk* (National Commission on Excellence in Education, 1983) and most subsequent reports have focused primarily on raising standards and graduation requirements, eliminating the "curriculum smorgasbord" of "soft" subjects in favor of a common core curriculum for all students and increasing the amount of time that students are expected to spend learning the "basics." The thrust is toward "getting tough" with students and teachers in order to increase the rigor in curriculum materials and instruction.

It can be argued that this discourse of "competitiveness" and "functional illiteracy" serves to make workers and educators scapegoats for the failures of North American industry in the 1980s and 1990s (e.g., Barlett & Steele, 1992). As Hodgkinson (1991) has suggested, the American educational reform movement diverts attention from the failure of government to allocate resources to the social infrastructure essential for healthy human development.

Some of the data presented by Hodgkinson (1991) are the following:

- 23 percent of preschool children (birth to age 5) in the United States live in poverty, the highest rate of any industrialized nation;
- About 350,000 children annually are born to mothers who were addicted to cocaine during pregnancy;
- The United States ranked twenty-second in global rankings for infant mortality with a rate of 10 deaths per 1,000 live births (1988 statistics);
- The number of reports of child abuse or neglect received annually by child protection agencies tripled between 1976 and 1987 to 2.2 million;
- Young males in the United States are five times as likely to be murdered as are their counterparts in other nations;
- A black male in the United States was about five times as likely to be in prison as a black male in South Africa (1988 statistics);
- More than 80 percent of America's 1 million prisoners are high school dropouts and each prisoner costs taxpayers upwards of $20,000 a year.

Hodgkinson points out that while America's best students are on a par with the world's best, "ours is undoubtedly the worst 'bottom third' of any of the industrialized democracies." He summarizes the situation as follows:

> About one-third of preschool children are destined for school failure because of poverty, neglect, sickness, handicapping conditions, and lack of adult protection and nurturance. There is no point in trying to teach hungry or sick children. (p. 10)

It is clear that while the rhetoric of raising educational standards and combating "functional illiteracy" flourishes, there is little interest in helping students and workers to make the transition from "reading the word" to "reading the world." In other words, the focus on "functional illiteracy" is intended to reinforce coercive relations of power in the society despite the increasingly apparent costs of this focus for the dominant group itself. As discussed in the next section, transmission models of instruction are essential to prevent the spread of cultural and critical literacies with their potentially "disruptive" social consequences.

Literacy Instruction in Schools It is clearly beyond the scope of this article to review even a fraction of the vast amount of documentation on this topic. However, the major trends that have emerged in the public debate about literacy instruction can be summarized as follows:

- A major culprit to emerge in the perceived decline of student literacy and numeracy is the alleged proliferation of "progressive" "child-centered" teaching methods and the unwillingness of educators to teach "basic skills" and content in a direct no-nonsense fashion (see Stedman & Kaestle, 1985, 1987, for an analysis of this perspective).
- When applied to reading instruction, this issue manifests itself in the perception that schools have virtually aban-

doned systematic instruction in phonics in favor of "whole language" methods that eschew direct instruction in the subskills of reading; since students are denied access to the building blocks of reading, it is not surprising (according to this view) that they don't learn to read very well (Adams, 1991).

◆ Although it has been less prominent in the public debate, a parallel argument is beginning to be heard against "process" approaches to writing instruction; since process writing instruction is alleged to have abandoned direct systematic instruction of vocabulary, spelling, and grammar in favor of allowing students to "discover" these aspects of literacy in the process of writing, it appears hardly surprising to critics of this approach that students have meager vocabularies and that their grammar and spelling are substandard.

◆ With respect to content instruction, there is a common perception (and some evidence [Ravitch & Finn, 1987]) that American students are profoundly ignorant of their own culture and history. This is usually attributed to the failure of American educators to transmit "cultural literacy" (in Hirsch's [1987] sense) to students; in other words, students have not had the opportunity to learn the essential shared knowledge base necessary to participate effectively in American society. The inference drawn by both academic and media commentators is that educators should desist from their permissive and "progressive" ways and start to *teach*.

The major point that I want to make in relation to these trends is that the current "back-to-basics" focus in literacy instruction associated with the educational reform movement is not a neutral stance based on educational research but rather part of the same sociopolitical agenda designed to limit the extent to which "reading the word" might lead students to "read the world." In other words, the goals of this conservative discourse are

a. to promote sufficient "functional literacy" to meet the needs of industry in an increasingly technological work environment;

b. to promote "cultural literacy" and cultural identities that are in harmony with the societal power structure so that what is in the best interests of the dominant group is accepted as also being in the best interests of subordinated groups;

c. to limit the development of critical literacy so that students do not develop the ability to deconstruct disinformation and challenge structures of control and social injustice.

Transmission approaches to pedagogy represent an essential component of this agenda.

Shannon (1989) points to the fact that basal reading programs have dominated the teaching of reading for most of this century. More than 90 percent of elementary school teachers rely on teacher's guide books and basal readers during 90 percent of their instructional time. As Durkin (1987) points out, the terminology and marketing strategies used to sell basal reading programs have changed over the years to reflect current pedagogical fashions but the programs themselves have remained essentially the same. Shannon's analysis suggests that school systems require teachers to use the basal materials and teacher's guidebooks as a means of controlling the production of literacy "outputs" which will be assessed by means of standardized achievement tests. Within this "production management" model of reading instruction:

> Teachers teach students what, when, where, how, and why to use the skill listed as next in the basal scope and sequence.... Questions asked during practice should be factual, encourage choral response from the group, and be carefully sequenced to lead students successfully to the goal without diversion. (Shannon, 1989, p. 90)

As Shannon points out, the argument that such approaches to reading are more effective than whole language approaches that substitute children's literature and creative writing for basal readers and "reading management systems" is ironic in view of the fact that whole language approaches are used almost universally in New Zealand, the most literate country in the world with very low rates of reading failure and minimal use of standardized tests. The predominance of teacher-controlled transmission of information has the effect of limiting the possibility any kind of critical thinking on the part of either teachers or students.

In summary, the common thread that runs through the current public discourse about literacy in schools is the intense effort to exclude from pedagogical practices any collaborative quest for meaning on the part of teachers and students. The only meanings that are appropriate to "discover" are those that have been prescribed and sanitized. This hierarchical control of the instructional process dictates the current pedagogical focus on passive reception rather than active exploration, the focus on out-of-context phonics rather than meaning, the focus on spelling and grammar rather than creative writing, and the focus on ingesting the "cultural literacy" of the dominant group rather than developing a critical literacy grounded in students' personal and cultural experiences.

Literacy and Subordinated Group Status In view of the fact that subordinated groups experience disproportionate academic failure, one might have expected educational reform efforts to be predicated on a causal analysis of this phenomenon. However, in a somewhat ironic twist, the public discourse has shifted to absolve schools and society from responsibility for minority group underachievement; continuing the tradition of "scientific" explanations of minority group school failure, commentators once again attribute school failure to minority students' own deficiencies (lack of academic effort), deficiencies of their families (parental apathy or inadequacy manifested in antisocial activity such as drug use, etc.) or, as discussed above, to cynical manipulation by minority group politicians (e.g., Hispanic "activists" forcing schools to implement ineffective bilingual education programs that deny children access to English). Thus, when the public debate stays at a general level, schools are castigated for their failure to promote adequate literacy and academic "excellence" and for their cavalier attitude to "accountability"; however, when the underachievement of minority students is specifically discussed, the blame shifts from the schools to minority students and their communities themselves.

The long-term effects of coercive relations of power are evident in the educational performance of groups that have been subordinated in the wider society over generations. Several theorists (e.g., Cummins, 1989; Ogbu, 1978) have pointed to the fact that minority groups that fail academically tend to be characterized by a sense of ambivalence about the value of their cultural identity and powerlessness in relation to the dominant group. This is what Ogbu (1978) refers to as "caste-like" status, and its educational effects are strikingly evident in many situations where formerly subjugated or colonized groups are still in a subordinated relationship to the dominant group.

Many students resist the process of subordination through "disruptive" behavior, often culminating in dropping out of school (Fordham, 1990; Willis, 1977). Others modify their cultural identity by "acting white" (Fordham, 1990)—often buying educational success at the expense of rejection by their peers and ambivalence about their identity. Still others are never given the opportunity in school to gain either academic confidence or pride in identity and, over time, internalize the negative attributions of the dominant group and live down to their teachers' expectations.

A central characteristic of colonial situations is that the dominant group uses its coercive power to define, and where necessary, confine. In other words, the dominant group defines the status and identity of the subordinated group and the subordinated group is expected to internalize this externally-imposed identity.

The phenomenon of "internal colonies" is exemplified by the fact that the three groups in the United States context that experience the most pronounced educational difficulty (African American, Latino/Latina, and Native American students) have each been subordinated for centuries by the dominant group. Similar patterns exist in Scandinavia where Finnish minority students in Sweden are reported to experience severe academic difficulties, a phenomenon not unrelated to the fact that Finland was colonized by Sweden for several hundred years (Skutnabb-Kangas, 1984).

This analysis has important implications for the promotion of literacy among subordinated groups. Approaches that focus only on technical skills of reading and writing (in either L1 or L2) are unlikely to be successful. If the root causes of educational failure and "functional illiteracy" are associated with a collective sense of ambivalence in regard to the group's cultural identity, resulting from the internalization of dominant group attributions, then to be successful, literacy instruction must address these root causes.

In a similar vein, Stedman (1987) has pointed out that much of the effective schools literature fails to focus specifically on schools that achieved and maintained grade-level success with low-income students. His reanalysis of the literature from this perspective highlights two aspects of effective schools that are omitted from most other accounts. The first of these is a focus on *cultural pluralism*, specifically, effective schools reinforce the ethnic identity of their students. The second is a focus on *academically rich programs* in which students are actively engaged in learning through tasks that can be related to their own experience. Similarly Lucas, Henze, and Donato (1990) emphasize a focus on *empowerment* as a central characteristic of high schools that were effective in educating Latino/Latina students in California and Arizona.

The vigorous opposition to bilingual education in the media and by groups such as *U.S. English* illustrates the reluctance by the dominant group to address the real causes of subordinated group underachievement. The institutionalization of bilingual education would provide access to jobs and upward mobility for members of subordinated groups. In addition, the valorization of minority languages and subordinated group identities in the interactions between educators and students would challenge the historically entrenched pattern of dominant/subordinated group relations in the broader society. As I have argued elsewhere (Cummins, 1989), the perceived potential of bilingual education to threaten the societal power structure has given rise to a campaign of disinformation designed to prevent educators, parents, and policymakers from "reading the world." Under the guise of helping minority students to "read the word" (i.e., achieve academically in English), opponents of bilingual education have sought to mystify research findings so that subordinated groups will acquiesce in the perpetuation of educational structures (e.g., English-only instruction) that constrict the possibilities for students' personal and academic development.

To acknowledge that bilingualism is a valuable cultural and economic asset would effectively reverse the historical pattern of devaluation of identity. The internal logic of the "international competitiveness" discourse might suggest that in an increasingly interdependent world, it is the monolingual/monocultural individual who is "culturally illiterate" and ill-equipped to prosper economically in "the new world order." Two-way bilingual programs for both majority and minority students illustrate very well the obvious potential of transforming coercive relations of power into collaborative relations. These programs develop bilingualism and biliteracy for both groups and significantly amplify the possibilities for knowledge generation and identity formation. By contrast, the present coercive structures attempt to render both groups "culturally illiterate" and deny minority students the possibility even of "functional literacy" in either of their languages.

In summary, the public debates on literacy and educational underachievement are orchestrated to build public support (or in Chomsky's [1987] terms "to manufacture consent") for educational structures that exert increased hierarchical control over the interactions between educators and students. The content of instruction is prepackaged, the options for gaining access to and interpreting information are predetermined, and the possibilities for critical thinking and transformative action are stifled. In addition, educational success and upward mobility for members of subordinated groups is extended only to those who bring their identities into conformity with dominant group prescriptions.

A framework for considering alternatives to the perpetuation of coercive relations of power in the educational system follows.

Challenging Coercive Relations of Power in the Educational System

PEDAGOGICAL AND SOCIAL ASSUMPTIONS UNDERLYING TRANSMISSION AND CRITICAL ROLE DEFINITIONS

The framework outlined in Table 1 attempts to map the pedagogical and social assumptions that reflect particular forms of institutional and individual educator role definitions. Conservative approaches to education that are reflected in much of the current focus on "educational reform" in North America tend to combine a transmission orientation to pedagogy with a social control orientation to curricular topics and student outcomes. The patterns of classroom interaction and their social implications are similar to Sirotnik's description cited above.

Within a transmission orientation, task analysis is typically used to break language down to its component parts (e.g., phonics, vocabulary, grammatical rules) and transmit these parts in isolation from each other. Knowledge is viewed as static or inert, to be internalized and reproduced when required. Approaches to learning associated with a transmission orientation reflect these views of language and knowledge in that learning is assumed to progress in a hierarchical manner from simple content to complex.

By contrast, within a collaborative critical inquiry orientation, educators encourage the development of student voice through critical reflection on experiential and social issues. Language and meaning are viewed as inseparable and knowledge is seen as a catalyst for further inquiry and action. This is consistent with a Vygotskian view of learning that emphasizes the centrality of the *zone of proximal development* (ZPD), where knowledge is generated through collaborative interaction and critical inquiry (Vygotsky, 1978). Expressed simply, the ZPD is the interpersonal space where minds meet and new understandings can arise through collaborative interaction and inquiry. Language use and interaction in the classroom reflect and elaborate on students' experience and are focused on *generating* knowledge rather than on the transmission and consumption of socially sanitized information more typical of most North American classrooms.

The ZPD represents a useful metaphor for describing the dual process of collaborative generation of knowledge and reciprocal negotiation of identity. Educators whose role definition encompasses challenging institutional structures that reinforce social injustice and that restrict culturally diverse students' options for personal and academic development will attempt to create conditions for interaction that expand students' possibilities for identity formation and critical inquiry. Rather than constricting the ZPD so that students' voices are silenced, educators who adopt this type of role definition will attempt to initially constitute the ZPD in such a way that students' voices can be expressed, shared, and amplified within the interactional process. Under these conditions, the ZPD will then be coconstructed by students and educators as they script their own identities and that of the society they envisage.

With respect to social outcomes of schooling and ways of achieving these outcomes, conservative approaches aim to (re)produce compliant and uncritical students, and to this end, they ensure that all curricular content that might challenge the view of reality favored by the societal power structure is expunged. By contrast, critical educators are focused on creating conditions that open possibilities for student empowerment and transformation of oppressive social structures. Thus, they attempt to select curricular topics that relate directly to societal power relations and encourage students to analyze these topics/issues from multiple perspectives.[1]

As one example of the very different pedagogical implications of conservative versus critical approaches, consider the ways in which the issue of Columbus's "discovery" of America might be treated. Traditional curricula have celebrated Columbus as a hero whose arrival brought "civilization" and "salvation" to the indigenous populations. In fact, as Bigelow (1991) points out, few North American texts mention that Columbus initiated the slave trade and cut off the hands of any indigenous people who failed to bring him sufficient gold. The "discovery" of America resulted within a few years in the genocide of the indigenous populations in the islands where Spanish rule was established. Critical educators would encourage students to explore the reality omitted from the sanitized accounts in traditional texts, critically inquire as to why the texts present the type of picture they do, and ask what are the parallels with current issues relating to power in our society. They would also explore the possibilities for taking action in relation to the issues raised through critical inquiry, as outlined by Bigelow (1991).

INTEGRATING FUNCTIONAL, CULTURAL, AND CRITICAL LITERACIES IN THE CLASSROOM

One framework that elaborates a critical literacy approach to the

Table 1 *Pedagogical and Social Assumptions Underlying Educator Role Definitions*

(Pyramid diagram with phases: Descriptive Phase, Personal Interpretive Phase, Critical Analysis Phase, Creative Action Phase)

BILITERACY: A TRANSFORMATIVE PEDAGOGY

education of culturally diverse students is presented by Ada (1988a, 1988b) on the basis of Paulo Freire's work. Ada's framework outlines how zones of proximal development can be created that encourage culturally diverse students to share and amplify their experience within a collaborative process of critical inquiry. She distinguishes four phases in what she terms "the creative reading act."[2] Each of the phases distinguished by Ada is characterized by an interactional process (either between the teacher and students or among peers) that progressively opens up possibilities for the articulation and amplification of student voices. The "texts" that are the focus of the interaction can derive from any curricular area or from newspapers or current events. The process is equally applicable to students at any grade level. Ada (1988a) stresses that although the phases are discussed separately, "in a creative reading act they may happen concurrently and be interwoven." (p. 103)

◆ **Descriptive Phase** In this phase the focus of interaction is on the information contained in the text. Typical questions at this level might be: Where, when, how did it happen? Who did it? Why? These are the type of questions for which answers can be found in the text itself. Ada points out that these are the usual reading comprehension questions and that "a discussion that stays at this level suggests that reading is a passive, receptive, and in a sense, domesticating process" (1988a, p. 104). When the process is arrested at this level, the focus remains on internalization of inert information and/or the practice of "reading skills" in an experiential and motivational vacuum. Instruction remains at a safe distance from any challenge to the societal power structure. This phase represents a focus on functional literacy isolated from both cultural and critical literacy.

◆ **Personal Interpretive Phase** After the basic information in the text has been discussed, students are encouraged to relate it to their own experiences and feelings. Questions that might be asked by the teacher at this phase are: Have you ever seen (felt, experienced) something like this? Have you ever wanted something similar? How did what you read make you feel? Did you like it? Did it make you happy? Frighten you? What about your family?

Ada (1988a) points out that this process helps develop children's self-esteem by showing that their experiences and feelings are valued by the teacher and classmates. It also helps children understand that "true learning occurs only when the information received is analyzed in the light of one's own experiences and emotions" (p. 104). An atmosphere of acceptance and trust in the classroom is a prerequisite for students (and teachers) to risk sharing their feelings, emotions, and experiences. It is clear how this process of sharing and critically reflecting on their own and other students' experiences opens up identity options for culturally diverse students. These identity options are typically suppressed within a transmission approach to pedagogy where the interpretation of texts is nonnegotiable and reflective of the dominant group's notions of cultural literacy. The personal interpretive phase deepens students' comprehension of the text or issues by grounding the knowledge in the personal and collective narratives that make up students' histories. It is also developing a genuine cultural literacy in that it is integrating students' own experiences with "mainstream" curricular content.

◆ **Critical Analysis Phase** After children have compared and contrasted what is presented in the text with their personal experiences, they are ready to engage in a more abstract process of critically analyzing the issues or problems that are raised in the text. This process involves drawing inferences and exploring what generalizations can be made. Appropriate questions might include: Is it valid? Always? When? Does it benefit everyone alike? Are there any alternatives to this situation? Would people of different cultures (or classes, or genders) have acted differently? How? Why? Ada emphasizes that school children of all ages can engage in this type of critical process, although the analysis will always reflect children's experiences and level of maturity. This phase further extends students' comprehension of the text or issues by encouraging them to examine both the internal logical coherence of the information or propositions and their consistency with other knowledge or perspectives. When students pursue guided research and critical reflection, they are clearly engaged in a process of knowledge generation; however, they are equally engaged in a process of self-definition; as they gain the power to think through issues that affect their lives, they simultaneously gain the power to resist external definitions of who they are and to deconstruct the sociopolitical purposes of such external definitions.

◆ **Creative Action Phase** This is a stage of translating the results of the previous phases into concrete action. The dialogue is oriented toward discovering what changes individuals can make to improve their lives or resolve the problem that has been presented. Let us suppose that students have been researching (in the local newspaper or in periodicals such as *National Geographic* and the *Greenpeace* magazines, etc.) problems relating to environmental pollution. After relating the issues to their own experience, critically analyzing causes and possible solutions, they might decide to write letters to congressional representatives, highlight the issue in their class/school newsletter in order to sensitize other students, write and circulate a petition in the neighborhood, write and perform a play that analyzes the issue, etc. Once again, this phase can be seen as extending the process of comprehension insofar as when we act to transform aspects of our social realities we gain a deeper understanding of those realities.

The processes described in Ada's framework are clearly compatible with Vygotskian approaches to learning. A context (or ZPD) is created in which students can voice their experience; meaningful and socially relevant content is integrated with active use of language in written and oral modalities; and students are challenged to use their developing language skills for higher-order thinking.

There is also a clear relationship with the *experience-text-relationship* (ETR) method (Au, 1979) insofar as each scheme focuses on relating culturally diverse students' experiences to the text. The ETR scheme makes the valid point that it is often useful to elicit students' experience prior to engaging in reading the text but it fails to highlight the importance of critical inquiry or creative action, which are central to Ada's scheme.

The representation of Ada's framework in Figure 1 highlights the fact that "comprehension" is not an "all-or-nothing" phenomenon; rather, it can take place at different levels and the process outlined by Ada represents phases in the progressive deepening of comprehension. This deepening of comprehension represents a progressive expansion of conceptual horizons. Thus, the more we process input or information, the more potential there is for deepening our understanding of the phenomena in question. The process of making

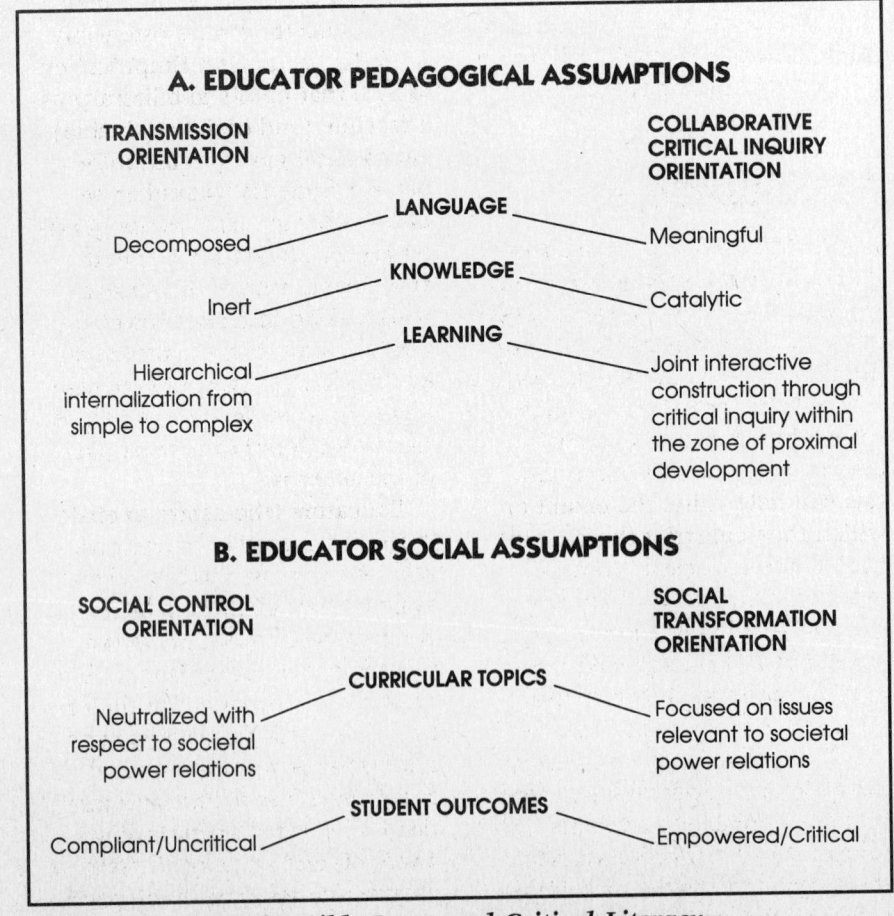

A. EDUCATOR PEDAGOGICAL ASSUMPTIONS

TRANSMISSION ORIENTATION		COLLABORATIVE CRITICAL INQUIRY ORIENTATION
	LANGUAGE	
Decomposed		Meaningful
	KNOWLEDGE	
Inert		Catalytic
	LEARNING	
Hierarchical internalization from simple to complex		Joint interactive construction through critical inquiry within the zone of proximal development

B. EDUCATOR SOCIAL ASSUMPTIONS

SOCIAL CONTROL ORIENTATION		SOCIAL TRANSFORMATION ORIENTATION
	CURRICULAR TOPICS	
Neutralized with respect to societal power relations		Focused on issues relevant to societal power relations
	STUDENT OUTCOMES	
Compliant/Uncritical		Empowered/Critical

Figure 1 *Comprehensible Input and Critical Literacy*

input comprehensible is an active constructive process that can be facilitated or inhibited by those we are interacting with (or by characteristics of texts we are reading).

In short, we cannot understand messages without acting on them. Initially, the action is usually internalized (Piaget's cognitive operations) but external actions will also contribute to the process of understanding. At the tip of the pyramid in Figure 1 is the descriptive phase, in which students' comprehension of the text (or phenomenon) is quite limited in that they have processed or acted on the text only to the extent that they are capable of reproducing the basic information it contains. Minimal cognitive action is involved. If the process is arrested at this phase (as it is in most classrooms), the knowledge will remain inert rather than becoming a catalyst for further exploration.

The personal interpretive and critical analysis phases represent internalized action on the text. While this internalized action can be carried out by individuals, the process will usually be enhanced when the action is collaboratively constructed in the context of social interaction. The personal interpretive phase deepens the individual's comprehension by grounding the knowledge in the personal and collective narratives that make up our experience and history. The critical analysis phase further extends the comprehension process by examining both the internal logical coherence of the information or propositions and their consistency with other knowledge or perspectives. Finally, the creative action phase constitutes concrete action that aims to transform aspects of our social realities. This external action to transform reality also serves to deepen our comprehension of the issues.

With respect to expansion of possibilities for identity formation, culturally diverse students engaging in the critical literacy process outlined in Figure 1 have the possibility of actively voicing their own realities and their analyses of issues rather than being constricted to the identity definitions and constructions of "truth" implicitly or explicitly transmitted in the prescribed curriculum. When classroom interaction progresses beyond the descriptive phase, students engage in a process of *self*-expression; in other words, by sharing and critically reflecting on their experience they collaboratively construct a ZPD that expands their options for identity formation.

Conclusion

I have argued that the construction of both knowledge and identity is jointly enacted by students and educators within the zone of proximal development. The ways in which educators define their roles with respect to culturally diverse students and communities will determine the extent to which they constrict the ZPD to limit students' possibilities for identity formation and knowledge generation or, alternatively, expand the ZPD to ground the curriculum in students' experiences such that a much broader range of possibilities for identity formation and knowledge generation are available to students. Educator role definitions reflect their vision of society, and implicated in that societal vision are their own identities and those of the students with whom they interact.

It is within this context that the debate on bilingual education must be understood. The history of the education of culturally diverse students in the United States and most other countries is a history of thinly disguised perpetuation of the coercive relations of power that operate in the wider society. The attempt to limit the framework of discourse so that promotion of biliteracy is not even considered as a policy response to the underachievement of Latino/Latina students illustrates the operation of coercive relations of power. Culturally diverse students are defined as deficient and confined to remedial programs that act to produce the deficits they were ostensibly intended to reverse. Empirical evidence that points to biliteracy as a feasible (and easily attainable) educational goal for culturally diverse students will either be distorted or ignored, as the quotation from Chavez (1991) cited at the beginning of this article makes clear. Maintenance of the lies of history and the facade of equity requires that bilingualism continue to be defined as part of the problem rather than as part of the solution.

Educators who aspire to challenge the operation of coercive relations of power in the school system must attempt to create conditions of collaborative empowerment. In other words, they must attempt to organize their interactions with students in such a way that power is generated and shared through those interactions. This involves becoming aware of, and actively working to change, the ways in which particular educational structures limit the opportunities that culturally diverse students might have for educational and social advancement. It also involves attempting to orchestrate the interactions with culturally diverse students in such a way that students' options for identity formation and critical inquiry are expanded rather than constricted. For Latino/Latina students, promotion of critical biliteracy is a necessary part of this empowerment process since, in the absence of critical biliteracy, they are unable to read either the word or the world in their two cultures.

NOTES

1. Within the continua sketched in Table 1, there are clearly many intermediate positions. For example, "whole language" approaches highlight the importance of meaningful language use and two-way interaction within the classroom; however, critical analysis of issues related to social justice tends not to be a focus of instruction in many "whole language" classrooms and has not been strongly emphasized by most "whole language" theorists (see Shannon, 1989). Thus, while "whole language" approaches are quite compatible with the critical and social transformation orientations sketched in Table 1, in practice they sometimes remain at the level of uncritical celebration of individual narratives and neglect issues of power and social justice (see Delpit, 1988, for a critique of whole language approaches applied to inner-city African American children).

2. I have slightly modified the labels given by Ada for the four phases in order to try and highlight certain aspects of the process. Although presented here in a linear format, the phases should not be thought of as requiring a linear or sequential approach. In other words, the process of collaborative critical inquiry can begin at any of the four phases and be incorporated in any manner into the instructional process. For example, as suggested in the *experience-text-relationship* method elaborated by Au (1979) and her colleagues (e.g., Mason & Au, 1986), an experiental or personal interpretive phase in which the teacher elicits students' personal experiences relevant to the text or topic can precede the descriptive phase. Ada's scheme is not in any sense formulaic but should be reinvented by individual teachers according to their perceptions and circumstances. The essential components are that students' experience and critical inquiry constitute the curriculum as much as any "text" since in the absence of students' experience and critical inquiry no text can become truly meaningful.

ABOUT THE AUTHOR

Jim Cummins (Ph.D. University of Alberta, 1974) is currently a professor in the Modern Language Centre of the Ontario Institute for Studies in Education. He has published several books related to bilingual education and minority student achievement including *Bilingualism and Special Education: Issues in Assessment and Pedagogy* (Multilingual Matters, 1984), *Bilingualism in Education: Aspects of Theory, Research and Policy* (Longman, 1986, with Merrill Swain), *Minority education: From shame to struggle* (Multilingual Matters, 1988, with T. Skutnabb-Kangas) and *Empowering Minority Students* (California Association for Bilingual Education, 1989).

REFERENCES

Ada, A. F. (1988a). Creative reading: A relevant methodology for language minority children. In Malave, L. M. (Ed.), *NABE '87. Theory, research and application: Selected papers*. Buffalo: State University of New York.

Ada, A. F. (1988b). The Pájaro Valley experience: Working with Spanish-speaking parents to develop children's reading and writing skills in the home through the use of children's literature. In Skutnabb-Kangas, T., and Cummins, J. (Ed.), *Minority education: From shame to struggle*. Clevedon, England: Multilingual Matters Ltd.

Adams, M. (1991). *Beginning to read: Thinking and learning about print*. Champaign, IL: Center for the Study of Reading.

Au, K. H. (1979). Using the experience-text-relationship method with minority children. *Reading Teacher*, vol. 32, pp. 677–79.

Baker, K. (1992). Comments on Suzanne Irujo's review of Rosalie Pedalino Porter's Forked tongue: The politics of bilingual education. A reader reacts .... *TESOL Quarterly*, vol. 26, pp. 397–405.

Barlett, D. L., and Steele, J. B. (1992). *America: What went wrong?* Kansas: Andrews & McMeel.

Bigelow, B. (1991). Discovering Columbus: Re-reading the past. *Our Schools, Our Selves*, vol. 3, no. 1, pp. 22–38.

Chavez, L. (1991). Let's move beyond bilingual education. *USA Today*, December 30.

Chomsky, N. (1987). The manufacture of consent. In Peck, J. (Ed.), *The Chomsky reader*, pp. 121–36. New York: Pantheon Books.

Collier, V. P. (1987). Age and rate of acquisition of second language for academic purposes. *TESOL Quarterly*, vol. 21, pp. 617–41.

Crawford, J. (1989). *Bilingual education: History, politics, theory and practice*. Trenton, NJ: Crane Publishing.

Cummins, J. (1991). Interdependence of first- and second-language proficiency in bilingual children. In Bialystok, E. (Ed.), *Language processing in bilingual children*, pp. 70–89. Cambridge: Cambridge University Press.

Cummins, J. (1989). *Empowering minority students*. Sacramento: California Association for Bilingual Education.

Cummins, J. (1981a). The public image of bilingual education. Report submitted to the Ford Foundation.

Cummins, J. (1981b). Age on arrival and immigrant second language learning in Canada: A reassessment. *Applied Linguistics*, vol. 2, pp. 132–49.

Delpit, L. (1988). The silenced dialogue: Power and pedagogy in educating other people's children. *Harvard Educational Review*, vol. 58, pp. 280–98.

DeVillar, R. A., and Faltis, C. J. (1991). *Computers and cultural diversity: Restructuring for school success*. Albany: SUNY Press.

Dunn, L. (1987). *Bilingual hispanic children on the U.S. mainland: A review of research on their cognitive, linguistic, and scholastic development*. Circle Pines, MN: American Guidance Service.

Durkin, D. (1987). Influences on basal reader programs. *Elementary School Journal*, vol. 87, pp. 331–41.

Ferdman, B. (1990). Literacy and cultural identity. *Harvard Educational Review*, vol. 60, no. 2, pp. 181–204.

Fishman, J. (1976). Bilingual education: What and why? In Alatis, J. E., and Twaddell, K. (Eds.), *English as a second language in bilingual education*, pp. 263–71. Washington, DC: TESOL.

Fordham, S. (1990). Racelessness as a factor in black students' school success: Pragmatic strategy or Pyrrhic victory? In Hidalgo, N. M., McDowell, C. L., and Siddle, E. V. (Eds.), *Facing racism in education*. Reprint series No. 21, *Harvard Educational Review*, pp. 232–62.

Freire, P. (1983). Banking education. In Giroux, H., and Purpel, D. (Eds.), *The hidden curriculum and moral education: Deception or discovery?* Berkeley, CA: McCutcheon Publishing Corporation.

Freire, P., and Macedo, D. (1987). *Literacy: Reading the word and the world*. South Hadley, MA: Bergin & Garvey.

Glazer, N., and Cummins, J. (1985). Viewpoints on bilingual education. *Equity and Choice*, vol. 2, pp. 47–52.

Hirsch, E. D., Jr. (1987). *Cultural literacy: What every American needs to know*. Boston: Houghton Mifflin Co.

Hodgkinson, H. (1991). Reform versus reality. *Phi Delta Kappan* (September), pp. 9–16.

Imhoff, G. (1990). The position of U.S. English on bilingual education. In Cazden, C. B., and Snow, C. E. (Eds.), *English plus: Issues in bilingual education*, pp. 48–61. The Annals of the American Academy of Political and Social Science, March.

Kirsch, I. S., and Jungeblut, A. (1986). *Literacy: Profiles of America's young adults*. Princeton, NJ: Educational Testing Service.

Lambert, W. E. (1975). Culture and language as factors in learning and education. In A. Wolfgang (Ed.), *Education of immigrant students*, pp. 55–83. Toronto: O.I.S.E.

Lindholm, K. J., and Zierlein, A. (1991). Bilingual proficiency as a bridge to academic achievement: Results from bilingual/immersion programs. *Journal of Education*, vol. 173, pp. 99–113.

Lucas, T., Henze, R., and Donato, R. (1990). Promoting the success of Latino language-minority students: An exploratory study of six high schools. *Harvard Educational Review*, vol. 60, pp. 315–40.

Mason, J. M., and Au, K. H. (1986). *Reading instruction for today*. Glenview, IL: Scott, Foresman and Company.

National Commission on Excellence in Education (1983). *A nation at risk: The imperative for educational reform*. Washington, D.C.: U.S. Government Printing Office.

Ogbu, J. (1978). *Minority education and caste*. New York: Academic Press.

Porter, R. P. (1990). *Forked tongue: The politics of bilingual education*. New York: Basic Books.

Ramírez, J. D., Pasta, D. J., Yuen, S. D., Billings, D. K., and Ramey, D. R. (1991). *Longitudinal study of structured English immersion strategy, early-exit and late-exit transitional bilingual education programs for language-minority children* (vols. 1–2, U.S. Department of Education Report, Contract No. 300-87-0156). San Mateo, CA: Aguirre International.

Ramírez, J. D., Yuen, S. D., and Ramey, D. R. (1991). Executive summary, Final report: Longitudinal study of structured English immersion strategy, early-exit and late-exit transitional bilingual education programs for language-minority children. Contract No. 300-87-0156. Submitted to the U.S. Department of Education. San Mateo: Aguirre International.

Ravitch, D., and Finn, C. E. (1987). *What do our 17-year-olds know? A report on the first national assessment of history and literature*. New York: Harper & Row.

Sayers, D. (1991). Cross-cultural exchanges between students from the same culture: A portrait of an emerging relationship mediated by technology. *Canadian Modern Language Review*, vol. 47, pp. 678–96.

Shannon, P. (1989). *Broken promises: Reading instruction in 20th century America*. South Hadley, MA: Bergin & Garvey.

Sirotnik, K. A. (1983). What you see is what you get—consistency, persistency, and mediocrity in classrooms. *Harvard Educational Review*, vol. 53, pp. 16–31.

Skutnabb-Kangas, T. (1984). *Bilingualism or not: The education of minorities*. Clevedon, England: Multilingual Matters Ltd.

Stedman, L. C. (1987). It's time we changed the effective schools formula. *Phi Delta Kappan*, vol. 69, pp. 215–24.

Stedman, L. C., and Kaestle, C. F. (1987). Literacy and reading performance in the United States from 1800 to the present. *Reading Research Quarterly*, vol. 22, pp. 8–46.

Stedman, L. C., and Kaestle, C. F. (1985). The test score decline is over: Now what? *Phi Delta Kappan*, vol. 67, pp. 204–10.

Swain, M. (1979). Bilingual education: Research and its implications. In Yorio, C. A., Perkins, K., and Schachter, J. (Eds.), *On TESOL '79: The learner in focus*. Washington, DC: TESOL.

Tikunoff, W. J. (1983). *An emerging description of successful bilingual instruction: An executive summary of Part 1 of the SBIF descriptive study*. San Francisco: Far West Laboratory.

Verhoeven, L. (1991). Acquisition of biliteracy. *AILA Review*, vol. 8, pp. 61–74.

Vygotsky, L. S. (1978). *Mind in society: The development of higher psychological processes*, Cole, M., John-Steiner, V., Scibner, S., and Souberman, E. (Eds.). Cambridge, MA: Harvard University Press.

Williams, J. D., and Snipper, G. C. (1990). *Literacy and bilingualism*. White Plains, NY: Longman.

Willis, P. (1977). *Learning to labor: How working class kids get working class jobs*. Lexington, MA: D.C. Heath.

Wong Fillmore, L. (in collaboration with C. Valadez) (1986). Teaching bilingual learners. In Wittrock, M. (Ed.), *Handbook of research on teaching*, 3d ed. New York: Macmillan.

Literacy Instruction through Spanish:
Linguistic, Cultural, and Pedagogical Considerations

Elly B. Pardo *and* **Josefina Villamil Tinajero**
Educational Consultant *University of Texas at El Paso*

In the United States, the structure and content of bilingual education programs has been a topic of scrutiny and heated debate for some 25 years now. Of greatest concern to educational practitioners, researchers, policy makers, communities, and families has been the scholastic achievement of linguistic minority children, particularly ways in which these youngsters successfully acquire and develop literacy skills in both their first and second languages (Cummins, 1989; Genesee, 1987; Lambert, 1984; Macedo, 1991). It is widely accepted that literacy is the cornerstone of all academic competencies (Cummins, 1987, 1989; Heath, 1983, 1989). For this reason, in both bilingual and nonbilingual classrooms, a primary instructional goal is to teach students how to use oral and written language for meaningful communication.

Pedagogical problems arise, however, in the interpretation of what constitutes meaningful language and literacy instruction for students who are dominant in a mother tongue other than English. One school of thought considers bilingual education to be a kind of *internment program* in which limited English proficient students (LEPs) must spend several years before learning enough English to survive in regular education settings. Proponents of the *internment* model promote a structured English immersion approach to literacy development (Baker & de Kanter, 1981; Dunn, 1987; Gersten & Woodward, 1985). This approach is focused strictly on providing LEP youngsters with sufficient oral, reading, and writing skills in English so that they can eventually transition to a regular education program where their more analytical literacy learning will occur.

Another school of thought treats bilingual education as a *buffer program* that helps transition students from their home language and culture to the language and culture of the classroom. LEP children in this type of educational setting are initially provided with language and literacy instruction in their mother tongue (their L1) while simultaneously acquiring oral language skills in English (their L2). Nevertheless, as soon as they have sufficient conversational and oral comprehension ability in their L2 (perhaps after a year or two) they are gradually transitioned into an English literacy curriculum, even though they may still remain in a bilingual classroom. For this reason, the *buffer* model of bilingual education is not designed with the purpose of fully developing and preserving the speaking, reading, and writing skills of LEP students in their mother tongue (Troike, 1978).

And finally, a third school of thought advocates bilingual education as a way of cultivating and maintaining the literacy proficiency of LEP children in both their first and second language. This method of bilingual instruction we shall call a *holistic* model of learning because it recognizes the societal value of developing literacy competence in a child's home language as well as in English. The rationale underlying the *holistic* model is that LEP children will have the best possible chance of becoming capable speakers, readers, and writers in both their L1 and L2 if they can transfer strong literacy skills from their native language to English (Cummins, 1981, 1987, 1989; Genesee, 1987; Krashen & Biber, 1988; Ramírez, Yuen & Ramey, 1991). For this reason, the model encourages long-term literacy instruction in both the L1 and the L2 as a means of sustaining literacy proficiency in two languages. It is the *holistic* method of bilingual education that will frame our discussion of the importance of native language instruction in promoting effective literacy skills in Spanish and English for Spanish dominant elementary school children.

The Connection Between Language and Literacy Learning

COGNITIVE AND ACADEMIC CONSIDERATIONS

Language is intimately linked both to conceptual development and social experience (Brown, 1973; Hakuta, 1990; Skutnabb-Kangas, 1981). It is therefore an important tool for processing information about one's surroundings and for organizing personal perceptions of self in relation to these surroundings (Vygotsky, 1962). It reflects how humans view and interact with their world—why they say what they say and why they think in certain ways. In other words, language is the filter through which all sociocultural experiences and understandings must pass (Alexander, Schallert & Hare, 1991).

Our discussion here will highlight the association between language background and literacy learning. In particular, it will underscore the importance of the mother tongue in teaching children to become competent readers, not only of words and phrases, but also of experience. Like others (Dechant, 1991; Smith, 1988), we argue that reading is an interactive process directed toward the sharing of meaning. To effectively engage in this process, readers must be able to comprehend a writer's text by drawing on their own literacy and sociocultural knowledge to reconstruct another's message. In other words, reading is intimately tied to comprehension and comprehension is directly related to what the reader already knows (Smith, 1988). What this means is that children cannot become proficient readers of another's experiences if their own background has not equipped them with the cognitive, linguistic, and social tools that are relevant to the information communicated in print.

Heath (1989) explains that "for all children, academic success depends less on the specific language they know than on the ways of using language they know" (p. 144). In the arguments that follow, we propose that with Spanish-speaking elementary school students, literacy instruction in their native language is the most pedagogically sound way of teaching them about the relationships between meaning and print in both Spanish and English. This is because empirical evidence has shown that Spanish dominant youngsters acquire academic language and literacy skills rapidly and better in both Spanish and English when they attain literacy proficiency in their mother tongue (Krashen & Biber, 1988; Ramírez, Yuen & Ramey, 1991). In keeping with this finding, we contend that if instruction in Spanish reading helps LEP children appreciate their linguistic heritage, develop positive literacy experiences, and attain competence in both academic Spanish and English, then long-term use of the native language for pedagogical purposes must be considered a viable alternative to an English-only curriculum.

NATURAL LANGUAGE LEARNING AND LITERACY COMPETENCE

The Goodmans (1979) explain that for young children, literacy acquisition is an extension of natural language learning. Natural language learning occurs when youngsters draw upon the lexicon and grammar of their mother tongue to organize their thinking and to communicate their thoughts and needs to people who understand their cultural experience. We have already noted that culture and language are closely intertwined—language serving to re-create or interpret the accumulated experiences of a social group (González, 1989). For this reason, effective literacy practices must be tied to the cultural norms, values, belief systems, and behaviors of a community of speakers. When literacy learning is not linked to familiar information, it will be at odds with children's natural learning processes, "will neutralize or blunt the force of their language learning strength, and may (even) become counterproductive" (Goodman & Goodman, 1979, p. 138).

The position of "natural learning" is central to our argument concerning reading instruction for Spanish-speaking students in the elementary grades. We propose that for Hispanic youngsters with little or no proficiency in English, the native language is the most appropriate vehicle for teaching them about the complexities of the relationship between speech and print. This is because reading requires that people match their linguistic and sociocultural knowledge to a text (Goodman, 1967). It is a process of "building a representation of text by relating what is on the page to one's own fund of experience" (Dechant, 1991, p. 6). In fact, reading is often thought of as reasoning through print (Smith, 1988) because it relies on "higher order" thinking skills that involve message interpretation, the association of print with past experience, and the construction of new meanings and relationships. It follows then that children learning to read in a language they do not speak well will spend much of their time on deciphering graphic input instead of on message interpretation. Reading for them will thus become a rote activity focused on sound and vocabulary recognition instead of on the interplay between words and the images and ideas that these words create.

Literacy learning is most effective, then, when it is a natural outgrowth of the world knowledge that students bring with them from their home environment to school. Heath (1983) observes that each community has its own rules for socializing children through language and that "ways of taking" meaning from print differ across communities. Therefore, when the literacy instruction of LEP students helps them to "take meaning" from their own reservoir of sociolinguistic experiences, the school is not only establishing continuity between home and school but is also validating the linguistic and cultural identity of these students.

Moreover, in terms of achievement, scholars have argued strongly that positive self-identification effects educational success (Lambert, 1987; Matute-Bianchi, 1986; Padilla, 1990). For this reason, using the language of the home as a tool for linguistic empowerment is the most natural way of cultivating the self-worth and intellectual potential that LEP children often abandon when they enter the culture of the school.

SOCIOLINGUISTIC PERSPECTIVES ON LITERACY COMPETENCE

When elementary school youth explore print in their mother tongue, they are learning about the lexical, grammatical, and semantic possibilities of a language that they already are able to use in purposeful speech. In other words, they have acquired a sociocultural perspective on how to explain, orient, prohibit, negate, mandate, and express emotions, etc., so that individuals in their speech community will think, feel, behave, or react in certain ways (Pardo, in press, pp. 147–50). "Writing is not simply the language of speech written down (but) has its own set of characteristic grammatical structures," and children "generally do not master the constructions of the written language until they themselves become fluent readers" (Perera, 1987, p. 101). As a result, youngsters must be reading extensively to encounter some of these constructions.

Given the multifaceted nature of the reading process, we propose that when Spanish dominant youngsters attain a level of reading proficiency in their L1 that enables them to do more than decode simple prose, they are learning a great deal about the science of linguistic communication. Specifically, they are gaining an analytical knowledge of the rhetorical potential of language: how to combine linguistic elements to develop cohesive arguments and how to create a mood and engage an audience through words. For this reason, providing young Spanish dominant children with sufficient literacy instruction in their L1 furnishes them with an understanding of the expressive possibilities of language that they can later apply to literacy learning opportunities in their L2. (See the discussion on the *linguistic interdependence principle* in the following section for a consideration of psycholinguistic factors affecting the transfer of language knowledge.)

Commenting on the importance of literacy instruction in the native language Snow (1990) observes:

> Practice in reading is possible only if children are willing to sit down and read, which is not likely if they are expected to read in a language they do not yet understand, or if they have to read material much below the level that interests them because of limitations on their language proficiency. (p. 69)

When LEP children must conduct their literacy activities in a language with which they have only little or moderate familiarity, they lose valuable opportunities to extract new ideas and forms of expression from texts that they can use in new language-based situations, both in their L1 and L2. We have already noted that printed material provides readers with numerous opportunities to discover how ideas are linked in ways that are not typical of everyday spontaneous speech. Pointing to the interplay between written and oral language, Perera (1987) explains that learning about the structural possibilities of written language enables readers to become more effective language users in general. She further notes that new structures "once mastered through writing . . . are available for use in speech . . . thereby increasing the power and flexibility of (an individual's) oral repertoire" (p. 115). It is clear then, that developing reading skills only in English with young students who are dominant speakers of Spanish may considerably reduce their linguistic potential. This is because when learning to read only in their L2, these students cannot internalize the same amount of grammatical, semantic, and stylistic information as they can when reading texts in their L1.

A plausible explanation for the inability of Spanish dominant students to process reading material in English as thoroughly as they are able to in Spanish stems from their limited exposure to the various contextual functions of English. The contextual functions of language refer to the culturally specific ways in which grammar and syntax are used in diverse social settings to convey meaning on a variety of topics to different audiences (Hymes, 1974). In order to be able to predict and identify with an author's message, a reader must therefore have strong *intuitions* about the structural and functional possibilities of the language he or she is attempting to comprehend. Nevertheless, when Spanish-speaking youngsters receive literacy instruction in their L2 before they acquire more than a superficial working knowledge of how to extract meaning from texts in their native language, they do not have well-developed intuition about either English or Spanish. Consequently, as mentioned earlier, their involvement with print is often directed more to the mechanics of literacy, i.e., decoding of sounds and word meanings, than to anticipating the ways that language elements can co-occur to create relevant messages.

The Connection Between Literacy Instruction in the Native Language and Achievement

CONVERSATIONAL AND ACADEMIC LANGUAGE

Jim Cummins has written extensively on the importance of developing children's literacy skills in their mother tongue (1979, 1981, 1987, 1989, 1991). Both on psycholinguistic and sociolinguistic grounds, he argues strongly that overall, nondominant speakers of English do better in school, in both their native language and English, if they are given ample opportunity to attain literacy proficiency through their L1.

Cummins (1989) has articulated an important linguistic distinction that highlights the relationship between language and achievement. This distinction, between *conversational* and *academic language*, describes a continuum of linguistic functions that children progressively acquire throughout their school years. At the lowest end of the continuum is conversational, or everyday, language in which both paralinguistic cues (e.g., gestures and facial expressions) and situational props facilitate the transfer of meaning among speakers and listeners. Conversational language, therefore, is highly *context embedded* (Cummins, 1981, 1987, 1989); meaning is understood not only by what is said but also by what is surrounding a discourse (i.e., extralinguistic information). For this reason, the syntax of context embedded speech is rather simple in comparison to that of other types of communicative events that do not rely on situational scaffolding.

As one moves towards the *academic* end of the continuum, however, the level of contextual support begins to decrease, and language exchanges eventually become *context reduced*. This means that as situational cues are gradually removed from a discourse, understanding must be achieved through more elaborate lexical, grammatical, and syntactic devices. Context reduced communication thus requires language specificity for clear expression and accurate comprehension. It is far more characteristic of instruction in the upper elementary grades and beyond than of the early primary grades. Examples of the conversational/academic distinction as they might occur, from simple to most complex, along the proposed continuum are face-to-face talk with friends, a telephone conversation between a student and teacher about a homework assignment, reading one's own essay at a school assembly, and writing a critique of a Shakespearean play.

Of relevance to the discussion here is that LEP children are frequently exited from bilingual education programs or moved into a predominantly English curriculum within a bilingual classroom on the basis of their ability to use and comprehend only conversational English (Collier, 1987; Cummins, 1981; Krashen & Biber, 1988). Their general knowledge of how to use their L1 in different settings for various purposes, however, is often quite limited and directed primarily to topics of a more concrete and descriptive nature. Ramírez (1992), however, highlights the importance of knowing several language varieties and specialized registers in order to attain *functional language proficiency* in academic subject matter:

> The acquisition of basic skills involves, in part, the learning of several language varieties that will allow the student to send (speak or write) or receive (listen or read) messages with different purposes (... write an essay to persuade, read an editorial for point-of-view). To acquire this competence the individual may need to know and understand the specialized register (specific language structures and technical terminology) of the subject. (p. 269)

Given that mastery of subject matter content is the most important criterion for success in school, students with an insufficient knowledge of academic classroom language, either in their L1 or L2, will not have the functional linguistic proficiency to grasp material that is abstract, decontextualized, and problem oriented. Otherwise, their involvement with more complex subject matter and learning materials will be superficial or restricted to less challenging information because they will not have the language and experiential background to understand and elaborate on a wide range of topics.

TRANSFER OF LANGUAGE KNOWLEDGE

A number of scholars (Cummins, 1987; Hakuta & Díaz, 1984; Lambert, 1984) have argued that the use of the native language to develop the academic skills of limited English proficient students is the best way of helping them avoid cognitive deficits and achievement lags in their school performance. In particular, Cummins (1989) explains that academic language learning requires two psycholinguistic prerequisites—concept formation and linguistic proficiency—and that these prerequisites constitute a global learning factor that he calls *common underlying proficiency* (CUP). CUP refers to the storage of cognitive and linguistic information that facilitates learning in general. In this way, the CUP model of bilingualism predicts that academic skills learned through one linguistic system will pave the way for the acquisition of skills in another. This is because, from an informational standpoint, the linguistic systems of bilinguals are *interdependent* (Cummins, 1989). Namely, when bilinguals use their language knowledge to construct and interpret meaning, they are drawing from a single storage space of information that funnels input into both their languages instead of from separate storage spaces for each language.

The *linguistic interdependence principle*, as Cummins describes the transfer of language knowledge from an individual's L1 to his or her L2, is useful in explaining why young, native Spanish speakers perform well in English when they attain literacy proficiency in their mother tongue (González, 1989; Krashen & Biber, 1988; Ramírez, Yuen & Ramey, 1991). Specifically, when these children learn about the intricacies of print relationships through materials that highlight their own language and social reality, the linguistic interdependence principle predicts that they will be able to extend their repertoire of literacy expertise to a range of language and social contexts in their L2. In fact, research shows that those students with high levels of literacy proficiency in their L1 perform better on tasks of academic English than do students with low levels of language and literacy proficiency in Spanish (Fischer & Cabello, 1978; Lindholm & Zierlein, 1991; Medina & de la Garza, 1989; Snow, 1990).

These findings then, provide pedagogical evidence that academic literacy skills acquired in the mother tongue will transfer positively to English if they are sufficiently developed in the native language. Data from the studies cited above also suggest that primary language instruction in literacy may be the most educationally sound method for helping Spanish-speaking LEP children learn about the academic uses of school English. The rationale that underlies this thinking is that when LEP children develop reading and writing competencies first in their mother tongue, they are not forced to address issues of language and meaning separately. In other words, they do not have to learn *about* a language before they can construct meaning in that language. Therefore, teaching Spanish-speakers about print relationships in their mother tongue enhances their opportunities to attend more to the semantic content of a writer's message and to the syntactic devices used to encode that message than to graphic input. Thus, acquisition of reading and writing skills and overall understanding of literacy as a tool for purposeful communication is not impeded by linguistic gaps.

The Connection Between Literacy Instruction in the Native Language and Pedagogy

Early in this paper we referred to a *holistic* model of bilingual education as one that cultivates and maintains the literacy skills of language minority children in both their L1 and L2. We explained that this model, which promotes literacy proficiency in both the home language and English, would frame our discussion on the importance of teaching Spanish dominant elementary school children to speak, read, and write competently in their primary language. In keeping with our purpose, we have presented evidence in the previous two sections to show: (1) that language is a vehicle for expressing the sociocultural behaviors of a community of speakers, (2) that prior linguistic knowledge determines the extent to which students can interact with information in a text, and (3) that children cannot become proficient readers if their past linguistic and social experiences are not relevant to the literacy materials they are using.

In this final section, we will comment on the importance of designing an educational curriculum that fosters linguistic pluralism as a means of enhancing the literacy skills of Spanish-speaking children. We will also consider the effect of classroom instructional practices in the native language on student learning and self-esteem.

LINGUISTIC AND CURRICULAR CONCERNS

Literacy can only be relevant and functional in the context of a relevant and functional curriculum. Such a curriculum allows for the natural acquisition of literacy and biliteracy by building on what learners know, their language, culture, interests, and common experiences. (Goodman, Goodman & Flores, 1984, p. 35)

If the purpose of literacy is meaning and meaning is tied to what readers know, then it follows that a relevant curriculum for Spanish-speaking elementary school children will build on information from their home, community, and school life (Wong Fillmore & Valadez, 1985). Krashen and Biber (1988) define literacy as "the ability to use language to discuss abstract ideas, to solve problems, (and) to clarify and stimulate thinking" (p. 22). A curriculum that fosters creative problem solving through Spanish will thus help bilingual youngsters achieve what English-only children achieve in an educationally stimulating environment. This is an awareness of how to use language to describe and reflect on one's own and others' actions, to organize thoughts through words, and to communicate ideas and intentions in a culturally appropriate way.

We have raised the issue of "creative" and "stimulating" literacy acquisition here because children develop a high degree of proficiency in speaking, reading, and writing only in educational settings where they are offered opportunities to become active participants in their learning experiences. Active literacy participation requires an identification with the topics and materials of the literacy event. Specifically, a literary curriculum that promotes a high level of student involvement enables all youngsters to raise questions about learning activities and to critically examine the content of their literacy interactions. Discussing the classroom environment of Spanish dominant bilinguals, Snow (1990) asserts that children will find literacy materials rich and challenging only in a language they speak well.

Of further importance to the literacy learning process is the way in which children are taught. The debate of the 1990s cannot be about the value of bilingual education for primary language students but instead about how to provide the most effective instructional environments for these students. For example, in a large-scale study of different program options available to Spanish dominant bilinguals in the elementary grades, Ramírez, Yuen, and Ramey (1991) discovered that those students who did not receive the long-term benefits of native language instruction exhibited a decrease in their rate of growth in English language achievement and reading after the third grade. This outcome suggests that as learning material becomes progressively more complex (or *context reduced*) across grade levels, the native language may be the best resource for teaching bilinguals about academic literacy skills of an analytical nature. In other words, when children have a solid linguistic foundation in their primary language, they are prepared to acquire increasingly abstract concepts in that language. Once learned through the mother tongue, these concepts will then provide the backdrop for expressing the kind of information in their L2.

Another pertinent issue concerning literacy instruction in bilingual settings addresses the need to explore how students achieve academic language competence in both their L1 and L2. Little is still known about the process bilinguals use to transfer information from one linguistic system to another and about which pedagogical environments best facilitate this transfer (Hakuta, 1986). To this end, Padilla (1990) suggests studying recent advances in the cognitive sciences and in educational technology to heighten our understanding of the way information is assimilated across languages and to articulate pedagogical practices with learning strategies.

LITERACY PRACTICES AND STUDENT SELF-ESTEEM

Certainly, no one would deny that professional accomplishment and socioeconomic mobility rest largely on an individual's skill at manipulating speech and print. Moreover, in a global society that relies heavily on international commerce and communication, there is a compelling need for individuals who are highly bilingual and biliterate. Nevertheless, when schools deny Spanish-speaking youngsters the tool that can be of greatest use to them in developing literacy proficiency—their native language—they are devaluing the self-worth of these youngsters and rejecting their most important personal asset for success in life. For this reason, Macedo (1991) asserts that "educators must develop radical pedagogical structures that provide students with the opportunity to use their own reality as a basis for literacy. This includes, obviously, the language they bring to the classroom." (p. 16)

All too often the success of bilingual education is judged by the number of LEP children who are reading in English or who are exited from bilingual programs into a regular education curriculum. The message these children receive, both overtly and covertly, from such instructional practices is that school achievement is measured primarily in terms of English competence. Bilinguals quickly learn that their native language and the cultural experiences it encodes have a low status in the classroom and in the society at large. Therefore, school personnel must seriously rethink how they transmit educational messages to students and whether the pedagogical practices they use in the classroom do, in fact, positively acknowledge the home background and cultural values of the students they serve.

A case in point comes from the Ramírez et al. study cited above. An examination of instructional personnel in different bilingual education program types shows that teachers in settings that promoted long-term study of literacy in Spanish generally had cultural backgrounds that were similar to those of their students. These teachers also had sufficient fluency in Spanish to be able to use the language as a medium of instruction. On the other hand, teachers in English immersion settings and in early exit bilingual education programs tended not to be Hispanic or to have the capability of teaching through Spanish. Their classroom behaviors thus reflected their pedagogical capabilities and the rationale underlying their respective program type.

To conclude then, we recognize, as have others (Ferdman, 1991; Skutnabb-Kangas, 1981), that the mother tongue is the primary vehicle for helping individuals establish their personal and social identity. It is the instrument that enables them to manage their thinking and the multitude of interactions, activities, and events in their surroundings. For this reason, if language minority children are to become competent readers, they must be able to share linguistic and cultural information with an author. Literacy instruction in their native language clearly helps them draw upon their own world knowledge to relate to texts in a meaningful way. When dominant speakers of Spanish learn to speak, read, and write proficiently in their primary language, they are building upon a firm foundation of linguistic, conceptual, and experiential information that paves the way for a high level of involvement with print. Snow (1990) underscores the need for schools to show sensitivity and appreciation for the language and cultural norms that young Spanish speakers bring with them to the classroom. Arguing this point on pedagogical grounds, she explains that by so doing, schools can maximize the self-esteem of students and that students with high self-esteem "work harder, learn better, and achieve more." (p. 64)

ABOUT THE AUTHORS

Elly B. Pardo received her Ph.D. in Education in 1985 from Stanford University, where her research focused on the first and second language learning patterns of Spanish-speaking children. She also has advanced degrees in Linguistics, Reading, and Spanish Literature from Stanford, Boston University, and George Washington University, respectively. Dr. Pardo has an extensive practical background in educational program evaluation and bilingual education. She has published in the areas of linguistics, developmental psycholinguistics, and educational testing; she has authored and contributed to many evaluation documents pertaining to the schooling of high-risk youth. Presently, Dr. Pardo works nationally as an educational consultant.

Josefina Villamil Tinajero is currently Associate Professor of Bilingual Education and Director of the Mother-Daughter Program at the University of Texas at El Paso. She is a fellow of the Kellogg National Fellowship Program and past president of the Texas Council of Reading and the Bilingual Child. Dr. Tinajero is an author of several reading programs published by Macmillan/McGraw-Hill School Publishing Company: *Mil maravillas, Campanitas de oro, Transitional Reading Program, A New View, The Write Idea,* and *Cuentamundos*. Currently, she serves as associate editor of *The Journal of Educational Issues of Language Minority Students* and on the editorial board of *Teacher Education and Practice*. She has also served on the editorial board of *The Reading Teacher*. Dr. Tinajero has prepared elementary teachers in bilingual, ESL, and reading and has been a consultant for numerous school districts throughout the United States. Currently, she is conducting research on the effects of cooperative learning on language minority students and on literacy and the transfer of learning.

References

Alexander, P. A., Schallert, D. L., and Hare, V. C. (1991). Coming to terms: How researchers in learning and literacy talk about knowledge. *Review of Educational Research*, vol. 61, no. 3, pp. 315–43.

Baker, K. A., and de Kanter, A. A. (1981). *Effectiveness of bilingual education: A review of the literature*. Washington, DC: Office of Planning and Budget, U.S. Department of Education.

Brown, R. (1973). *A first language: The early stages*. Cambridge, MA: Harvard University Press.

Collier, V. P. (1987). Age and rate of acquisition of second language for academic purposes. *TESOL Quarterly*, vol. 21, pp. 617–41.

Cummins, J. (1991). Language shift and language learning in the transition from home to school. *Journal of Education*, vol. 173, no. 2, pp. 85–97.

Cummins, J. (1989). *Empowering minority students*. Sacramento: California Association for Bilingual Education.

Cummins, J. (1987). Bilingualism, language proficiency, and metalinguistic development. In Homel, P., Palij, M., and Aaronson, D. (Eds.), *Childhood bilingualism: Aspects of linguistic, cognitive and social development*, pp. 57–73. Hillsdale, NJ: Lawrence Erlbaum Associates, Publishers.

Cummins, J. (1981). *Schooling and language minority students*. Los Angeles: California State University; Evaluation, Dissemination and Assessment Center.

Cummins, J. (1979). Linguistic interdependence and the educational development of bilingual children. *Review of Educational Research*, vol. 49, pp. 222–51.

Dechant, E. (1991). Understanding and teaching reading: An interactive model. Hillsdale, NJ: Lawrence Erlbaum Associates, Publishers.

Dunn, L. (1987). *Bilingual Hispanic children on the U.S. mainland: A review of research on their cognitive, linguistic, and scholastic development*. Circle Pines, MN: American Guidance Service.

Fischer, K., and Cabello, B. (1978). *Predicting student success following transition for bilingual programs*. Los Angeles: Center for the Study of Evaluation.

Ferdman, B. (1991). Literacy and cultural identity. In *Language Issues in Literacy and Bilingual/Multicultural Education*, pp. 347–71. Cambridge, MA: Harvard Educational Review.

Genesee, F. (1987). *Learning through two languages*. Cambridge, MA: Newbury House Publishers.

Gersten, R., and Woodward, J. (1985). A case for structured immersion. *Educational Leadership*, vol. 43, no. 2, pp. 75–79.

González, L. A. (1989). Native language education: The key to English literacy skills. In Bixler-Marquez, D. J., Green, G. K., and Ornstein-Galicia, J. L. (Eds.), *Mexican-American Spanish in its societal and cultural contexts*. Rio Grande Series in Language and Linguistics, no. 3, Pan American University at Brownsville.

Goodman, K. S. (1967). Reading: A psycholinguistic guessing game. *Journal of the Reading Specialist*, vol. 4, pp. 125–35.

Goodman, K. S., Goodman, Y., and Flores, B. (1984). *Reading in the bilingual classroom: Literacy and biliteracy*. Washington, DC: National Clearinghouse for Bilingual Education.

Goodman, Y., and Goodman, K. S. (1979). Learning to read is natural. In Resnick, L. B., and Weaver, P. A. (Eds.), *Theory and practice of early reading*, vol. 1. Hillsdale, NJ: Lawrence Erlbaum.

Hakuta, K. (1990). Language and cognition in bilingual children. In Padilla, A. M., Fairchild, H. H., Valadez, C. M. (Eds.) *Bilingual education: Issues and strategies*. Newbury Park, CA: Sage Publications.

Hakuta, K. (1986). *Mirror of language*. New York: Basic Books.

Hakuta, K., and Diaz, R. M. (1984). The relationship between degree of bilingualism and cognitive ability: A critical discussion and some new longitudinal data. In Nelson, K. E. (Ed.), *Children's language*, vol. 5, pp. 319–44. Hillsdale, NJ: Lawrence Erlbaum Associates, Publishers.

Heath, S. B. (1989). Sociocultural contexts of language development. In *Beyond language: Social and cultural factors in schooling language minority students*. Los Angeles: California State University; Evaluation, Dissemination and Assessment Center.

Heath, S. B. (1983). *Ways with words*. Cambridge: Cambridge University Press.

Hymes, D. (1974). *Foundations in sociolinguistics: An ethnographic approach*. Philadelphia: University of Pennsylvania Press.

Krashen, S., and Biber, D. (1988). *On course: Bilingual education's success in California*. Sacramento: California Association for Bilingual Education.

Lambert, W. (1987). The effects of bilingual and bicultural experiences on children's attitudes and social perspectives. In Homel, P., Paliu, M., and Aaronson, D. (Eds.), *Childhood bilingualism: Aspects of linguistic, cognitive, and social development*, pp. 197–221. Hillsdale, NJ: Lawrence Erlbaum.

Lambert, W. (1984). An overview of issues in immersion education. In *Studies in immersion education: A collection for U.S. educators*, pp. 8–30. Sacramento: California State Department of Education.

Lindholm, K. J., and Zierlein, A. (1991). Bilingual proficiency as a bridge to academic achievement: Results from bilingual/immersion programs. *Journal of Education*, vol. 173, no. 2, pp. 99–113.

Macedo, D. (1991). English only: The tongue-tying of America. *Journal of Education*, vol. 173, no. 2, pp. 9–20.

Matute-Bianchi, M. E. (1986). Ethnic identities and patterns of school success and failure among Mexican-descent and Japanese-American students in a California high school: An ethnographic analysis. *American Journal of Education*, vol. 95, pp. 233–55.

Medina, M., Jr., and de la Garza, J. V. (1989). Bilingual instruction and academic gains of Spanish-dominant Mexican American students. *NABE Journal*, vol. 13, no. 2, pp. 113–23.

Padilla, A. M. (1990). Issues and perspectives. In Padilla, A. M., Fairchild, H. H., and Valadez, C. M. (Eds.), *Bilingual education: Issues and strategies*, pp. 1–26. Newbury Park, CA: Sage Publications.

Pardo, E. B. (in press). Prerequisites for developing effective oral language skills. In Wheelock, A. (Ed.), *Crossing the tracks: How untracking can save America's schools*, pp. 147–50. New York: New Press.

Perera, K. (1987). *Understanding language*. One of a series of occasional papers published by the National Association of Advisers in English.

Ramírez, A. G. (1992). Language proficiency and bilingualism. In Padilla, R. V., and Benavides, A. (Eds.), *Critical perspectives on bilingual education research*, pp. 257–76. Tucson, AZ: Bilingual Review/Press.

Ramírez, J. D., Yuen, S. D., and Ramey, E. (1991). *Final report: Longitudinal study of structured English immersion strategy, early-exit and late-exit transitional bilingual education programs for language-minority children*. U.S. Department of Education, Contract No. 300-87-0156. San Mateo, CA: Aguirre International.

Skutnabb-Kangas, T. (1981). *Bilingualism or not: The education of minorities*. Bodmin, Cornwall: Robert Hartnoll Ltd.

Smith, F. (1988). *Understanding reading: A psycholinguistic analysis of reading and learning to read*. New York: Holt, Rinehart and Winston; Hillsdale, NJ: Lawrence Erlbaum Associates, Publishers.

Snow, C. E. (1990). Rationales for native language instruction. In Padilla, A. M., Fairchild, H. H., and Valadez, C. M. (Eds.), *Bilingual education: Issues and strategies*, pp. 60–74. Newbury Park, CA: Sage Publications.

Troike, R. C. (1978). Research evidence for the effectiveness of bilingual education. *NABE Journal*, vol. 3, pp. 13–24.

Vygotsky, L. S. (1962). *Thought and language*. Cambridge, MA: MIT Press.

Wong Fillmore, L., and Valadez, C. (1985). Teaching bilingual learners. In Wittrock, M. C. (Ed.), *Handbook of research on teaching*, pp. 648–85. Washington, DC: American Educational Research Association.

We Speak in Many Tongues

Language Diversity and Multicultural Education

Sonia Nieto
University of Massachusetts at Amherst

Introduction

The United States is on the road to becoming a truly multilingual nation, if not in policy at least in practice. While the battle by the conservative right to make English the sole and official language of the country rages on, our classrooms, communities, and workplaces are becoming more linguistically diverse.[1] The increase in the number of students who speak a native language other than English has been dramatic and is expected to remain so. For instance, immigration to the United States during the 1970s and 1980s was among the largest in this nation's history. Legal immigration alone between 1980 and 1990 was almost 9 million, equalling that of the peak immigration decade of 1900–1910. About one-third of this immigration has been from Asia and another third from Latin America. In addition, it is estimated that the number of students who speak a language other than English will increase from just over 2 million in 1986 to over 5 million by 2020. Another indication of the enormous changes taking place in our society is the prediction that by the year 2050 the Latino population will have tripled in number and the Asian population will have increased tenfold.[2]

These statistics are cause for concern for the many teachers who must grapple with the dilemmas posed by the linguistic and educational differences that students bring to our schools. The purpose of this chapter is to explore the growing linguistic diversity in our society and schools in order to propose a different and more productive way of approaching the issue. Rather than continuing to view linguistic diversity as a problem to be corrected, we must change our thinking and consider it an asset for our classrooms and for society in general. Research focusing on the importance of native language development in school achievement will also be reviewed. Finally, I will propose several implications for school policies and practices based on the research reviewed and on a reconceptualization of language diversity within schools.

Language Diversity and Multicultural Education: Expanding the Framework

To understand language issues in a more comprehensive way, we need to expand the framework with which we view linguistic diversity. I will propose several ways in which to do this:

- understanding language diversity as a positive rather than as a negative condition;
- developing an awareness of the key role that language discrimination has played in U.S. educational history;
- removing the compensatory status of programs for linguistically diverse students;
- understanding the crucial role of bilingual education within a multicultural perspective; and
- redefining the benefits of linguistic diversity for all students.

Viewing Bilingualism as an Asset In the United States, we have generally been socialized to think of language diversity as a negative rather than as a positive condition. Yet in most other countries in the world, bilingualism and multilingualism are the order of the day. The prestige accorded to language diversity is a highly complex issue depending on the region of the country, the country itself, the language variety spoken, where and when one has learned to speak, and of course, the ethnicity and class of the speaker. Sometimes bilingualism is highly regarded. This is usually the case with those who are well educated and have high status within their society. At other times, bilingualism is seen as a sign of low status. This is usually the case with those who are poor and powerless within their society, even if they happen to speak a multitude of languages.[3] It is evident that issues of *status* and *power* must be taken into account in reconceptualizing language diversity. This means developing an awareness that racism and ethnocentrism are at the core of policies and practices that limit the use of languages other than the officially recognized high-status language in schools and in society in general. That is, when particular languages are prohibited or denigrated, the voices of those who speak them are silenced and rejected as well.

Within the United States, the language of power is English. For those who speak it as a native language, monolingualism is an asset. In our society, bilingualism is usually considered an asset only for those who are dominant in English but have learned another language as a second language.

On the other hand, those who speak a language associated with low prestige and limited power as their native tongue are often regarded as deficient. Speaking with a Parisian French accent may be regarded as a mark of high status in some parts of the country, while speaking Canadian French or Haitian Creole usually is not. Likewise, speaking Castilian Spanish tends to be regarded more positively than speaking Latin American or Caribbean Spanish, which are often viewed within the general population as inferior varieties of the language.

For some groups, then, bilingualism is seen as a handicap. This is usually the case with our Latino, American Indian, Asian, and Caribbean students, those who represent the majority of the language minority students in our classrooms. Linguistically, there is nothing *wrong* with the languages they speak. That is, for purposes of communication, these languages are as valid as any others. However, socially and politically, they are accorded low status. Students who speak these languages are perceived as having a "problem," and the problem is defined as fluency in a language other than English. Because society in general and schools in particular define this as a problem, the purpose of education becomes to wipe out all signs of the native language. This is often done by well-meaning educators who perceive their students' fluency in another language as a handicap to their learning English and moving up the social ladder.[4]

BILITERACY: A TRANSFORMATIVE PEDAGOGY

Developing an Awareness of Linguicism
United States educational history is replete with examples of language discrimination or what Skutnabb-Kangas has called *linguicism*. Specifically, she defines linguicism as "ideologies and structures which are used to legitimate, effectuate and reproduce an unequal division of power and resources (both material and nonmaterial) between groups which are defined on the basis of language."[5] Entire communities, starting with Indian nations and enslaved Africans, have been prohibited the use of their native languages for either communication or education. This is evident in policies forbidding the use of other languages in schools, and in the lack of equal educational opportunity for youngsters who could not understand the language of instruction.[6] While this is particularly evident with racially and economically oppressed groups, linguicism has not been limited to these but has in fact been a widespread policy with *all* languages other than English in our society. The massive obliteration of the German language is a case in point. While German was almost on a par with English as a language of communication in the United States during the eighteenth and nineteenth centuries—and was in fact one of the most common languages used in bilingual programs during parts of our history—it was largely wiped out by xenophobic policies immediately prior to, during, and after World War I.[7]

Because of the tremendous pressures faced by those who spoke languages other than English, the fact that giving up one's language is a terrible and unnecessary sacrifice was often not questioned. Even today, it is still common to hear of children punished for speaking their native language, or of notes sent home to parents who barely speak English asking them not to speak their native language with their children. While nowadays there is more of an awareness of the extreme ethnocentrism of such practices, the fact that they continue to exist is an indication of our ingrained reluctance to perceive language diversity in positive terms. In developing a more positive framework for linguistic diversity, it is absolutely crucial that we learn how language discrimination has been used to discredit and disenfranchise those who speak languages other than English.

Removing the Compensatory Label from Linguistic Diversity Generally speaking, approaches geared toward students who speak a language other than English are compensatory in nature. That is, they respond to language diversity as if it were an illness to be cured. Thus, most approaches emphasize using the native language only as a bridge to English. When English is learned sufficiently well, the reasoning goes, the bridge can be burned and the student is well on her or his way to achieving academic success.

There are several problems with this reasoning. First, a compensatory approach assumes only that students are *lacking* in something, rather than that they also possess certain skills and talents. Instead of perceiving fluency in another language as an asset to be cherished, it is seen as something that needs fixing. Using the students' literacy in their native language as a basis for the development of literacy in their second language is not usually considered a viable option. Thus, students are expected to start all over again. Not only do they flounder in English, but they often forget their native language in the process.

In addition, even when language minority students are in bilingual programs, they are frequently removed too quickly and often end up in special education classes.[8] Most of the approaches used to help language minority students in school are based on this compensatory framework.[9] Yet, research in this area has suggested that in general students need between five and seven years to make a successful transition from their native language to English.[10] Ironically, when they fail to achieve, the blame is often placed on bilingual programs rather than on premature "exiting" from bilingual programs. Schools need to turn around preconceived notions of language diversity that may lead to policies and practices that jeopardize the very students we are trying to reach.

In order to expand our framework for linguistic diversity, then, we need to develop practices that build on students' language skills rather than tear them down. Programs such as *maintenance* or *developmental bilingual education*, in which students are encouraged to develop literacy and continued use of both English and their native language, represent a very different approach to language diversity. In programs such as these, students' native language is not considered a "crutch" to lean on until they master the "real" language of schooling. Rather, their native language is recognized as valid not only while they learn English but also in the acquisition of knowledge in general. *Two-way bilingual programs*, in which language minority students and monolingual speakers of English are integrated, afford another way of validating both languages of instruction. In addition, students in these programs learn to appreciate the language and culture of others and to empathize with their peers in the difficult process of developing fluency in a language not their own. Such programs have also been found to be successful in promoting academic achievement.[11]

Linguistic Diversity and Multicultural Education In expanding the framework for language diversity, we also need to redefine it within the field of multicultural education. One of the primary goals of multicultural education is to build on the strengths that students bring to school. Unfortunately, even within multicultural education, the strengths of language diversity are rarely considered. Even the most enlightened and inclusive frameworks for multicultural education fail to take into account the significance of language differences. Although race, class, and gender are often considered integral to multicultural education, language, which does not fit neatly into any of these categories, is not.[12] While it is true that most language minority students within U.S. schools are also from racially and economically oppressed communities, language differences cannot be relegated to either racial or class distinctions alone. Language diversity in and of itself needs to be considered as an important difference through which we can better understand both the talents and the needs students bring to school.

The failure of many proponents of multicultural education to seriously consider linguistic diversity or of supporters of bilingual education to understand the goals of multicultural education leads to a curious schism: in one corner, we have multicultural education while in the other we have bilingual education. This artificial separation often results in the perception that multicultural education is for African American students and other students of color who speak English, while bilingual education is only for Latino students and other students who speak a language other than English as their native language. This perception is reinforced by the fact that each of these fields has its own organizations, political and research agendas, and networks. Of course, this kind of specialization is both necessary and desirable because the questions we need to ask and the approaches we develop for each may be quite distinct. On the other hand, by positing the fields of bilingual and multicultural education as fundamentally different and unconnected ones, their common agendas are denied and each is left scrambling for limited resources. The unfortunate result is that proponents of bilingual and multicultural education sometimes become enemies with separate constituencies who know little about the other and may therefore respond with ignorance and hostility to one another.

Teachers need to understand that bilingual education is part and parcel of multicultural education. By allowing these two fields to be isolated from each other, the natural links between them are obscured. Language is one of the most salient aspects of culture. If the languages students speak, with all their attendant social meanings and affirmations, are either negated or relegated to a secondary position in their schooling, the possibility of school failure is increased. Because language and culture are so intimately connected, and because both bilingual and multicultural approaches seek to involve and empower the most vulnerable students in our schools, it is essential that we foster their natural links. This is not to imply that either bilingual or multicultural education is reserved for particular groups. On the contrary, both should be understood as necessary for *all* students. Nevertheless, given their roots and historical context, it is true that they began as responses to demands for improving the education of African American, Latino, Native American Indian, and Asian American students.

Redefining the Beneficiaries of Linguistic Diversity Generally speaking, programs that meet the needs of language minority students require the separation of these students from others. In fact, the dilemma posed by this kind of isolation has been seen as one of the knottiest questions facing the proponents of bilingual education. Landry has maintained that while the problems of race, class, gender, and disability discrimination are best resolved by integration, quite the opposite is true for language discrimination.[13] That is, bilingual education demands the opportunity to *separate* students, at least for part of their education. This makes it particularly troublesome in a democratic society that purports to afford all students an equal educational opportunity. While this claim of equal education is far from real, it is nevertheless an important ideal to strive for. Thus, we need to face the dilemma of segregation that bilingual education presupposes.

There are several ways that the needs of limited English proficiency and monolingual English speakers can be served at the same time. One is through two-way bilingual education, as previously mentioned. Other approaches include setting aside times for joint instruction and developing bilingual options within desegregation plans and magnet schools. Much remains to be done in expanding these options. Perhaps the most important shift in thinking that needs to take place is that *bilingual classrooms, teachers, and students are a rich resource for nonbilingual classrooms, teachers, and students.* When this shift happens, our schools will have taken the first step in commiting society to making bilingualism and even multilingualism central educational goals for *all* students. This is hardly the case right now. For language minority students, for example, English language acquisition, often at the expense of their native language, is the primary goal rather than bilingualism. Even for our English monolingual students, the goal of bilingualism is an elusive one because foreign language courses are delayed until secondary school and are often ineffective. However, when language diversity becomes a benefit to all, we can be quite sure that the persistent underfunding of bilingual education will be eliminated and all students will benefit as a result.

We also need to mention, however, that bilingual education and other support services need to be understood as ensuring educational equity, particularly for language minority students. The issue is not simply one of language but goes much deeper than this. Bilingual education is a civil rights issue because it provides one of the few guarantees that children who do not speak English will be provided education in a language they understand. Given the increasing number of students who enter schools speaking a language other than English, it is clear that bilingual education will become even more important in the years ahead. Just as desegregation has been considered an important (and as yet unattained) civil right for those doomed to receive an inferior education because of inequality of resources, bilingual education is understood by language minority communities as an equally important civil right. Thus, in expanding the framework for linguistic diversity so that all students can benefit from it, we need to remind ourselves that for limited English proficient students, bilingual education is not a frill but *basic* education.

Native Language and School Achievement

Because language diversity has so often been viewed as a deficit, the positive influences of knowing a language other than English have frequently been overlooked.[14] Nevertheless, some recent research has examined the role of a native language other than English on the literacy development and academic achievement of students. Let me begin by stressing that the lack of English skills alone does little to explain the poor academic achievement of students classified as limited in their English proficiency. For example, Cuban students have the highest educational levels of all Latinos, yet they are also the most likely to speak Spanish at home.[15] Cubans are also the most highly educated and upwardly mobile of all Latino groups. It is clear then that speaking Spanish is not the problem. Rather, how language is viewed by the school and the larger society, how students themselves feel about their language, and most importantly, the economic class and professional background of parents seem to play key roles in the academic performance of students.

Given this caveat, research nonetheless suggests that native language maintenance seems to improve rather than jeopardize academic achievement. A study by Dolson, for instance, found that in measures of academic achievement, students who used Spanish at home generally outperformed their peers whose families had switched to only English. Clearly, the home language of these students gave them a distinct advantage in learning.[16] Another study found that recent Mexican immigrants were more successful in school in the United States than were longtime Mexican American residents. The same has been found with recent Puerto Rican arrivals as compared with those who have been here through all or most of their schooling.[17] Thus, the longer they are here, the worse their academic achievement. A major study of immigrant and nonimmigrant students in San Diego had similar findings. They concluded that Latino, Filipino, and Asian immigrants who were just becoming fluent in English were more academically successful than their U.S.-born counterparts.[18] Clearly, then, language differences are not the major problem.

Other recent research bolsters these findings. For example, studies by Moll and Díaz on successful reading and writing learning environments for Latino students found that the students' native language and culture did not handicap their learning. Instead, they concluded that the problems linguistic minority students face are generally due to instructional arrangements in schools that fail to capitalize on the strengths, including linguistic and cultural resources, that they bring to school.[19] In her research with four Mexican American students, Commins also found that the classroom setting for linguistic minority students can work as an intervening variable to support or to weaken students' perceptions of themselves and can thus contribute to their linguistic and academic development or lack of it. In fact, one of the major themes demonstrated by the student profiles was the ambivalence they experienced about their bilingualism.[20]

Thus, speaking a language other than English is not necessarily a handicap; on the contrary, it can be a great asset to learning. How such language use is interpreted is the real issue. For example, bilingual and other support services for students with a limited English proficiency frequently have a low status. Even their physical placement within schools is indicative of this. These programs are often found in large windowless closets, hallways, or classrooms next to the boiler room. Little surprise then that even the parents of children in these programs press for a quick exit for their children.

Yet, the fact is that bilingual education and other programs that support native language use, even if only as a transition to English, are generally more effective than programs such as ESL alone. This is true not only in terms of learning content in the native language, but in terms of learning *English* as well. This seemingly contradictory finding can be understood if one considers the fact that students in bilingual programs are provided with continued education in content areas *along with* structured instruction in English. In addition, they are building on their previous literacy and thus it becomes what Lambert has called an *additive* form of bilingual education. *Subtractive* bilingual education, on the other hand, is when one language is substituted for another, and true literacy is not achieved in either.[21] This often happens in programs where the students' native language is eliminated and English grammar, phonics, and other language features are taught out of context with the way in which real day-to-day language is used.

Even in programs where English is not used or used minimally, results show dramatic gains in students' achievement. Campos and Keatinge, for instance, found that Latino children enrolled in a Spanish-only preschool program developed more skills that would prepare them for school than children in a bilingual preschool program where the main goal was to develop proficiency in English.[22] A comparative evaluation of bilingual and ESL-only programs also found that students in bilingual programs consistently outperformed those in ESL-only programs even in their English-language performance.[23] Ironically, the more native-language instruction students received, the better they performed in English! It is clear then that even if the primary purpose of education in our society is to learn English (a debatable position at best), bilingual programs seem to work more effectively than programs in which only English is used because bilingual programs use students' acquired literacy as the basis for learning English. These findings have been consistently reported by researchers working in the field of bilingual education. Thus, when students' language is used as the basis for their education, when it is respected and valued, students tend to succeed in school.[24]

Although not explored as thoroughly with culture, a number of studies point to the same conclusions. For example, in a study of successful Punjabi students, Gibson found that parents consistently admonished their children to maintain their culture and made it clear that not doing so would dishonor their families and communities.[25] In addition, a major study of Southeast Asian students found an intriguing connection between grades and culture: higher grade-point averages were positively related to the maintenance of traditional values, ethnic pride, and close social and culture ties with members of the same ethnic group.[26]

In my own research with academically successful students, I found that maintaining language and culture were essential in supporting and sustaining their academic achievement. In a series of in-depth interviews with these linguistically, culturally, and economically diverse students, one of the salient features accounting for school success was a strong-willed determination to hold onto their culture and native language. Their pride in culture and language, however, were not without conflict. That is, most of these young people expressed both pride and shame in their culture. Given the assimilationist messages of our society, this is hardly surprising. What was surprising, however, was the steadfastness with which they maintained their culture and language in spite of such messages. Yet, for the most part, these were students who would not be expected to succeed in school given their disadvantaged economic position.[27]

What can we learn, then, from research focusing on the importance of language and culture in the academic achievement of students? One intriguing conclusion is that the more students are involved in resisting assimilation while maintaining their culture and language, the more successful they will be in school. That is, cultural and linguistic maintenance seems to have a positive impact on academic success. This is obviously not true in all cases, as we can all think of examples of people who have felt they had to assimilate in order to succeed in school. The case of Richard Rodríguez, who felt compelled to choose between what he considered "public" and "private" worlds, comes to mind. That is, in order for him to succeed, he felt that he needed to reject his Mexican culture and the Spanish language.[28] We can legitimately ask whether his represents a healthy success, for in the bargain he lost part of himself. Thus, while it is important not to overstate that linguistic and cultural maintenance seem to have a positive impact on academic achievement, it is indeed a real possibility and one that severely challenges the "melting pot" ideology that has dominated U.S. schools and society throughout this century. The notion that assimilation is a necessary prerequisite for success in school and society is severely tested by current research.

Implications for Classroom Practice

The conclusion that maintaining native language and culture positively influences student achievement turns on its head not only conventional educational philosophy but also the policies and practices of schools that have done everything possible to effectively eradicate students' culture and language in order, they maintained, for all students to succeed in school. It would mean that rather than attempting to erase culture and language, schools should do everything in their power to use, affirm, and maintain them as a foundation for students' academic success. School policies and practices that stress cultural pride, build on students' native language ability, and use the experiences, culture, and history of the students' communities as a basis for instruction would be the result. We can even say that when their language and culture are reinforced not only at home but in school as well, students seem to develop less confusion and ambiguity about their ability to learn. Thus, regardless of the sometimes harsh attacks on their culture and language (as is the case in communities in which there are strident campaigns to pass "English-only" legislation), students whose language and culture are valued within the school setting pick up affirming messages about their worth.

If we move our thinking from *language diversity as deficit* to *language diversity as asset*, the implications for policy and practice become quite different from what they are at present. When linguistic diversity is seen as a handicap to be "fixed," policies and practices that focus on doing away with students' language differences are in operation. On the other hand, when linguistic diversity is seen as a valuable resource for students, schools, and communities, policies and practices reinforce the importance of and necessity for bilingualism and multilingualism. Three key implications of the reconceptualization of linguistic diversity in our schools become clear: strengthening bilingual programs, developing comprehensive multicultural education, and actively seeking ways to involve the parents of linguistic minority students in their children's education. Let us briefly review each of these.

1. Bilingual Programs Need to Be Valued and Strengthened

Bilingual education has always been a controversial program within U.S. schools, especially during the past 25 years when it has become such an important option for students with limited English proficiency. It is clear that a rethinking of the very goals of bilingual education needs to take place in order to reinforce the crucial role it has proven to have in supporting both English acquisition *and* native language maintenance. Thus, not only should these programs be promoted, but they should also be accorded more visibility and respect within schools. This implies at least the following:

- more funding for bilingual programs;
- availability of such programs for all students with limited English proficiency;
- changing the "quick-exit" mentality of bilingual programs; and
- more two-way programs in which bilingualism is promoted for all students.

2. Comprehensive Multicultural Programs Should Be Developed

Reconceptualizing language diversity as an essential component of multicultural education also means that the way in which schools view multicultural education needs to be changed. Multicultural education in many schools is reduced to a "Holidays and

Heroes" approach where making exotic masks, eating ethnic foods, and commemorating safe heroes are the primary activities. Nevertheless, the research reviewed here has made it clear that if culture and language are to be respected and affirmed, a comprehensive approach to multicultural education needs to be developed. This means that linguistic differences of students not in bilingual programs need to be respected as well. In fact, most students who speak a language other than English are not in bilingual programs, at least not for most of their schooling. Strategies that would send these students the message that their language is important and worthy of respect might include:

- encouraging students to use their native language with language peers, both in academic and social situations;
- pairing students with a buddy more fluent in English and encouraging each to teach the other;
- motivating students to teach their peers about their language and culture;
- inviting guests who speak a variety of languages to the classroom; and
- using bilingual classrooms as a valuable resource for nonbilingual classrooms.

In addition, teachers who learn at least a working knowledge of one or more languages are telling their students that they appreciate the difficult work it takes to learn another language.

3. Parent Involvement of Linguistic Minority Students Should Be Promoted

The key role that parent involvement plays in the education of all students has been proven time and again.[29] In the case of linguistic minority students, this role can be even more central. That is, because the parents of these children are often directly involved in their native language literacy, their support of and participation in native language maintenance are crucial. Although parents are the first and most important teachers of their children, the secondary status accorded to parents of linguistic minority students has impacted on their involvement in school in negative ways. Schools and teachers need to develop strategies that welcome parents as important partners in the education of their children. This means seeking ways to involve them both in school and out, and to reaffirm the role they have in nurturing and maintaining children's literacy in their native language. One way of respecting the languages they speak as languages of knowledge and learning is to use these languages in activities that promote literacy both in school and at home. This reasoning was behind the literacy project developed by Ada in her research with Mexican American parents. Working with the parents of young elementary school children, she initiated a discussion-oriented project on children's literature. In the process of dialogue, reading, and writing, parents developed confidence and greater abilities in using the resources at their command, particularly their language and culture, to promote the literacy of their children.[30]

It is obvious from such research that parents can have a decisive effect on their children's literacy development and on their academic success in general. Schools need to acknowledge this important role and to seek innovative strategies to use the talents, hope, and motivation of parents in constructive ways. The view that poor parents and those who speak a language other than English are unable to provide appropriate environments for their children can lead to condescending practices that reject the skills and resources that parents do have.

Conclusion

Language is one of the fundamental signs of our humanity. It is "the palette from which people color their lives and culture. Intimately connected to the human experience, language oils the gears of social interactions and solidifies the ephemera of the mind into literature, history and collective knowledge."[31] While linguistic diversity is a fact of life in U.S. schools and society, many languages are not given the respect and visibility they deserve. Because English is the language of power in our society, monolingualism is perceived as an asset. Those who speak a language other than English are generally viewed as having a problem that must be solved. At the core of such perceptions are racist and ethnocentric ideas about the value of some languages and not others.

Given recent trends in immigration, the shrinking of our world, and the subsequent necessity to learn to communicate with larger numbers of people, it is clear that a reconceptualization of the role of languages other than English within our schools and society in general has to take place. Such a reconceptualization needs to have the following components:

◆ a redefinition of linguistic diversity as an asset rather than a deficit;

◆ building on students' strengths, including their language and culture, rather than tearing these resources down;

◆ actively seeking out involvement by parents and other community people representing the linguistic diversity our students bring to school;

◆ understanding bilingual education and other language approaches and services as important and necessary components of multicultural education; and

◆ developing an awareness that all students can benefit from linguistic diversity, not only those with limited English proficiency.

Given this kind of reconceptualization, the policies and practices that schools have in place need to be reexamined. Those that build on students' diversity should be strengthened, while those that focus on differences as deficits should be eliminated. This means, at the very least, that bilingual and multicultural programs *for all students* have to be comprehensively defined, adequately funded, and strongly supported.

About the Author

Dr. Sonia Nieto is Associate Professor in the Cultural Diversity and Curriculum Reform Program, School of Education at the University of Massachusetts at Amherst. Born and raised in Brooklyn, Dr. Nieto was educated in the New York City public school system. She received her B.S. in elementary education from St. John's University and her M.A. in Spanish literature from the New York University Graduate Program in Spain. Dr. Nieto has taught at the elementary and junior high school levels and at P.S. 25, the first bilingual school in the Northeast, where she was also a curriculum specialist. Before receiving her doctorate in curriculum from the University of Massachusetts in 1979, she was a member of the faculty of the Puerto Rican Studies Department at Brooklyn College.

Dr. Nieto has received a number of fellowships and awards, including the Ford Foundation and Title VII doctoral fellowships, the *Human and Civil Rights Award* from the MTA (Massachusetts Teachers Association) in 1988, and the *Outstanding Accomplishment Award* from the Hispanic Committee of the American Association of Higher Education (1991). Dr. Nieto is married and has two daughters.

Notes

*The title of this chapter refers to a statement made by Dr. Luis Reyes ("We speak in many tongues, but we are not confused") in response to *The New York Times Magazine* article entitled "A Confusion of Tongues." It was reported in *Speaking Out About Bilingual Education: A Report on the Testimony Presented at the Community Speak-Out on Bilingual Education* (Puerto Rican/Latino Education Roundtable, c/o Centro, Hunter College, New York City, June 15, 1983).

I would like to thank Jerri Willet for reading an earlier version of this chapter and providing helpful and critical suggestions for improving it.

1. The National Education Association, among many other organizations, has taken a strong stand against the "English Only" movement. See *Official English/English Only: More Than Meets the Eye* (Washington, DC: NEA, 1988). For in-depth reviews and analyses of the history and purposes of "English Only," see Harvey A. Daniels, ed., *Not Only English: Affirming America's Multilingual Heri-*

tage (Urbana, IL: National Council of Teachers of English, 1990); and "English Plus: Issues in Bilingual Education," *Annals of the American Academy of Political and Social Science* 508 (March 1990).

2. See, for example, John B. Kellogg, "Forces of Change," *Phi Delta Kappan* (November 1988): 199–204; Thomas Muller and Thomas Espenshade, *The Fourth Wave* (Washington, DC: Urban Institute Press, 1985); the National Coalition of Advocates for Students, *New Voices: Immigrant Students in U.S. Public Schools* (Boston, MA, 1988); Gary Natriello, Edward L. McDill, and Aaron M. Pallas, *Schooling Disadvantaged Children: Racing Against Catastrophe* (New York: Teachers' College Press, 1990); and E. Emily Feistritzer, *Teacher Crisis: Myth or Reality? A State-by-State Analysis, 1986* (Washington, DC: National Center for Education Information, 1986).

3. For a more comprehensive explanation of this, see Howard Giles, Klaus R. Scherer, and Donald M. Taylor, "Speech Markers in Social Interaction," in Klaus R. Scherer and Howard Giles, eds., *Social Markers in Speech* (Cambridge, England: Cambridge University Press, 1979); Einar Haugen, "The Language of Imperialism: Unity or Pluralism?" in N. Wolfson and J. Manes, eds., *Language of Inequality* (New York: Mouton Publishers, 1987); and Robert Phillipson, "Linguicism: Structures and Ideologies in Linguistic Imperialism," in Tove Skutnabb-Kangas and Jim Cummins, eds., *Minority Language: From Shame to Struggle* (Clevedon, England: Multilingual Matters Ltd., 1988).

4. See the research by Aida Hurtado and Raúl Rodriguez for a more comprehensive description of this phenomenon, "Language as a Social Problem: The Repression of Spanish in South Texas," *Journal of Multilingual and Multicultural Development* 10 (5): 401–19.

5. Tove Skutnabb-Kangas, "Multilingualism and the Education of Minority Children," in Tove Skutnabb-Kangas and Jim Cummins, eds., *Minority Language: From Shame to Struggle* (Clevedon, England: Multilingual Matters Ltd., 1988), p. 13.

6. For examples of language discrimination in our history, see Meyer Weinberg, *A Chance to Learn: A History of Race and Education in the U.S.* (Cambridge, England: Cambridge University Press, 1977); and Jim Cummins, *Empowering Minority Students* (Sacramento, CA: California Association for Bilingual Education, 1989). Language discrimination was the basis for the unanimous Supreme Court decision in *Lau v. Nichols* (*Lau v. Nichols*, 414 U.S. 563, St. Paul, MN: West Publishing Co., 1974).

7. See, for example, Diego Castellanos, *The Best of Two Worlds* (Trenton, NJ: State Department of Education, 1983); and Gary S. Keller, and Karen S. van Hooft, "A Chronology of Bilingualism and Bilingual Education in the United States," in Joshua Fishman and Gary Keller, eds., *Bilingual Education for Hispanic Students in the United States* (New York: Teachers College Press, 1982).

8. For an explanation of the relationship between premature removal from bilingual programs and special education, see Jim Cummins, *Bilingualism and Special Education* (Clevedon, England: Multilingual Matters Ltd., 1984).

9. For a review of program models in bilingual education, see Carlos J. Ovando and Virginia P. Collier, *Bilingual and ESL Classrooms: Teaching in Multicultural Contexts* (New York: McGraw-Hill Book Co., 1985).

10. See Jim Cummins, "The Role of Primary Language Development in Promoting Educational Success for Language Minority Students," in Office of Bilingual Bicultural Education, *Schooling and Language Minority Students: A Theoretical Framework* (Sacramento, CA: Evaluation, Dissemination, and Assessment Center, California State University, Los Angeles, 1981); and Virginia P. Collier, "How Long? A Synthesis of Research on Academic Achievement in a Second Language," *TESOL Quarterly* 23 (September 1989): 509–31.

11. Virginia P. Collier, "Academic Achievement, Attitudes, and Occupations Among Graduates of Two-Way Bilingual Classes." Paper presented at the annual meeting of the American Educational Research Association, San Francisco, CA, March 1989.

12. See, for example, Christine E. Sleeter and Carl A. Grant, "A Rationale for Integrating Race, Gender, and Social Class," in Lois Weis, ed., *Class, Race, and Gender in American Education* (New York: State University of New York Press, 1988).

13. Walter J. Landry, "Future *Lau* Regulations: Conflict Between Language Rights and Racial Nondiscrimination" in Raymond V. Padilla, ed., *Theory, Technology, and Public Policy on Bilingual Education* (Washington, DC: National Clearinghouse for Bilingual Education, 1983).

14. For extensive reviews of the research on bilingualism as a deficit, see Cummins, *Empowering Minority Students*; and Kenji Hakuta, *Mirror of Language: The Debate on Bilingualism* (New York: Basic Books, Inc., 1986).

15. Ray Valdivieso and Cary David, *U.S. Hispanics: Challenging Issues for the 1990s* (Washington, DC: Population Trends and Public Policy, 1988).

16. David P. Dolson, "The Effects of Spanish Home Language Use on the Scholastic Performance of Hispanic Pupils," *Journal of Multilingual and Multicultural Development* 6 (2): 135–56.

17. María E. Matute-Bianchi, "Ethnic Identities and Patterns of School Success and Failure Among Mexican-Descent and Japanese-American Students in a California High School: An Ethnographic Analysis," *American Journal of Education* 15 (1): 233–55; and Joseph O. Prewitt-Díaz, "A Study of Self-Esteem and School Sentiment in Two Groups of Puerto Rican Students," *Educational and Psychological Research* 3 (Summer 1983): 161–67.

18. Ruben G. Rumbaut and Kenji Ima, *The Adaptation of Southeast Asian Refugee Youth: A Comparative Study* (San Diego, CA: Office of Refugee Resettlement, 1987).

19. Luis C. Moll and Stephen Díaz, "Change as the Goal of Educational Research," *Anthropology and Education Quarterly* 18 (December 1987): 300-11.
20. Nancy L. Commins, "Language and Affect: Bilingual Students at Home and at School," *Language Arts* 66 (January 1989): 29-43.
21. W. E. Lambert, "Culture and Language as Factors in Learning and Education," in A. Wolfgang, ed., *Education of Immigrant Students* (Toronto: OISE, 1975).
22. S. Jim Campos and H. Robert Keatinge, "The Carpinteria Language Minority Student Experience: From Theory, to Practice, to Success," in Skutnabb-Kangas and Cummins, eds., *Minority Language*.
23. The study by Virginia P. Collier and Wayne P. Thomas was reported by James Crawford in "Study Challenges 'Model' E.S.L. Program's Effectiveness," *Education Week*, April 27, 1988.
24. See, for example, the research cited by Jim Cummins, *op. cit.*; see also Stephen Krashen and Douglas Biber, *On Course: Bilingual Education's Success in California* (Sacramento, CA: California Association for Bilingual Education, 1988); Shirley Brice Heath, "Sociocultural Contexts of Language Development," in *Beyond Language: Social and Cultural Factors in Schooling Language Minority Students* (Los Angeles, CA: Evaluation, Dissemination, and Assessment Center, Office of Bilingual Education, California State Department of Education, 1986); Carole Edelsky, "Bilingual Children's Writing: Fact and Fiction," in Donna M. Johnson and Duane H. Roen, eds., *Richness in Writing: Empowering ESL Students* (New York: Longman, 1989).
25. Margaret A. Gibson, "The School Performance of Immigrant Minorities: A Comparative View," *Anthropology and Education Quarterly* 18 (December 1987): 262-75.
26. Rumbaut and Ima, *The Adaptation of Southeast Asian Refugee Youth*.
27. Sonia Nieto, *Affirming Diversity: The Sociopolitical Context of Multicultural Education* (New York: Longman, 1991).
28. Richard Rodríguez, *Hunger of Memory: The Education of Richard Rodríguez* (Boston: David R. Godine, 1982).
29. Anne T. Henderson, *The Evidence Continues to Grow: Parent Involvement Improves Student Achievement* (Columbia, MD: National Coalition of Citizens in Education, 1987).
30. Alma Flor Ada, "The Pájaro Valley Experience," in Tove Skutnabb-Kangas and Jim Cummins, eds., *Minority Education: From Shame to Struggle* (Clevedon, England: Multilingual Matters Ltd., 1988).
31. William F. Allman, "The Mother Tongue," *U.S. News & World Report*, November 5, 1990.

BILITERACY: A TRANSFORMATIVE PEDAGOGY

BECOMING CRITICAL:
Rethinking
Literacy, Language, and Teaching

Catherine E. Walsh
University of Massachusetts

The world we inhabit is palpably deficient: There are unwarranted inequities, shattered communities, unfulfilled lives. We cannot help but hunger for traces of utopian visions, of critical or dialectical engagements with social and economic realities. And yet, when we reach out, we experience a kind of blankness... How are we to move the young to break with the given, the taken for granted—to move towards what might be, what is not yet? (Greene, 1986, p. 427)

Maxine Greene speaks to a reality and a concern that, as educators of Spanish-speaking children, many of us share. With each year the contradictions between our students' lived lives and the content, context, and relations of schooling seem to become more visible and tenacious. The isolation and marginalization they experience affects us as well—as bilingual teachers we are classified, alienated, and kept in the margins. While each one of us, in our own way, may hunger for change and to "break with the given," we often feel that we cannot do it alone. And if we could, where would we begin? What visions might we conjure and pursue? What different contexts, relations, and approaches might we imagine and carry through?

This chapter explores the theoretical and practical tenets that underlie a more critical understanding of and approach to language, literacy, and teaching with Spanish-speaking children. It addresses the questions of why we need, and what it means, to become "critical" by presenting the problematic treatment of Spanish-speaking students and of language and literacy in U.S. public schools.

Finally, it offers thoughts about how we might "break with the given" to challenge and engage our students and ourselves in ways that promote critique and afford hope, commitment, and transformation.

Spanish-speaking Children in U.S. Schools

A walk down the corridor of most any urban public school in the United States verifies what numerous demographic reports have been telling us. Populations have diversified in terms of racial/ethnic composition so that in many cities students of color are more often than not the majority. Latino students make up a significant proportion; linguistically, Spanish is clearly the second language. Between 1979 and 1989 the native Spanish-speaking population over the age of 5 grew by 65 percent to 14,489,000 (Waggoner, 1992). Estimates suggest that as many as 8 million are school-aged children (Pérez & Torres-Guzmán, 1992).

The increasing presence of Spanish-speaking students in U.S. public schools has done little to improve their overall social or educational condition. Latino students remain disproportionately poor—38 percent compared to 18 percent for non-Latinos (U.S. Department of Commerce, 1991). Fifty-seven percent of Puerto Rican students are poor; their poverty rate is the highest of any other Latino group. Latinos are also the most undereducated. Drop-out rates for Latinos are greater than for any other group. In fact, as a recent study by the American Council on Education found, high school completion rates for Latinos are actually declining: from 60.1 percent in 1984 to 55.9 percent in 1989 (Flores, Tefft Cousin & Díaz, 1991). Anecdotal information suggests that as many as 80 percent leave urban high schools before graduation. Furthermore, 56 percent of Latino 17-year-olds are classified as functionally illiterate (compared to 13 percent of whites) (Fueyo, 1988). What are schools doing to and for these students?

From the day they enter the school door, most Spanish-speaking students are classified as "at risk" for failure. This labeling has more to do with issues of race/ethnicity, class, and language status than it does with academic ability or potential. It is the "difference" from the institutionalized, expected, tacit norm—that is, from white, middle-class native English speakers—that situates Latino students in a deficit position from the beginning. The "at risk" label carries with it a whole series of beliefs and expectations about what students cannot (as opposed to what they can) do; it also serves to rationalize failure when it happens (Flores, Tefft Cousin, & Díaz, 1991; Oakes, 1985).

School practices have much to do with why many Latino students do not do well in school. Numerous studies and reports have demonstrated the connection between such practices as remediation, grade retention, and tracking and school failure. Edelman (1988), for example, maintains that these practices increase the likelihood that students will never become truly literate, will drop out, become teen parents, and be unemployed as adults. Similarly, studies have pointed to the inherent biases of standardized tests and their inability to measure the real academic potential of poor and minority students. Yet, schools continue to use these practices and forms of assessment. Latino students are disproportionately the victims: Latinos are more likely to be retained in-grade, to be in low-track classes or groupings, and to enter high school overage. As a recent study by the National Council of La Raza found, 28 percent of Latino children in the first four grades are enrolled below grade level; 12- to 15-year-olds are 2.5 times more likely than whites to be two or more grades behind; and by the age of 17, one in six Latinos are at least two years behind the expected grade (Wheelock, 1990). Three-quarters are placed in nonacademic tracks. Latino students also have the lowest rate of educational achievement on standardized English tests (Hispanic Policy Development Project, 1988). And as compared to other groups, they have a disproportionately high rate of referral for Chapter 1 and other remedial services.

The practices, beliefs, attitudes, and assumptions that help structure the educational reality of Spanish-speaking students in our nation's schools need to be examined, questioned, deconstructed, and challenged. Central to this effort is a rethinking of why language, literacy, and teaching are so essential. Such critique is important in our coming to understand the complex ways that policies and pedagogies differentially position students. Also, the relations of power and control that are explicitly and implicitly at work in the educational institution must be accounted for and transformed. These are steps towards "becoming critical."

BILITERACY: A TRANSFORMATIVE PEDAGOGY

Language—Conflict and Struggle

I remember being caught speaking Spanish at recess—that was good for three licks on the knuckles with a sharp ruler. I remember being sent to the corner of the classroom for "talking back" to the Anglo teacher when all I was trying to do was tell her how to pronounce my name. "If you want to be American, speak 'American.' If you don't like it, go back to Mexico where you belong." . . . Attacks on one's form of expression with the intent to censor are a violation of the First Amendment. El Anglo con cara de inocente nos arranca la lengua. Wild tongues can't be tamed, they can only be cut. (Anzaldua, 1987, pp. 53–54)

Spanish-speaking children have always met rejection in this nation's schools. Gloria Anzaldua's personal acccount helps us to recapture and recall that of countless others. It evokes us to ask: in the course of history, how many names have been changed? Identities confused or hidden? How many Spanish tongues, under the guise of Americanhood, have public schools "cut"? And how many have struggled and resisted these attempts at control and assimilation?

Language is a central element of who we are, how we think of ourselves, and how others see us. It is tied in a myriad of ways to the history of generations past and to the present-day struggles of culture, identity, and communication in homes, communities, schools, and a variety of other social institutions. Although we may not always recognize it, language is also a place where power is realized, for it is through language that values, meanings, identities, and subjectivities are shaped and positioned. Schools illustrate this language and power relation well—by treating some meanings, interpretations, and experiences and one communicative form (English) as universal and standard (Walsh, 1991b).

At the same time, the growth in Spanish-speaking communities, along with the enactment of bilingual education legislation, have forced most public schools to acknowledge that Spanish language instruction can have a momentary place in classrooms. Its function, however, is never akin to the English "mainstream." Rather, its focus is typically an attempt to ease transition. While developmental bilingual programs (sometimes called Two-Way or Spanish Immersion) attempt to position Spanish differently by eliminating a requisite mainstreaming and including native English speakers, English still retains the higher, universal status. It constitutes the norm which is generally considered as that to which immigrant students aspire. The sad fact is that most school boards, administrators, and teachers would not be displeased if bilingual education disappeared tomorrow. The accompanying hope, of course, is that Latinos would somehow disappear with it. Two examples serve as illustrations:

◆ In a Massachusetts city where the public school population is now 70 percent Latino, the majority Puerto Rican, and the private school population is 90 percent white, white city residents recently picketed a school board meeting with signs that read MAKE THEM SPEAK ENGLISH and SEND THEM HOME. At the ballot box, these same white residents voted down a tax override that would have helped the city schools, now the poorest in the state; instead they voted to put their tax dollars into trash removal.

◆ In a nearby town, over 400 parents recently signed a petition barring anyone "not thoroughly proficient in the English language in terms of grammar, syntax, and most importantly the accepted and standard use of pronunciation" from being hired "for the purpose of educating" elementary schoolchildren. The petition, which has received the endorsement of the mayor (who has a Greek accent) was the result of a transfer of a native Spanish-speaking bilingual teacher to a "mainstream" classroom.

While language serves as the identified site of much of the struggle around and towards Spanish speakers, it is not simply the speaking of Spanish (or a Spanish accent) that is the primary issue. Society and schools, however, would have us think so. As the SEND THEM HOME sign above suggests, the real issue is that which Spanish signifies and represents, and in the xenophobic attitudes that accompany demographic change, the fear of loss of power and (linguistic, cultural, and sociopolitical) control, the disdain that Latinos do not "melt" as other past and present immigrants, and the fact that the number of Latinos and of Spanish speakers just keeps growing. Within this complex mesh of attitudes, emotions, and racial/ethnic, class, identity, and power relations, language becomes much more than just what one speaks—it becomes a territory in which cultural, political, and ideological struggles are waged. Certainly the multimillion dollar campaign to make English the "official" language is one clear example.

What does it mean to begin to understand language in this more critical way? To recognize language as a site of conflict and struggle? What does it require us to consider with regard to our students as well as ourselves? And what does it suggest in terms of literacy and teaching?

Beginning to see language in a more critical way requires, from the very outset, a challenging of the assumption that in bilingual education, it is language that is the major issue of pedagogy and identity and of debate and defense. In this assumption, language becomes reified, in a sense, severed from the broader social, political, and ideological context, treated as a monolithic, ahistoric form. Students (and instruction) are simply categorized as Spanish or English. In challenging this, we need to tease out the complex ways that language does and doesn't define us. This means exploring how our own and our students' identities are multiple and contradictory, and how they frequently shift. It also means considering how we position ourselves in relation to our language or languages, and to our race/ethnicity, gender, age, etc. How do our students do their positioning?

We must attend to the differences among Spanish-speaking students and to the complex ways that language, particularly for Puerto Rican and Chicano students, is interwined with history, politics, and power, with resistance, and with cultural and identity struggles that emerged as a response to past and present colonization. Such attention is important for it helps bring to the fore the real-life impact of history, politics, and power on people's lives, language, and consciousness and the creative possibilties that come out of resistance and struggle. It helps us begin to understand why Spanish immigrants are more likely to abide by and achieve the expected school norms than are U.S.-born Puerto Ricans and Chicanos. Further, it helps us challenge and understand in a different way schools' (and possibly some of our own) value judgments and negative assumptions about students' varied, expressive language forms. The existence, connotation, and use of laden terms like "alingualism," "semilingualism," "Spanglish," "pochismos"— Spanish words distorted by English that suggest contamination, interference, "deslenguado," "el español deficiente" (Anzaldua, 1987; Flores, Attinasi & Pedraza, 1981)—are examples.

In coming to a critical understanding, we need to ask what it is about "other" language use that draws such ire and emotion. We need to question whose interests those individuals and organizations that attack multilingualism, bilingual, and multicultural education represent and what it is they are really trying to control and dismantle. We also need to think differently about what it is we teach and defend—in other words, to see Spanish and English in less of a binary and more in a dialogic and problematic light, to recognize the indelible ways that Spanish and English are inscribed onto and within one another in the United States, and to seek out the oppositional and creative meanings and messages that the languages may produce and present. This means challenging static views of bilingualism and language shift—the shift from the native language to English that all immigrant children supposedly experience—for more dynamic views that recognize a spectrum of language ability and use (including language mixing, i.e., codeswitching) across a variety of contexts and situations.

Such views raise questions about the efficacy of language proficiency tests as well as of the programatic walls and instructional delivery designs that separate Spanish-speaking bilingual students from their possibly equally language-able Latino peers in monolingual classrooms.

Taking on a more critical language perspective demands that we think more carefully about language's significance, pedagogy, and use. It also pushes us to realize that simply teaching in Spanish is not enough. The underlying assumptions of the curricula and the instructional approach must also change, otherwise any communicative form can be used to impart the same dominant, tacit standards.

Literacy— Assumptions and Approaches

The interface of language and literacy is one with which bilingual educators are quite familiar. We know the benefit of teaching

BILITERACY: A TRANSFORMATIVE PEDAGOGY

reading and writing in the native language first and how to begin to go about making the transfer of skills to English. Yet, given the questions and issues that I have previously raised, why might we need to think beyond this? Should we be concerned that school-based literacy seldom takes into account the varied and multiple literacies at work in Spanish communities? And what about the development of other literacies as well—including those necessary to "read," deconstruct, and challenge the societal and school practices and policies of marginalization, oppression, and othering? How do existing approaches limit these more critical and enabling concerns?

Literacy instruction in elementary classrooms can be overwhelmingly categorized into two approaches: the traditional skills-based (basal) approach and the whole language approach. While whole language has made inroads into a number of individual monolingual and bilingual classrooms, the traditional approach remains the most prevalent on a systemwide level. Commercial basal readers and their accompanying scripted guides, workbooks, charts, tests, and ditto masters are in use in over 90 percent of U.S. elementary classrooms (Shannon, 1989). Ramírez (1991) in his national study of Spanish bilingual programs similarly found traditional approaches to be the standard.

The Traditional Approach

Traditional approaches are based on the view that learning is teacher-directed and fact-oriented (Pahl & Monson, 1992). Anyone who has attended or taught in U.S. elementary schools is familiar with the method and orientation. However, explicitly stating some of the beliefs and assumptions that underlie the approach can help reveal why it is problematic (Walsh, 1991a).

First, let us consider how such approaches view knowledge and, as a result, teaching and learning. Traditional approaches treat knowledge as a neutral and universal entity that is separate from people and their actions, experiences, and social contexts. It is considered quantifiable and verifiable information that must be formally acquired and taught. Textbooks and curricula form its substance and control its dissemination. As I have pointed out elsewhere (Walsh, 1991a):

> Implicit in this conception is a theory of how individuals learn and, as a result, how teachers should teach. The acquisition or "learning" of knowledge is treated as deductive and deterministic; instruction breaks "it" down into discrete pieces and feeds it to students in a systematic way. Learning thus become synonymous with an unquestioned absorption. Consequently, teaching is relegated to a transmission-oriented task, dependent not on the teacher's creativity or engagement with the students and the material but on the skill of imparting decontextualized matter so that students might replicate it in "standardized" tests of achievement. (p. 9)

Second, consider how experience is treated and understood. In traditional approaches, experience is thought to be separate from and transcendent of lived experiences; there is little or no connection between the knowledge and skills being conveyed and the practical aspects of real life.

The experiences that students bring to the classroom are considered, within traditional approaches, to be generally unrelated and inconsequential to the knowledge being presented and to the tasks of teaching and learning. This is because the writers and publishers of basal texts assume that all children bring to the classroom a somewhat common set of concepts and a similar repertoire of literacy-related experiences. Of course, the concepts and experiences they assume are those typically conveyed and supported in white, middle-class, English-speaking, suburban, male-dominated households (e.g, see research by Heath 1983, 1986, and Anderson and Stokes 1984 that confirms this). The curricula thus favors these students by setting them as the "standard." This tends to be so even in Spanish language basals. When students' backgrounds do not match the "standard," remediation—in the form of Chapter 1, special education, or reading specialists—is called for. Experience thus becomes of consequence only when it is a problem; the solution is to dissolve or to remove it so that the transmission of knowledge can go on as normal.

Why are traditional approaches problematic for Spanish-speaking students? Put directly, traditional approaches tend to exacerbate the racial/ethnic, language, class, and gender stratifications of schools and classrooms, deny what it is children do know, and track students into levels that tend to inscript and predict their success and failure.

Whole Language

Whole language carries with it a different set of beliefs and assumptions. Knowledge, for example, is considered in whole language approaches to be connected to the student, and her/his social context and personal/social needs. It is understood as the reflection of interaction and experience. Knowledge is acquired as part of a natural meaning making process in which students actively draw from prior knowledge and lived experiences to construct meaning and make sense out of the text and/or the world around them. Acquisition, in other words, comes from real use. Information and skills are not broken down into small manageable chunks but are learned in a holistic and authentic manner.

Whole language classrooms also promote a different understanding of learning and teaching. In contrast to the passive, text-based banking method (Freire, 1970) at work in traditionally oriented classrooms, whole language treats learning as active, student centered, and process-oriented. Teachers serve as catalysts and facilitators and texts afford a supplement to and an extension of students' own experience and discovery.

Experience is central to the process of learning for all students in whole language classrooms. Instructional activities (e.g., dialogue journals, language experience, process writing, literature-based study, etc.) are structured to draw students' personal experience out and to push them to explore and extend it. All experiences are treated as equal, valid, and worthy of inclusion as are different social, cultural, and text-based perspectives and "readings."

With its focus on the natural interconnectedness of knowledge, people, and experience, whole language challenges the artificial, disjointed nature of traditional approaches. As Harmon & Edelsky (1991) point out:

> Whole language intends reading and writing to be seen by students as useful and relevant—as both possible to acquire and worth acquiring. . . . It focuses on the ideas students have rather than the ones they lack; it assumes the expansion of roles so that students teach and teachers learn; it sets high but flexible standards; it emphasizes language repertoires rather than right answers; and it fosters questioning, analyzing, speaking up, and writing down. (pp. 130–131)

Whole language affords the potential for a classroom and literacy learning environment in which students, as independent and active learners, assume a more authoritative and responsible stance; where a sense of valor and personal power is fostered.

The problem with whole language theory and practice, from a critical perspective, is its lack of sociopolitical critique. In the process of constructing knowledge and interpreting experience in whole language classrooms, students are not usually pushed to consider the social and cultural dynamics, the lived realities, and the personal and collective struggles actually involved in the interpretation, definition, and understanding of the experiences. Similarly, teachers are not encouraged to explore these connections in their own or their students' lives or within the educational institution. All experience is treated as neutrally lived and equally accepted despite the fact that in the real-life social world, in the school, and in the communities from which bilingual students come, it is not. The power relations and power inequities of race/ethnicity, language, class, and gender are played down and instead a kind of cohesive plurality is celebrated (Harmon & Edelsky, 1991). This neither helps students understand the structural components and changing power relations that are explicitly and implicitly present in their lives nor allows for the need to take some kind of action to address and change oppressive conditions.

Critical Approaches

How does a critical approach to literacy differ from existing traditional or whole language perspectives? Critical approaches recognize knowledge as always partial and problematic, as bound in complex ways to the social, political, historical, cultural, linguistic, and economic conditions that operate both upon and within society. Thus while knowledge is grounded in the meanings, experiences, and lived lives of students, these meanings, experiences, and lives are shaped by the relations of power and control that are explicitly and implicitly present in everyday living. They are not fixed—that is, there is no single set of meanings or experiences that are Spanish, Latino, or even Mexican or Puerto Rican. And it is precisely this fact that meaning is not fixed that critical approaches take up and utilize as a basis of dialogue and critique in the classroom.

Such understandings and treatment of knowledge contrast with the "given" notion of knowledge in traditional approaches and the humanistic, whole language view of knowledge as the mere reflection of interaction and experience (i.e., meaning). Critical approaches give attention to the ways that schools, curricula, and texts organize and present knowledge and to how this organization and presentation work to reproduce and maintain dominant interests. They challenge teachers and students to figure out where they fit within this social order and to think critically about the complex and often contradictory nature of their experiences, identities, actions, and interpretations inside and outside the educational institution. Peterson (1991) provides a good account of what this challenging looks like in an upper elementary Spanish bilingual classroom.

The goal of critical approaches is to help students read both the word and the world (Freire & Macedo, 1987) and in doing so, to read between the lines, questioning and imagining what is not immediately visible. It is to help students understand the personal and the social worlds in which they live and to believe their actions alone and together can make a difference. At a time when the disproportionate achievement and drop-out rates for Latino students and the level of marginalization of Latino communities are of major concern, such goals of empowerment and social transformation are particularly crucial.

In practice, critical approaches challenge teachers and students to work together in more participatory and democratic ways; to individually and collectively question and examine, in light of one's own and others' experiences, the information that texts and schools present; and to construct new and sometimes different ways of interpreting, understanding, reading, writing, and acting in the classroom, with one another, and in the world. They demand that we not just think differently about what and how we teach but that we also think differently about ourselves as literacy and language teachers, bilingual educators, and as Latinos/Latinas or non-Latinos/Latinas.

Critical approaches push us to ask questions such as: How do we understand what we understand? What enables or discourages this understanding? What does it mean to reposition ourselves and our students as knowers? What does this repositioning require and suggest in terms of the content, context, and social character of literacy instruction? What does it mean in terms of our own teaching and practice and our own identities?

Becoming Critical: Considerations for the Classroom and the Profession

The popular myth is that teaching is an eight to three job. With summers off and periodic vacations during the year, it is assumed that teachers have it easy. Yet, as the statistics at the beginning of this chapter reveal, the context of schooling is much different from that typically considered; schools, teaching, and learning are contentious, problematic places and spaces because all of society lives there.

What does it mean to become a critical (bilingual) educator within this enigmatical reality? There are two directions that I think need to be considered: what it means in terms of classroom pedagogy and what it means as a professional in the field.

Some educators that work from a critical perspective have been careful to point out that there is no single critical pedagogy nor is there a step-by-step recipe to follow. However, there are published examples of what some critical teachers have done in their classrooms (Arrastia, 1991; Bigelow, 1989; Peterson, 1991; among others). There are also some common elements that can be considered (Walsh, 1991b).

The first element is a belief in the participatory nature of learning. Critical classrooms move beyond familiar cooperative learning activities by engaging students in collective modes of investigating, questioning, and production. These classrooms are participatory not merely because students are involved but because there is a real-life function, purpose, and outcome of their involvement.

The second element is the use of dialogue to foster an open exchange through which students come to better understand their own and others' realities. This does not mean just letting students talk—it means sculpting a classroom context in which students engage in thoughtful exchange around a particular problem, text, or situation. Teachers that promote real dialogue in their classrooms believe that students learn as much if not more from their peers than they do from passively reading texts or listening to teachers.

Taken together, dialogue and participatory learning require that teachers let go of some of their authority and learn to become active listeners and co-earners. They also require that students be permitted and encouraged to use the language forms most conducive to communication.

The third element is a redirecting of the curriculum so that it is based on generative problem-themes that derive from students' concerns and interests. Content area subject matter and skills development are tied to the themes rather than vice versa. In introducing and developing the themes, teachers use questioning and problem-posing techniques that draw out students' personal experiences and push them to reach beyond, look for what is absent, make connections with others, and develop strategies for resolving or addressing problems in real life (Aguiar et al., 1990; Walsh, in press).

Finally, there are the two elements of reflection and action. Reflection means creating numerous opportunities whereby students can personally and collectively reflect on the material being studied and make connections to themselves, their communities, and the broader society. Action means that in critical classrooms, students and teachers never idly sit back. Rather, they see the need and assume the responsibility for acting in ways that can positively impact problems, situations, contexts, environments, and the world around them. The goal of this action, although realized differently in early childhood and upper elementary classrooms, is to tranform problematic and oppressive conditions.

Becoming critical, however, means also challenging our own roles, positions, and perspectives. Positioning oneself as a bilingual teacher or as a teacher of Spanish-speaking children, for instance, requires an examination of our own social location in relation to our students. In other words, we must consider how our race/ethnicity, class, and language abilities and forms, as well as where and how we have lived (i.e., in ethnic-specific communities, in urban versus rural versus suburban areas, etc.) and gone to school are similar to or different from the background, experiences, and positions of students in our classrooms. And we must consider what these similarities or differences mean in terms of how we view ourselves and how others—administrators, teachers, parents, and students, as well as the broader society—view us.

For example, if we are native, English-speaking, and white, we must recognize that we occupy a position of privilege in U.S. society; our lived experiences in childhood and adulthood and as teachers are thus qualitatively different from our Latina/Latino, African American, or other colleagues of color, as is our relationship to the tacit norms and the language that the school and curriculum present. This does not mean that native English-speaking whites should not teach Spanish-speaking children, but it does mean that we must be constantly aware of who we are, how we position ourselves and how others position us, and the internalized values and assumptions that we carry. In becoming critical, we must engage in a personal reflection and questioning about our own values and assumptions and we must seek ways to engage with our colleagues both inside and outside bilingual education about ours and theirs. We should also endeavor to extend this process to the classroom, with our students.

Because of racism, Latina or Latino teachers share with their students a marginalized position in schools and in society. The lived reality of racism, oppression, and marginalization makes most Latina/Latino teachers more sensitive to the ways that their students are limited and held back by school policies and practices and curricular exclusions. Yet ethnic and class differences or varied life and community experiences may still result in teachers seeing themselves in a very different manner from their students and their parents. And, even for those teachers who consider themselves as from the community, students and parents may see them differently.

Becoming critical (bilingual) educators necessitates a recognition of and an attention to our positions as individuals, to one another, and as teachers in an "othered" field. It summons us to dialogue so that different histories, experiences, and locations can be engaged, alternative understandings and relationships can be created, and new alliances can be formed. It prompts us to be attentive to the multiple ways that bilingual students, bilingual teachers, and bilingual education are devalued, silenced, and oppressed, as well as to the ways that we permit and sometimes even support this oppression. Most importantly, it demands that we take responsibility within and for bilingual education by making "critical" both our relations and involvement and our language and pedagogy, by challenging those individuals and practices that serve dominant interests, and by taking action in classrooms, schools, the educational field, and in the broader society to dislodge the relations and structures of power that constrain us, our practice, and our students.

To become critical is to grasp onto that utopian vision of a more just world where "unwarranted inequities, shattered communities, and unfulfilled lives" no longer reside. Becoming critical means that we can no longer be naive, passive, or silent bystanders to that which is. It means becoming spirited, conscious, creative, and committed actors in rethinking and constructing that which might be.

About the Author

Catherine E. Walsh is the Coordinator of the New England Multifunctional Resource Center for Language and Culture in Education and an adjunct associate professor at the University of Massachusetts in Amherst and Boston. She has taught Spanish-speaking children, youth, and adults in the United States and Latin America. She is a longtime advocate and activist for bilingual education and language rights and is the author of numerous articles on language, literacy, and bilingual education. Her book *Pedagogy and the Struggle for Voice: Issues of Language, Power and Schooling for Puerto Ricans* was published in 1991.

References

Aguiar, C., Alcantar, L., Florian, H., Hernandez, J., Matos, A., and Rodriguez, R. (1990). *El arrepentimiento de Julian/Julian's regrets*. Somerville, MA: Multicultural Education Training and Advocacy, Inc.

Anderson, A., and Stokes, S. (1984). Socio and institutional influences on development and practices of literacy. In Goelman, H., Oberg, A. and Smith, F. (Eds.) *Awakening to literacy*. Portsmouth, NH: Heinemann, pp. 24–37.

Anzaldua, G. (1987). *Borderlands. La frontera. The new mestiza*. San Francisco: Spinster.

Arrastia, M. (1991). Community literature in the multicultural classroom: The mothers' reading program. In C. E. Walsh (Ed.), *Literacy as praxis: Culture, language, and pedagogy*. Norwood, NJ: Ablex, pp. 133–54.

Bigelow, W. (1989). Discovering Columbus: Rereading the past. *Rethinking School*, vol. 4, no. 1, pp. 12–13.

Edelmann, M. W. (1988). Forward to the *Children's Defense Fund Budget*. Washington, DC: Children's Defense Fund.

Flores, B., Tefft Cousin, P., and Díaz, E. (1991, Sept.). Transforming deficit myths about learning, language, and culture. *Language Arts* (68), pp. 369–79.

Flores, J., Attinasi, J., and Pedraza, P. (1981). La carreta made a U-turn: Puerto Rican language and culture in the U.S. *Daedalus* 110, pp. 193–217.

Freire, P. (1970). *Pedagogy of the oppressed*. New York: Seabury.

Freire, P., and Macedo, D. (1987). *Literacy: Reading the word and the world*. New York: Bergin and Garvey.

Fueyo, J. M. (1988). Technical literacy versus critical literacy in adult basic education. *Journal of Education* 170 (1), pp. 107–18.

Greene, M. (1986, Nov.). In search of a critical pedagogy. *Harvard Educational Review* (56) 4, pp. 427–41.

Harmon, S., and Edelsky, C. (1991). Risks and possibilities of whole language literacy: Alienation and connection. In C. Edelsky (Ed.): *With literacy and justice for all. Rethinking the social in language and education*. Philadelphia: Falmer, pp. 112–26.

Heath, S. B. (1986). Sociocultural contexts of language development. In California Department of Education (Ed.), *Beyond language: Socio and cultural factors in schooling language minority students*. pp. 143–86. Los Angeles: Evaluation, Dissemination Assistance Center.

Heath, S. B. (1983). *Ways with words: Language, life and work in communities and classrooms*. New York: Cambridge University Press.

Hispanic Policy Development Project (1988). *Closing the gap for U.S. Hispanic youth*. Washington, DC: Author.

National Council of La Raza (n.d.). Reversing the trend of Hispanic undereducation. Washington, DC: Author.

Oakes, J. (1985). *Keeping track: How schools structure inequality*. New Haven: Yale University Press.

Pahl, M. M., and Monson, R. J. (1992, April). In search of whole language: Transforming curriculum and instruction. *Journal of Reading* (35) 7, pp. 518–24.

Pérez, B., and Torres-Guzmán, M. (1992). *Learning in two worlds: An integrated Spanish/English biliteracy approach*. New York: Longman.

Peterson, R. (1991). Teaching how to read the world and change it: Critical pedagogy in the intermediate grades. In C. E. Walsh (Ed.), *Literacy as praxis*. Norwood, NJ: Ablex, pp. 156–82.

Ramírez, J. D. (1991). *Longitudinal study of structured English immersion strategy, early-exit, and late-exit bilingual education programs*. Washington, DC: U.S. Department of Education.

Shannon, P. (1989). *Broken promises. Reading instruction in twentieth century America*. New York: Bergin and Garvey.

U.S. Department of Commerce (1991). *The Hispanic population in the United States: March 1991*. Washington, DC: Bureau of the Census.

Waggoner, D. (1992). *Numbers and needs: Ethnic and linguistic minorities in the United States*, 2 (3) May. Washington, DC: Author.

Walsh, C. E. (in press). Engaging students in their own learning: Literacy, language, and knowledge production with Latino adolescents. In D. Spener (Ed.), *Biliteracy: Theory and practice*. Englewood Cliffs, NJ: Prentice-Hall Regents.

Walsh, C. E. (1991a). Literacy as praxis: A framework and introduction. In C.E. Walsh (Ed.), *Literacy as praxis: Culture, language, and pedagogy*. Norwood, NJ: Ablex, pp. 1–22.

Walsh, C. E. (1991b). *Pedagogy and the struggle for voice: Language, power and schooling for Puerto Ricans*. New York: Bergin and Garvey.

Wheelock, A. (1990). *The status of Latino students in Mass. public schools: Directions for policy research in the 1990s*. Boston: Mauricio Gaston Institute for Latino Community Development and Public Policy.

Making Our Whole-Language Bilingual Classrooms Also Liberatory

Mary S. Poplin
The Claremont Graduate School, Claremont, California

Exciting new whole-language techniques are flourishing in bilingual education where classrooms have been transformed into writing and reading workshops. Books in various languages brighten every spot on counters, bookshelves, desks, and tabletops. These books are written by authors from all corners of the world; written in every language; drawn from various publishers of trade books and anthologies; imported from around the world and translated into multiple languages. The writings of children and adolescents in their primary and secondary languages cover the walls like ribboned wallpaper. Portfolios show off drafts of creative writing, favorite poems, journals of all kinds; letters and notes give these classrooms a museum appeal. (For excellent texts on whole-language classrooms for bilingual/second language learners, see: Benesch, 1988; Edelsky, 1986; Edelsky, Altswerger & Flores, 1990; Freeman & Freeman, 1992; Hayes, Bahruth & Kessler, 1991; Hudelson, 1989; LHEA, 1988; Rigg & Allen, 1989.) No longer is remediation the order of the day in bilingual classrooms. Bilingualism instead is recognized in these classes as a gift, one on which this country's future depends. The new educational approaches associated with whole language have emerged full blown in our classes in order to multiply the talents of our students who are already well on their way to becoming biliterate, bicultural citizens. Here in the whole-language classroom all languages are valued and citizens become literate in their own language and ultimately in English. They do so through real books and in real writing—individually and cooperatively (Ada, 1988; Flores, Cousin & Díaz, 1991).

BILITERACY: A TRANSFORMATIVE PEDAGOGY

But what of the world in which we live, what of the fact that many schools and communities still view bilingualism as a threat, or worse, as a disability (Cummins, 1984, 1989; Flores, Cousin & Diaz, 1991; Skutnabb-Kangas & Cummins, 1988)? The want ads demonstrate that bilingualism is no disability in the real world and the threat this nation faces is associated more with its monolingualism than with its bilingualism. How do our whole-language classrooms prepare our students for the reality of a society that currently accepts them only partially and often treats their gifts as disabilities? How can whole-language bilingual teachers equip their students with the necessary tools to combat the racism they will face throughout their lives? How can we help them to deal with the subtle and overt disparagements about their accents, their ethnicity, and their communities? How can they become active players in the achievement of social justice so that their gifts be honored, their communities flourish, and they can make contributions fully to our free and democratic state? One way that holds much promise is to add a critical or liberatory perspective to our existing whole-language environment.

This chapter will begin an exploration and, hopefully, a dialogue among educators like ourselves about how we take our whole-language bilingual classrooms one step further toward social justice. To do this we must encourage our students to recognize and use their own power to become the best persons they can and to contribute to making the best possible society. First, I will briefly review the roots of whole-language bilingual classrooms and liberatory education. Secondly, by using examples drawn from bilingual classrooms and programs, similarities and differences between whole-language and liberatory whole-language bilingual classes will be explored.

The Roots of Bilingual Whole Language

The bilingual whole-language movement is based on (1) studies of the natural acquisition of second languages and on (2) a learning theory called *constructivism*. Through the study of how people naturally develop a second language came bilingual whole-language pedagogies (Cummins, 1984, 1989; Krashen, 1981, 1982, 1985; Skutnabb-Kangas & Cummins, 1988). We understand that second languages develop much like first languages and that first languages provide important bases upon which second ones emerge. By observing children and adolescents develop languages, it became clear that it is best to fully develop one's first language and teach important content in the primary language while gradually developing the second language. In fact, the basis of good bilingual education is also constructivist. Communicating messages takes precedence over grammar, natural communication over skills instruction, real reading over skills work, process writing over worksheets, and natural activities between children and between children and adults over synthetically contrived language activities that teachers give to children.

Constructivists observed the way in which children naturally develop and learn various things (e.g., number knowledge, movement, moral reasoning, language, and second languages). Based on these observations, constructivists offered a definition of learning that was in stark opposition to the way schools have traditionally been structured and the way we have thought about the task of teaching. *Constructivism suggests that students do not acquire knowledge from outside information given to them, but rather they learn by constructing new meanings from new and old experiences in a context of rich social interactions.* Language teachers then must create classrooms in which students can experiment and play with language. Students must be called on *to construct their own meanings rather than memorize someone else's.*

Bilingual whole-language classrooms then use a variety of activities designed to draw out student meanings through various language and literacy activities in social contexts. These classrooms frequently use thematic interdisciplinary units so that meanings can be constructed in large contexts and easily connected by students to their lives. Within these units there is a great deal of literature read to and by students in their primary language and later in second languages. There are many choices about what is read. Students work in cooperative groups to encourage the social interactions among peers that bilingual whole-language teachers know are essential to learning and to language development. Various forms of the writing process are evident: I-search papers (Macrorie, 1984), dialogue and dialectic journals, personal journals, letter writing, invented spellings, and reader response narratives. Reciprocal teaching (Palincsar, 1988–1989; Ruíz, 1989) and cooperative learning, where students become teachers, call for students to become even more actively engaged in meaning making. Music, art, interpersonal, and bodily kinesthetic intelligences are also integrated into the classroom in an effort to address the multiple talents and interests of all youngsters.

This whole-language bilingual class functions first to help students become literate and educated in their own language while gradually adding a second language. In these classes, reductionistic methods of assessment are replaced with authentic portfolios, Primary Language Records (Barrs, Ellis, Hester & Thomas, 1989), rich annotations, and student self-assessments (see Thomas, in press). Levels and grades that have divided our students before (usually determined by strict adherence to reductionistic language assessments) give way to more flexible groupings where older students or more proficient students help mentor younger ones. Here, time and space are created where one can learn at one's own pace.

Constructivism suggests that the natural sequence in which children and adolescents (all of us) construct new meanings is from whole to part to whole. The parts, for example, the specific skills of reading and writing, must be broken down by the learner, not the teacher, and learned as skills are needed within the context of real books and stories and writing activities. Thus, whole-language bilingual educators de-emphasize the early teaching of skills in preference for experiencing the whole of reading and writing first—reading and writing in the primary language. The skills of spelling, word attack, phonics, etc., are naturally developed as students move between the romance and desire to read and write and the experience of reading and writing for real purposes. During the phases when students actively try to sort out parts (specific skills), the teacher plays an important role in helping students or arranging for students to help others in demonstrating and guiding the student in an examination of the self-chosen part or skill. Skill instruction prior to a student being ready causes students to become dysfluent just as second language instruction prior to primary language understanding often results in illiteracy in both languages. The relationship of whole to part to whole is a very tricky one, one that takes those of us who teach a great deal of time to sort out for ourselves and then to adjust to the various individuals in our classes. Skill instruction separate from the literacy activities in which a student is actively involved, such as synthetic worksheet activities, rarely make any real sense to students whose language skills are developing and thus do not become integrated into the rest of what they are learning about language (Poplin, 1988a, b).

The last whole in this process comes as one has accumulated much real experience and both understands the whole and has sorted through some of its parts and can function in language (in our instance) without having to concentrate much on the parts. In this stage, one more fully understands the whole of language, is fluent in one's primary spoken and written language. Whitehead called these three stages "romance, precision, and wisdom." Once an individual is operating in the third stage (wisdom) in his/her first language, the second language can emerge more easily using the cognitive academic and basic interpersonal skills from the first language to support the ideas and the construct of language in the second. If, however, one is stunted in his/her first language, extensive research suggests that chances are the second language will be similarly impacted (Cummins, 1989). On the other hand,

Cummins and others have demonstrated that students who are fully bilingual are more cognitively flexible, have more concepts with which to think through issues and more ways to express single concepts. Stone (1992) finds evidence that bilingual, bicultural students are more creative in divergent thinking activities as well.

A second principle of constructivism suggests that the learner transforms new experiences through what he/she currently knows and believes. Thus, in whole language as in other constructivist techniques, there is an emphasis on what students currently know and care about. Because people construct new meanings based on what they have experienced, meanings often differ from person to person. Especially different will be the meanings developed by an upper-middle-class English-speaking child growing up in a privileged suburb. However, it is very likely that she/he will be more able to approximate the meaning determined to be "correct" in the text or test because her/his experiences are more likely to match that of the curriculum or test writer. For this reason, there is a healthy distrust of "correct" answers to "reading comprehension" activities and tests. We all construct different meanings to different texts, even different from our friends and others similar to us. This does not mean there is no overlap in our understandings or that our meanings are so different that we cannot understand one another, as is often feared by conservative educators who advocate standardized curricula for all—usually exclusively Euro-American.

A third principle of constructivism suggests that learning is self-regulated and self-preserving (not teacher or curriculum regulated). Thus, choice and self-assessments are critical to the bilingual whole-language class. A person's construction of meaning is naturally about the things one cares about. Choice of text and the active involvement of students and their peers in whole-language classrooms fuels this particular principle of constructivism. Students learn best what they have chosen to learn, what is somehow connected to their lives.

To the constructivist, even errors are important. For it is in error, self-noted error, that one's learning is truly advanced. Whole-language teachers notice when students realize the errors they make, that is why spelling in whole-language classes is allowed to emerge naturally versus taught directly. Much constructivist research suggests that there is a very natural sequence in which students regulate their own learning to spell (and other knowledge of the specific part skills in language). In alphabetic languages, for example, one can expect that children will first spell by using only consonants. Even though the spelling of one language spills over to the other, gradually people sort these differences out over time and through many experiences with written tests (books and writing) (Hudelson, 1989; Rigg & Allen, 1989). The notion that students can and do regulate their learning is critical to whole-language bilingual classrooms. The silent period, well documented in the second language development research, is also evidence of this self-regulatory process of learning.

To the constructivists, meanings are constructed not only individually but socially. In fact, many believe that meanings are constructed primarily through social interactions. The notion that knowledge is socially constructed leads constructivists to suggest that knowledge is to some degree unique across cultures and communities. For example, in child rearing some cultures encourage more cooperation (versus competition) among siblings. Consequently, there is an emphasis on cooperative learning strategies in the bilingual whole-language class. Whole-language bilingual classes strive to make second language learning like first language learning, which is accomplished in rich social interactions within the family. The importance of natural and nonthreatening social interaction in bilingual classes cannot be overestimated.

Constructivists have as their major goal individual cognitive development. Because language is inextricably linked to cognition, language classrooms have benefited greatly from the insights of constructivist theory. The classroom has also given life to that theory in the form of multiple exciting activities developed within these classrooms where children and adolescents experiment with, play with, and develop new meanings by using primary and later second languages in the richest social and literary contexts possible.

The Roots of Liberatory Education

The major purpose of liberatory education (often called *critical pedagogy* in North America) is not simply the cognitive and linguistic development of the individual. It is the understanding of oneself within the broader social context and a working out of how one's gifts can contribute to the development of a more just community, society, and world. Liberatory education does begin with similar constructivist assumptions among learning, but goes one step beyond them. In liberatory pedagogies one draws out student voices around issues central to their community and society and puts these voices in contact with: (1) others' voices in that same community, (2) the voices of texts, and (3) the voices of others inside and outside the community (Apple, 1987; Darder, 1991; Freire & Faundez, 1989; Freire & Macedo, 1987; Giroux, 1988; McLaren, 1989; Park, 1989; Shor, 1980; Walsh, 1991; Weiler, 1988).

In liberatory education, bilingualism is seen not only as a cognitive process of learning primary and second languages but as a political, economic, and social issue. The politics of bilingualism and biculturalism are made explicit to the learner, as well. Paulo Freire once answered the question of whether a teacher should teach a standard dialect or dominant culture's language by saying:

> Yes, the liberatory teacher has to know this, or see the language problem in this way. The so-called standard is a deeply *ideological* concept, but it is necessary to teach correct usage while also criticizing its political limitations.
>
> Now the question is, knowing all these things, does the liberating educator have the right not to teach standard usage? Does he or she have the right to say, "I am a revolutionary so I don't teach the 'good' English?" No. In my point of view, she or he will have to make it possible for the students to command English but here is the big difference between him or her and the other revolutionary teacher. While the traditionalist teaches the rules of the *famous English* (laughs) he or she *increases* the students' domination by elitist ideology which is inserted into these rules. The liberatory teacher teaches standard usage in order for them to survive while discussing with them all the ideological ingredients of this unhappy task. Do you see? This is how I think teachers can reflect on their fear of student rejection and also their fear of standard usage. (Shor & Freire, 1987, pp. 71–72)

Because bilingualism is important to the creation of a larger and more humane world community, bilingualism holds social value beyond mere cognitive and pragmatic individual values.

Factors that are associated with bilingual, bicultural knowledge are also critiqued in liberatory pedagogy. Racism, sexism, monoculturalism, and the unequal distribution of power and wealth are all topics for the classroom. The content of liberatory education is life, and the world and one's place in it. Thus materials are drawn from broader contexts and literacy encompasses more than reading and writing as it is generally thought of in schools. The technologies of reading and writing are viewed as tools to learn and act in society not as ends (or subjects) in and of themselves. There is a recognition in liberatory education that one must critique what one teaches. Inherent in the choices people make are hidden biases (the hidden curriculum) that prioritize one culture's language, literature, and knowledge over others and define dominant culture knowledge as "high status" and thus most appropriate for instruction, while all else is relegated to a "lower status" (see Aronowitz & Giroux, 1988).

According to liberatory educators, teaching is a political act. This is especially true for those of us who teach persons from communities with little power. As we teach, we must recognize that we either are acting for things to stay the same or acting to change them. The overt purpose of liberatory education is liberation of all peoples from oppression (e.g., economic, social, racial, gender, and political). These words often make teachers nervous until they begin to realize that all that is done in schools, the very structure of schooling into which we walk each day, is a political structure which consciously or unconsciously uses the assumptions and power of dominant peoples to make all its decisions.

An important concept for liberatory bilingual whole-language teachers is how to help students understand how oppression works against themselves and their communities. Erickson (1987) defines hegemony as:

> routine actions and unexamined beliefs that are consonant with the cultural system of meaning and ontology within which it makes sense to take certain actions, entirely without malevolent intent, that nonetheless systematically limit the life chances of stigmatized groups, Were is not for the regularity of hegemonic practices, resistance by the stigmatized would not be necessary. Were it not for the capacity of the established to regard hegemonic practices as reasonable and just, resistance could be more overt. Resistance could be informed by an explicit social analysis that unmasks the practices as oppressive. Yet currently neither the oppressors nor the oppressed face squarely the character of their situation, and resistance is often inchoate just as oppression is not deliberately intended. (p. 352)

An example of a hegemonic practice in bilingual education is the assumption by many educators that bilingual instruction is synonymous with remedial education. The overrepresentation of bilingual students in "basic" or "special education" programs is often the result of the belief that having a different first language is detrimental or deviant (Poplin & Phillips, in press).

So the liberatory teacher must help develop an awareness of these oppressive processes and practices through *the way* literature is discussed and writing is directed. Rather than read Sandra Cisneros' *House on Mango Street* as a text full of beautiful language and funny stories, we must teach it as those things *plus* a narrative about poverty, bilingualism, and attempting to find one's place in the world. We must also teach about Cisneros' life and how she acts to make the world a better place.

Similarities

Both whole-language (constructivist) and liberatory educators begin with students' primary language for both cognitive *and* sociopolitical reasons. We know that learning happens faster and more efficiently when primary languages are taught and used for instruction first. We know that society is best served when more people can communicate in more languages. We know that through different languages people can express different ideas, thus bilingual, bicultural peoples are often more creative and cognitively flexible (Cummins, 1989; Stone, 1992).

Whole-language and liberatory educators each begin with students' own stories or voices. Cognitively, starting with students' own lives provides a grounding to new experiences, a place to begin in one's own mind from which new meanings might be best constructed. Socially and politically one must develop one's voice in order to know oneself and be able to act in a larger community and society.

Both whole language and liberatory educators provide rich literate environments. There is an emphasis on real literature drawn from various cultures and written in both students' native and second languages. The richness of the literacy includes student writings written both individually and collectively. Language experience stories, the study of authors, and texts of all genre grace both rooms; in addition there are the texts of the real world—oral storytelling, newspapers, videos, comic books, magazines, community newspapers, and reference texts written in multiple languages. These texts are all a part of the whole-language bilingual and liberatory class.

Both emphasize real reading for real purposes and real writing for real purposes. Exercises designed solely for the study or practice of skills are not used in these classes. Rather these classrooms write letters to friends, community members, newspapers, and businesses. Students write essays about their own opinions and try their hand at various forms of creative writing. Grammar, spelling, punctuation, and word skills are taught *within* the context of one's own real literacy. Activities not often associated in people's minds with literacy support the literacy activities in these classrooms as well. These activities include dramatic plays, mock economic systems, art projects, and mock trials that call on students to be active participants in the construction of knowledge.

Examples

Examples of liberatory whole-language activities help delineate the differences between whole-language and liberatory whole-language classrooms. The first example is the well-known Pajaro Valley literacy project in which Alma Flor Ada helped teachers develop a project where bilingual children wrote about their families to stimulate primary literacy (Ada, 1988). Many liberatory literacy projects begin with writing one's own text from one's life versus beginning with a text created outside. The texts developed by these students contain pictures and drawings of family members, relay favorite family stories, require children to interview their parents, and are written in the child's primary language. This project allows the child's life, his/her community, the significant people in his/her life, his/her language, and his/her own voice to be brought to the classroom. The significant people in these children's lives, become, in Alma Flor's words, "the protagonists of the texts." This project effectively addressed all the principles outlined above as constructivist whole language. Children began with their lives and their language; with the whole of their story; *they* broke it into the literacy skills of expression; *they* used their primary language in a cognitive academic manner; *they* accomplished this within the context of rich social interactions that were comfortable; *they* transformed what they knew into text and learned more about themselves in the process; and *they* used real reading and writing. The project also addressed liberatory principles by reversing the unusual power configuration in the class. The students were the experts and knew the answers. The protagonists were not selected by others, they were people whose lives rarely make it into the official histories. They raised what was generally considered "low" status knowledge to "high" status. The activities placed the children at the center of their community as viewers and participants of action and, in the course of all this movement, students were placed in interaction with one another.

Basically bilingual whole-language and liberatory bilingual whole-language activities differ in purpose and therefore in practice. Liberatory activities do not just concern one's cognitive academic development but one's whole life. Being bilingual, especially bilingual and a person of color, in this country calls on one to have to fight for one's own and communal empowerment. Our students must be equipped to understand and act on this oppression. Additionally, bilingual, bicultural students bring great gifts to the nation that often go unused because of oppressive conditions of poverty and unequal distribution of power. Students are bombarded with conflicting messages all day. From MTV to the president, they must be able to see their way through and have the confidence and skills they need to make critical decisions. In short, they need more than reading and writing to become the best persons they can become. The incorporation of liberatory pedagogy into our already exciting whole-language bilingual classroom allows for students to become fully engaged bicultural citizens. This keeps us from engaging in what Lourdes Arguelles (1992) calls "a shallow pedagogy of hope," one that does not validate the despair that often accompanies a subordinated position in society.

BILITERACY: A TRANSFORMATIVE PEDAGOGY

In order for a teacher to exercise what Toinette Eugene calls "the liberation ethic of care" with her/his students, the teacher must be cognizant of the content of the material she/he brings into class as well as the strategies used in implementing classroom activities. The very selection of content is often different between whole-language and liberatory whole-language bilingual classes. Does the content represent only one story; is the literature largely translations of Euro-American texts? Is the content carried beyond its simple story value? Does it leave out certain people's stories?

It is interesting to note that constructive and liberation educators often use the same strategies but for different reasons. These reasons, however, often shape the strategy in one way or another. For example, one can use the strategies of cooperative learning in any number of ways for any number of reasons. As the reasons one uses any particular method varies, so does its execution in the classroom. We have all seen very reductionistic teachers use cooperative learning arrangements to accomplish synthetic activities, such as the questions at the end of a chapter or worksheets. Constructivists, because they believe that learning is accomplished best in social situations, use cooperative learning to enhance cognitive functioning, thus students are grouped to accomplish cognitively rich and complex activities that contain a great deal of discovery, experimentation, and discussion. To be liberatory that activity must also be critical and involve the thinking through and acting on a socially significant idea, event, or concept. Each of these looks very different in the classroom and each requires a different level of investment and involvement by students.

Additionally, liberatory whole-language activities frequently involve the community by either bringing the community into class or designing real projects to go out. How different is homework that draws from and gives to the community versus homework contrived for the practice of literacy. The more curriculum is integrated with community needs, strengths, and issues the more liberatory real whole language can be.

No matter how poor or how troubled a community looks in our eyes, there are great gifts there that we as teachers must come to know and use. To do this teachers must first examine their own culture and come to an understanding that it embodies only one way of seeing and being; that there are other ways to be in the world. We must lose our fear of things we don't understand to the process of coming to know. We must listen to our students, to their families, and to their communities so that we can understand the goodness and the struggle inside their communities. Then we can truly educate students to act responsibly in a free democracy, to become the best they can become, and to make the world a better place. If we are not liberated ourselves from our own unselfconscious monocultural and usually liberal stances, we cannot help others empower themselves.

Liberatory classroom teachers generally see their role as teaching students to read the world, not just the word (Freire & Macedo, 1987), and thus literacy has a far larger definition. We expand it to mean the ability to read between the lines of advertising, to read the racist and sexist messages in our songs, to read the violence in our media and to read themselves into that world as actors who can work for a more just, safe, and moral society. We expand it to mean visual literacy, the literacy of the arts, the knowledge of the body, popular culture literacy, the total awareness of things around us and our place in the world. In liberatory classrooms, students use language to talk about the current world, their place in it, and their ideas for the making of a better world. These are the conversations held inside liberatory classrooms where children and adolescents express their values, concerns, thoughts and dreams. These are the things that make up the examined life and these are the ideas that engage all of us, no matter our age.

Liberatory teachers understand that their role is one of longevity, that they are not just teaching cognitive skills so the child can progress to the next grade, but are allowing space and time for students to build upon their own values and talents. We all act politically, even those like myself who used to say I never wanted to be involved in the politics of schooling. Finally, I had to admit that everything I did had political and social implications for my students and their communities. There are no safe apolitical havens. To not act to change things is to act to keep them the same.

Students also begin to view themselves as actors in community and in society—as people who can write letters, organize groups of peers, influence others, and make a difference. This is a far cry from students who see themselves primarily in the context of the evaluation of themselves by school authorities and texts. Student voice is more than creative writing in liberatory whole-language bilingual classes, it is the way one comes to be and present oneself in the world. It is not about mice who live in the country nor animals that come out in the night; it is not simply delightful stories and rich novels; it is about life and being in the world, about making the world a better place through our being. Being a liberatory teacher is not only life-giving to others, it is life-nourishing for ourselves as well.

About the Author

Mary Simpson Poplin is a professor on the Faculty in Education of The Claremont Graduate School in Claremont, California. After teaching elementary students in north Texas for a number of years, Mary received her Ph.D. from the University of Texas at Austin in 1978. Her early work was in the field of special education. For the past ten years, she has concentrated on the preparation of teachers and teacher educators for multiethnic and multilingual urban environments. During the spring of 1990, she also taught second language students every morning in an urban high school. Her professional publications center on the exploration of nonreductionistic pedagogies in diverse educational settings, including constructivist, critical or liberatory, and feminine pedagogies.

References

Ada, A. F. (1988). The Pájaro Valley experience: Working with Spanish-speaking parents to develop children's reading and writing skills through the use of children's literature. In Skutnabb-Kangas, T., and Cummins., J. (Eds.), *Minority education: From shame to struggle*, pp. 223–36. Clevedon: Multilingual Matters Ltd.

Apple, M. (1987). *Teachers and texts*. New York: Routledge & Kegan Paul.

Arguelles, L. (1992, April). *Transforming education*. Address to Spring Seminar, Institute for Education in Transformation, Claremont Graduate School, Claremont, CA.

Aronowitz, S., and Giroux, H. (1988). Schooling, culture, and literacy in the age of broken dreams: A review of Bloom and Hirsch. *Harvard Educational Review*, vol. 58, no. 2, 172–94.

Barrs, M., Ellis, S., Hester, H., and Thomas, A. (1989). *Primary language record*. Portsmouth, NH: Heinemann.

Benesch, S. (1988). *Ending remediation: Linking ESL and content in higher education*. Alexandria, VA: Teachers of English Speakers.

Cummins, J. (1989). *Empowering minority students*. Sacramento, CA: California Association for Bilingual Education.

Cummins, J. (1984). *Bilingualism and special education: Issues in assessment and pedagogy*. London: Multilingual Matters Ltd.

Darder, A. (1991). *Culture and power in the classroom: A critical foundation for bicultural education*. New York: Bergin & Garvey.

Edelsky, C. (1986). *Writing in a bilingual program: Había una vez*. Norwood, NJ: Ablex Publishing Corp.

Edelsky, C., Altswerger, B., and Flores, B. (1990). *Whole language. What's the difference?* Portsmouth, NH: Heinemann.

Erickson, F., (1987). Transformation and school success: The politics and culture of educational achievement. *Anthropology and Education Quarterly*, vol. 18, pp. 335–56.

Eugene, T. (1989). Sometimes I feel like a motherless child: The call and response for a liberational ethic of care by African American feminists. In Brabeck, M. (Ed.), *Who cares? Theory, research, and the educational implications of the ethic of care*, pp. 45–62. New York: Praeger.

Flores, B., Cousin, P. T., and Díaz, E. (1991). Transforming deficit myths about learning, language, and culture. *Language Arts*, vol. 68, pp. 369–79.

Freeman, Y. S., and Freeman, D. E. (1992). *Whole language for second language learners*. Portsmouth, NH: Heinemann.

Freire, P., and Faundez, A. (1989). *Learning to question: A pedagogy of liberation*. New York: Continuum.

Freire, P., and Macedo, D. (1987). *Literacy: Reading the word and the world*. South Hadley, MA: Bergin & Garvey.

Giroux, H. A. (1988). *Teachers as intellectuals: Toward a critical pedagogy of learning*. Granby, MA: Bergin & Garvey.

Hayes, C. W., Bahruth, R., and Kessler, C. (1991). *Literacy con cariño. A story of migrant children's success*. Portsmouth, NH: Heinemann.

Hudelson, S. (1989). *Write on. Children writing in ESL*. Englewood Cliffs, NJ: Prentice-Hall Regents.

Krashen, S. (1985). *The input hypothesis: Issues and implications*. New York: Longman.

Krashen, S. (1982). *Principles and practice in second language acquisition*. Oxford: Pergamon Press.

Krashen, S. (1981). *Second language acquisition and second language learning*. Hayward, CA: Alemany Press.

London Higher Education Authority (1988). *Stories in the multilingual primary classroom. Supporting children's learning of English as a second language*. London: London Higher Education Authority.

Macrorie, K. (1984). *Telling writing*. Upper Montclair, NJ: Boynton Cook.

McLaren, P. (1989). *Life in schools*. New York: Longman.

Palincsar, A. (1988–89). Collaborative research and the development of reciprocal teaching. *Educational Leadership*, vol. 40, no. 4, pp. 37–40.

Park, P. (1989). *What is participatory research: A theoretical and methodological perspective*. Unpublished paper. Northampton, MA: Center for Community Education & Action, Inc.

Poplin, M. (1988a). The reductionistic folly in learning disabilities: Replicating the past by reducing the present. *Journal of Learning Disabilities*, vol. 21, no. 7, pp. 389–400.

Poplin, M. (1988b). Holistic/constructivist principles of the teaching/learning process: Implications for the field of learning disabilities. *Journal of Learning Disabilities*, vol. 21, no. 7, pp. 401-16.

Poplin, M., and Phillips, L. (in press). Sociocultural aspects of language and literacy: Issues facing educators of the learning disabled. *Learning Disability Quarterly*.

Rigg, P., and Allen, V. G. (Eds.) (1989). *When they don't all speak English. Integrating the ESL student into the regular classroom*. Urbana, IL: National Council of Teachers of English.

Ruíz, N. (1989). An optimal learning environment for Rosemary. *Exceptional Children*, vol. 56, no. 2, pp. 130–44.

Shor, I. (1980). *Critical teaching in everyday life*. Chicago: University of Chicago Press.

Shor, I., and Freire, P. (1987). *A pedagogy for liberation: Dialogues in transforming education*. Portsmouth, NH: Heinemann.

Skutnabb-Kangas, T., and Cummins, J. (Eds.) (1988). *Minority education: From shame to struggle*. Clevedon: Multilingual Matters Ltd.

Stone, S. (1992). *Divergent thinking: Nontraditional or creative talent of monolingual, bilingual and special education students in an elementary school*. Unpublished dissertation. The Claremont Graduate School, Claremont, CA.

Walsh, C. E. (1991). *Pedagogy and the struggle for voice: Issues of language, power, and schooling for Puerto Ricans*. New York: Bergin & Garvey.

Weiler, K. (1988). *Women teaching for change: Gender, class and power*. South Hadley, MA: Bergin & Garvey.

Part II
DEVELOPING LITERACY

DEVELOPING LITERACY

LISTENING TO Children's Voices:
Opening the Door Through Fairy Tales

Barbara Dube Moreno
The Los Angeles Unified School District, California

In the spring of 1989, I was privileged to work, as both teacher and researcher, with a class of 30 second-grade urban students. The focus of our twelve-week study involved using folktales as a vehicle for personal empowerment, utilizing both Freire's Theory of Critical Pedagogy and Alma Flor Ada's Creative Reading Method. Although almost all of these multiethnic children were English speaking, the lessons we shared could easily be applied in a bilingual setting. I believe that any second-grade class, taken through a similar process, might come up with the same kind of responses.

While Hispanic children have realities and specific needs of their own, they share a social and cultural reality with other urban children. The complex world of the urban child and of ethnic and minority language children is both rich and full of potential for reflection. These children need the opportunity to validate and dialogue about their own life experiences in order to understand themselves and begin to take charge of their own destiny.

Although the activities in the study described were originally conducted in English, they can and should take place in the first language of the children. This program and the insights gained can be useful with children everywhere. They may, in fact, be especially helpful when working with Spanish-speaking children, who often feel disenfranchised and who need the opportunity to speak and to be heard in order to gain a strong sense of self and personal empowerment.

In order to share the process, as well as the valuable perceptions of the children who participated in the study, I will first present a chronological account of our everyday procedures in order to involve the reader in the classroom experience. This chronology serves both as an example of an integrated theme approach to teaching and a model of how the methodologies presented were utilized. While the particular folk/fairy tales in this study were read in English, they can be presented in any language. They are simple stories to translate if Spanish language versions are not available—it is the essence of the stories that is important, not the specific language itself. Folk/fairy tales have been handed down, person to person, over the centuries as an oral tradition. It is appropriate that the tradition continue.

> **Teachers must be able to reach beyond their own world to touch that of their students and assist students to do the same.... To do this, we must listen to their stories and hear who they are. We must learn to listen and listen to learn.**
>
> —Cynthia Chambers Erasmus

71

Following an overview of the process, some examples of the children's reflections will be presented as a demonstration of both Critical Pedagogy and the Creative Reading Methodology, showing ways in which they work and how the children, through their involvement, became empowered as both thinkers and as students.

As educators, it is imperative that we listen carefully to these young voices. Seven- and eight-year-old children do reflect on interactions, responsibilities, and interpersonal relationships in their own private worlds and in the world around them. They can become empowered decision makers and change agents and thoughtful, active participants in the shaping of their own lives.

I chose folktales as the vehicle toward empowerment because they reflect both a culture's uniqueness and the universality of human experience. They deal with life's most simple, yet most enduring, aspects—joy and sorrow, hope and disappointment, weakness and strength. Folktales address basic human needs and experiences—thirst and hunger, the natural order of birth, marriage, and death. They hold out the hope that good will always triumph over evil, that victory is not dependent on size, age, or gender, and that clear thinking and brain power can win out over mere physical strength. Well told tales, which have been passed on by word of mouth, provide the reader/listener with rich language and imaginative literature, as well as potent models of how people think, make choices, and find the cleverness and strength inside themselves to significantly change their lives (Buchan, 1931).

Folktales recognize that human beings shape their own destiny and provide a natural way to emulate thinking patterns. They construct a bridge between the ongoing problem solving modeled by folk heroes and heroines and the actual problems presented by contemporary life. Using the characters as models, listeners can become active protagonists, creating their own life stories. Folktales become, in a sense, metaphors that lend strength and direction for one's own life journey. Through critical reflection, the reader can evaluate and analyze how fairy tale protagonists successfully or unsuccessfully solve their dilemmas. In turn, those resolutions can provide alternative solutions for resolving similar real-life predicaments.

Folktales provide an opportunity to observe cultural diversity. They foster higher-order thinking skills when devices such as predicting outcomes, analyzing character behavior, and comparing and contrasting different cultural versions of the same tale—such as the numerous variants of Cinderella—are incorporated (Carlson, 1972).

Utilizing folktales as a basis for dialoguing with young children provides an avenue for personal empowerment. The interactive, shared experience of a story, a folktale, or a fairy tale encourages children to think and reflect both on the story and what it may imply for their own lives. This moves the teaching experience away from the traditional "banking education" (Freire, 1970) into a "problem-posing" mode. As Freire tells us about dialogue:

> Only dialogue, which requires critical thinking, is also capable of generating critical thinking. Without dialogue there is no communication and without communication there can be no true education. (p. 81)

It is important that this process of critical reflection be presented to all children, regardless of age. Alma Flor Ada accurately states that "It is never too soon to begin to encourage children to reason, to ask questions, to search for alternatives, to develop their own judgments" (Ada, 1990). Empowering young children to think and act critically through folk tales is one such possibility.

DEVELOPING LITERACY

Throughout this experience in Critical Pedagogy, I utilized Alma Flor Ada's Creative Reading Method for guiding the dialogue (Ada, 1987). It is simple and direct and can be learned easily, and it can be varied to suit the individual teacher/facilitator.

The dialogic reflection, which followed frequent folk/fairy tale sessions, began by simply acknowledging ways a particular story was relevant to the children's own personal lives. They were then guided, one step further, into examining ways in which they might take action to affect or change their lives. As a result of their reflections, they found themselves "beginning to assume responsibility for their own lives, for their relations with others and for conduct within their sphere of action" (Ada & Olave, 1986, p. 16).

The children's reflection moved through the four phases of the Creative Reading Method. These phases are not necessarily sequential, and they grow naturally out of the dialogue with the children.

In the first phase, the Descriptive Phase, the children answer the essential, yet standard *who? what? where? when? why?* and *how?* kind of questions. Next, in the Personal Interpretive Phase, the students use their own experiences as a gauge to examine the textual information. The questioning is more personal, such as "Have you done something similar?", "What would you have said?", and "How did you feel after reading this?" Here the essential process of reflection begins. In the third phase of the Creative Reading Method, the Critical Phase, the student is asked to both reflect and infer from the information: "Could this have turned out differently?" "Who benefits from this decision?" (Ada, 1987)

Ada takes this thinking process one critical step further in her Creative Phase, where she suggests that students use this newfound critical awareness to make decisions about their own lives. Here children are encouraged to take responsibility for their own actions and to determine ways they can feel satisfied and make their own lives more enriched and gratifying.

This fourth phase was the main focus of our dialogues and, used in conjunction with the fairy tales, it provided a consistent base for reflection, out of which the children's significant themes emerged.

The Storytelling Process

During the actual storytelling process, the children seated themselves in a semicircle on the carpet around a low chair in which I sat. After the children settled in, I introduced the book in a variety of ways. Sometimes I would show the cover and ask if they could guess what the book was going to be about. Other times I told them the story title and discussed the illustrator, mentioning other books illustrated by the same person. Sometimes they would have a task while listening to the story, such as "Each time you hear this refrain, say it with me" or "Look for the picture of the black cat. He is on almost every page. See if you can figure out what he is doing." Occasionally it was necessary to give a little warning such as "This story might be a little scary. Can you guess why?"

When they had questions in the middle of the story that could not wait, I would stop to clarify their dilemmas. After the story was finished, we would begin the dialogue. Sometimes they had questions or comments, and sometimes they were ready to move on to a new activity.

I tried to bring each discussion to a formalized closure. Occasionally the students had nothing more to say and were unwilling to participate in the summarizing process. They had already moved on to a new idea. Once they had finished talking, it was futile to pursue the subject. Since this is a common experience in the primary classroom, I usually took the children's lead and proceeded from that point.

On some days, the children could sit for 30 minutes, listen to a story, and become involved in a thoughtful dialogue. Other days they could only sit through the story and sit no longer. Often, the discussion would begin and distractions by children with a shorter attention span or more pressing concerns would limit the dialogue time. Sometimes the dialogue came abruptly to an end.

At optimal fairy tale sessions, I would read the story aloud. This would then be followed by a dialogue, sometimes completed on paper. For example, one day after discussing Hansel and Gretel's stepmother, the children wrote about what made them feel mean and their responses to that mean feeling.

The fairy tales were presented as an integrated curricular unit of study and became the overall classroom theme, with particular stories and activities woven throughout. During each week to ten-day period, several versions of one particular folk/fairy tale were introduced. One variant was presented each day in a read aloud situation. The study of some fairy tales was concluded by viewing the *Faerie Tale Theatre* video version.

Their interest in many of the stories carried over far past the time they were presented, partly because the fairy tale books were available in the classroom library.

The whole class was invited to work through the first stage of reflection after hearing each story. This involved a cursory examination of characters, events, and story details as shown through text and illustrations. It also included some initial reflection on the consequences of character decisions.

Even though several renditions of one story were presented over a relatively short period of time, the opportunity for additional reflection came later in two or three subsequent stages, often through writing or in subsequent dialogues.

Listening and Reacting to Fairy Tales

The initial group of books were about Little Red Riding Hood. The well-known Trina Schart Hyman (1982) version was introduced first. The class listened and responded politely but were unwilling to work past a cursory Descriptive Phase discussion. They simply were not excited by the story.

The next version they heard was *The Gunniwolf* (Harper, 1967), which contains a catchy sing-song refrain. While the children enjoyed singing the refrain, they did not enthusiastically respond to the story itself.

The children clearly stated that they already understood the concept of not talking to strangers; they were well aware of the dangers of venturing out alone. They made it clear that any further discussion was futile. They agreed to hear two more versions, *Little Red Cap*, illustrated by Lisbeth Zwerger (Crawford & Zwerger, 1983), and *Red Riding Hood*, retold by Beatrice Schenk De Regniers (1977), and then the children pushed for a different fairy tale.

Subsequent to hearing the Little Red Riding Hood stories, the concept of "red" was integrated throughout the curriculum. The children wrote "Red Poems," which were posted on a red bulletin board. They collected and categorized red objects in cooperative math groups. They celebrated a "Red Day" when each child wore something red to school and created a red painting. The children were definite, however, about not wanting to hear the story again.

The next fairy tale presented was *The Three Bears*. There were numerous versions with rich, diverse illustrations. I assumed these would stimulate an extended dialogue about the danger of breaking into people's houses, the need to follow directions, and the idea of natural consequences. They were clearly thinking—but not in a direction I had imagined or planned. The lessons concerning following your mother's directions, not going into the strangers' houses, and not taking and using other people's belongings seemed as familiar to them as the warnings from Little Red Riding Hood and were equally as uninteresting.

The story initiated individual science reports on bears. This involved viewing several *National Geographic* tapes and reading aloud science books with simple, basic information about a variety of bears. The children also completed bear art projects, learned to count by threes, and culminated this unit with a "Teddy Bears Picnic."

They did become quite enchanted with the illustrations of Jan Brett (1987) and Lorinda Bryan Cauley (1981). They would pore over the pages admiring the detailed artwork, and argue over which version was their favorite. Overall, the basic plot and characters did not hold much interest for them.

Several versions of *Jack and the Beanstalk* stories were also introduced (Cauley, 1983; De Regniers, 1985; Galdone, 1982b; Still, 1977) and were diverse enough so that the details could be utilized to engage in a rather sophisticated comparison-and-contrast Venn Diagram exercise. The students were not eager to discuss the righteousness of Jack's theft but were much more interested in the mother's treatment of Jack.

Jack and the Beanstalk was used to motivate a science lesson in which the children grew and dissected lima beans. They also grew potato vines and made paper lima bean blossoms for a bulletin board, where they posted their observations of the lima bean growth process. Those activities generated much more interest than the story.

They also enjoyed the fairy tale *Puss in Boots* (Galdone, 1976). Their dialogue focused on financing a college education and how having children at an early age might have an impact on achieving higher education goals. Their dialogue exhibited a worldliness I did not anticipate, not realizing that these were issues second graders might already be considering.

During the initial reading of *Hansel and Gretel* (Scribner & Adams, 1975), I realized that the overt violence and child abuse in the story were more graphic than I had remembered. I questioned my own good judgment, but much to my surprise, they enthusiastically applauded the story and begged to hear it read again immediately.

Additional versions of *Hansel and Gretel* were then introduced over the next three week period (Crawford & Zwerger, 1980; Galdone, 1982a; Lobel, 1971). The children eagerly asked to hear yet another *Hansel and Gretel*, and these stories elicited considerable interest and discussion. The children wrote responses to the story, letters to the stepmother, and their interest culminated in writing their own versions.

The last folk/fairy tale introduced in the study was the traditional European Cinderella story, with additional variants reflecting a number of other cultures. The Galdone (1978) version, presented first, painted a fairly standardized story of Cinderella and her family, who all live happily ever after following Cinderella's marriage to the prince. The children seemed comfortable with this familiar version and their discussion centered on the stepsisters' treatment of Cinderella and the stepfamily's jealousy.

The next version presented was the Grimm's telling of *Cinderella* (Svend, 1978), which portrayed the stepfamily as cruel and abusive. In this book, the stepsisters mutilate their feet in order to fit into the slipper the prince has brought. In retribution for their unkind treatment of Cinderella, their eyes are pecked out by doves. The children applauded the punishment of the stepsisters and demonstrated a concern about the ideas of justice, fairness, and retribution in the story.

They enjoyed *Mufaro's Beautiful Daughters* (Steptoe, 1987), an African Cinderella story, and were quite taken by the rich and detailed illustrations. The children saw the comparison to and difference from the traditional European Cinderella immediately and made a clear distinction between the two sisters in this story: the kind, generous one who becomes the queen and the mean, selfish one who ends up as her sister's servant. They expressed a clear understanding again about jealousy and its natural consequences.

In *The Indian Cinderella* (Phenix, 1985), the children immediately understood the correlation between this and the traditional Cinderella story. They expressed concern that Little Burnt Face is abused by her real sisters rather than stepsisters. Also, the father, who is present, does not intervene in their mistreatment of her. The themes of jealousy and punishment were brought up once more as well as appropriate sibling relationships. This version turned out to be a favorite Cinderella story for many children.

Vasilisa the Beautiful (Whitney, 1970) is a Russian folktale with a Cinderella character. Vasilisa's mother dies and leaves her a magical doll who can help solve her problems. Her father remarries a terrible woman and then disappears from the story. The children turned all their attention to the absent father, trying to analyze why he would have abandoned his daughter.

Yeh-Shen (Louie, 1982), the oldest recorded Cinderella story, held their rapt attention. There was a quiet, reflective moment when I finished reading. Then they tried to figure out Cinderella's real name since they now had so many possibilities from which to choose. They also questioned why the Cinderella character always had to work.

Tattercoats (Steel, 1976), an English version of Cinderella, was the last presented in this story cycle. It tells of a young girl whose grieving grandfather will have nothing to do with her after her mother, his favorite daughter, dies in childbirth. She is saved by a magical goatherd. The grandfather's treatment of his granddaughter became the primary topic of conversation. The children exhibited a good understanding of the grandfather's grief in statements such as "She was born on the same day his best daughter died—he was mad at her because he thought she killed her." At the same time, they realized that his behavior toward his granddaughter was unacceptable: "I think he was wrong." "He should have treated her right. The girl never did anything to him." While the children showed remarkable empathy with the grandfather's grief at having lost his favorite daughter, they did not condone his behavior.

Retribution

The children displayed an explicit sense of what was fair retribution for abusive behavior. In the Grimm's version of *Cinderella* (Svend, 1978), clearly a favorite, they held a firm concept of just punishment for the stepsisters and the stepmother. The children did not accept the treatment of Cinderella and sought assurance that this kind of wrongdoing would not go unattended. Even in reaction to the first and mildest version of Cinderella (Galdone,1978), they expressed mistrust of people who behave in such a "mean" manner. Only one child showed any magnanimity. When asked, "What do you think of how the story ends?" she was willing to forgive and forget. "Good that she let them move in 'cuz she could've been mean to them like they was mean to her." Another child was clear about the way events should have transpired: "As soon as Cinderella moved in, they all should have helped do the work."

The last story read to the class during the study was a final version of Hansel and Gretel (Jeffers, 1986), still their favorite. The children had two basic issues with this story that were yet unresolved. One was whether the stepmother and the witch were one and the same person. The other was the father's treatment of the two children. They were finally ready to concede that the father was mean because "he took Hansel and Gretel out into the forest" and "he yelled at them." They had struggled with the father's responsibility since hearing the first version and finally came to an acceptable resolution. As to the witch/stepmother combination, there was no definitive conclusion. After all, who really knows for sure?

Writing as Reflection

As previously mentioned, the fairy tale sessions frequently included a corresponding writing exercise. Prior to the writing sessions, the assignment was discussed and the writing process was modeled on the chalkboard. This became, in fact, a method of reflection on earlier dialogues. For example, after listening to *Hansel and Gretel*, the children discussed the stepmother's behavior. Initially, they dictated a list of all the things that could have caused her meanness. This was written on the chalkboard and then transferred to a chart. The same process was followed to list what they might do to help the stepmother change her behavior patterns.

When the letter writing idea was presented, the children dictated a class letter first. They reviewed the letter writing format as well. They reviewed the previously dictated lists of what could have caused the stepmother's aberrant behavior and what they might do to help her make behavior modifications. The lists were posted on the chalkboard and they were asked if they had anything to add. A few additions were made. After the children had written their own letters to the stepmother, they had an opportunity to share them aloud with the class.

There were other fairy tale-related writing activities. These included creating their own version of The Three Bears, Cinderella, and Hansel and Gretel and writing a dialogue for two hands, in which each traced hand discussed its favorite fairy tale with the other, explaining the reasons for their choice. They wrote about the reasons they selected one particular version of Cinderella as their favorite and ended the semester by composing an original fairy tale.

As it turned out, the children moved back and forth throughout all four phases of the Creative Reading Method as the dialogue naturally evolved. They could, with a few questions provided by the teacher, set their own dialogue agenda, based on their interests and needs. The discussions touched on all levels of questioning and the children began to take charge of their own learning, elaborating on the issues of most concern to them.

Real-Life Problem Solving

The children had a well-stocked cache of how to effectively solve everyday problems. After the first reading of *Hansel and Gretel* (Scribner and Adams, 1975), they had several practical suggestions as to how the woodcutter and his wife could avoid starvation. Some children realized immediately that the family had many resources in their own environment that they had not utilized. One child said that "They could've gone into the woods and got some nuts and berries." Two children suggested that "they could have gone fishing" or "gone hunting too." Even if they didn't have a gun, as one boy suggested they might not, another understood that "they could've set a trap or something or they could've looked for fruit trees." The children were knowledgeable about what it takes to survive "in the woods" and one verbal young girl took their ideas one step further and suggested that "They could've planted some seeds and grown some food to eat," a very pragmatic idea.

Some children felt that monetary remedies were in order, such as to get "a job somewhere so they could get some money" or "move to the city" so the father could find work. Cause-and-effect relationships seemed to present no hurdle for these young children. They were well-schooled in the correct course of action needed to provide for life's necessities.

In the event that finding a job or hunting, harvesting, and gathering failed, the children realized there were other solutions to the problem: "They could've gone and asked their neighbors did they have any food 'cuz their kids was hungry." And if one clear thinking girl was correct in her assumption that "They didn't have no neighbors; they lived in the woods," another was certain that "they could've gone into town where there was people that could help them." The children's message, through their problem solving, was that if you find yourself in a tough spot, you always have options: you can ask people to help you or you can find ways to help yourself. They never implied that giving up was even a possibility. They suggested that if you have a problem, you simply need to solve it. Their suggestions were tenable and well-grounded in reality. It is easy to speculate that if these children had been Hansel and Gretel's parents, the story would have taken an entirely different turn.

Compassion and Ways to Heal Human Wounds

During their discussion of how to help the stepmother out of her dilemma, the student's compassionate suggestions reflected an understanding about ways to heal human wounds. Their ideas ranged from the practical—"Give her some food"; "Talk to her"; "Send her to a psychiatrist"; "Send her to a hospital"—to the supportive—"Counsel her"; "Send her a good letter"; "Invite her to dinner"; and of course, "Hug her." Many ideas showed creative imagination and caring, such as "Get her fancy clothes"; "Take her to a fitness center"; "Buy her a bird to sing to her when she was in a bad mood."

Willingness to Act in Support of Others

Following the discussion about how they could help the stepmother, the class followed up on the suggestion to "Write her a good letter." They translated their concerns into letters in which they admonished the stepmother for her behavior and yet supported her healing. Initially, the class wrote a group letter (in part to review letter writing form) and dictated the following:

May 8, 1989

Dear Stepmother,

Why did you have to take the children into the woods? Next time, don't take the children into the forest because their father cares for his children. Next time, think before you act.

Were you mean because your parents were always complaining about you and hurting you and making you very mad? Why did you do it back to the children? You shouldn't have copied your parents.

I would like to help you out. I will take you to a psychiatrist to talk to you so you will feel better. I will also take you to the movies to make up for your bad days. I will invite you to my house for dinner and give you a hug.

Room One

In their individual letters to the stepmother, the children reflected on previous class discussions and also on the model letter. They wrote to her with anger and passion—and even forgiveness—about genuine issues that concerned them. Here the children exhibited their own strong codes of morals and ethics. They were clear about what led to the stepmother's abandoning Hansel and Gretel and what the students could do to help prevent a reoccurrence.

Almost all of the children began their letter using the same format as the model, asking the stepmother a question. They wanted to know "Why are you so mean and selfish?"; "Why did you give your kids a little to eat?"; " Why did you take the kids out in the forest and left them out there?"; "Why don't you help them instead of torturing them?"

They continued, through their letters, to attempt some understanding of the stepmother's behavior. "If someone gave you food would you be nice?" "Did your mother and father hypnotize you to do that when you were young?" Was it "because your parents yelled at you" or "because you hate children"? "Are you mean because your mom and dad were fighting over who gets you the most?"

They offered her practical suggestions ("You don't have to copy your mom and dad") that indicated their perception of how childhood experiences can affect adult behavior. They also explained the consequences of unacceptable behavior: "If you were nicer, I would give you food and tell you funny stories." One thoughtful girl included an important insight into interpersonal relations when she wrote, "You are not the right kind of women that people like. They hate you and you need to be nice like some other people." Another summed it up with "I would love you if you were nice."

In their letters the children were earnest in their need to understand what might have caused such aberrant behavior. They were sincere in their desire to help this poor, faltering stepmother find a better path. Their comments reflected an understanding of the responsibilities of motherhood and of an appropriate relationship between a mother and child. In another discussion, one of the children brought up the fact that she was not the "real mother" but only the stepmother. Several children immediately retorted that she still shouldn't have treated the children that way—"That's not a right way to be." One child articulately pointed out that "The mother is supposed to love her childrens and take care of them, not send them out to the woods for those wolves to eat."

Hope for Transformation

It was fascinating to note that despite what the stepmother had done, the children saw hope for her transformation. During this part of our dialogue, not one child expressed the idea that it was too late or that it was hopeless or that she was just that kind of person. They seemed to hold a firm belief that even a "child abuser" could recover with some professional help and some love. This would have been considered sound advice coming from a trained counselor; it is important to note how grounded in practicality and in humanity these young children were.

Contemporary Life as It Impacts Young Children

Throughout this process, the children discussed many aspects of their everyday life. Their use of fairy tale characters as a vehicle to resolve daily fears can be seen in one particular dialogue. While discussing the witch in *Hansel and Gretel*, many children expressed their fear of her and described how frightened they would be if they had been caught in a situation similar to that of Hansel and Gretel.

When asked what was more frightening than the witch, a number of children described Freddie from the film *Nightmare on Elm Street* and Jason from the movie *Friday the Thirteenth*. These two popular horror film characters stalk, terrorize, and murder their victims with no sense of conscience or wrongdoing.

The children reported having recurring nightmares about these diabolical personalities. When asked what they could do if they actually encountered such a person, many of the children were silent and seemed almost paralyzed by the notion. A few finally said, "Hide" or "Run away," others said, "Call my parents" or "Call the police." These modern horror movie creatures seemed to have created a genuine terror, which was now incorporated into these young children's lives.

It is important that they learn to combat the Freddies and the Jasons, who live not only in their imaginations—but less dramatically—in the real world. Fairy/folk tales provide an opportunity to explore these possibilities. The children can confront the idea of evil and abuse in a nonthreatening situation and plan out solutions for choices, if later faced with potentially threatening or paralyzing situations. Subsequently, they can apply this kind of critical decision making to real life situations.

These young children are still mastering the thinking process. They are also learning ways to affect their own reality and become strong, active protagonists in their own lives. Fairy tales have facilitated that process.

Other Outcomes

There were other changes in the children that took place as a natural outgrowth of our work together. When we first began, the children "told" on each other with great frequency, looking for someone else to be the arbitrator or problem solver. By June, most had begun their own problem-solving process and only reported major conflicts such as hitting and missing belongings—a significant change from their earlier behavior.

This change was highlighted in a recess situation when a few girls were squabbling in the yard. Finally one asserted to the others, "You're just jealous and actin' just like those stepsisters. If you don't watch out, you gonna get your eyes pecked out for being so mean." She then stalked away in a huff. The Cinderella story had given her some verbal leverage; the girls on the receiving end of her anger understood that they had overstepped their boundaries. Prior to the fairy tales and related dialogues, this situation probably would have been handled with pushing, shoving, and crying. This second-grade protagonist had been empowered enough by metaphorical language to walk away from a potentially explosive situation and feel victorious in the process. She had, after all, thrown the ultimate insult.

By June many children also had stretched their writing skills from simple one-page stories to complex stories as long as six or eight pages. Also the depth and quality of their writing had vastly improved. They were able to take the vocabulary from the fairy tales and claim it as their own so that words such as *famine* and *precious* and *pebbles* became a working part of their vocabulary. They gained an innate sense of story and by the end of the school year were able to write their own fairy tales easily with a clear understanding that each story had a beginning, a middle, and an end, a conflict and a resolution.

The Need for Dialogue

In most classrooms, there are few times during the curriculum-oriented day when children are able to share their feelings or their experiences. Their dialogue around Hansel and Gretel and Cinderella opened the door for the children to engage in a new kind of communication.

Children need a place and an opportunity to discuss their feelings and reactions to situations that have taken place in their lives, as well as other issues that concern them. Dialogues allow them to make statements about their own importance in the world. They become empowered by having the value of their own life experiences recognized. A fairy tale is a safe starting place for children and can be both successful and useful in stimulating this significant kind of conversation.

Significance of the Dialogues

The perceptions of this particular group of children suggest that they had not been isolated from the realities of their own worlds. They had, from a seven- or eight-year-old perspective, a clear notion of how the "universe" functions. They often generated solutions for given situations revealing a sophistication in their thinking and experience that I had not anticipated.

They demonstrated an understanding of social systems and relationships and of the skills required to survive in the world. They verbalized a myriad of reasons about the possible causes of child abuse and what might be done to help transform a child abuser. They seemed to grasp several causes of jealousy and disclosed numerous experiences with the problems of sibling rivalry. They clearly explained their conception of adult financial responsibilities and what steps are necessary to finance a college education. They conveyed the importance of strong, positive interpersonal relationships and the responsibility one person has for another. Their perceptions were well developed and indicated that these students had established a world view long before the fairy tale dialogues. This process merely provided an arena in which they could voice their opinions and clarify their feelings.

These children carried a clear and accurate understanding of the rules of fair play, as well as ways to solve modern-day problems. In short, their perceptions may stem from only seven or eight years of experience, yet they've set their parameters straight by establishing an ethical framework useful for the rest of their lives. They also exhibited a tenderness, mixed with their worldliness, which made their words even more poignant and pressing. As McLaren (1989) so aptly states, "Teachers need to understand how experiences produced in the various domains of everyday life produce in turn the different voices students employ to give meaning to their worlds." (p. 227)

The enthusiasm with which the seven- and eight-year-olds participated and the thoughtfulness of their dialogues demonstrate the appropriateness of this process. When given the opportunity to voice an opinion, seven- and eight-year-olds have a great deal to say. These children welcomed a chance to reflect on issues that were important to them. Perhaps what they needed most was a validation of those problem-solving abilities and a recognition that their observations have value, thus empowering them to build on those skills.

Both Critical Pedagogy and the Creative Reading Method work as vehicles for the empowerment of young children. Used in tandem, they can validate students' perceptions and the significance of their own lives. By dialoguing with students in their native language about issues that are important to them, children can be challenged to discover ways to affect their own lives and that of their community. They can become empowered critical thinkers who will begin to live with a sense of dignity and worth and who can—and will—begin to shape their own destiny.

About the Author

Barbara Dube Moreno completed her doctoral studies in Multicultural Education at the University of San Francisco, under the guidance of Alma Flor Ada, who was her mentor. She is currently working at The Open School, Center for Individualized Instruction, in Los Angeles, as a fifth- and sixth-grade teacher. Here she is able to apply much of what she learned about empowering young children as learners and decision makers. She is also a poet and is working on a book for children titled *Miguel, Miguel*.

References

Ada, A. F. (1990). Class Lecture. University of San Francisco.

Ada, A. F. (1987). *Workshop: A children's literature-based whole language approach to creative reading and writing*. Unpublished manuscript.

Ada, A. F. (1986). Creative education for bilingual teachers. *Harvard Educational Review*, vol. 56, pp. 386–94.

Ada, A. F., and Olave, M. P. (1986). *Exploramos (hagamos caminos)*. Menlo Park, CA: Addison-Wesley.

Brett, J. (1987). *Goldilocks and the three bears*. New York: Dodd, Mead, & Company.

Buchan, J. (1931). The novel and the fairy tale. In Haviland, V. (Ed.), *Children and literature: Views and reviews*, pp. 221–29. IL: Scott, Foresman.

Carlson, R. K. (1972). World understanding through the folktale. In Carlson, R. K. (Ed.), *Folklore and folktales around the world.* Newark, DE: International Reading Association.
Cauley, L. B. (Illus.) (1983). *Jack and the beanstalk* (from story by J. Jacobs). New York: Putnam's.
Cauley, L. B. (1981). *Goldilocks and the three bears.* New York: Putnam.
Crawford, E. D. (Trans.), and Zwerger, L. (Illus.) (1980). *Hansel and Gretel.* New York: Morrow.
Crawford, E. D. (Trans.), and Zwerger, L. (Illus.) (1983). *Little Red Cap* (from story by J. Grimm and W. Grimm). New York: Morrow.
De Regniers, B. S. (1985). *Jack and the beanstalk.* New York: McElderry.
De Regniers, B. S. (1977). *Red Riding Hood.* New York: Atheneum.
Freire, P. (1970). *Pedagogy of the oppressed.* New York: Continuum.
Galdone, P. (Illus.) (1982a). *Hansel and Gretel.* New York: McGraw-Hill.
Galdone, P. (Illus.) (1982b). *Jack and the beanstalk* (from a story by J. Jacobs). New York: Clarion.
Galdone, P. (1978). *Cinderella.* New York: McGraw-Hill.
Galdone, P. (Illus.) (1976). *Puss in Boots* (from a story by C. Perrault). New York: Clarion.
Harper, W. (1967). *The Gunniwolf.* New York: Dutton.
Hyman, T. S. (1983). *Little Red Riding Hood.* New York: Holiday House.
Jeffers, S. (Illus.) (1986). *Hansel and Gretel.* New York: Dial.
Lobel, A. (Illus.) (1971). *Hansel and Gretel.* New York: Delacorte.
Louie, A. (1982). *Yeh-Shen.* New York: Philomel Books.
McLaren, P. (1989). *Life in schools.* New York: Longman.
Phenix, J. (1985). *The Indian Cinderella.* Holt, Rinehart and Winston of Canada.
Scribner, C., Jr. (Trans.), and Adams, A. (Illus.) (1975). *Hansel and Gretel.* New York: Scribner's, 1975.
Steel, F. A. (1976). *Tattercoats.* New York: Bradbury, 1976.
Steptoe, J. (1987). *Mufaro's beautiful daughters.* New York: Scholastic.
Still, J. (1977). *Jack and the wonder beans.* New York: Putnam's.
Svend, O. (Illus.) (1978). *Cinderella* (from a story by Grimm). New York: Larousse.
Whitney, T. P. (1970). *Vasilisa the beautiful.* New York: Macmillan.

Second Language Literacy and Immigrant Children

◆◆◆

The Inner World of the Immigrant Child

Cristina Igoa
Hayward Unified School District, California

This article attempts to speak to the culture shock, the uprooting experience, and the unique perspective of the immigrant child where the acquisition of a new language and culture is concerned. How this process is handled in the classroom plays a large part in determining whether the immigrant child successfully achieves second language literacy and becomes capable of thriving within the dominant culture.

The inner world is that deeper part of the child from whence thoughts and feelings emerge. Perhaps the inner world can be defined as the truth within the individual whether or not that "truth" has any basis in reality—nevertheless, it is what the child feels and believes. It is where fears and unreasoned joyousness, fantasies, and intuition move and speak. For us as adults, it is a surprising world; the forgotten world of our own childhood where imaginary, grotesque, or obscure characters can influence the drama of self-creation or self-destruction.

If the child is to live freely, creatively, and acculturate to a new social environment, then the deeper part of the child needs to surface and his or her mask needs to be removed through warmth, reverence, understanding, and a penetrating listening on our part.

If we are to understand the inner world of immigrant children, then we need to go to them, listen carefully to their deeper feelings, love them, and take what they have to say seriously so that in collaboration with them, we can design programs that will empower them fully.

What the Professionals Have to Say

The psychological trauma that immigrants experience when uprooted from their own soil is less visible and less easily measured than their language proficiency. Having left behind the whole system of communication, cultural beliefs, and the sense of identity that once gave meaning to their lives, many immigrants experience a deep sense of anxiety.

Heidegger says that without the language that maintains a connection with the past, without that ability to name, the past ceases to exist or to have any reality for a person (Heidegger, 1971). Yet, belief in the concept of progress has led to the incredibly naive idea that people can free themselves from their past, that it is possible for people to exchange one culture for another in the same way people can exchange commodities (Bowers, 1984).

There is a complex of sentiments built up around a language. When a group hangs tenaciously to its own language, more is involved than mere difficulty in learning English (Brown, 1969). Contacts with the culture in which someone's human nature has been developed tend to keep that person adjusted until he or she is organized in terms of a new social milieu (Brown, 1969). Without a cultural code of some kind, a person cannot think or communicate. So holding on to their language, with all its associations, may be one way immigrants attempt to ease anxiety. Skutnabb-Kangas (1981) emphasizes the importance of the mother tongue even as the new language is mastered. In this light, the native language bridges the learner's experience with the new environment. Consciousness and mastery are expanded, not dislocated.

Successful acculturation, which includes second language acquisition, is a process rather than an event, and it must be allowed to take place as a "both/and," rather than an "either/or," proposition. The adjustment entails coexistence of old values and traditions with the new; making concessions to the requirements of a new society without necessarily giving up cherished cultural values of the old (Bhatnager, 1981).

Cultural conflict of interest can often lead to demoralization and disorganization. Disorientation has resulted from the effort on the part of some people to lose their cultural identity, and the immigrant who tries to live in two cultures may not be stabilized in either. An immigrant child caught in such a dilemma may try to conform to one culture at home and another at school, often vacillating between the two (Brown, 1969). However, when an important cultural attitude—an attitude that one sees as one's fabric of being—is neglected, the person suffers (Henderson, 1984).

Entering the Inner World of the Immigrant Child

The transition the immigrant child must make in order to become oriented to a new language and culture is formidable. Traditionally, we have relied upon schooling as the dominant means of bringing immigrant children into mainstream U.S. culture. However, there are four potential and typical shortcomings of systems designed to help immigrant children: (1) the program may treat immigrant children as anomalies, or as guests; (2) the program may emphasize assimilation rather than integration within the educational system and society at large; (3) the program may be guided by the belief that the immigrants should ignore or reject their native culture in favor of the new culture; (4) the program may not take into account that there may be little or no emotional support at home, since adult members of the family may themselves be experiencing culture shock.

When we rely too much on results of skills tests or other observations that compare immigrant children's language skills to the ideal, immigrant children may appear dysfunctional, inoperative, unwilling, or even "dumb." But immigrant children have a rich inner life, and when we tap into this world, there is a wealth of information about what the child's experience has been and about what the child needs. Even if the teacher cannot really communicate in the spoken language of the child, it is still possible to establish emotional bonds that permit the child to articulate in some way where the problem may lie.

The child's perspective on immigration and second language literacy is well known to me, for my childhood was shaped by two uprooting experiences—first, in temporary transplant from a Spanish-speaking home in the Philippines to South America as a 5-year-old—and later, in my permanent immigration from the Philippines to the United States as a 13-year-old. However, it was not until I began to teach immigrant children myself that I embarked upon a serious reflection about my personal experience and the importance of recognizing the feelings of my immigrant students as I sought to teach them content. I found that what succeeded most was when I tried to give them what I would have liked teachers to have given me as an immigrant.

As a young kindergarten child in a school in Colombia, South America, I felt uprooted from the known warmth and familiar images of my native country. Although I spoke the language of the new country, I needed the closeness of a teacher, I needed friends, I needed to be taken by the hand and shown how to write my name. I recall staring at a blank piece of paper, feeling inadequate and at a loss regarding what to do. I convinced my parents that schooling was too painful an experience and that home was a safer place.

As a 13-year-old in America, once again I felt the uprooting; a deep sense of loss of familiar signs, friendships, and customs. I withdrew into silence because of the culture shock. In the Philippines, we greeted each other with a kiss on the cheek; in America, with a handshake. Each time I would encounter an unexplained difference, I would feel awkward, confused, ashamed, or "inadequate." These innumerable differences had nothing to do with language because I was raised as a bilingual. Cultural differences, the loss of cultural identity, and the feelings of inadequacy would well up in me as I sat in class. There was an unexplained void, an emptiness inside. I read well. I could illustrate. But these were mere skills. What I needed was a cultural connection. I was constantly adapting to the system. I needed the system to meet me halfway, to collaborate, to include my thoughts and feelings.

Ten years ago, I directed a language intervention center in San Francisco. One project that seemed to be a particularly effective means of helping students develop language skills and a means to express their thoughts and feelings involved the production of filmstrips based on illustrations and stories created by the children. I realized at the time that the filmstrip contents revealed much more than the child's command of grammar and syntax. Those images—a vulnerable little egg, the staring yellow eyes of a tiger, a lonely bear, an "upside-down world"—stirred deep feelings within me of my own uprooting experience.

I had long understood that immigrant children inevitably experience a period in which culture shock, limited language skills, and the expected stresses of childhood combine to produce a deep sense of isolation and vulnerability. Some years later, I began to ask myself how I could get anyone to understand the depth of these feelings. If these overwhelming emotions could in some way be identified and named, would it help us to help the children find their way? In the filmstrips, I thought I began to see a way to clearly communicate the feelings and needs of the immigrant child to others. I decided it was important to confirm my interpretations and determined to reacquaint myself with my former students, who were now on the verge of adulthood. I contacted school counselors at the local high school to find out how many of the former students were in attendance. I found most of the students, and they were available and enthusiastic about being a part of a study to delve deeply into the inner world of the immigrant experience.

What the Children Have to Say

The methodology used was dual dialogic retrospection. This methodology is based on principles stated by Freire (1984), who proposes that research should be a form of giving voice to the voiceless, of acknowledging human beings as capable of knowing. Dialogic retrospection has been described in detail by Kieffer (1981). In my own study, Kieffer's methodology was expanded by the fact that I was both the researcher and a former participant in the experience, thus allowing for dual dialogic retrospection. The students and I reviewed the filmstrips and re-created their experience of having participated in the language center as new immigrants. From every angle, we

DEVELOPING LITERACY

explored the simple question, "What are the feelings and thoughts of immigrant children?" In the course of these discussions, we attempted to identify the mechanisms the children adapted to overcome difficulties, and reflected upon the implications of the immigrant child's experience for educational systems.

The results of this examination not only formed the basis of my doctoral dissertation (Igoa, 1988), but helped me develop an improved classroom approach to help immigrant children achieve second language literacy. By their application, the immigrant children I now teach continue to achieve measurably improved reading and writing skills.

This collection of quotes is representative of what some of the immigrant children I have worked with had to say about their first encounters in a new country shortly after the uprooting from their homeland.

> This is a totally different environment than I have been used to. The change is different because it upsets the kind of life I had. It was different back home. School was different, teachers were different. I feel depressed because I miss my friends in my country.
>
> I want to stay close to my family, I am afraid to leave them, but I must go to school. It is hard to go into a classroom. It is new and I feel as if everyone is looking at me and staring at me.
>
> I am having a difficult time adjusting. I don't like going to school. I am not sure I will make it. I can't speak English. I don't understand what they are saying. I am scared, afraid to express the emotions.
>
> I am afraid people will laugh and make fun of me because I am feeling different from others. I have no friends. I am lonely and alone and sad.
>
> I need someone to care for me, to hold my hand, and say, "It's all right, I'll help you. Don't be afraid." I need someone to set me on the right track. I need her caring so that I can be stronger. I just need enough confidence so that I can begin to do things on my own.

In his introduction to Frances Wickes's *The Inner World of Childhood*, Carl Jung explains, "What this book provides is not theory, but experience." Much of what I have to say comes directly from the hearts and minds of those who have experienced the uprooting process. Wickes (1966) established that loving, secure relationships with parents are important for a child's growth and well-being. You will find an extension of this concept in all my recommendations for school administrators, in all my suggestions for teachers, in every facet of my working model of an immigrant children's language center.

Understanding the Silent Stage

> I felt different from everyone else.... I couldn't really be with anybody because they couldn't understand me and I couldn't understand them. There was no way I could try to make things better for myself. It was hard just feeling bad.
>
> I felt it was hard for me to tell them all that I felt; express it all; so I just kept some feelings inside myself.

If there is one characteristic of the uprooting experience that appears to be shared by all immigrant children, irrespective of nationality, economic status, family stability, or any other factors, it is what some have characterized as "the silent stage."

In the silent stage, immigrant children may appear to be retiring, moody, fearful, even terrified, but not because they do not wish to socialize or cooperate. Immigrant children long to blend in and to be like others, and to join in the activities of other children. But the fear of ridicule, a deep loneliness, loss of cultural identity, and the pressures of the new school system and the new culture can combine to render feelings of helplessness, alienation, exhaustion, and inadequacy. To get themselves through the period of adjustment in which these feelings dominate, the immigrant child adopts the mechanism of self-imposed isolation.

This phase may last from one to two years and more if the child finds no connection in friendships or with the teachers.

The silent stage need not be a negative experience and even has its innate advantages. As I met with the teenagers who recalled their feelings and experiences, it became clear to me that during the period in which these children had been trapped in helpless silence by their inability to communicate in the dominant language, they had become insightful observers of their own human condition and of life around them. In that silence, they had developed strong listening skills. Moreover, they can now articulate beautifully what had been pent up inside at the time, for they keenly value language as a way of self-expression. They do not take language for granted, because there was a time in their lives when they were silent, and a time when they experienced the sheer joy of breaking that silence.

I look upon the silent stage as a period of incubation in which the child must be provided with a warm and nurturing environment that makes it safe to break out of that shell and to be culturally different. Ultimately, supporting the child through this period is more efficient than a sink-or-swim approach or the concept of constantly moving the child to a "better" class, and subsequently making the child relive the uprooting experience again and again.

There is little the teacher can do to prevent an immigrant child from entering the silent stage, but there is much the teacher can do to see that the silence does not evolve into unguided introversion or morbid introspection that shuts the child away from the world of human activity and human relationships (Wickes, 1966). If the teacher can look into the child's inner world and identify the cause behind the silence, she may be able to increase the chances of identifying, as well, what type of support the child needs to emerge from that silence.

The teacher can also examine her own attitudes toward immigrant children. For in the silent stage children are keen in picking up their teachers' unconscious feelings toward them. If the teacher believes the student will not succeed, the student senses this, believes it, and will most likely fail. Immigrant students have expressed that the teacher is one who walks with the student down the road of acculturation and that a positive relationship between teacher and student is essential for students' academic progress.

> Teachers should be more patient with immigrants because it is very difficult for a person to be in a new country and to learn a new language. If a teacher feels there's no hope, then the child will think, "Well, if the teacher who's helping me thinks that I can't go anywhere, then I might as well give up myself." If the teacher even gets tired of helping, then this person will give up. The most important thing is for the teacher to have patience and for the student to think positively.

The Fear of Ridicule

For some immigrant children, the silence is related to a fear of ridicule. Ridicule discredits a person and evokes feelings of shame; it attacks a person's feeling of equality in relationships and robs him or her of personal dignity and competence. The fear of ridicule is linked to forces in the collective unconscious that can make a person feel as if he or she were in the clutches of some unknown terror (Wickes, 1966). As two of my early immigrant students expressed to me some years later:

> I was afraid to say anything. I was afraid people would make fun and laugh at me because of my feeling different from the others. I kept quiet.

> It was really hard [back then] for me to go into a classroom. It was new and I felt as if everyone was looking at me and staring at me.

One of the most meaningful filmstrips I have seen produced by an immigrant child is called "Near the Mountain." Here is a reproduction of the filmstrip made by one of the children, accompanied by the audio portion:

DEVELOPING LITERACY

Start

Near the Mountain
by
Dennis Yee

One day my friend and I went walking in the mountain.

We were so tired, we sat down on the ground.

Soon it was nighttime.

Then we saw two yellow eyes.

We went to the yellow eyes.

And it was gone.

We went to look and look. It was a tiger.

Then the tiger was chasing us.

We ran so fast from the tiger. (gasps)

And soon morning came.

Then I saw a house near the mountain.

We went inside.

And we saw a woman in the house.

She was cooking something.

My friend said, "I am so hungry."

And the woman saw us.

I said, "Can we go in?"

The woman said, "Oh, sure."

And the woman let us eat some cookies. (eating sound)

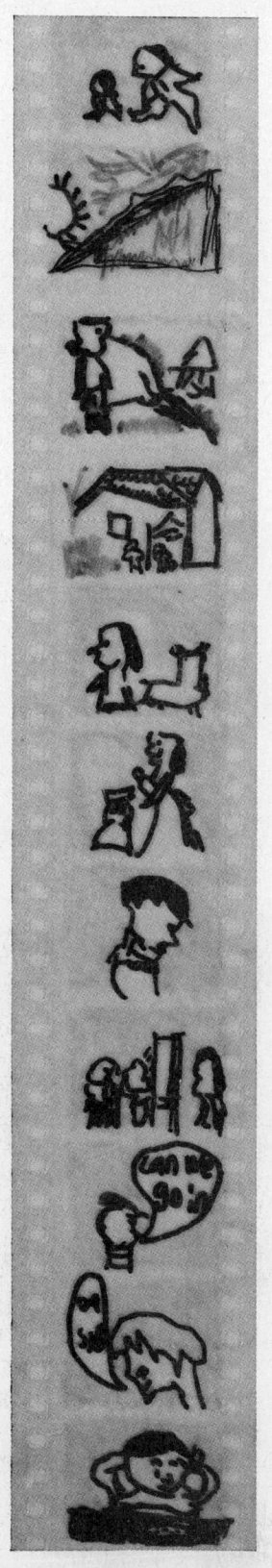

After, a man came home. We said to the man, "We saw a tiger near the mountain."

At nighttime, the man saw the tiger. He shot the tiger, and the tiger was dead.

The End

This story is rich in symbols and meaning. The tiger could be said to represent danger and the wish to hide. The mountain evokes the difficult road an immigrant child must travel, the feeling that life can be tough and dangerous. On the other hand, there is some sense of adventure—the boys go to look at, not away from, the yellow eyes. The yellow eyes represent the immigrant child's fear that others are "staring at him" whether or not this fear is based on reality.

Most of all, the filmstrip externalizes wish fulfillment—a relationship with a friend, the presence of adults who offer warmth and refuge, the elimination of the source of fear. Friendship and a nurturing environment are important factors in survival and overcoming fear. The elimination of the tiger could be seen to free the child to be more confident, to bridge the gap between the known and the new. The boy who wrote the story later reflected:

> The tiger—the man shot the tiger—and so the tiger is like a fear and so now there are no more fears. [The man] is the person who helps the immigrants, the teacher, in this case it's you that helped him get through, blend into a new culture so at the end there are no more fears. They feel that they are part of the new culture. The tiger is the fear of the new country, the change, the people in the new country. The man shot the tiger. The two boys started to blend into a new environment and a new culture. So at the end, the fear was gone.

Isolation and Loneliness

Another aspect of self-imposed silence may be a feeling of isolation, described by one immigrant child as follows: "When I first came to school in America, nobody played with me. I was alone. Nobody liked me because I was from another country."

Whether or not such a statement is true, that feeling is the child's reality. It is difficult to socialize when you feel that your language and your culture are useless, and the feeling is compounded when you are unable to articulate the feeling to others outside one's silent world.

A child with this feeling may seem passive, uncommunicative, unwilling to learn to read or write. It is not unusual to find, however, that the child who seems "unwilling" to learn has little or no support system at home or in the school, and that the adults at home are themselves traumatized by culture shock and feelings of inferiority. There are endless stories of adult immigrants who have had to go from being doctors to car attendants, from teachers to servants, or from homemakers to sweatshop workers as part of their transition to the new world. How can these adults even have the time to hear about the child's loneliness and confusion, when they themselves are struggling to survive?

The filmstrip story "The Lonely Bear" is one immigrant child's expression of her longing for connection.

Start

The Lonely Bear
(name withheld)

DEVELOPING LITERACY

One day, there was a bear.

He was so lonely because he did not have any friends to play with.

So, he decided to take a walk.

When he was walking, he heard something. So he went to find out what it was.

And then he saw something tiny. A little squirrel was lying on the ground.

The little squirrel was hurt. He had fallen off the tree.

The bear picked it up and took it home.

He took care of it day . . .

and night.

When morning came, the little squirrel was running around the cave.

When the bear woke up, he was happy that the little squirrel was feeling better.

But soon the bear was feeling sad because he thought that the little squirrel was going to leave him.

The little squirrel went to the bear and thanked him.

And the little squirrel went out . . .

and ran to call his friends.

They followed him.

He wanted them to meet his new friend,

the bear. And they all became friends.

The End

By the time the child who wrote that story came to my language center, she had been in America for several years and had been bounced from school to school and classroom to classroom because of her lack of fluency in English. Both parents worked constantly and had little time for her; she had made no friends and knew no children other than her sister, with whom she did not get along. When asked how long it was before she found a real friend she responded, "seven years." This was an unusually long silent period.

When this student retrospectively considered this filmstrip, she recognized how well the story reflected her unresolved loneliness and her inability to integrate happily with her family and society.

> The bear had no friends, and no one was around for him . . . [and] I was lonely and alone and sad. I wasn't sure I'd make it in school.

By the time she was interviewed, the long unresolved loneliness had made her introverted and deeply unhappy. As expressed so poignantly in her fictional story, friendship and bonding are the solutions that enable the immigrant child's real story to have a happy ending. But unfortunately in real life, this child dropped out in her last year of high school. Without the necessary emotional support from home, friends, and school, she couldn't make it. She did express that a school counselor had taken an interest in her, but after a year, he left. She was convinced then that, had she continued feeling the support of that counselor, she would have graduated along with the others.

Exhaustion and Culture Shock

Another recurring theme in the inner world of the immigrant child is a feeling of exhaustion from exposure to the continual parade of strange sights and events. As one child put it:

> It was so different. I consumed so many different incidents, that I felt really stressed out. I was not quite set to find out about all these things.

The opening of the filmstrip with the tiger found the two boys walking the mountain and becoming "so tired, we sat down on the ground." The filmstrip story, "The Upside-Down Morning," also illustrates another immigrant child's similar feeling about her new culture.

Start

The Upside-Down Morning
by
Cindy Wu

One morning when I woke up, I saw the sun coming through my window.

It was going to be a good day, I thought.

When I went downstairs, everything was upside-down.

Wow! I was so hungry, I opened the refrigerator . . .

and things began falling down.

I went to the table to get a cup.

When I opened the faucet to get a drink, the water went right through my cup.

I started to go and take a walk around the block.

Well, I saw many more strange things.

DEVELOPING
LITERACY

I saw a horse riding in a car.

And I saw funny looking houses.

I saw fish swimming on sidewalks. Could you imagine, swimming on your sidewalk?

I saw bubbles coming out of the girl's head.

I saw a flower growing on top of a bird's back.

When I walked around one block, I saw a cat that had a mustache.

I was so scared I ran home.

I got tired from that walk. I went to take a nap.

When I woke up, everything was back to normal.

The End

The impressions are not frightening or depressing, but express how different and strange the surroundings are—nothing makes sense any more; nothing is as expected. The protagonist projects a feeling of tiredness and a desire to find out that the strangeness is all over—in this case, that it was all a dream. The tiredness in the dream can indicate depression; the uneasiness about the unknown may be associated with a lack of relevant experience to fall back upon, compounded by the absence of familiar signs and symbols.

The term *culture shock* has frequently been used to describe what people experience when they attempt to cope with an entirely different culture (Ekstrand, 1981). Immigrant children keenly feel the environmental differences between their new reality and their homeland, not only in terms of language barriers, but also in terms of events and how people look and behave. Some immigrant children are confused by having a choice of two cultures in the United States, as one child noted:

> There is no "American" way, right? Because everyone ... America is like a melting pot, right? So everyone, every nationality, is ... if you come here and you get used to everything and you become a citizen, then you are American, technically, [but] I see myself as somewhere in between. I'm caught in between.

These children "caught in between" adapt by behaving one way at school and another way at home. This adaptation lasts as long as there is some form of intervention.

The Struggle in School

At one point or another, culture shock inevitably manifests itself as a struggle in school for the immigrant child. All of the students who have participated in my research described feelings of being rushed, particularly in academic matters.

> I was always being pushed to adapt to be American. Do this and do that. While I was trying to adapt to one stage, it's time to move on to the next, and I was falling behind. It's hard—it's like fast-forward and you're in slow motion. Somebody was trying to fast-forward me.

Some children handle culture shock by "hiding." Hiding can take the form of silence or a complete retreat into the native culture, or the child may even attempt to find a hideout or pretend not to understand English. One student said she tried to spend all her free time in the library because it was so quiet, an escape from what she experienced as the din and confusion of American culture. One boy confided that he repeatedly attempted to avoid school by locking himself in his room, and another made a habit of arriving late to school. One girl felt so insecure about moving on in school that she intentionally failed tests to stay behind.

While the phenomenon of culture shock is unavoidable, the pressure to adapt can be eased by a warm acceptance and appreciation of the original culture as the immigrant learns to accept the new culture. A child who most beautifully articulated the need to keep contact with one's heritage while receiving the nurturance to feel safe told the story of "The Little Egg."

Start

The Little Egg
by
Dung Nga Le

One day in a little town in America, there was an egg sitting in a nest on a branch of a tree.

It just sat there all winter,

all spring,

all summer,

and all fall.

When the next year came, it still sat there all winter again.

In the spring, it hatched into a beautiful bird.

It started to fly around the tree.

Soon, it began to fly farther away from the nest.

It flew and it flew and it flew to Vietnam.

It landed on the window of a house . . .

that belonged to a little girl.

The little girl's name was Tai Hing.

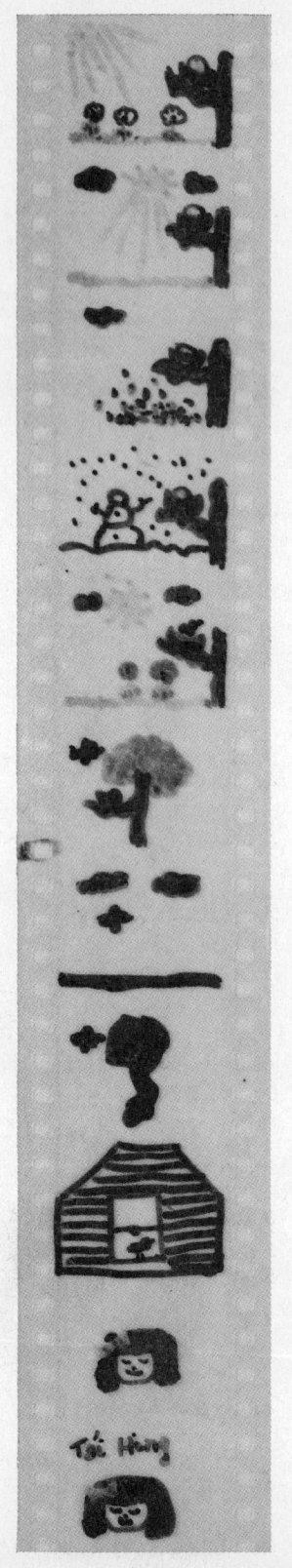

DEVELOPING LITERACY

In the morning, she looked out the window and saw a tired-out little bird.

She picked it up slowly and gently and brought it to her room.

She cared for it, fed it, and kept it warm.

The bird began flying all around the house.

The bird grew bigger and bigger . . .

and soon it was time to let it go. She put it on the open window and the bird flew away.

Soon, the bird found a mate,

and they made a big nest.

The two birds came to visit Tai Hing every year. She was expecting them every year.

The End

This filmstrip was drawn by a Vietnamese child. Hispanic children and children of other cultures have related to the story's theme because it speaks to the universal desire of all immigrant children to keep in touch with their roots.

Setting the Stage

How does a teacher create a nest that will give the child a sense of security while stimulating him or her to acquire enough of the majority language to leave the nest? What can be done to alleviate the child's feelings of cultural and personal isolation? What must be done if the child is stuck in the silent stage or seems unwilling to learn?

There is no one formula for working with immigrant children; different children require different approaches and the teacher must be somewhat analytical and even research oriented, ready to try new ideas when the first idea doesn't work. I personally find it helpful to keep a running journal of my observations and to make many preparations before I meet the student.

The day before I am to meet new students, I reflect upon what I will say to them because I know that on this first day I set the stage for the remaining year. I prepare my introduction carefully, think about my own philosophy of education, and plan first-day activities. I make a conscious effort to get in touch with the feelings of curiosity and enthusiasm I experienced when I first started teaching.

On the first day, students are most eager to know something about their teacher and how things will "work." Students enter the classroom and engage in nervous chatter; then suddenly there is dead silence as I present myself in front of the class. I know this is the only time of year I can get this degree of attention and focus, and I try to make the most of it.

I set the stage for the year's drama and discoveries and speak of hopes, expectations, and limits. Perhaps the message I try to convey is one of "We are in this together." The room is theirs as well as mine. There needs to be reverence, respect, and caring for one another if we are all to make it.

Building the Nest

I have learned that my immigrant students learn quickly if they feel "at home," not only with me, but in "our" room. It is particularly important in the Spanish culture to give a person the sense of feeling welcome. *Mi casa es tu casa*—my house is your house—is a Spanish way of inviting someone to feel at home, to be themselves whilst respecting others' needs to be "at home" as well. I try to convey the message that although we are all welcome to feel at home, it is also a serious place for learning.

It is a place where I can act as their guide, and where I also can learn from them as they learn from me. Initially, some immigrant children are surprised or even skeptical of this concept of teacher as "student," but it is an important source of empowerment that they soon embrace.

In working with immigrant children, I am aware that they come to me with a valuable cultural history and language. I take the time to read beforehand about their country, and to locate books they will find culturally relevant. The more I show interest in who they are and what riches they have brought to this country, the more I open the door for their curious minds to ask questions and seek information about the new environment.

Opening the Door to Dialogue

Shortly after I have gotten acquainted with the entire class, I prepare quiet, productive activities on which children can work individually or in pairs without my direct participation. I prepare two to four mature students to be "student teachers," so that if questions need answering or directions need clarification, the student teachers can act as monitors. I give these student teachers the opportunity to take small responsibilities in responding to their peers' needs, such as giving permission to sharpen a pencil or giving support to the insecure.

I then use these quiet times to meet with each student for a one-on-one dialogue. At the university level, it is often a given for a student to meet individually with professors to clarify mutual expectations, discuss academic concerns, and bring up any matters that might affect attainment of goals. In my own classroom, during these quiet times in which the student teachers are in charge, I find it helpful to give my students that same type of opportunity. These dialogues are an important methodology in working with immigrant children. The teacher must find a way of connecting with the child as a unique individual to validate the child's cultural history and establish a trusting, respectful, and warm relationship.

I set up a little "office" space around my desk and meet with each student for about 15 minutes. During the dialogue, I specifically inquire into the style of teaching and method of learning used in the child's country of origin. I find out if the child is coming from an academically supportive home. If in the process of our meeting, the child shares his or her inner world and needs more time, I schedule a meeting at a later date and perhaps in a more private location. If the child confides to me about a troublesome or economically difficult home situation, I express concern and tell the child I will make referrals if needed.

If an immigrant child is in the silent stage, I enter the immigrant child's silent stage myself by respecting the silence and waiting for the child to come forth. If there is resistance, if a child is not ready to talk, I honor that resistance, but we still spend time together in order to establish trust and warmth. I speak very directly to the child and try to find out what I can do to make it safe for the child to speak to me. If I can figure out what the child is feeling, I can understand his or her behavior.

Validating the Child's Culture

Once I have completed the dialogue with each child and have read up on each child's cultural heritage, we prepare for a celebration. We set a day for the students to bring their native food, music, and costumes, and invite those who have learned cultural dances to add to the festivities. Just as it is a naive idea that people can free themselves from their past and can exchange one culture for another, so it is naive to believe that all Spanish-speaking children embrace one culture. These festivities honor the differences.

Having opened a safe channel for the children to share their inner world with me, and in preparation of the celebration to validate their cultural identities, I ask the children to write what they can about where they came from and what brought them to the new land. Like people from many cultures that have extended families, the Hispanic is very receptive to working in groups and assisting one another where language limitations prevent some of them from writing what they want to express. In their writing, they include drawings of their flags, their foods, or their costumes.

I also show them how to use tape recorders, which the children take turns bringing home with the assignment of working with their families to capture the sounds of their culture—their language and its music. Engaging their families in this project is one more way of validating the culture and giving the child a connection between home culture and school culture.

I often find that by this time, I begin to receive invitations to visit the home. I leave my calendar open to visit those families who wish to have me, for it gives me the opportunity to learn even more about the child's inner world and how I can better support the child's needs.

Making the Desk a Home

The room now is decorated with their writing, their artifacts, and their pictures. The room has become a nest of familiar, and therefore comforting symbols. The children are ready for even more individual expression.

During the dialogic interviews, I find that the children consciously and unconsciously take in everything about me, because part of their developmental stage is to mirror the adult they respect and who respects them. My desk has a vase with a flower, a pencil holder, and other personal expressions, and the children bring to school their own meaningful symbols to create their own "office space" around their desks—a decorated trash can, photographs, miniatures. When this happens, I am moved because I know that they are feeling at home in their classroom.

Once a principal asked me if I was not concerned that the children may become distracted during lessons and play with the objects on their desks. My response was that I have found that the comfort these artifacts bring to the children actually frees them to become totally involved in the work. If the children feel ill at ease, that is when their attention wanders.

Again, I look to what we adults do to humanize our environments. In businesses, employees decorate their offices and cubicles with photographs, plants, and souvenirs that give not just pleasure, but also a sense of identity. Many studies have found that employees who are granted some level of control to feel "at home" with themselves in the work environment are more industrious and productive than those who are stripped of individuality. If recognizing the needs of the individual to exist in the workplace helps adults work better, why not children? Are not children as human as adults?

Encouraging Peer Bonding

In reflecting upon their immigrant experience, my students agree that the teacher is their closest friend at first and is sometimes the only person the child can really turn to. However, it is important to encourage peer bonding as well. Peer bonding is a necessary stage of childhood development. Friendships with other children not only ease feelings of isolation and fear, but stimulate learning in that the learning children acquire through friends is effortless, unconscious, and continuous. Learning becomes a matter of identity, of how we see ourselves (Smith, 1992).

This is not just theory. Immigrant children who have achieved second language literacy always identify the significance of friends in having helped them adapt to the "new reality." Friends help validate them, act as counselors, and stimulate oral language. Friends are the bridge that will cross them over to a new class, to a new school.

I find that I can simultaneously assist with peer bonding and help with the struggle in school by setting up after-school study groups. To set up a study group, I first teach the children how to study with each other in the classroom. From my dialogues and some additional research, I determine which children can best study with each other according to where they live in the neighborhood. One student is designated with the responsibility for obtaining assignments, arranging for study sessions, and seeing that members of the group come to class prepared.

Using this cooperative learning strategy, students can academically support each other, particularly in cases where the adults at home cannot speak English. At the same time, the immigrant child is given a needed sense of belonging.

Helping the Child Embrace Biculturalism

In our one-on-one communication, I also try to get the child to look forward. I realize that feelings of inadequacy can be internalized by the child from exposure to subtle monolingual/monocultural attitudes that one language or culture is the only way, or the best way. In our "nest," the immigrant child learns that the door is open to maintain his or her own language and culture even as he or she learns to live within his or her new environment.

I speak to the children's inner feeling that learning to read in a new language is an extension of what they already know in their own language, and that their life is richer for being able to articulate in more than one way. I encourage flexibility and divergent thinking by presenting the outlook that multiple cultures represent a "both/and," rather than an "either/or," set of choices.

I must stress how crucial it is to help the immigrant child cope with pressures to replace rather than supplement his or her native language and culture. The child who responds to unconscious monocultural attitudes is in danger of overidentifying with the new culture and sabotaging important roots. If immigrant children are not validated to become bilingual, if they don't learn to deal with their bilingual selves at an early stage, they come to regret the loss of their language and culture later in life.

After I help students focus on the richness and rewards of the opportunity to become bilingual and bicultural, I empower them to become active participants in their own education. Each child in my classroom has a written oath to take individual responsibility for his or her own learning. I give the children memo cards to help them keep track of what they need to work on. I help the children identify guidelines to compete with themselves, to be sensitive to others, and to share their knowledge.

Reflections on Instructional Methodologies

Although instructional methodology is important to second language literacy, the real key is to help the child to deal with the fears and anxieties that block learning. To respond first to the inner world, the immigrant child's thoughts and feelings is uppermost in my mind. Once the children feel at home in my classroom and have said everything they have to say—verbally and nonverbally, written or drawn—about who they are and where they have come from, then I know they are ready to listen to me and ready to learn how to read and write.

If I can get the immigrant child over the emotional hurdle of accepting the new culture without rejecting his or her own, if I can free the child from the emotional burdens of loneliness, isolation, fear of ridicule, helplessness, and anxiety, it becomes really very easy to teach the child to read and write. The great methodology debates—whole language or phonics approach, basal readers or literature-based textbooks—fade in importance once the child is truly ready to learn.

Summary: What Immigrant Children Have to Say

Immigrant children need a safe and nurturing environment in which they can cope with the language barrier until they are ready to express themselves within the new culture. The mechanisms immigrant children adapt when the integrity of their cultural identity is challenged include self-imposed silence and academic failure, the creation of escape hatches, and over-embracement of American culture to the exclusion of native culture.

To lessen the impact of culture shock, immigrant students need a transitional place, a nest, in which they can "incubate" and grow emotionally as well as intellectually. Without a caring teacher and other forms of intervention, patterns of loneliness, anxiety, and helplessness continue to persist. Value must be placed on the immigrant child's own language and heritage so the opportunity for self-expression and the feeling of belonging are not denied during the acculturation process.

The teacher must have a flexible, creative attitude to find ways to reach the children; the teacher must be prepared to continually function as a researcher and analyst. Every immigrant child brings with him or her another new truth about the uprooting experience that must be examined.

Empower children to succeed and they will succeed. Immigrant children do not want to be outsiders, they want to belong to their new reality without having to discard the cultural heritage that gives structure and meaning to their lives. To the degree these needs are met, they will be psychologically healthy and happy children who are predisposed to the successful acquisition of language and the desire to contribute to their new society.

About the Author

Cristina Igoa was one of the founders of the Mission Reading Clinic in San Francisco in 1972. She established a language center for immigrant children in 1980, which won the J. Russell Kent award for exemplary programs in San Mateo County, California. She obtained her Ed.D. at the University of San Francisco as a Title VII Doctoral Fellow. She was a supervisor of student teachers at San Francisco State University, recently appeared as guest lecturer for the teacher training program at the College of Notre Dame, and currently teaches in the Hayward Unified School District as part of a team of teachers working on process reconstruction at Tyrrell Elementary School. She has a book in progress tentatively titled "The Inner World of Immigrant Children."

References

Bhatnager, J. (1981). Multiculturalism and education of immigrants in Canada. In Bhatnager, J. (Ed.), *Educating immigrants*, pp. 69–95. New York: St. Martin's Press.

Bowers, C. A. (1984). *The promise of theory: Education and the politics of cultural change*. New York: Longmans, Green & Co.

Brown, L. G. (1969). *Immigration: Cultural conflicts and social adjustments*. New York: Arno Press. (Originally published in 1933.)

Ekstrand, L. H. (1981). Unpopular views on popular beliefs about immigrant children: Contemporary practices and problems in Sweden. In Bhatnager, J. (Ed.), *Educating immigrants*, pp. 184–213. New York: St. Martin's Press.

Freire, P. (1984). *Pedagogy of the oppressed*. New York: Continuum Press.

Heidegger, M. (1971). *On the way to language*. (P. Hertz, Trans.) New York: Harper & Row. (Originally published in 1959.)

Henderson, J. L. (1984). *Cultural attitudes in psychological perspective*. Toronto: Inner City Books.

Igoa, C. (1988). *Toward a psychology and education of the uprooted: A study of the inner world of immigrant children*. Unpublished doctoral dissertation, University of San Francisco.

Kieffer, C. (1981). *Doing dialogic retrospection: Approaching empowerment through participatory research*. Paper presented at the International Meeting of the Society for Applied Anthropology, University of Edinburgh, Scotland.

Skutnabb-Kangas, T. (1981). *Bilingualism or not: The education of minorities*. (L. Malmberg and D. Crane, Trans.) Great Britain: Hartnoll, Ltd.

Smith, F. (1992, February). Learning to read: The never ending debate. *Phi Delta Kappan*, vol. 434.

Wickes, F. G. (1966). *The inner world of childhood* (rev. ed.) New York: Appleton-Century. (Originally published in 1955.)

Cultural Integration of Children's Literature

Elba Maldonado-Colón
San Jose State University, California

Abstract

Three strategies to enhance the language, reading, and writing abilities of second language learners are modeled. Selection of issues present in children's literature and the incorporation of semantic maps and Venn diagrams are illustrated as effective tools for the development of reading insights and cross-cultural understandings. These strategies are recommended for classes where the native language and/or English are used. This type of instruction accommodates second language learners in the most effective manner.

Cultural Integration of Children's Literature

Research and practice suggest to teachers of bilingual students that the integration of children's literature becomes an effective vehicle to enhance language (speaking, listening, reading, and writing) as well as cognitive development. The interrelationship between language and cognitive development suggests that an optimal medium for dual development can be an environment in which the participants are socially involved in making meaning, communicating to share and learn, and developing questions and hypotheses for further investigation. Such is the image of a Vygotskian classroom where learners enthusiastically meet challenges, exchange information, and celebrate discoveries.

This article will describe three types of strategies for native speakers and second language learners. The strategies are to be incorporated into a framework characterized by the use of children's literature and extensive group discussions around problems arising from the content, or form, of the pieces selected. Individually, or together, they are aimed at assisting the development of oral and written language skills as well as the interpretation of the role of the reader when approaching narratives that require bringing personal and/or previous experiences to bear upon what is being read.

The two sections that follow deal with theoretical support, the challenges that exist in the education of second language learners, and the three strategies recommended to enrich this developmental process. The bibliography assists readers to further investigate each strategy.

The Development of a Base

Learning is a complex process that becomes a greater challenge for second language learners educated through the weakest of two languages. If new information is to be effective and integrated, the learning process requires interacting, experiencing, and understanding. Learners must be taken from the present learning level and be brought to higher levels (Krashen, 1982, 1986) through careful guidance, observation, and participation in teaming for problem solving (Moll, 1990a, b; Vygotsky, 1987).

Reading for Meaning: Meaning for Reading

Reading and language acquisition are not independent of culture. It is the familiar images, language, and concepts that readers and writers rely on to draw meaning from, or convey meaning through, the printed message. This shared information base constitutes the framework that enables them to interpret the message without dedicating undue efforts to focusing on unfamiliar details. When the structure and background become transparent, the overall message can be understood. When the language and culture are not familiar to the teacher or the student, the learning and discovery rate are affected by ambiguity; as a result, anxiety increases and a sense of inability might overcome the learners. This is the case with many students who are turned off by what is available for them to read, or to practice their developing reading skills. Significant amounts of ambiguity (in text, language, background, and culture) do not enhance their learning opportunity. The integration of the learner's culture/background and the use of cultural resources in teaching (Moll & Díaz, 1987) is not a new trend in instruction, but it definitely has captured teachers' interest because of the changing profile within public schools.

Throughout the previous years, it has been common practice to develop either vocabulary or an aspect of the theme of a story before students read the story in round-robin style or independently in silent reading. Many second language learners lose interest in the process. As a consequence, incomplete information networks exacerbate limited reading skills. This leads to less than optimal understanding of concepts among some learners. Others do not have sufficient English language skills to structure their answers once they have completed the assigned reading. Another group does not perceive any relationships between their personal experiences and the discussion of a reading assignment. To the members of all these groups, reading and life become parallel rather than intertwined processes, as they are naturally. Thus, motivation to interpret or to appropriate the written message is significantly lower. This reflects in passive participation in reading and language arts classes. Smith (1988) would identify them as those who chose not "to belong to the reading club."

In their study of literacy supports for linguistically and/or culturally different students, Moll (1989, 1990a, b) and Moll et al. (1990) found that classroom practices underestimate the potential and knowledge of Latino students: "It is our contention that existing classroom practices underestimate and constrain what Latino (and other) children are able to display intellectually" (p. 1). Further, Moll and his colleagues found that high teacher expectations and dialogue with students on topics that tapped their personal, cultural, and linguistic experiences did make a difference in participation, motivation, and growth, which are considered indicators of *learning* within school settings. Thus, they advocate "strategic application of cultural resources" in order to turn around the academic underachievement of these students and to "demonstrate convincingly how their ample language, cultural, personal, and intellectual resources could form the basis of their schooling" (p. 2).

Hence, language arts work with second language learners requires careful selection of topics and strategies that develop or tap familiar concepts and experiences in order to stimulate dialogue. Students are to be challenged to delve into a literary piece. Personal analysis and response to it by reflecting on and discussing what has been read is a powerful learning tool. Re-creating it from a different perspective can enhance understanding. This is achieved by seeking information to extend what has been read. Creating a parallel piece of their own production that integrates their personal experiences develops an image of authorship, control, and power. A classroom that operates under this perspective empowers, provides opportunities to practice critical thinking strategies, and influences students' choices now and later. It gives students practice in studying information, making choices, assuming responsibilities for the choices followed, anticipating shortcomings, and overcoming expected and unexpected limitations. It helps students become familiar with other cultures and personal perspectives, thus becoming an avenue toward liberation (Freire, 1973) from the limitations imposed upon minorities by schooling and society at large, and increases the chances of these children having an active voice in the control of their future.

Three Strategies for Integration and Control

In the following section, I will propose the integration of three strategies to generate discussion, achieve involvement, stimulate self-reflection, and increase the amount of shared information among class participants. This constitutes an interpretation of a way to implement the concept of *strategic application of cultural resources* (Moll, 1992). The first strategy is the identification of issues weaved in the fabric of selected pieces of literature. The second is the use of a semantic map to capture individual information related to issues in a story or poem and to develop shared information for all students. And the third is the use of the Venn diagram to help students visualize themselves in relation to the issues in the literary piece(s) read and discussed.

In Search of a Literary Piece with a Potentially Familiar Issue

Critical pedagogy is crucial for second language learners, especially if they are part of certain linguistically and/or culturally different groups (Cummins, 1984, 1986, 1989; Moll, 1989, 1990a, b; Moll et al., 1990). Critical pedagogy is the pedagogy of personal and intellectual growth and development (Ada, 1990). How is one to implement aspects of this powerful teaching/learning philosophy in the classroom? The following example will illustrate a strategy. Begin by scanning children's literature, looking for issues that are meaningful and relevant to these students[1]— issues that will tap their funds of personal experiential knowledge, issues that will enable them to perceive through their dialogue different perspectives and instances of actualization. Thus, varying personal examples emerge through open class discussion and/or small discussion groups.

As a teacher, read stories and poems. After enjoying the piece for its own literary merits, reread it, looking for material appropriate to generate dialogue among your second language learners. Look for meaningful issues that would involve students at their zone of proximal development.[2] By following this suggestion after reading two legends by Tomie de Paola, *The Legend of the Bluebonnet* (1983) and *The Legend of the Indian Paintbrush* (1988), an issue such as *giving* was identified. Such an issue would generate a lot of discussion among class members. Students, especially refugees and new arrivals, as well as those oppressed by economic forces, endlessly *give*. They *give up* and *give to*. Thus, this is an ideal opportunity to tap their personal experiences, weaving them into the fabric spun by classroom dialogue.

Once the issue has been identified, the focus of the discussion to introduce the two legends becomes the meaning and/or thoughts one associates with the word or concept of *giving*. A semantic map that begins with the word *giving* would serve as a starter. It never fails to arouse interest. We all have given up and given to in our lives. To some it is natural and easy, to others it is difficult and unnatural. A healthy dialogue emerges. Thoughts proceeding from different participants are listened to and contrasted. In this way, diversity is listened to, respected, and further understood in a safe reflective environment. Figure 1 represents the starter and the comments provided by fifth graders in a bilingual classroom.

Once *giving* has been explored, particularly the feelings related to *giving*, the first of the legends is introduced. Perhaps the easier in which to identify the message of *giving* and its consequences is *The Legend of the Bluebonnet*. In it, a little girl chooses to give up her most treasured possession in order to secure the welfare of her tribe. Our students know about this. Both *giving up* and working toward the benefit of the group are common themes in their lives. Because the author does not go into the feelings of the little girl nor the thinking that went on before she decides to give up, the legend provides the teacher an excellent opportunity to engage students in dialogue about what could possibly have gone on in the girl's mind and heart. This also reveals to students one of the secrets of reading—you bring your personal experiences to bear on the text and its interpretation. Often, the author does not tell you everything. The author sketches images with words. The reader fills in the images. Powerful insights about reading are gained from a discussion of a charming story.

The second legend fulfills the same role but from a different perspective. In *The Legend of the Indian Paintbrush*, the main character is a boy who wants to become and to share his abilities with his group. Not being able to do it as he first thought he would, he settles for a more realistic way of becoming, sharing a talent he has recently discovered. Great dialogues emerge from a study of the issues involved in sharing abilities and talents. Aspects covered include: how to share, the joy of sharing and *giving to* others, unrecognized contributions/sharing, and *giving up* one dream to pursue another. All people have shared these experiences. They are weaved in the fabric of the old and new traditions that our students bring to class. Once again, the avid participant is confronted with the understanding that we place ourselves into what we read through our personal experiences and those of others.

Not only do second language learners benefit from the natural sharing of insights, but their oral language seems to improve significantly when participating in meaningful discussions. The issues selected are self-motivating, and motivation, as we know, is a powerful force in learning. As Krashen (1986) would argue, one learns by using the language in a meaningful, unstressful manner; in this process, more language is acquired and edited. The issues selected through this activity involve students in dialogue and other activities developed around these two pieces of literature.

Since oral language, listening, reading, and writing are interrelated, a strategy such as the one suggested above becomes an avenue for empowerment among an increasing and marginal population coexisting in classrooms where instruction does not take into consideration the information that they bring with themselves as they enter our schools (Cummins, 1989; Moll, 1990a, b; Moll et al., 1990). These discussions provide an additional vehicle to tap into mainstream cultural knowledge. Some of the populations are unfamiliar with our ways of organizing and structuring learning opportunities, thus reducing their chances to be successful in our system. This strategy can be a vehicle to validate their previous knowledge and bring forth points of organization and learning that are important for schooling in the United States.

In the Spanish language-arts class period, the teacher can parallel this strategy by using similar stories written in, or translated into, Spanish. For example, the issues of *giving to*, *giving up*, and sharing are part of the following stories: *La moneda de oro* (Ada, 1991), *El prado del tío Pedro* (Puncel, 1983), *El último árbol* (Zavrel, 1988), and *El señor Viento Norte* (de Posadas Mañé, 1984). In *La moneda de oro*, by sharing her time, meager resources, and knowledge, an old woman goes around helping those who need her. She tends to those in need, and time after time, gives up the only thing she has—a gold coin. Following her around is a young man desiring to acquire the woman's treasure. As he follows her around, he also learns about *giving to* and *giving up* by sharing his talents and his newly acquired wealth—a gold coin.

Other books in English that deal with the issues of sharing, *giving to*, and *giving up* are: *Kite Flyer* (Haseley, 1988), *The Great Kapok Tree* (Cherry, 1990), *The Circuit* (Jiménez, 1984), *The Giving Tree* (Silverstein, 1964), and *The Seal Mother* (Gerstein, 1988). The teacher can guide students from the simpler of these to those more complex in language and content. Other related issues to be explored are moving, family separation, changing lifestyles, taking care of others, losing and making friends, entering new groups, and loneliness. The field is rich, it needs only to be plowed.

Development of Strong Information Networks through Semantic Maps and Venn Diagrams

Broader information networks, personalized learning experiences, and greater interface with the mainstream population will facilitate for second language learners psychosocial integration into the established system. Greater amounts of shared information make transparent the learning opportunity and the materials selected to facilitate learning. A strategy that accepts several perspectives can help students in getting to know what other members of the group have experienced, or think, and can help resolve social conflicts, as well as academic difficulties.

In learning efficiency, experts are distinguished from novices, among other aspects, in their capacity to categorize and collapse new and old information into more accessible and simpler coding systems. This is what we want for our second language learners. Thus, semantic maps and Venn diagrams become effective strategies teachers use to develop common funds of information. In addition, they become tools for second language learners to negotiate information that is not clearly understood because of limitations in language proficiency, experiential background, or absence of personal experiences dealing with the language, the culture, or the structure of the selection or material being read.

Semantic mapping and the Venn diagram become focusing tools for second language learners. They not only capture visually a series of apparently unrelated concepts, but display a set of collected or aggregated information which lends itself rather well for further reflective thinking and critical dialogue. For example, in the case of the two legends discussed above, the teacher could begin and end with diagrams like those suggested below (Figures 1 and 2).

After deciding on issues and stories to be shared, a mini-unit that begins with the introduction of the framework in the form of a semantic map could be developed. It only includes an advanced organizer, that is, the phrase *give up*. It is presented to the students as an issue to be discussed and explored. Presenting the word, or concept, as an issue which is of importance to all opens the door to dialogue. Questions can follow the pattern of *Who has given up something today, yesterday, or this past week? What have you given up? What motivated or forced you to give up? Feelings are important; how did you feel before and after you gave up?* Students' comments are plotted in the frame either as a word or phrase (see Figure 1).

As a learning group striving to identify common threads within

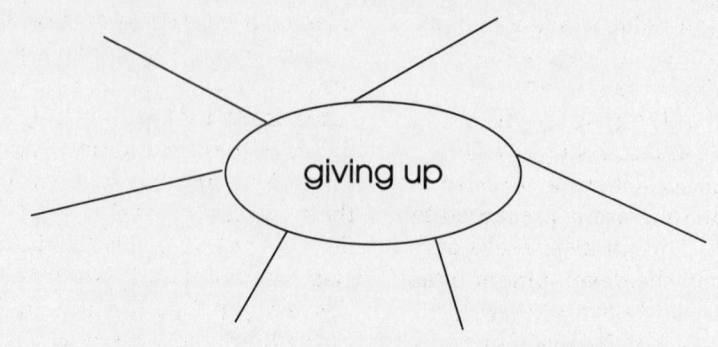

Semantic map to introduce the theme and first story

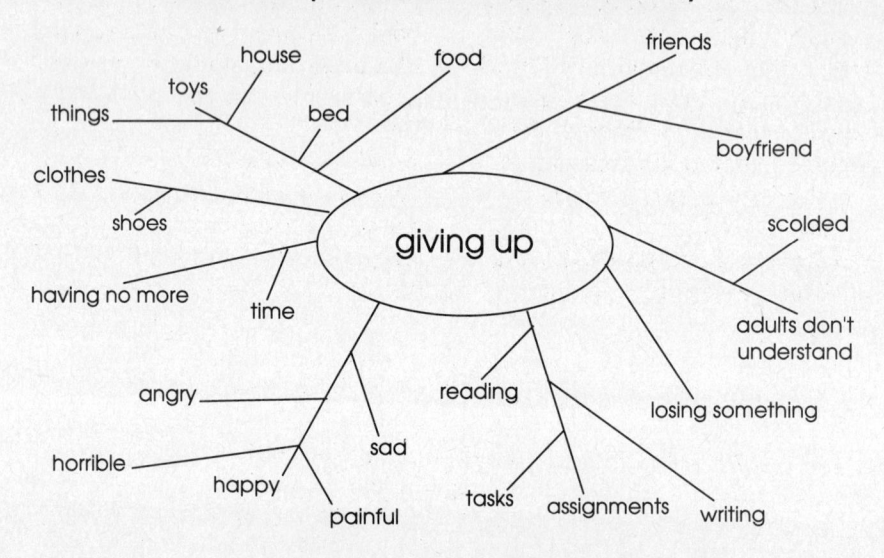

Semantic map with students' comments

Figure 1 *Semantic maps of an issue selected for mini-unit*

the class, look for common feelings, experiences, and things that have been given up. Talk about commonalities and differences. Introduce the story and suggest to students that they should listen not only to enjoy the piece, but to reflect on the feelings and actions of the main character(s). Discussion follows when the oral reading concludes.

Many students have experienced similar situations of loss and oppression by circumstances beyond their control. Discuss how those experiences could be shared through writing, and how one could try to get readers to identify with the feelings of the characters. This process generally yields the origin of narratives of personal experiences or stories heard from family members. With older learners, it could spin off into the creation and need for myths and legends. Discussing current myths and legends proves engaging and revealing in regard to linguistic skills and personal/cultural perceptions. This is a way semantic mapping, along with appropriate selections from the world of children's literature, can become powerful tools in facilitating the education and validation of the experiences of language minority students. (For other uses and types of semantic maps see Pehrsson and Robinson, 1985.)

The Venn diagram is another frame that engages students in exploration, comparison, and dialogue (see Figure 2). After reading and discussing two or more stories sharing a common issue, the diagram is presented to students. This strategy seeks to strengthen the development of associations and new information gained through discussion and the readings covered in class. Students strengthen the insight that integration of old and new knowledge is an obligatory strategy to advance learning. Through dialogue on shared information, personal involvement is attained.

Asking students to find commonalities among stories first and then among themselves, their lives, and the stories forces reflection, dialogue, and judgment in the selection of words. It also provides familiarity with a tool that will free them from the tyranny of not knowing how to organize their words or thinking when dealing with comparisons in the classroom. Figure 2 presents the answers provided by fifth graders in the bilingual classroom.

Notice that along with the two books that were selected as part of a mini-unit, students' personal experiences also find their way into the schema. Together, they provide for individual students a coherent whole rather than fragmented impressions fostered by traditional reading practices, in which the focus is solely a summary of the story and identification of details. An additional gain in this situation is the motivation that leads students to record personal experiences through the development of parallel stories,[3] original stories, or entries in their interactive journals. This results in the appropriation of books/stories to negotiate feelings and concerns. Thus, participatory learning, learning that challenges, and teaching opportunities that are above students' present level (Moll, 1989) but can be negotiated together are part of what is possibly the best pedagogy for the empowerment of language minority students, especially for those older students who are not at grade level in their reading.

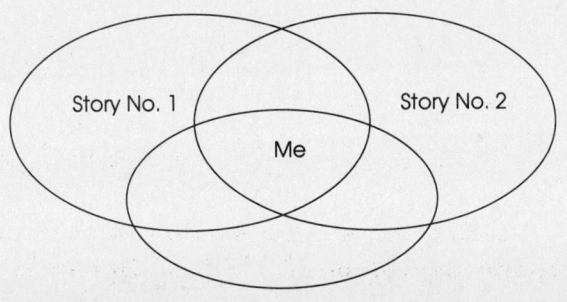

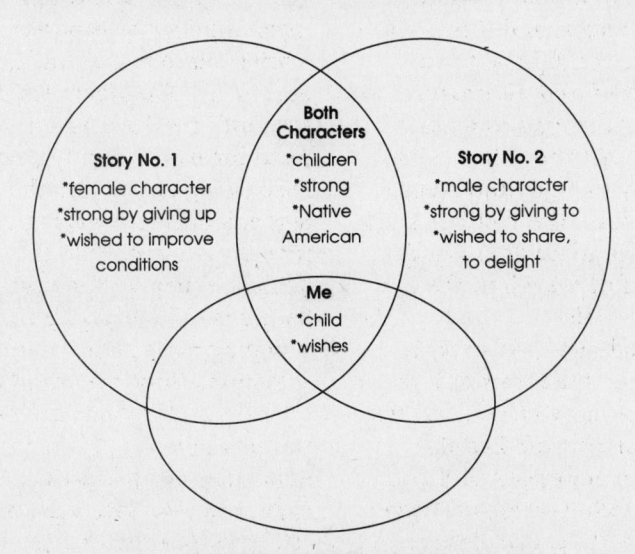

Conclusion

Second language learners need to penetrate the message and story structure of children's literature as published in the United States as part of their empowerment process. They need to develop a stronger base of shared information. They also need to continue enhancing their language skills as well as their reading abilities. Validation of personal experiences is a critical need in the bilingual classroom. This article has presented three strategies that succeed in engaging students' interest, increasing their desire to participate actively through dialogue and written expression (in the form of interactive journals), and in developing broader *funds of knowledge*.[4] Such an approach provides fertile ground for students to extract all kinds of insights related to themselves, other members of other cultural or linguistic

Figure 2 *Venn diagram of two stories in a mini-unit*

groups, and particularly, to the reading and writing processes that are critical for academic success and for what Abi-Nader (1991) identifies as participation in the future socioeconomic/professional order of a shrinking world.

NOTES

1. Meaningfulness is achieved by researching the history and sociocultural perspective(s) of the target groups of people.
2. The zone of proximal development is a Vygotskian construct that defines a level of development at which the learner is ready to profit from advanced instruction if the opportunity provides for social interaction through issue or problem resolution. It is a concept similar to the instructional level, with the understanding that it requires meaningful social interaction with at least one more person of advanced knowledge or abilities. For further clarification and operationalization of this concept, see Moll (1989).
3. Using the same format provided by the author, but changing characters and/or other elements of the story. (This can also be done with poems and songs.)
4. This concept has been developed by Moll and his associates (1990) at Arizona State University in Tucson.

ABOUT THE AUTHOR

Dr. Maldonado-Colón is an associate professor at San Jose State University in both the Division of Teacher Education/Bilingual Program and the Division of Special Education/Bilingual Special Education Program. The courses she teaches and has taught include Bilingual Language Arts, ESL Methodologies, Speech and Language Development, Multicultural Education, and The Bilingual Student in Special Education. She has published papers on these subjects. Her research interests are in the areas of language acquisition and the development of reading competency among bilinguals. She has been a bilingual teacher for 20 years at both public schools and college levels. Dr. Maldonado-Colón has taught at the University of Texas at Austin, Teachers College (Columbia University), and the University of Massachusetts in Amherst.

REFERENCES

Abi-Nader, J. (1991). Creating a vision of the future: Strategies for motivating minority students. *Phi Delta Kappan*, vol. 72, no. 7, pp. 546-49.

Ada, A. F. (1991). *La moneda de oro*. Madrid: Editorial Everest.

Ada, A. F. (1990). *A magical encounter: Spanish language children's literature in the classroom.* Compton, CA: Santillana.

Cherry, L. (1990). *The great kapok tree*. San Diego, CA: Harcourt, Brace, Jovanovich.

Cummins, J. (1989). *Empowering minority students.* Sacramento, CA: California Association for Bilingual Education.

Cummins, J. (1986). The role of primary language development in promoting educational success for language minority students. In *Schooling and language minority students: A thematic framework* (pp. 3-49). Los Angeles: California State University; Evaluation, Dissemination and Assessment Center.

Cummins, J. (1984). *Bilingual education and bilingual special education.* Great Britain: Multilingual Matters.

de Paola, T. (1988). *The legend of the Indian paintbrush.* New York: G. P. Putnam's Sons.

de Paola, T. (1983). *The legend of the bluebonnet.* New York: G. P. Putnam's Sons.

de Posadas Mañé, C. (1984). *El señor Viento Norte.* Madrid: Ediciones SM.

Freire, P. (1973). *Education for critical consciousness.* New York: Continuum.

Gerstein, M. (1988). *The seal mother.* New York: Dial Books for Young Readers.

Haseley, D. (1986). *Kite flyer.* New York: Four Winds Press.

Jiménez, F. (1984). The circuit. In Anaya, R. A., and Márquez, A. *Cuentos chicanos: A short story anthology*. Albuquerque, NM: New America.

Krashen, S. D. (1986). Bilingual education and second language acquisition theory. In *Schooling and language minority students: A thematic framework* pp. 3-49. Los Angeles: California State University; Evaluation, Dissemination and Assessment Center.

Krashen, S. D. (1982). *Principles and practice in second language acquisition.* Oxford: Pergamon Press.

Moll, L. C. (1992). Bilingual classroom studies in community analysis: Some recent trends. *Educational Researcher*, vol. 21, no. 2, pp. 20-24.

Moll, L. C. (1990a). *Community-mediated instruction: A qualitative approach.* Paper presented at the Annual Meeting of the American Educational Research Association, Boston, April 1990.

Moll, L. C. (1990b). *Vygotsky and education: Instructional implications and applications of socio-historical psychology.* New York: Cambridge University Press.

Moll, L. C. (1989). Teaching second language students: A Vygotskian perspective. In Johnson, D. M., and Roen, D. H., (Eds.), *Richness in writing: Empowering ESL students* pp. 55-69. New York: Longman.

Moll, L. C., and Díaz, R. (1987). Teaching writing as communication: The use of ethnographic findings in classroom practice (pp. 195-221). In Bloome, D. (Ed.), *Literacy and schooling* pp. 55-65. Norwood, NJ: Ablex.

Moll, L. C., Vélez-Ibáñez, C., Greenberg, J., Whitmore, K., Saavedra, E., Dworin, J., Andrade, R. (1990). *Community knowledge and classroom practice: Combining resources for literacy instruction* (OBEMLA contract no. 300-87-0131). Tucson, AZ: University of Arizona.

Pehrsson, R. S., and Robinson, H. A. (1985). *The semantic organizer approach to writing and reading instruction.* Rockville, MD: Aspen Systems Corporation.

Puncel, M. (1983). *El prado del tío Pedro.* Madrid: Ediciones SM.

Silverstein, S. (1964). *The giving tree.* New York: Harper and Row.

Smith, F. (1988). *Joining the literacy club.* Portsmouth, NH: Heinnemann.

Vygotsky, L. S. (1987). Speech and thinking. In Rieber R., and Carton, A. (Eds.), *L. S. Vygotsky, collected works*, Vol. 1 (pp. 39-285). New York: Plenum.

Zavřel, S. (1988). *El último árbol.* Madrid: Ediciones SM.

DEVELOPING
LITERACY

Contemporary Trends

in Children's Literature Written in Spanish in Spain and Latin America

Alma Flor Ada
University of San Francisco, California

The cultural products of people who speak Spanish are very diverse. Many of these products reflect multiple influences to different degrees: indigenous American, African, European, Middle Eastern, etc.

In the case of Latin America and of Spain as well, these influences and the people that they represent have not come together easily; rather they were historically brought together through a process of invasion and slavery. As a result, they have always been shaped by oppression and domination as well as by resistance.

As Spanish-speaking people from Latin America find themselves in the United States (either as immigrants or, in the case of Chicanos and Puerto Ricans, through subsequent invasions), it becomes important to reflect and focus on the common elements that allow us to have a dialogue and bridge our differences. One of these elements is the Spanish language.

This same element—the Spanish language—is also a link with Spain, problematic as that link may be. Latin Americans have often, and with good reason, perceived Spain exclusively as the oppressor. It is important to note, however, that Spain itself has been the subject of invasions throughout its history, and that it is not an ethnically monolithic reality. Not only are there many other languages besides Spanish spoken in Spain, but the people who speak those languages have a long history of struggle to maintain their ethnic identity. Moreover, the official Spain has been an object of contention throughout the centuries as general popular movements have sought to revindicate the rights of the people. The most salient example of this is the Spanish Civil War.

Thus, while the Spanish language has been, and still is, often used as a tool of oppression, the premise of this article is that the language and the literature within it can be used as a tool of liberation. The emphasis on the Spanish language does, however, have inherent limitations, especially when it comes to fully representing many Latin American children's realities. However beyond the scope of this article, it is crucial to emphasize the importance of children's literature written in indigenous American languages and in the vernacular of Latin Americans of African descent.

All literature begins with the oral tradition, which is a representation of a people's culture. The stories were told to shorten the long winter nights, after the work in the fields had been completed or the cattle enclosed. The ballads and yaravís, each in their own way singing the pains of impossible love, and the lullabies that soothe the mother's babe to sleep are expressions of a certain interpretation of reality. "Oral literature" is a product of the feelings of a people, their remembrance of and perspective on their historical experiences, their willed or unwilled contact with other cultures, and their responses to the demands of everyday life.

The Hispanic oral tradition is very rich, as it bears the influences of many different cultures. Spain itself, as mentioned previously, has been a battlefield for much of its history. The indigenous inhabitants of the Iberian Peninsula were invaded first by the Latin Romans and then by the Germanic Visigoths. Later, the peninsula was invaded by successive waves of Muslim warriors in a "jihad," or "holy war," of religious expansion. The Muslims remained and developed a culture on the Iberian peninsula for the next 800 years. A significant number of Jews lived on the peninsula both during Arab rule and the subsequent Christian kingdoms that slowly descended from the north and began to take over the territory in the name of "reconquering the land for Christianity." All of these influences were present in the oral tradition of what later came to be known as the nation-state of Spain.

In their colonial expansion across the Atlantic, the Spaniards encountered, invaded, and attacked some very highly developed civilizations as well as many tribal cultures with very rich oral traditions. Many of the myths and legends of the indigenous cultures of the Americans were incorporated into the oral tradition of the resulting new cultures. These new cultures were also influenced by other strong mythologies that originated in Africa, mainly of Yoruba, Lucumi, Mandingo, Congo, and Carabalí origin. The African influence transformed forever much of Latin American literary expression by endowing it with a distinctive musicality and rhythm.

This rich tradition of oral literature, which was enjoyed by adults and children alike, required only the people's sensitivity to be shared and preserved and to grow as the stories became diversified in retellings or new ones were created in response to new realities. In contrast, the written literature for children had a very different development. While the oral folklore lived in the telling, requiring only a voice and an ear to create a written literature, it was not enough that sensitive people wanted to develop and share a common heritage. The task presented different demands of skills and resources. It was also geared to a specific segment of the population—those who knew how to read and who could afford books. On the other hand, in France, Perrault initiated a written literature for children based on the popular tradition, as did the Brothers Grimm in Germany. There was no comparable figure in Spain or Latin America to bridge the span between the oral and written traditions.

While adult literature thrived in nineteenth-century Spain, and writers developed who obtained recognition worldwide, no children's writer appeared who had the stature of Andersen in Denmark, Carroll in England, or Collodi in Italy. There was some literature published for young readers, but the most significant publication in Spanish for children in that century was written in New York.

While in exile, the great Cuban author José Martí wrote, between July and October of 1889, four issues of a magazine for children, *La edad de oro* (*The Golden Age*), which have been reprinted many times in book format (Martí, 1979). This work, as all of Martí's, was very much ahead of its time, both in the quality of the language (simple and engaging) and in the variety of the content. It included poetry and prose, free retellings of stories by other writers (Andersen's story "The Two Nightingales"), and folktales, as well as his own original stories and descriptive pieces.

In *La edad de oro,* Martí offered Latin American children the opportunity to reflect about the differences brought about by economic class in works such as the ballad *Los zapaticos de rosa* (*The Pink Shoes*), the poem *Los dos príncipes* (*The Two Princes*), and the story *Bebé y el señor Don Pomposo* (*Bebé and Mr. Pompous*). Latin American children also could recognize their own multiple ancestry as Martí invited them to reflect on their Indian heritage in *Las ruinas indias* (*Indian Ruins*), which shows the great development of pre-Hispanic cultures, and in *El padre Las Casas* (*Father Las Casas*), where the cruel treatment those same people received is examined. The acknowledgement of the African heritage is poignantly present in *La muñeca negra* (*The Black Doll*). But Martí goes beyond; he wants all boys and girls to recognize that they are part of a wider world. In a most beautiful piece, *Un paseo por la tierra de los Anamitas* (*A Tour of the Land of the Vietnamese*), after an extraordinary retelling of the traditional tale of the four blind men and the elephant, he expresses:

> And so are men, each one believing that only what he thinks and sees is the truth, and saying in prose and verse that no one should believe but what he believes, just like the four blind men and the elephant.
>
> When, indeed, what one should do is to study with love everything that human beings have thought or done, and that gives great happiness, seeing that all human beings have the same sorrows, and the same history, and the same love. The world is a beautiful temple, where all human beings of the earth can gather together in love, because they all have wanted to know the truth, and they all have written in their books that it is useful to be good, and they have all suffered and struggled to be free, free in their lands, and free in their thoughts. (Martí n/y; the translation is my own.) (p. 146)

Unfortunately, in spite of its enormous influence, *La edad de oro* was not the beginning of a strong production of books for children in Latin America. Plagued by colonialism, these countries continued to look to Europe first—and to the United States later—for literary models for children. For the first 40 years of this century, the majority of what was published were translations.

A wonderful book not written for children was appropriated by them through the mediation of the schools. *Platero y yo (Platero and I)* (Jiménez, 1973), the lyrical sketches of Juan Ramón Jiménez's youth in Moguer, Spain, became a classic among Latin American children, aided by the presence of the poet in Puerto Rico, where he lived in exile after the Spanish Civil War.

During the next four decades, literature for children in Spain suffered from the same restrictions that were imposed there on all artistic and intellectual life. An example of the tensions of the country can be seen in two significant works produced in the period of Franco's rule.

The first is a book that received great attention both inside and outside of Spain. It is a story that probably only a society with such Catholic roots would have found appropriate for children. In *Marcelino, pan, y vino* (*Marcelino, Wine, and Bread*), José María Sánchez Silva (1952) tells how a young orphan boy, raised in a monastery, is befriended in his loneliness by a life-size image of Christ that had been tucked away in an attic. The young boy, Marcelino, brings his friend bread and wine; Christ in turn grants him his wish of dying in order to be with his mother once more.

The other is a play, *Historia de una muñeca abandonada* (*The Story of the Abandoned Doll*), by the best of the contemporary Spanish playwrights, Alfonso Sastre (1962). Inspired by Brecht, Sastre is able to create an enchanting play that raises the moral issues of private ownership and social responsibility. Solomon's judgment is reenacted between two young girls who claim ownership of the same doll, which was abandoned by a rich girl and subsequently cared for by the cook's daughter. The play has become a model of children's theater for its well-developed characters, the agility of the action, and the delicate and humorous use of the polymorphic verses of Spanish classical theater.

In Latin America, books originally written in Spanish for children in the first half of the century tended to have very little distribution outside of the country of publication and the editions tended to be limited. In contrast, translated works abounded. My generation, and that of my students during my first years as a teacher, grew up reading Italy's D'Amici and Salari, France's Verne, Britain's Dickens, Switzerland's Spyri, and America's Alcott and Stevenson.

Yet two exiled Spanish refugees made excellent contributions to Latin American children's literature during this time. In Cuba Herminio Almendros did a beautiful job retelling traditional stories, while in Mexico Antonio Robles continued publishing his stories, taking on Mexican characters and scenery.

In Chile the Nobel Prize winner Gabriela Mistral wrote delicate poetry for children. Meanwhile in Argentina, one of the countries with a stronger publishing tradition, writers of children's books were developing a new voice, a more contemporary approach to action and character development, and especially, a good sense of humor—an element that had been lacking in much of the previous writing for children. Conrado Nalé Roxlo (1963, 1988) with *La escuela de las hadas* (*A School for Fairies*), Javier Villafañe (1986), well-known for his work as a puppeteer, and the excellent poet María Elena Walsh (1987), who incorporated the limerick into literature written in Spanish, are some of the many writers who can be acknowledged. Their efforts are being continued by a new generation of excellent writers: Laura Devetach (1989), Graciela Montes (1988a, 1988b), and Gustavo Roldán (1986).

But while it was possible then to find individual writers, there was not yet a strong movement devoted to publishing for children. Specialized publishing houses or collections and awards dedicated to children's literature produced in Spanish were few or nonexistent in most countries.

This scenario has changed dramatically in the last three decades. One interesting development took place in Cuba, where the Cuban Revolution assumed as one of its more important goals the development of a literate citizenry. Not only was a highly successful literacy campaign conducted in Cuba, but it was recognized that in order to have readers, it was imperative to have books. Numerous publishing houses appeared, some of them devoted exclusively to children's publications. Various awards were established, contributing to the legitimization of a genre that had long been considered a sort of distant cousin, not a true form of literature. Casa de las Américas, the Cuban publishing house that offers some of the most prestigious literary awards in Latin America, began to offer a children's literature award, which further legitimized the genre throughout the Spanish-speaking world.

The search for local color and a literature for children rooted in the Latin American reality developed differently but consistently in the various countries. It was apparent that, just as adult writers have felt the need to describe Latin American reality and give it an international status, similar work was necessary in children's literature.

For readers throughout Latin America and Spain, the names Paris, London, or New York could easily convey a distinct mental image of those cities, but the same was not true of the names Caracas, Lima, or Santiago. Just as apples, peaches, pears, nightingales, oaks, and spruce—having appeared in multiple literary references—have a well-recognized literary image, the same was not true, and probably still isn't, when it comes to guavas, mangoes, algarrobos, ceibas, armadillos, lizards, cocuyos, and tlacuaches.

Thus Latin American children could more easily read and think about animals, plants, and, for that matter, cities and countries exotic to them than about those that belonged to their own reality. It seemed dignified to write about grapes, but not about cashews. However, the trend has begun to shift. For example, in Puerto Rico Isabel Freire de Matos (1968) wrote an ABC book illustrated with woodcuts by Antonio Martorell, with a poem for each letter of the alphabet related to the Puerto Rican flora, fauna, and culture.

In Venezuela, a nonprofit organization, Banco del Libro, began to publish legends of the Pemón and Guajiro Indians as well as contemporary realistic stories of Venezuelan cities and countryside under the logo Ekaré. *Ni era vaca ni era caballo* (*It Wasn't a Cow nor a Horse*) written in 1984 by Miguel Angel Jusayú, a Guajiro Indian, denounces the effects of the destructive penetration of white men into the territories of the Indians.

El cocuyo y la mora (*The Firefly and the Mulberry Bush*) (Kurusa & Uribe, 1978a), *El rabipelado burlado* (*The Fooled Possum*) (Kurusa & Uribe, 1978b), and *La capa del morrocoy* (*The Turtle's Cape*) (Kurusa, 1982) were among the first books to incorporate Latin American animals and landscape in picture books of a design and quality that did not envy foreign publications. *La calle es libre* (*The Streets Are Free*) (Kurusa, 1981), one of the few Latin American children's books to have been published abroad in English, shows life in one of the shantytowns on the outskirts of Caracas. A group of children request a place to play from the authorities. When their request receives media coverage, all kinds of promises are made to them. But since the promises remained unfulfilled, the community takes matters into its own hands.

In Mexico, the Secretaría of Educación Pública (SEP) has sponsored several important initiatives. One of them was the publication of a children's magazine *Colibrí* (published in 1979, in collaboration with Editorial Salvat), which not only offered children valuable information in an engaging format, but also served to develop a number of graphic artists specializing in illustration for children. Some issues, dealing with various periods of Mexican history, were reprinted in book format in 1987 by the program Libros del Rincón, another initiative of SEP. This program reprints books from other publishers as well as printing original books that then are provided as a classroom library to the public schools. One specific aim of the program is to publish books that are varied in format, reading level, and content so as to offer diversity to children and have something for each one of the students in the class.

The selections are consistently excellent. Of particular interest are, of course, those that depict the Mexican reality. There are books inspired by old turn-of-the-century photographs, like *Joaquín y Maclovia se quieren casar* (*Joaquín and*

Maclovia Want to Get Married) (Hinojosa & Meza, 1987) or *Por el agua van las niñas* (*Little Girls Fetch Water*) (Romo, 1988), and books that tell what it is like to be an Indian child in today's Mexico, like *Soy Náhuatl* (*I'm Náhuatl*) (Román Lagunes & Dolores, 1988) or *Soy Huichol* (*I'm Huichol*) (González, 1988).

Private publishing houses also began to recognize the rich Mexican heritage and to publish beautifully illustrated versions of traditional legends and poetry. *De tigres y tlacuaches* (*Of Tigers and Tlacuaches*) (Kurtycz & Kobeh, 1981) is an example of a book inspired by the autochthonous tradition, while *El espejo de obsidiana* (*The Obsidian Mirror*) (Goldsmith, 1982) is part of a unit of six stories, each set in a different period of Mexican history.

The publishing house Editorial Amaquemecan has also made a contribution to the publication of original Mexican writing with a collection that has a simpler format but excellent literary content. *El maravilloso viaje de Nico Huehuetl a través de México* (*The Wonderful Trip of Nico Huehuetl Through Mexico*) (Muria, 1986), a spinoff of Selma Langerloff's classic, recognizes the rich diversity of Mexico and the need for children to be informed of it. In *Pok a Tok. El juego de pelota* (*Pok a Tok: The Ball Game*) by Gilberto Rendón Ortiz (1986), Mayan mythology is woven into contemporary stories.

In Cuba the encouragement of the previously mentioned awards and specialized collections, government subsidies to make books very inexpensive, and the printing of very sizable editions have contributed to the development of a very ample body of children's literature by significant writers. The phenomena of a great poet writing for children is not uncommon in the Spanish-speaking tradition. Nicolás Guillén (1978) adds to that tradition with his book *Por el mar de las Antillas anda un barco de papel* (*Through the Caribbean, There Sails a Paper Ship*). Mirta Aguirre (1984) is unquestionably one of the very best among the many good poets who write specifically for children in this century. Her poetry, collected under the title *Juegos y otros poemas* (*Games and Other Poems*) is as light and bright as butterfly wings. Her ability to create images by fusing two words has had a significant influence on younger poets.

Nersys Felipe has twice won the prestigious Casa de las Américas award. She has been able to master, in *Cuentos de Guane* (*Tales from Guane*) (Felipe, 1976a), the difficult task of creating a book of childhood memories truly appealing to children. Her book *Román Elé* (1976b) is one of the few books in Spanish for children that has treated the issue of slavery adequately. The protagonist is a boy whose grandfather was a slave and who himself grew up under a despotic landowner in conditions reminiscent of slavery. But nothing robs Román Elé of the dignity he has learned from his grandfather nor of his ability to love, to hope, and to struggle for his freedom.

Other poets worth mentioning are David Chericián, author of *Caminito del monte* (*A Road in the Forest*), who writes of serious topics with a lively African-Caribbean musicality; and Dora Alonso, author of *La flauta de chocolate* (*The Chocolate Flute*) (1984) and *Los payasos* (*The Clowns*) (1985), who writes children's poetry with the voice of a great poet. Julia Calzadilla (1976), in *Cantares de la América Latina y el Caribe* (*Songs of Latin America and the Caribbean*), another Casa de las Américas award-winning book, takes on the challenge of uniting all the Latin American countries. Her poetry is rich in regionalisms and toponyms that celebrate the diversity of the people who live in Latin America and the Caribbean. Alga Marina Elizagaray (1988), one of the critics who has extensively promoted the new Cuban literature outside of Cuba, has retold a series of African folktales that have taken hold in the Caribbean in a book published in Mexico by Amaquemecan, *Fábulas del Caribe* (*Caribbean Fables*).

DEVELOPING LITERACY

In Spain the new freedom obtained after Franco's death brought about much new growth in publishing, and children's books were not an exception. Many publishing houses initiated collections specifically devoted to that genre. Books began to be published in the other three official languages: Gallego, Basque, and especially Catalán. A large number of publishing houses are in Cataluña, of which Barcelona is the capital, and many writers and illustrators are of Catalán origin.

During the Franco regime, authors were not allowed to publish in Catalán. Now that there is the freedom to do so, a large number of books are published originally in Catalán and only afterward translated into Spanish.

One example of these books is the story *La conejita Marcela* (*Marcela, the Little Rabbit*). In this story, the writer Esther Tusquets (1987) treats the theme of oppression brought about by discrimination. Marcela, a beautiful black rabbit, flees her home in order to escape from an oppressive situation. In her valley, the white rabbits live upstream and push, bite, and kick any black rabbit that happens to cross their path. Marcela ends up finding another valley where it turns out that the conditions are reversed. It is the black rabbits that live upstream and dominate the white rabbits. Marcela is troubled, as conditions have changed yet not really changed at all. When, in order to belong, she finally forces herself to attack a white rabbit, a surprising thing happens and she ends up siding with him against the others. The pair flees and finds an unpopulated valley, which will not remain without rabbits for long, yet the rabbits will no longer be all white nor all black.

The theme of multiple heritage is a historical reality for Hispanics. The novelist José María Merino, surprised that the historically significant experiences of the invasion and colonization of Latin America were not represented in the literature for young readers, attempted to respond to the challenge. His trilogy of novels has as a protagonist a young boy who is the son of a Spanish conquistador and an Indian mother. Unfortunately there remains a lack of other books that attempt to address this subject matter.

Recognizing that the rich folklore of Spain was beginning to disappear and be relegated to scholarly compilations, three writers have done considerable work to ensure that the best of the folklore will continue to be accessible to children. Carmen Bravo-Villasante (1978, 1984a, 1984b) has collected lullabies, rhymes, tongue twisters, and other language games, which have been published in beautifully produced books. The folklorist Antonio Rodríguez Almodóvar (1987) has rewritten for children many of the popular tales he personally collected in small towns and villages. He was able to keep the traditional style of oral narrative that mixes fantasy and realism, humor, dramatic tension, simplicity, and tenderness. Finally, Arturo Medina (1987) has done an excellent compilation of the games that children play, accompanied by songs that, in the Hispanic tradition, are mostly segments of old medieval ballads.

But contemporary Spanish children's literature does not remain focused on the past. Contemporary issues also can be found. There are books that discuss ecological issues for children of different ages, like María Puncel's *El prado del tío Pedro* (*Uncle Pedro's Pasture*) (1983), a picture book that invites the young reader to choose between three possible solutions to an ecological problem, and *El río del los castores* (*The River of the Beavers*) (Martínez Gil, 1984) for older readers.

Other important social issues are also becoming the theme for children's books. The abandonment of the small villages creates the environment for *El amigo oculto y los espíritus de la tarde* (*The Hidden Friend and the Afternoon Spirits*) (López Narváez, 1986), centered on the struggles of a young boy to survive in hiding in his own village, and the conflict he faces over whether to accept having strangers move into the town, destroying by their presence the memories he has carefully preserved, or to simply have the houses crumple and decay from lack of care. The migration to the cities and the adjustment that this demands of older people is also explored in Pilar Mateos's *El cuento interrumpido* (*The Interrupted Story*) (1986).

In Spain, sensitive personal issues are also being brought to bear in children's literature. The author and illustrator Asun Balzola (1984a, b) has created a character, Munia, a young girl who awakens to the understanding of her own growing body, the need to understand her own feelings and to learn how to ask forgiveness, and who finds an original friend, a crocodile, who helps her overcome the nightmares brought on when she begins to lose her teeth. It's hard for Munia to believe that her teeth will grow back—after all, her grandmother's haven't!

The issue of death, always difficult to discuss, has been delicately treated by María Martínez Vendrell (1983) in *Yo las quería* (*I Loved Them*), and beautifully illustrated by Carmen Solé Vendrell. A young girl has to have her braids cut during her mother's illness. The braids that she carefully saves will become a memory of her mother and symbol of her tenderness. And the fact that she is told that her short hair makes her resemble her mother gives her the strength to begin to overcome her sorrow.

In summary, it could be said that never before have Spain or Latin America published as many books for children as they are publishing today. A great many of the titles published are still translations, both of the classics and of contemporary books written in Europe and the United States. The prevalence of translations, however, is not without benefit. Due to Spain's tendency to be less insular than the United States, there are many excellent European children's books—notably German and Italian ones—available in the Spanish language, which are not available in English. Yet the number of writers producing original works in Spanish for children continues to increase substantially.

The quality of the editions, the good art accompanying the texts, the development of collections specializing in children's literature under the care of experts, and the increase in awards have all given children's literature recognition and validity.

The history of Spain and Latin America has begun to be a literary subject for young readers. The recognition of our multiple heritage is emerging in historical fiction and symbolically in fables, although it remains to be addressed in contemporary realistic fiction.

There is recognition of the great richness of traditional folklore of Spanish, Indian, and African descent that is being rediscovered and returned to children in beautiful editions. In Latin America, especially, there is a conscious effort to validate the presence of autochthonous flora and fauna as well as the vernacular use of the language in literature.

Much is yet to be done. The examples given are only a small portion of what still needs to be published. I can look back and remember the absence of available books when I wanted my students to find representations of themselves, their families, and their communities as protagonists in the stories they read. I rejoice and find my energies renewed every time a book that can be celebrated is published.

In the time frame of the five-hundredth anniversary of the European invasion of this continent, the subsequent 500 years of indigenous resistance, and the painful birth of the resulting new cultures, we have much to think about. As a people, we have deep wounds to heal, and many social injustices, both current and long-standing, to address. It is only when we do so that we shall be able to carry out the hope of the great African-Cuban poet Nicolás Guillén, and allow our grandparents to embrace in forgiveness. Looking back honestly at our history and honoring and defending the expression of diversity among us and within us will give us the strength to join together to shape our future. To paraphrase the Peruvian writer Cesar Vallejo: "Hay, hermanos y hermanas, muchísimo que hacer" ("There is, brothers and sisters, much work to be done").

About the Author

Alma Flor Ada is an internationally acclaimed author and teacher. Since publishing *Sonrisas* in 1967, she has written many books including the 1991 Christopher Award winner, *The Gold Coin, La canción del mosquito* and *Abecedario de los animales*. Currently director of Doctoral Studies, International Multicultural Program at the University of San Francisco, Alma Flor is considered the foremost U.S. authority on children's literature in Spanish and has lectured extensively around the world on topics including multicultural education, bilingualism, children's literature, and critical pedagogy. *Serafina's Birthday, My Name is María Isabel* and *The Rooster Who Went To His Uncle's Wedding* are some of her recent children's books.

References

Aguirre, Mirta (1984). *Juegos y otros poemas*. Havana, Cuba: Gente Nueva.
Alonso, Dora (1985). *Los payasos*. Havana, Cuba: Gente Nueva.
Alonso, Dora (1984). *La flauta de chocolate*. Havana, Cuba: Gente Nueva.
Balzola, Asun (1984a). *Munia y el cocodrilo naranja (Colección algunas veces Munia)*. Barcelona, Spain: Ediciones Destino.
Balzola, Asun (1984b). *Munia y la señora piltronera (Colección algunas veces Munia)*. Barcelona, Spain: Ediciones Destino.
Balzola, Asun (n/y). *Los zapatos de Munia (Colección algunas veces Munia)*. Barcelona, Spain: Ediciones Destino.
Bravo-Villasante, Carmen (1984a). *El libro de las adivinanzas*. Ilustraciones Carmen Andrada. Valladolid, Spain: Susaeta.
Bravo-Villasante, Carmen (1984b). *Una, dola, tela, catola. El libro del folklore infantil*. Valladolid, Spain: Susaeta.
Bravo-Villasante, Carmen (1978). *Adivina, adivinanza. Folklore infantil*. Madrid, Spain: Interduc/Schroedel.
Calzadilla, Julia (1976). *Cantares de la América Latina y el Caribe*. Ilustraciones Ricardo Reymena. Havana, Cuba: Casa de las Américas.
Chericián, David (n/y). *Caminito del monte*. Havana, Cuba: Gente Nueva.
Colibrí (1987). *Historia. Mayas y aztecas (Libros del Rincón)*. Dirección General de Publicaciones y Bibliotecas. SEP.
Colibrí (1979). *Enciclopedia Infantil*. Mexico City, Mexico: Dirección General de Publicaciones y Bibliotecas. SEP.
Devetach, Laura (1989). *Monigote en la arena (Libros del malabarista)*. Buenos Aires, Argentina: Ediciones Colihue.
Elizagaray, Alga Marina (1988). *Fábulas del Caribe*. Ilustraciones Patricio Gómez. *(Colección nogales)*. Amaquemecan, Mexico: Editorial Amaquemecan.
Felipe, Nersys (1976a). *Cuentos de Guane*. Ilustraciones Manuel Castellanos. Havana, Cuba: Casa de las Américas.
Felipe, Nersys (1976b). *Román Elé*. Ilustraciones Tomás Borbonet. Havana, Cuba: Casa de las Américas.
Freire de Matos, I. (1968). *ABC de Puerto Rico*. Sharon, CT: Troutman Press.
Goldsmith, Patrick (1982). *El espejo de obsidiana*. Ilustraciones Felipe Ehrenberg *(Colección Fonapás)*. Mexico City, Mexico: Organización Editorial Novaro.

González, Refugio (1988). *Soy Huichol (Libros del Rincón)*. Mexico City. Mexico: Secretaría de Educación Pública.

Guillén, Nicolás (1978). *Por el mar de las Antillas anda un barco de papel*. Ilustraciones Rapi Diego. Havana, Cuba: UNEAC.

Hinojosa, Francisco, y Meza, Alicia (1987). *Joaquín y Maclovia se quieren casar (Libros del Rincón)*. Mexico City, Mexico: Secretaría de Educación Pública.

Jiménez, Juan Ramón (1973). *Platero y yo*. In *Antología de la literatura infantil en la lengua española*. Madrid, Spain: Doncel.

Jusayú, Miguel Angel (1984). *Ni era vaca ni era caballo*. Ilustraciones Monika Doppert. Caracas, Venezuela: Ediciones Ekaré-Banco del Libro.

Kurtycz, Marcso, y Ana Garcia Kobeh (1981). *De tigres y tlacuaches. Leyendas animales*. Mexico City, Mexico: Organización Editorial Novaro.

Kurusa (Adapt.) (1982). *La capa del morrocoy*. Ilustraciones Cristina Keller. Caracas, Venezuela: Ediciones Ekaré-Banco del Libro.

Kurusa (1981). *La calle es libre*. Ilustraciones Monika Doppert. Caracas, Venezuela: Ediciones Ekaré-Banco del Libro.

Kurusa, y Uribe, Verónica (Adapt.) (1978a). *El cocuyo y la mora*. Ilustraciones Amelie Areco. Caracas, Venezuela: Ediciones Ekaré-Banco del Libro.

Kurusa, y Uribe, Verónica (Adapt.) (1978b). *El rabipelado burlado*. Ilustraciones Vicky Sempere (1978). Caracas, Venezuela: Ediciones Ekaré-Banco del Libro.

López Narváez, Concha (1986). *El amigo oculto y los espíritus de la tarde. (Cuatro Vientos)*. Barcelona, Spain: Noguer.

Martí, José (1979). *La edad de oro*. (Facsimile edition). Havana, Cuba: Editorial Letras Cubanas.

Martí, José (n/y). *La edad de oro*. Ilustraciones Enrique Martínez Blanco. Havana, Cuba: Gente Nueva.

Martínez Gil, Fernando (1984). *El río de los castores (Cuatro Vientos)*. Barcelona, Spain: Noguer.

Martínez Vendrell, María (1983). *Yo las quería*. Ilustraciones Carmen Solé Vendrell. Barcelona, Spain: Destino.

Mateos, Pilar (1986). *El cuento interrumpido*. Barcelona, Spain: Noguer.

Medina, Arturo (1987). *Pinto Maraña: Juegos populares infantiles*. Ilustraciones Carmen Andrada. Valladolid, Spain: Susaeta.

Montes, Graciela (1988a). *Tengo un monstruo en el bolsillo*. Ilustraciones Elena Torre. Buenos Aires, Argentina: Libros del Quirquincho.

Montes, Graciela (1988b). *La verdadera historia del Ratón Feroz*. Ilustraciones Elena Torre. *(La ratona cuentacuentos)*. Buenos Aires, Argentina: Libros del Quirquincho.

Muria, Anna (1986). *El maravilloso viaje de Nico Huehuetl a través de México*. Ilustraciones Felipe Dávalo. Amecameca, Mexico: Editorial Amaquemecan.

Nalé Roxlo, Conrado (1988). *La escuela de las hadas (Libros del malabarista)*. Buenos Aires, Argentina: Ediciones Colihue.

Nalé Roxlo, Conrado (1963). *La escuela de las hadas*. Ilustraciones Leonardo Helablian. Buenos Aires, Argentina: Editorial Universitaria de Buenos Aires.

Puncel, María (1983). *El prado del tío Pedro (Cuento de la torre y la estrella)*. Ilustraciones Teo Puebla. Madrid, Spain: Ediciones SM.

Rendón Ortiz, Gilberto (1986). *Pok a tok, el juego de pelota*. Ilustraciones Felipe Dávalo. Amecameca, Mexico: Editorial Amaquemecan.

Rodríguez Almodóvar, Antonio (1987). *Cuentos de la media lunita*. Sevilla, Spain: Algaida.

Roldán, Gustavo (1986). *El monte era una fiesta (Libros del malabarista)*. Buenos Aires, Argentina: Ediciones Colihue.

Román Lagunes, Rosa, y Dolores, Jesús Vitorino (1988). *Soy Náhuatl (Libros del Rincón)*. Mexico City, Mexico: Secretaría de Educación Pública.

Romo, Marta (1988). *Por el agua van las niñas (Libros del Rincón)*. Photos by C. B. Waite. Mexico City, Mexico: Secretaría de Educación Pública.

Sánchez Silva, José María (1952). *Marcelino, pan, y vino (Colección la ballena alegre)*. Madrid, Spain: Doncel.

Sastre, Alfonso (1962). *Historia de una muñeca abondonada. (Colección Girasol-Teatro)*. Ilustraciones Felicidad Orquín. Salamanca, Spain: Anaya.

Tusquets, Esther (1987). *La conejita Marcela*. Ilustraciones Wenceslao Masip. Barcelona, Spain: Lumen.

Villafañe, Javier (1986). *Cuentos y títeres (Libros del malabarista)*. Buenos Aires, Argentina: Ediciones Colihue.

Walsh, María Elena (1987). *Palomita de la puna*. Ilustraciones Vilar. Buenos Aires, Argentina: Sudamericana.

DEVELOPING LITERACY

STRATEGIES for Working with OVERAGE STUDENTS

Carrol Moran
Educational Consultant

Josefina Villamil Tinajero
The University of Texas at El Paso

Judy Stobbe
Pajaro Valley Unified School District, California

Ignacio Tinajero
Ysleta Independent School District, Texas

Joining the Community of Learners

Increasingly in our schools today we are asked to deal with recent immigrants to the United States, some of whom have had little or no schooling either here or in their home country. Often these students come from troubling experiences in their home country, such as war, poverty, or political persecution, that may affect their emotional as well as academic preparation for schooling. Their unique backgrounds will present a special challenge to you and will bring great reward. Each student will bring his/her own background, personality, and experiences to our classrooms. Overage students often bring real world experiences that will enrich our classrooms and provide the foundation for accelerated learning. Our job is to tap the potential and build upon it to ensure successful learning opportunities for these students.

The first, most crucial, step is to provide a nurturing, supportive transition for the overage student to bring him/her into your community of learners in a positive way. These students thrive in environments where they are accepted, respected, made to feel that they belong, and given opportunities to be in charge of their own learning.

It will be important for you as the teacher to build a personal relationship with the student. If possible, meet the family and learn as much as you can about the student's background, not only their educational background, but experiences, interests, and strengths that you can use during learning activities. We know that lowering the affective filter is critical to allow learning to take place, so the stronger the relationship you can forge with the student, the more comfortable he/she will feel in the learning environment, and as a result, greater learning will happen.

The learning community includes your other students. It is often difficult for students to accept someone who is different from them. Work with all your students to learn supportive attitudes toward differences, both academic and social. Be honest, sensitive, and forthcoming about the kinds of experiences your new student has had and why he/she may not have the same level of skills or knowledge as the norm. Perhaps a writing assignment or a visualization might help students to put themselves in the place of the new student and empathize with what the new student is facing in this new environment. Ask students what they can do to help the new student become accustomed to this new country, school, classroom, and life. Try to follow through on their suggestions and bring them into a cooperative effort at making the new student have the most supportive and enriching learning opportunities possible.

In the context of your classroom, there will be many opportunities for the overage student to share his/her expertise with other students. Notice special capacities such as artistic abilities, manual dexterity, or special knowledge. Try to provide leadership opportunities for the student to share these strengths with others. Set up an "elective day" on which certain students can teach other students how to do something they know how to do well. Be sure to include the overage student as a teacher. At times, it may be possible to teach the overage student expert knowledge that he/she can, in turn, teach the rest of the class, such as how to conduct a science experiment or the steps for a craft or cooking project.

With a student who has had little or no knowledge of the institutional aspects of school, it will be necessary to guide them in learning about school rules and procedures. Often students from backgrounds such as these will have had a great deal of responsibility for themselves or younger siblings, or even experience in a workplace. They may not understand that the freedom of choice of what you can do, and when, may be different in an elementary school. Use the arrival of the new student to have your class role-play rules and procedures to familiarize the new student with the expectations of the school community and classroom. Ask an experienced student to take the new student on a tour of the school that will include not only becoming familiar with places but also school personnel.

As well, a student who has had no school experience may not have had the opportunity to use some of the materials that we take for granted that students who come to us have used. Even the simplest tools, like scissors, staplers, and glue, may be new for this student. Set aside some time and a helper to introduce these items to the student. The introduction could be part of a language development lesson in which the new student creates a project using these items, then talks about what he/she did, and finally, creates a language experience log of the project. Creative play may not have been part of the child's experience, so provide puppets, puzzles, blocks, dolls, etc. These could be free-time choices for the student when his/her work is done.

The arrival of an immigrant student in your classroom is a special challenge. While it may seem like a great burden to get a new student with such special needs, the time and energy that you spend making this student a productive and valued member of your class will bring you enormous joy as you see the progress he/she makes toward becoming a successful student capable of thriving in the dominant culture.

The home/school connection is an important concern in working with overage students who are being motivated to learn at an accelerated rate. The following have been found to be successful:

◆ Home visits, ideally before the start of the school year, to meet the family and learn as much as possible about the student's background—not only educational background but also experiences, interests, and strengths that you can tap

◆ Home visits when students are absent or appear to be overly frustrated in the classroom

◆ Working with parents early in the year to establish a daily time and place for study (regardless of whether or not homework has been assigned) and to encourage them to participate during that study time. In order to maximize participation, make suggestions that address the time—and education—limits parents may have. Explicitly stress to them the importance of structured study time.

◆ Invitations to parents to the classroom, not only to observe but also to discuss a relevant topic

◆ Coordinating with parents to establish neighborhood study groups where several students can meet

Motivating Overage Students

Beyond their needs for academic skills, overage students also have emotional and motivational needs that must be addressed. These needs are often magnified in importance where there are cultural and linguistic differences between home and school. They include students' needs to feel a sense of identity, to belong, to be understood by and to communicate with significant others, and to succeed in environments in which they are accepted and respected (Igoa, 1993).

A primary way in which we can provide motivating and supportive learning environments is for classroom environments to provide overage, linguistically diverse students with opportunities to use their own language and worlds of reality as the bases for learning and as the initial tools for reflection, critical thinking, and building conceptual foundations in the acquisition of new ideas and language.

Igoa (1993) states that "value must be placed on the immigrant child's own language and heritage so the opportunity for self-expression and the feeling of belonging are not denied during the acculturation process" (p. 99). More important, the use of students' own language allows them the opportunity to reconstruct their history and their culture (Macedo, 1991), to express their thoughts and ideas, and to talk about their feelings. Igoa also points out that "It is difficult to socialize when you feel that your language and your culture are useless, and the feeling is compounded when you are unable to articulate the feeling to others outside one's silent world" (p. 90). Cummins (1989) and Krashen and Biber (1988) also identify the need for first language support in order to promote academic success and the building of self-esteem of language minority students.

Another critical way to motivate students is to communicate to them that they are important and that we, as teachers, have very high expectations of them: failure is impossible with a good attitude and with a good self-concept.

The physical and social environments in the classroom communicate to students what we think and what we expect of them. In many successful classes such as Mr. Ignacio Tinajero's (a sixth-grade class for recent arrivals and overage students), the walls are filled with students' work, their own pictures and chosen careers, and words of wisdom such as "It is your attitude, not your aptitude, that determines your altitude" and "Failure is impossible!" Bulletin boards display pictures of successful Hispanics and newspaper articles showing powerful role models (Hispanics with *ganas*).

Igoa suggests that teachers should examine their own attitudes toward immigrant students: "For in the silent stage children are keen in picking up their teachers' unconscious feelings toward them. If the teacher believes the student will not succeed, the student senses this, believes it, and will most likely fail" (p. 88). Mr. Tinajero empowers his students to become participants in their own education, having each student take a written oath to assume individual responsibility (the affirmation is recited daily).

Effective Strategies to Integrate the Overage Student into the Core Curriculum

First, we must consider the realities and limitations of classroom teaching (for example, the amount of available teacher time for individualized instruction) while designing optimal learning opportunities for overage students. As much as possible, we want to find strategies that allow the overage student to participate in regular classroom activities yet require minimal modifications to the basic lesson, and we want to minimize isolation of the overage student from his/her peers.

With this in mind, Macmillan/McGraw-Hill's *CUENTAMUNDOS* Spanish reading program offers a flexible format that will allow you to tailor instruction to meet the needs of a wide range of students—including emergent readers chronologically beyond the primary grades. The program includes:

- High-quality, high-interest core literature that is both multicultural and draws heavily from the rich Hispanic oral tradition. Illustrations and photos support the text. This combination facilitates comprehension and retelling of selections and language development.

- A bibliography for each unit in the core program of easier-to-read trade books related to the respective theme of the unit. These books—carefully selected so as to be both manageable textwise and age-appropriate—can be used during individual or small group lessons to develop reading fluency. If teacher time is not available, the help of (properly informed) teacher aides, librarians, parents, and even student tutors might be solicited.

- Recordings of the selections and poems in the pupil edition on audiocassettes so that students can hear the literature that they cannot yet read independently. This allows them to participate in whole-class discussions and develop literary concepts such as genre, story structure, and interpretive and creative thinking skills.

- Activities in the basic lesson plan that are particularly effective with emergent readers, for example:
  — Language experience
  — Shared reading
  — Interactive reading (modeling, think-aloud strategies, development of vocabulary within meaningful contexts)

- Activities within the basic lesson that incorporate students' own experience and language in developing background and that provide for discussions in cooperative groups, small groups, and as a whole class. Thus, overage students receive a maximum of oral-to-print experiences through graphic organizers, such as semantic, story, and character maps, in order to develop relationships between ideas, concepts, and events.

As we think about what school experiences our students bring to us at our level of teaching, we need to ensure that the overage student can experience the same kind of interactions with materials and print that our other students have had years to experience. Think in terms of making the curriculum real to the new student without using printed material. Of course, at the same time you will be working to develop the new student's literacy skills, but for other concepts the class is studying try to provide experiences that allow for a meaning-centered understanding of the content of the lesson. Modifications of the basic curriculum to engage and integrate the overage student are often simply a matter of deciding which activities that are already outlined will be more effective with *all* students and then sequencing the activities to get the most out of them. Following are some ideas for accomplishing that.

It always seems there is so much to do and not enough time or personnel to give each student the individual attention he/she needs. This will be especially true for the overage student who will not have the literacy skills to participate in certain lessons at the level of your other students. Cooperative learning can assist this student to feel a part of the regular classroom curriculum. It is important that the other students have empathy for this student's needs when working on a cooperative task to which he/she cannot contribute with reading and writing skills. Assign the overage student a cooperative buddy. These two can be used as one person in a cooperative group, with the buddy performing the reading and writing tasks and the overage student other tasks.

Research other possibilities for additional personnel to give the overage student the extra attention he/she will require. Some possibilities may include: community people, grandparents, a paraprofessional who has a spare 20 minutes, the principal who may want to spend some time teaching, the custodian who may need help with some task and can spend some time conversing with the student, and business people or cross-age tutors from another class. Set up regularly scheduled, clear activities that these people can do to help the student.

Use as much realia as possible to bring to life a particular unit of study. Set up class museums, displays, science experiments, and the like. Ask other students to be the curators of these displays and discuss them with the new student. Ask new students to keep a learning log about these discussions, using their emerging literacy skills to keep track of what they have learned. Make use of other teaching strategies that enhance other intelligences besides the linguistic and the logico-mathematical. Provide multisensory opportunities for your entire class. Music, drama, and visual arts activities will enhance the understanding of concepts and allow the overage student to participate as an "equal" with classmates.

Music can be a great community builder and the basis of oral-to-print experiences for the overage student. Learn songs that relate to your unit of study and then have the overage students use these as reading material when the words have been memorized. Ask cooperative groups to create another verse for a song, make a large chart, illustrate it, and perform it for the rest of the class. Use rhythm instruments. To strengthen the home/school connection, ask students to bring in songs from their homes and have them teach those songs to the class.

Songs leave lasting impressions on children. They make teaching and learning fun. For students with limited experiences with reading and writing, a song can serve as a springboard to a variety of literacy activities. Whatever the purpose, the following guidelines are helpful in selecting songs for use with overage students. The songs should:

◆ be appropriate for the age and grade level of the students

◆ correlate with themes/concepts being developed in the unit

◆ provide opportunities to enrich and extend the reading selections

◆ be culturally relevant

◆ provide multiple opportunities for oral-to-print experiences

◆ be easy to sing and listen to

◆ include repetitive phrases or verses

Some songs can be used simply to set the tone—for example, listening to Calypso music before reading a story set in the West Indies. Students may listen to the song as background music or they might develop a semantic map to develop vocabulary and concepts. Follow-up activities should provide for additional interaction and reflection about the song, including its application/relevance to the theme.

Dramatic arts also can be used to integrate the overage student into the regular curriculum. Through heterogeneous grouping, simple drama such as choral reading can give the overage student a low-anxiety way to participate successfully in the core curriculum and improve oral reading. Acting out stories allows the student to participate in a personal response to literature as well as build the sense of story so critical to successful reading. Dramatizing historical events and abstract notions such as liberty, or depicting character traits will allow the student to demonstrate and practice comprehension of important concepts. Drama is also a way to involve all the students in an enriching experience without isolating the overage student with a separate tutor. The visual arts will also be a place to integrate your overage student into the regular curriculum. Drawings, paintings, sculpture, and other artistic creations will not only provide a way for the student to demonstrate comprehension of learning objectives but also provide the basis for discussion and the creation of language experience literacy materials the student can use to develop reading and writing skills. The visual arts can be used as "learning logs" for nonliterate students by allowing them to record what they know and have learned with mediums other than paper and pencil.

Creating an environment where the overage student can be involved in the regular learning activities that go on in the classroom and receive the special assistance needed to gain the basic skills he/she is lacking is made possible through the expansion of the learning opportunities *for all your students* through realia, manipulatives, drama, and the arts. This allows overage students to participate and to gain valuable knowledge and skills toward becoming literate themselves. The key to success will be in making these students feel they are productive and valuable parts of the community of learners.

Emergent Literacy Activities

ASSESSMENT STRATEGIES

Put yourselves in the shoes of the overage student coming to a new place with new rules, procedures, language, etc. Couple that sense of strangeness with the fact that you cannot do the work that your peers do because you don't know how to read and write. Think of the stress and frustration that you would feel. It is important to keep these feelings in mind when you begin to design literacy opportunities for these emergent readers beyond the primary grades. Make the curriculum as challenging, age appropriate, and interesting to the student as possible. Be honest about what needs to be learned, yet encourage taking risks in order to get better. It is critical to maintain high expectations.

A first step in designing the curriculum for the overage student will be to engage in some meaningful assessment of the student's knowledge about print. Observation and analysis of the results of meaningful tasks will give you some ideas about what to do with this student to improve literacy. It is likely that the student has had some experience with print, probably basic sight words such as street signs, package labels, etc., but may have had little or no interaction with literature or content area material. Start with what you know the student knows and proceed from there to observe and record anecdotal information.

Reading Behaviors and Knowledge

◆ Recognizes own name in a variety of contexts

◆ Recognizes some words (e.g., names of classmates, signs, cereal boxes)

◆ Handles a book appropriately
   — turns pages front to back
   — demonstrates top-to-bottom orientation

◆ Tracks print from left to right

◆ Shows an interest in looking at books and an understanding of their organization

◆ Can retell a known story in sequence

◆ Engages in discussions about what he/she has heard read or read himself/herself

Writing Behaviors and Knowledge

◆ Makes drawings that tell a story

◆ Writes name

◆ Uses proper pencil grip

◆ Writes from left to right

◆ Uses
   — letterlike forms
   — invented spelling
   — some conventional spelling

◆ Can read back own writing

In addition to observing the student and analyzing work samples, conduct an interview with the student. Try to set aside a block of uninterrupted time so you can get to know the student. You will want to focus this interview on what the student knows about reading and writing. It can set the tone of future attitudes about your willingness to accept the student as a risk taker in the literacy process. Keep the interview upbeat and positive, acknowledging how much the student already knows and how you will work together to help him/her learn more. Some possible questions to ask might be:

- *What kind of books do you like best?*
- *What is reading?*
- *Why do people read?*
- *What can you read?*
- *How did you learn to read?*
- *What do you do when you look at books?*
- *What is writing?*
- *Who do you see who writes?*
- *Why do people write?*
- *What can you write?*

Initial Literacy Experiences

If, through this process of observation and interview, you find that the student has no experience with print or the written word, it will be important to provide the student with a great deal of input on how the printed word works. Begin by arranging for the student to be read to as frequently as possible in a one-to-one situation. Use volunteers, peers, or anyone you can find to provide as many "lap reading" experiences as possible. Focus the student's attention on the print, encouraging him/her to pick out known words and/or use oral cloze, in which the student fills in the word that the reader leaves out. Collect audiocassettes of picture books to which the student may listen during class time when he/she is not participating in the regular program. Use wordless books to have the student tell you the story using the pictures as a guide. Write down the student's story and encourage him/her to read it back to you. Make arrangements with library personnel to send the student to the library to pick out books that are of interest to him/her. Read aloud the literature that the rest of the class is reading. The key here will be to surround the student with print.

To initiate the student into the writing process, begin a dialog journal with the student. The focus of this journal is on communication between you and the student. The secondary use of the dialog journal is as an ongoing assessment of the emerging generalizations the student is making about print. Thirdly, the dialog journal will allow you to model on an individual basis how writing works. The process is as follows:

- Each day the student "writes" (drawing should be viewed as writing in the initial stages of literacy development).

- Ask the student to tell you (or a volunteer) what he/she has written. Then, you respond in writing to what the student has told you. The student should watch while you write; you should slowly vocalize what you are writing to enable students to observe and hear the phonemic elements of the words. This response will be most effective if it induces a thoughtful response in the student. For example, asking "why" questions or asking for elaboration are thought-provoking responses. Begin to encourage the student to respond to you in writing as his/her sense of the alphabetic principle emerges.

- Accept all responses. This is not the place for error correction. Use this individual activity to introduce the next step the student needs in the form of mini-lessons.

Provide opportunities for the overage student to be involved in activities in which they can see other children write and hear their own writing read aloud. As much as possible, involve the overage student with his/her classmates in hands-on, interactive activities relating to the literature and themes the class is studying so that they can understand the concepts and content.

General Strategies for Reading Development

In order for the student to gain emergent literacy skills, it will be necessary to provide time for individual or small group instruction that is designed to meet assessed needs. The focus of this instruction should be based on real literature.

In each unit of the *CUENTAMUNDOS* program, teachers will find lists of titles of trade books that relate to the theme of the unit and are at an easier reading level. The bibliography appears in the lesson planning pages at the beginning of the unit. The suggested titles relate to the theme being developed in the core literature, resulting in coherent teaching and learning. These titles may be used following the general strategies listed below.

◆ Begin any lesson with a piece of literature by having the students predict what they think the selection will be about, using the cover illustration and/or title as a prompt. Ask the students to justify their ideas, tapping their own background knowledge as reasonable justifications.

◆ Brainstorm what the students know about the theme of the selection. Create a semantic map together. Revise this after the selection has been read.

◆ Read the book. As you read, stop and ask students to predict what will happen next. If appropriate to the text, use oral cloze to have students predict what word or phrase will come next. This will be particularly appropriate in a selection that contains predictable text, rhymes, or patterned writing. While reading, track the print as the students watch. This will be more effective if you use a Big Book, but with a small group of students a trade book will suffice. Just make sure that all students can see the print.

◆ Ask the students to respond orally to the book. Engaging in "instructional conversations" is an important learning activity. Probe with higher-order questions to elicit a discussion, not just to check comprehension. Talk about story structure or predictable text or the "whys" of character development. Use graphic organizers to keep track of your discussions. Graphic organizers are also important because they offer further opportunity to see the spoken word in print. (Always vocalize slowly as you write. This allows students to see and hear how phonemes are written.)

◆ At another small group session, reread the selection, this time having the student read the words. Accept all attempts at trying to read the text. For some, this activity will be a retelling using the pictures to guide what is said. For others who have a greater understanding of print, some of the text will be read conventionally. Use this opportunity to develop print awareness with techniques such as:

— Cloze readings, in which you cover a word in the text. Ask students to predict what the word might be, given the context of the story, then uncover the initial sound or syllable and have them revise their guess using graphophonics.

— Ask the student to track the words while you read aloud. Stop and ask the student to supply a word or phrase.

— Have the student listen to an audiocassette of the selection, then choose part or all of the text to practice reading for fluency. Recordings may be available commercially or recorded by sufficiently talented and capable volunteers.

◆ A follow-up activity should be designed to provide opportunities for reflecting and responding to the selection. Some possibilities are:

— Do an art project related to the selection.

— Design flannelboard characters to use in retelling the story to a younger student.

— Sequence the pictures from the selection, then dictate or write a summary of the story. Use this as reading material for fluency development.

— Innovate on predictable text to create an "original" story. Publish and illustrate the new story.

— Hold a literature discussion with a peer who has read the same story.

— Create a drama that other students can participate in.

— Research more about the theme of the story and prepare an oral report to give to the class or a buddy.

Literature that is appropriate for an overage student with little or no prior schooling/literacy might begin with wordless books in which they create the text, predictable books, pattern books, poetry, and songbooks.

General Strategies for Writing Development

Reading and writing development go hand in hand. You should view every reading opportunity as an opportunity to develop writing skills and vice versa. Students need to be encouraged to take risks and try out emerging strategies and generalizations they have about written language. Fluency should be valued over form. In the initial stages, drawing is writing, although this will change as the student learns more about the alphabetic principle. With young children, the stage after drawing would be using letterlike forms instead of pictures, then letter strings with little or no relation to the phonemes they represent. Overage students may skip these stages and move right into invented writing (aka approximated spelling). With the overage student, this developmental process will be difficult to keep in perspective.

Daily you will be confronted with the lack of skills, the lack of knowledge, etc., and be tempted to circumvent the developmental process by correcting every error. Resist this urge! You must trust that the student will learn to write conventionally if you surround him/her with print, provide meaningful opportunities to engage in real reading and writing, and wisely and sensitively engage in the stages of the writing process with editing as the final stage. Most likely, the progress you see will be rapid and encouraging.

Yet there are others who argue the need for direct instruction—that is, skills-specific intervention—at the same time the benefits of whole language and process teaching are reaped and reported. María de la Luz Reyes (1991), for example, cautions that in addition to the benefits of whole language and process teaching, teachers must consider the culture and expectations for learning that immigrant students—and parents—bring to American classrooms. She reports:

> Minority groups who hold teachers in high regard, for example, may rely on and expect some direct guidance from teachers—a feature not so evident in process classrooms where teachers function more as facilitators than as interveners (Pearson, 1989). Macías's (1989) work with Hispanic students and Siddle's (1986) work with African-American students indicate that these minority pupils expected that if they needed to learn something, teachers would point it out. (p. 160)

Reyes (1991) cites a case study of sixth graders' dialog journal and literature log writing in which "the students did not, in fact, attend in any lasting manner to correct form in their writing." These results are contrasted to the success stories reported by Atwell (1987) for mainstream students in process classrooms.

> Students failed to see a connection between the lessons and their writing in dialog journals and literary logs and so continued to make the same mistakes. The teacher's attempts at indirect mediation are contrary to the explicit guidance that children from nonmainstream backgrounds may expect. (Reyes, 1991, p. 166)

The following are some contexts for writing:

◆ Spoken word to print

— Brainstorming to create word banks

— Brainstorming to create semantic maps

— Language experience with wordless books, story summaries, literature, or content logs of experiences

— Innovations on predictable and patterned literature

- Independent, self-selected writing
  - Dialog journals
  - Writer's workshop
  - Personal response to literature/content area lessons through logs or journals

A general plan to use when writing with these emergent students is:

- Hold discussions prior to writing to tap background knowledge and clarify topic selection.
- Brainstorm words the student will need to write about the topic. Create a word bank or a semantic map for students to draw from as they work more independently.
- Ask student to draft ideas using their best guesses for spelling. If necessary, ask students to leave a blank for words they do not wish to attempt. It will be up to you to encourage fluency. Try not to give in to student demands to spell words.
- Ask the student to read the piece to you or a response group. Provide feedback on the content and allow time for revisions.
- Edit with the student. Use this opportunity to teach one or two writing conventions that you deem appropriate for the student at this time.
- Publish the piece by transcribing the student's words into conventional print.
- Use the writing for further reading experiences with the overage student.

Approaches for Word Attack and Decoding with Younger Students

Word attack and decoding skills are important to a student's becoming a successful independent reader. Nevertheless, we need to consider these skills in the larger context of literacy development. To be literate means to be able to get the meaning out of the printed word for the purpose of getting information and to be able to communicate through the written word. According to Goldenberg (1990), some research has shown that:

> For many children, instructional and other opportunities to learn bottom-up skills make positive contributions to literacy development. There is, therefore, no reason to exclude from beginning literacy programs opportunities for children to learn about letter-sound associations and how letters combine to form syllables and words. (p. 595)

In addition, it is important to remember the role of semantics (context: what makes sense here) and syntax (what sounds right grammatically) in unlocking new words and figuring out the meaning of a passage. Keep this in mind when working with overage emergent literate students. It will be tempting to say to yourself: "This student is so far behind the others that I must teach her the letter sounds right away so she can begin reading." Yet phonics proficiency, in and of itself, cannot produce comprehension of text. Put phonics in perspective.

First, in the previous steps in the reading/writing process found in the beginning pages of this article, we focused on moving from whole to part strategies. The same is true of instruction for word attack skills or phonics. Teaching letters and sounds in isolation is not adequate. Barrera (1983) maintains that:

> Spanish phonics training does not guarantee simple and instant literacy for all children.... It seems imperative, therefore, that teachers in bilingual education make phonics teaching only one dimension of several in Spanish reading instruction. Knowledge of letter-sound relationships is only one of the cueing systems that should be available to the reader as she or he goes about identifying words to get at meaning. (p. 168)

There are many meaningful contexts for the teaching of phonics if you follow the reading/writing process guidelines. A good

DEVELOPING LITERACY

rule of thumb is to base your explicit teaching of phonics on what naturally comes out of the literature. That way, the small bit (phonetic part) is taken out of a whole text and can be put back into its whole while preserving meaning. As well, those are the phonics skills that students will need to be able to read that particular text.

Your attention should be focused on the *contexts* and the *strategies* you will find in your classroom to do explicit teaching of phonics/word-attack skills with overage students. Some are:

◆ Shared reading (using a Big Book or a piece of text the student can see when reading aloud)

◆ Cloze activities (masking a word, leaving the beginning sound/syllable visible, and asking the student to predict the word from the initial sound)

◆ Poems and songs

◆ Reading and rereading

— During reading or rereading of a text that the student is able to read somewhat effectively, do a minilesson on an explicit sound/letter relationship you know will assist the student to read more fluently.

◆ Shared writing (when you are writing aloud)

— When writing in front of the student in a dialog journal or as part of a language experience story, take time to teach a sound/symbol correspondence. For example, in responding to the student's journal writing, you might say after pronouncing the words as you write your response: "Can you find a word here that begins like your name, Lupe? What word do you think that is? That's right, it is *lago*. What sound do you think this letter makes? (Cover all but the *l*.) Can you think of something else that starts like that sound? Yes, Lizet starts like *lago*. How do you think you would write Lizet?" Then, slow down the sounds as you say them and encourage the student to write the sounds he/she hears.

◆ Guided reading (when the student is reading with your guidance)

— Use the cloze technique (covering a word in the text and encouraging the student to predict the word from context, then semantics, then confirm with graphophonics).

— When you read with the students, encourage them to use known words to work out unknown words.

As phonetic elements come up in the natural reading and writing in your classroom, assist the emergent student to make a personal phonics booklet. The student will use this book to write words containing the phonics elements he/she has noticed and studied during the above contexts. Have the student put the words that you have been studying or noticing during reading and writing into this book and use it to make generalizations about other words. The important thing here is that these should be words the student has noticed, not words that you are giving the student.

By attending to the student's daily reading and, especially, what you see in their daily writing, you will be able to note what phonics generalizations the students have mastered. This will guide you in what you need to teach explicitly. As there is no set-in-cement order for teaching sound/letter correspondences, the following should be viewed as just a guide that has come from observing students:

◆ vowels

◆ consonants

◆ blends (*br, cr, fr*, etc.)

◆ digraphs (*ll, rr, ch*)

◆ diphthongs (*ie, ue, ei, au*, etc.)

Instruction should always have meaning for the student and not just follow a prescribed sequence. You will be surprised at the rapid progress of your students if you let them guide you as to what they need to know!

Approaches for Word Attack and Decoding with Older Emergent Readers

As pointed out in the previous section of this article, research with culturally diverse students (Delpit, 1988; Reyes, 1991) suggests that it may be beneficial to modify the whole language process approach to literacy and to more explicitly teach certain aspects of literacy such as decoding skills. The older the student with little or no prior schooling, the "truer" the need exists for direct, explicit instruction since learning must occur at an accelerated pace—often without the advantage of individualized instruction.

The information that follows for helping Spanish readers learn the range of sound/symbol correspondences does not constitute a traditional structural approach to decoding. Rather, it is based on a process of assessment of students during authentic reading and writing, discussions with students about the patterns in sound/symbol relationships, and activities and experiences that reinforce an understanding of the alphabetic principle. This approach organizes the decoding elements into logical chunks. It provides an academic vocabulary (*vowel, blend,* etc.) so that students can speak articulately about relationships between the internal parts of words in identifying them and figuring out their meaning. It promotes inductive thinking and high-level discussion rather than the rote teaching of skills. Overage students in the upper grades are thus provided a vocabulary to talk about printed language so that literacy will include an understanding of *how print functions* in embodying spoken and written language.

It is not suggested here that decoding become a focus for reading instruction, but rather that it be woven in—ten minutes a day, once or twice a week, for example—to discussions motivated by assessment of students' needs and/or the elements that the literature lends itself to focus on.

Upper-grade classrooms generally rely heavily on the assumption that students can read and write at or close to grade-level standards. It is critical that teachers assess the literacy realities of their students, particularly the overage ones, in order to get a true sense of where students are in their literacy development and to design a curriculum that fosters high self-esteem and rapid growth. The assessment process itself should begin with experiences in which students successfully and confidently share their strengths and weaknesses. Ongoing assessment will involve watching the student's interaction with print in the classroom, setting up specific tasks, and discussions with the student.

In addition to the suggestions for assessment provided at the beginning of this article, you might consider including the following when assessing students in the upper grades. Given the limitations of time for both student and teacher, the goal is to identify and teach that which is lacking, not what students already know.

Miscue Analysis Start with a very simple piece of text (just a few words) and listen to the student read. Note the words students are able to read and those that they cannot. Progress with increasingly difficult and lengthy passages to the point where the student clearly is having difficulty. Be sure to praise students for whatever they do successfully.

Writing Analysis Ask students to draw a picture and write a story about their picture. Do one such picture and story as a whole class to provide a model. Analyze their invented spelling to identify conventions they have developed and others they still have not. Depending upon the confidence level of the student regarding writing, give a brief dictation to see the resultant sound/symbol relationships you are concerned about. You will want to include words that have the consonant contrasts (hard and soft *c*, for example) as well as vowel combinations.

Below is an organizational chart for letter-sound correspondences in Spanish that may be useful in analyzing student miscues and writing. The chart organizes elements

DEVELOPING LITERACY

in such a way that you can see instantly the areas of difficulty for students acquiring literacy in Spanish. This will facilitate identifying which elements to teach explicitly. As stated, there will not be time for, or value in, teaching every element. This reality will be important in selecting literature that highlights those elements that need to be covered. The vowels and single consonants that are constant will come easily. Spelling problems may result with the contrasts; use visual memory cues to help students learn and remember how to spell the contrasts. Blends and digraphs will require a few discussions and focused activities (context rich, not skill-and-drill type). Understanding the vowel combinations will help students decode and spell and will be necessary to master accentuation.

In working with the literature, incorporate the suggestions provided earlier in this article to develop story comprehension and provide for authentic reader response. This should happen *before* moving into decoding and other word-attack skills. When students are familiar with the selection as a whole, assign them small passages to break into lines and into words. Cutting sentences into words to scramble and unscramble will help students see word divisions. You might want to picture-code some of the words to help students initially.

LA CORRESPONDENCIA ENTRE LAS LETRAS Y LOS SONIDOS

LAS CONSONANTES

CONSONANTES	GRUPOS CONSONÁNTICOS	DIAGRAMAS
m l ch p rr v t ñ z d b n f s y w k j h ll	br bl cr cl fr fl gr gl pr pl tr dr	ll rr ch
Contrastes y - ll k - q - c rr - r j - g - x n - ñ b - v z - s - x - c h (a e i o u)	tl	

LAS VOCALES

SINGULARES ABIERTAS CERRADAS	HIATOS	DIPTONGOS TRIPTONGOS
a e o i u (y)	ae ea oa ee ao eo oe ie ía ío íu úe úa úo úi eí aí oí aú oú eú	ie ia io iu iai ue ua uo ui iai ei ai oi iei au ou uei eu ay ey oy

From *Making the Transition from Spanish to English* by Robin Avelar La Salle, Robert Calfee, and Carrol Moran (Pajaro Valley Unified School District, California). Reproduced by permission.

Have students look for and discuss similarities and differences in words. As with any field of study, they will need to know specific related terminology in order to discuss internal patterns in words. CAUTION: The recommendation that students acquire this terminology (*vowel, blend,* etc.) should not be construed as a return to outdated structural approaches to teaching decoding. If students don't have the term *vowel combinations*, they will have an impossible time trying to compare words and make generalizations regarding spelling and grammatical patterns. To impart this explicit academic vocabulary, build on a linguistic base that is experientially meaningful (and ideally interesting and fun) for the students. For example, to help students understand the concept and term *vowel*, use a familiar song such as "Una mosca parada en la pared" and have students watch what happens to each other's mouths as they change the vowels to "Unu muscu purudu un lu purud." This visual activity will help students understand why in Spanish *a, o,* and *u* are called strong, or "open," vowels and *e* and *i* are called weak, or "closed," vowels. That information will be important when students learn the rules for accentuation in Spanish.

When students are beginning to write words that have blends, you may notice that initially they only record one of the letters in the blend. This observation should prompt you to look for a story or poem with words that have blends in order to have a literary base from which to focus student attention on blends. In working with other decoding elements, use mnemonic devices to help students remember (for example, *Uso* c *en* círculo *porque* c *casi es un círculo*).

Almost all students—including the above-grade-level readers—can benefit from discussions about letter-sound relationships. This meta-understanding of reading will help them when they all read in English, which has a much more complex decoding system. Including all students in at least some of these discussions will allow overage students to be part of a group that is learning something new about literacy.

Conclusion

Emerging literacy is one of the most exciting phenomena to watch develop. Literacy is the key to success, both in the educational system and in the pursuit of lifelong learning. Celebrate with your overage student each of his/her accomplishments toward becoming literate. The process will be rewarding for you and your other students as you see, hear, and read progress towards opening up the world of literacy.

ABOUT THE AUTHORS

Carrol Moran is an educational consultant specializing in bilingual education (for Spanish and Portuguese speakers) and second language literacy. She has worked in education for 20 years, teaching preschool through college levels. During her 14 years with the Pajaro Valley School District in Watsonville, California, she worked as a classroom teacher, reading and language specialist, and resource and mentor teacher.

Carrol is the author of several books, including: *The Keys to the Classroom: A Teacher's Guide to the First Month of School*; *The Bridge: Spanish to English*, a guide to teaching literacy in a bilingual setting; and *Colors of the Earthquake*, a rhyming book illustrated by children about the Loma Prieta earthquake. In addition she has written curriculum for kindergarten through eighth grade in math, social studies, science, and language arts and writes adaptations of curriculum for students acquiring English for major textbook publishing companies. Presently, Carrol is a Title VII Fellow in Stanford's doctoral program in Language, Literacy and Culture.

Judy Stobbe (BA University of California, Santa Cruz; MA in Education, University of San Francisco) has worked in bilingual education since 1976 as a classroom teacher, resource teacher, and teacher trainer. As a mentor teacher and Supervisor of Teacher Education at the University of California, Santa Cruz, she has worked with many bilingual teachers to improve the quality of education for students acquiring English.

Currently she teaches at Alianza School, a magnet bilingual school in the Pajaro Valley Unified School District, Watsonville, California. She is a sought-after educational consultant and free-lance writer in the areas of emergent literacy, second language acquisition, and bilingual education. She coauthored *The Keys to the Classroom: A Teacher's Guide to the First Month of School*, as well as many articles, curriculum guides, and classroom materials.

Josefina Villamil Tinajero is a noted authority on bilingual education. Josie is Associate Professor of Bilingual Education at The University of Texas at El Paso, past president of the Texas Council of Reading and the Bilingual Child, and director of the nationally acclaimed "Mother-Daughter Program" at UTEP. Her additional interests include emergent literacy, integrated language arts instruction, cooperative learning, teacher preparation, and links between home, school, and community.

Ignacio Tinajero's educational experience extends for over 20 years and includes responsibilities as a recruiter, rehabilitation counselor, physical educator, seven years as an assistant principal, and the last three in the Ysleta Independent School District, El Paso, Texas, as a bilingual teacher for "at-risk" students. He is presently at Ramona Elementary as a fifth- and sixth-grade teacher for recent immigrants. His major concern as a teacher is to effectively transmit affection and foster a positive self-concept as a basis for students' active participation in a process that promotes growth for the parent-teacher-student partnership. In doing so, it is his desire to offer our society better human elements to help transform it into one that is more humane and just.

REFERENCES

Atwell, N. (1987). *In the middle: Writing, reading, and learning with adolescents*. Portsmouth, NH: Boynton/Cook.

Barrera, R. B. (1983). Bilingual reading in the primary grades: Some questions about questionable views and practices. In T. H. Escobedo (Ed.), *Early childhood bilingual education: A Hispanic perspective*. New York: Teachers College Press.

Cummins, J. (1989). *Empowering minority students*. Sacramento, CA: California Association for Bilingual Education.

Delpit, L. D. (1988). The silence dialogue: Power and pedagogy in educating other people's children. *The Harvard Educational Review*, vol. 58, no. 3, pp. 280–98.

Goldenberg, C. (1990, October). Research directions: Beginning literacy instruction for Spanish-speaking children. *Language Arts*, vol. 67, pp. 590–97.

Igoa, C. (1993). Second language literacy and immigrant children: The inner world of the immigrant child. In J. V. Tinajero and A. F. Ada (Eds.), *The power of two languages: Literacy and biliteracy for Spanish-speaking students*. New York: Macmillan/McGraw-Hill School Publishing Company.

Krashen, S., and Biber, D. (1988). On course: Bilingual education's success in California. Sacramento, CA: California Association for Bilingual Education.

La Salle, R. A., Calfee, R., and Moran, C. (1987). *Making the transition from Spanish to English: The historical-structural method to decoding-spelling*. Unpublished handbook for bilingual teachers, developed under the auspices of READ in conjunction with the Pajaro Valley Schools Mentor Program.

Macedo, D. (1991). English only: The tongue-typing of America. *Journal of Education*, Boston University, Vol. 173, no. 2.

Reyes, M. (1991). A process approach to literacy instruction for Spanish-speaking students: A best fit. In E. H. Hiebert, *Literacy for a diverse society: Perspectives, practices, and policies*. New York: Teachers College Press.

INNOVATIVE Assessment IN Traditional Settings

JoAnn Canales
University of North Texas

Portfolios, authentic assessment, student observations, and performance-based assessments are all commonly used jargon among today's educators. In part, this is an adverse reaction to the skills-based testing that so many claim is an inaccurate and biased picture of students' actual level of academic achievement. It's also a reaction to the need for alternative assessment measures that more closely reflect the innovative classroom practices intended to develop responsible, articulate, and critical-thinking students.

Undertaking innovative assessment practices is much like asking classroom teachers to undertake research initiatives. Like researchers, they will be responsible for determining the important questions to ask about student performance, the corresponding data to support the evidence, the data collection format and procedures, and the analysis and interpretation of the data. Unlike researchers, they will be subject to a much more collaborative effort that requires all of the participants in the educational community to have a common understanding of the "research" efforts because of the implications of the findings—namely, student achievement and academic progress.

Toward a Common Definition

The dilemma in attaining a common understanding of alternative assessment strategies is multifold. First and foremost, is the issue of *definition* (Zessoules & Gardner, 1991; Meyer, 1992). A common language that is to transcend classroom level instruction requires common terminology with common definitions. Second, the classroom instruction must correlate to the new assessment methodology, both of which require considerable staff development. Third, the subjectivity inherent in atraditional assessment practices must be minimized. This requires that teachers work collaboratively at the campus and district level to

DEVELOPING LITERACY

standardize the procedures for documenting academic progress. Fourth, the innovative procedures must be in concert with the reporting practices of the district. This will require that the district either totally revamp the reporting system to parents or that the innovative practices be infused into the traditional reporting system. Either of these approaches necessitate many ongoing parent training/sharing sessions to acquaint them with any new assessment practices implemented. Because these practices will be such a departure from parents' experiences, many of them may be initially confused, bewildered, or even hostile about the purpose or the wisdom of such practices.

Therefore, in the interest of minimizing change and newness, a gradual transition from traditional to atraditional assessment and reporting practices is strongly recommended until all of the stakeholders affected are comfortable with the approach, the strategies, and the results of the new accountability process.

Thus, this article will define and describe three innovative assessment measures (IAMs) that not only validate innovative classroom practices but also serve to document students' academic progress. These IAMs include portfolios, performance-based assessments, and student observations. Additionally, a process for translating a student's score on the IAMs to a traditional reporting format will also be detailed.

Innovative Assessment Practices

PORTFOLIOS

This assessment strategy can best be defined as a collection of works produced by the student. Traditionally, this collection of works usually resulted in "the notebook" that was divided by tabs into sections labeled classwork, homework, quizzes, and tests, and was supposed to be a compilation of ALL work accomplished by the student during the year.

Unlike "the notebook," the portfolio contains only a predetermined set of examples of student work accomplished during a predetermined time period. This seemingly simplistic process must first address several questions at three different levels. The questions include:

Who makes the decisions?

What will it look like?

When will it be accomplished?

Where will it be kept?

How will it count?

The three levels include the district, the campus, and the classroom. A graphic representation of the interaction between these questions and the three levels is presented on the following page. An elaboration of the points contained in the chart is presented below.

Who Makes the Decisions? Central and essential to an effective assessment practice is a collective understanding and decision-making process. This process, in turn, will ensure uniform standards within a common entity. Many would argue that this uniformity and standardization process negates the very essence of the flexibility and creativity inherent in authentic assessment practices.

Regardless of the philosophical positions and beliefs present, there are certain realities prevalent in an educational community that require a common framework for assessing student learning. Some of those realities include:

- a common core of academic standards that may be statewide or districtwide,
- the mobility of students within a district, and
- the accountability standards being established at the state level.

To achieve the standardization necessary and yet maintain the flexibility desired, decision makers may wish to utilize the inverted triangle approach. This approach enables a broad framework to be developed at the district level and allows for additional specificity to be developed at the campus and classroom levels based on the needs of the respective population of students. The role of the decision makers at the district level is to determine the parameters for the authentic assessment practices in the following areas: types of practices, time frames for collecting the data, resources for managing the data, and categories

Chart 1

	District	Campus	Classroom
Who makes the decisions?	Campus and district representatives and parents	Grade and subject representatives and parents	Teachers and students
What will it look like?	Define the parameters—disciplines, categories, number of items, the quality of the items.	Refine the district parameters, periodically review their utility and appropriateness; discuss the nature and contents with parents.	Adapt the parameters.
When will it be accomplished?	Define the time frame.	Formulate the implementation of the assessment.	Adhere to the time frame.
Where will it be kept?	Provide appropriate resources to facilitate storage, maintenance, etc.	Provide appropriate support to facilitate documentation.	Allocate space and access to the portfolios to facilitate individual student responsibility for maintaining the portfolios.
How will it count?	Develop a common accountability system for portfolios vs. grading policy and define the parameters for the system.	Refine the parameters; train the faculty and inform parents regarding accountability/ grading system.	Adapt the parameters and inform students of accountability/grading system.

of criteria for analyzing and interpreting the data. The role of the campus level decision makers is to further refine these parameters based on the campus activities and the student population. The role of the classroom teacher is to adapt the parameters to fit the subject matter and the makeup of the classroom population.

What Will It Look Like? Individuals in the "arts" have utilized the portfolio system extensively. They include samples of their best works that typify their expertise and their level of accomplishment, as well as their potential. For classroom purposes, the decision makers first need to consider the purpose of the portfolio. Some salient questions requiring consideration and consensus include:

◆ Should the portfolio include *only* a student's best work?

◆ What kind of work should be included, e.g., writing samples, self-analytical reflective audiotapes, performance videotapes accompanied by peer and self-critiques, teacher observation checklists/narratives?

◆ What criteria would be used to determine a student's best work?

◆ Who would decide which work was best—the teacher or the student?

◆ Should the portfolio include a sampling of a student's work over time, e.g., beginning of semester/year, midsemester/year, end of semester/year?

◆ Should the sampling include all stages of the final product?

Following is an example of one district-level scenario:

> A portfolio will consist of a sampling of the student's work. It will include four (4) samples taken during September, January, and May. Three will be thematic unit products. The fourth will be the student's selection. This piece can be accomplished at any time during the year. The remaining decisions about the contents of the portfolio should be made at the campus and classroom levels.

When Will It Be Accomplished? A specific time frame periodically interspersed throughout the academic term is important to ensure comparability of all students' level of achievement. A two-week time period is recommended at each data collection point. This two-week window allows sufficient time for students to accomplish a writing process, for students to make up missed work, or for the usual interruptions common in a dynamic workplace.

Minimally, three data collection points should be identified with the first data point serving as the baseline. Additional data points would include a midyear point and an end-of-the-year point. Ideally, if there is districtwide uniformity with respect to thematic unit organization and implementation, work samples should be obtained and included in the portfolio for each theme covered. Various forms of authentic assessment should be considered, e.g., performance-based tasks, observation checklists, reflective audiotapes, writing samples.

Where Will It Be Kept? Maintaining these portfolios can be an arduous task unless appropriate storage containers, file folders, and labels are available. The district should consider purchasing these in bulk so that all teachers and students can have access to the necessary materials. Such access will help ensure that students learn responsibility for their maintenance. In some instances, if the grading will be shared between a language arts teacher and a math, science, or history teacher, students will need to transport them back and forth in order to receive the appropriate credit.

How Will It Count? Defining the criteria and the value of each criterion is the final step in the decision-making process. At the district level, parameters need to be determined for the criteria that will be included in the "grading" process and its corresponding value with respect to the district's reporting format.

Priestly (1992) has developed numerous formats for documenting students' authentic work. Among his suggestions is a form for evaluating portfolios that address three categories of criteria—contents, attributes, and other. It serves as an example of the kinds of parameters that could be established at the district level. The category *Other* would enable the campus and classroom decision makers to refine and adapt the form to meet their individual needs.

In the case of limited English proficient students, the *Other* category should include opportunities for teachers to rate students' linguistic competencies in each of the five areas of communication skills—listening, speaking, reading, writing, and nonverbal.

Following is a modified sample of the Portfolio Evaluation Form adapted to reflect the progress of students in bilingual programs.

Name: _____   Language of Instruction: _____
Subject: _____   Date: _____

PORTFOLIO EVALUATION FORM

	Needs Work	Fair	Good	Excellent
CONTENTS				
1. Completeness. Meets all requirements.	1	2	3	4
2. Variety. Includes a variety of pieces.	1	2	3	4
3. Focus/Purpose. Meets intended purposes.	1	2	3	4
ATTRIBUTES				
4. Effort. Demonstrates concerted effort.	1	2	3	4
5. Quality. Illustrates appropriate level of quality.	1	2	3	4
6. Creativity. Shows imagination and creative ideas.	1	2	3	4
7. Risk Taking. Takes risks in creating/choosing works that go beyond minimum expectations.	1	2	3	4
8. Growth. Shows improvement.	1	2	3	4
9. Reflection. Shows signs of personal reflection.	1	2	3	4
10. Self-Evaluation. Shows awareness of strengths and weaknesses.	1	2	3	4
LINGUISTIC COMPETENCE				
11. Listening Skills. Shows appropriate use of posture and behaviors.	1	2	3	4
12. Speaking Skills. Demonstrates native fluency.	1	2	3	4
13. Reading Skills. Illustrates appropriate level of quality.	1	2	3	4
14. Writing Skills. Illustrates appropriate level of quality.	1	2	3	4
15. Nonverbal Skills. Shows appropriate use of gestures and facial expressions.	1	2	3	4
TEACHER'S COMMENTS				
16. _____	1	2	3	4
17. _____	1	2	3	4
STUDENT'S COMMENTS				
18. _____	1	2	3	4
19. _____	1	2	3	4

TOTAL Points = _____   76 total possible points (4 × 19)
Equivalent Grade = _____   19 minimum number of points (1 × 19)

Range of Points	Grade
64 – 76	A
51 – 63	B
38 – 50	C
19 – 37	D

Adapted from Priestly, Michael. *Performance Assessment Handbook.* New York: Macmillan/McGraw-Hill Publishing Company, 1992.

DEVELOPING LITERACY

PERFORMANCE-BASED ASSESSMENTS

Performance-based assessments can be the basis for the ratings in the portfolio evaluation form described in the previous section. These measures can assess oral and written products of individual students. In other words, teachers can observe students as they work independently or in groups during the final week of the assignment. This should give students ample time to employ the skills to be assessed. Further, it will give the teacher ample time to observe students as they accomplish their tasks.

These performance-based assessments should include the three categories of criteria central to programs designed for limited English proficient children. The categories of criteria include academic competencies, linguistic competencies, and affective competencies (Canales, 1992; Mercado & Romero, in press). The academic criteria can be drawn from state, district, local, or textbook stated objectives regarding the salient content to be acquired. In an integrated unit team teaching situation, the academic (or cognitive) criteria could be scored by the science, history, or math teachers. The linguistic criteria could be scored by the language arts and language development teacher, and the affective criteria could be scored by the student's homeroom teacher.

On the following page is a sample form to assess performance. It is called a Competence Evaluation Form because the teacher is asked to rate the student's level of competency on specific skills.

As with the Portfolio Assessment Form, the ratings are converted to a point system that can be subsequently converted to a traditional grading system. Also, as with the Portfolio Assessment Form, the specific criteria within each category should be defined at the district level, refined at the campus level, and adapted at the classroom level.

STUDENT OBSERVATIONS

As teachers learn to facilitate learning for students and organize classroom tasks so as to allow for more collaborative group work versus strictly direct teaching or independent seat work, student observations will become more feasible. This form of assessment differs from the performance-based assessment in two distinct ways. First, it is accomplished as students interact in a collaborative group setting. Second, this type of assessment should be ongoing, i.e., formative in nature. Systematic documentation of students' behaviors, as they are actively engaged in learning, should also be included in a portfolio. Such assessments are valuable for several reasons. They:

1. communicate to students that all objectives—academic, linguistic, and affective—have value;

2. validate time, energy, and resources spent on developing good productive citizenship skills, e.g., interpersonal, self-concept, and communicative skills;

3. enable individual students to reflect on their personal as well as their cognitive growth;

4. enable facilitators of learning (teachers) to become more familiar with their students and their needs;

5. provide a means of documenting student behavior in group work; and

6. assist in decision making regarding program placement, i.e., tutorial, English as a Second Language, Bilingual Education, Special Education.

Name: _____ Language of Instruction: _____
Subject: _____ Date: _____

COMPETENCE EVALUATION FORM

	Needs Work	Fair	Good	Excellent
ACADEMIC				
1. Organizes information.	1	2	3	4
2. Summarizes and draws conclusions.	1	2	3	4
3. Makes inferences.	1	2	3	4
4. Compares and contrasts.	1	2	3	4
LINGUISTIC				
5. Follows directions (listening).	1	2	3	4
6. Retells what is read (speaking).	1	2	3	4
7. Uses appropriate vocabulary (writing).	1	2	3	4
8. Uses decoding strategies (reading).	1	2	3	4
AFFECTIVE				
9. Listens to others' comments during discussion.	1	2	3	4
10. Speaks in turn.	1	2	3	4
11. Offers constructive suggestions during group work.	1	2	3	4
12. Analyzes own work reflectively.	1	2	3	4
TEACHER'S COMMENTS				
13. _____	1	2	3	4
14. _____	1	2	3	4
STUDENT'S COMMENTS				
15. _____	1	2	3	4
16. _____	1	2	3	4

TOTAL Points = _____   64 total possible points (4 × 16)

Equivalent Grade = _____   16 minimum number of points (1 × 16)

Range of Points	**Grade**
53 – 64	A
41 – 52	B
29 – 40	C
16 – 28	D

A Student Observation Form should reflect specific defined behaviors. These behaviors should be explained to students and students should be aware of the assessment instrument and the implications of their behavior ratings on their individual and group grade.

DEVELOPING LITERACY

Following is an example of how an observation form can be used for group and individual grading purposes.

| Name: _____ | Language of Instruction: _____ |
| Subject(s): _____ | Date: _____ |

STUDENT OBSERVATION FORM

	Student #1	Student #2	Student #3	Student #4	TOTAL
Makes eye contact					
Extends thinking of peers					
Utilizes praise appropriately					
Takes turns speaking					
Contributes to group task					
TOTAL					Sum of either

NOTE: The shaded cell should be the sum total of either the row or column labeled TOTAL. Users of this form may wish to verify their addition by separately totaling the row and column labeled TOTAL.

These forms can be completed either by the teacher or by individual students serving as "Performance Observers" for the day. Students in this role should not be included in the overall team scores or it may contribute to bias on the part of the observer.

Individual students receive a mark for every time they are observed engaging in one of the specified behaviors. The frequency with which each behavior is observed in *all* students determines the corresponding grade. For example, if each group member is observed accomplishing all of the behaviors three (3) or more times during the group activity, then the group's total point score is 60+.

    3   occurrences of behavior
× 5   (# of behaviors)
× 4   (# of students in group)
= 60+ occurrences of behaviors by the group collectively

A midpoint of acceptable group behavior might be a total point score of 32.

    2 occurrences of behavior
× 4 (4 out of 5 behaviors)
× 4 (# of students in group)
= 32 occurrences of behaviors by the group collectively

A low point of group behavior might be a total point score of 12.

    1 occurrence of behavior

× 3 (3 out of 5 behaviors)

× 4 (# of students in group)

= 12 occurrences of behaviors by the group collectively

A range of points could then be determined to correspond to the use of the traditional grading system. In order for each group member to get a specific grade, the collective team score would need to be within the following range:

A = 60+ pts.

B = 32–59 pts.

C = 12–31 pts.

D = below 12

In this particular example, all of the skills to be observed are affective. These can be varied to focus on either academic, linguistic, or affective skills, or the skills can be a combination of the three. Of primary concern is that they reflect the specific behaviors important to appropriately accomplish the activity/task.

There are two questions frequently asked regarding students' participation in group work. One concerns a student's *unwillingness* to participate in group work. The second question concerns the issue of penalizing a group because of one "freeloader."

It is not unreasonable to expect that some, if not all, students will occasionally prefer to work independently and will simply "not feel like" group work. It is unreasonable, however, to allow this kind of behavior without a corresponding consequence. After all, the effectiveness of a workplace is dependent on the effectiveness of the interdynamic nature of its workers. While we may not always *feel like* being cooperative, learning to work cooperatively in groups is very important if students are to become functional, contributing members of society.

Although I am not suggesting that *all* work must be group work, one way to ensure participation in group work is to let students know that they have the option to not participate. However, there is a limitation on the number of options that can be exercised during a given period. Once these options are exercised, students are required to participate in group work as assigned. This is the equivalent to "personal leave days" in the workplace. The number of options should be determined by the teacher, or collectively with students, at the beginning of the school year and explicitly stated and posted visibly in the classroom.

In response to the second question, teachers should not penalize a group due to the behaviors of the freeloader. The range of points will need to be redone if the number of group members is altered. However, the "freeloader" should not receive credit that was not earned. If a student refuses to participate and "carry his/her weight," alternative measures such as teacher/student conferencing or counseling may be required.

DEVELOPING LITERACY

INNOVATIVE ASSESSMENT PRACTICES AND TRADITIONAL REPORTING PRACTICES

As illustrated in the previous sections, it is possible to utilize alternative assessment measures in the classroom and still maintain a traditional reporting format. Extensive use of such alternative assessment measures will require a form that readily summarizes the individual measures.

Following is a summary grading chart modified from an example provided by Priestly (1992). It facilitates record keeping and can be kept in a student's portfolio, a record/notebook, or in a teacher's file for easy access. Decision makers will want to specify if the form should be subject- or theme-specific. The organization of the instructional delivery system should inform this decision.

Name: _____ Language of Instruction: _____
Subject/Theme: _____ Date: _____

SUMMARY GRADING CHART

Innovative Assessment Measure	Grade	Notes
Average Grade		

Grading Legend

A = 95
B = 85
C = 75
D = 65

Comments:

Adapted from Priestly, Michael. *Performance Assessment Handbook: A Guide for Language Arts Teachers*. New York: Macmillan/McGraw-Hill Publishing Company, 1992.

The grade/numerical equivalents found in the section labeled *Grading Legend* should correspond to the reporting/grading policy already established by the district-level decision makers.

CONCLUSION

Although many questions may surface among statisticians regarding the validity and reliability of such a practice, the suggestions provided in this chapter are constructive for several reasons.

First, they offer classroom practitioners a way to document observable behaviors. Second, they reduce the amount of subjectivity in the assessment process by specifically stating the performance and grading criteria. Third, they offer students and their parents specific information regarding their performance not available from traditional grading practices. The impact of this information will be more meaningful if the forms used for the IAMs are written in the language of the home as well as in the language of instruction. Fourth, it enables the traditional promotion practices to remain in place. Otherwise, decision makers would have to wrestle with yet another major issue—that of determining how many skills and which skills warrant promotion versus retention.

Finally, as long as accountability is in the forefront of the educational scene, assessment results will greatly influence nonpractitioners' perceptions of the schooling process and thus assessment practices will drive instruction. Alternative ways must be sought to make the search for appropriate innovative assessment measures a productive journey—productive for students, productive for educators, and productive for society.

About the Author

Dr. JoAnn Canales is an assistant professor at the University of North Texas. Currently she is working with inner-city schools serving Hispanic students in Dallas, Texas, as part of a collaborative effort between the university, the public schools, the public sector, and the private sector. She is a specialist in curriculum and instruction especially related to special populations of students. She has worked extensively in the areas of program evaluation and student assessment, both cognitive and linguistic. In addition to her professional work, JoAnn is also a very active community volunteer as well as an advocate for Hispanic children.

References

Canales, J. (1992). Innovative practices in the identification of limited English proficient students. In *Proceedings of the second national research symposium on limited English proficient (LEP) student issues: Focus on evaluation and measurement,* vol. 2, pp. 89–122. Washington, DC: United States Department of Education Office of Bilingual Education and Minority Languages Affairs (OBEMLA) August, 1992.

Mercado, C. I., and Romero, M. (in press). Pupil assessment in bilingual education. In *NSSE yearbook on bilingual education.*

Meyer, C. A. (1992, May). What's the difference between *authentic* and *performance* assessment? In *Education Leadership,* vol. 49, no. 8, pp. 39–41.

Priestly, M. (1992). *Performance assessment handbook.* New York: Macmillan/McGraw-Hill Publishing Company.

Zessoules, R., and Gardner, H. (1991). Authentic assessment: Beyond the buzzword. In Perrone, Vito (Ed.), *Expanding student assessment,* pp. 47–71. Alexandria, VA: Association for Supervision and Curriculum Development.

Suggested Reading

Bernstein, D. K. Assessing children with limited English proficiency: Current perspectives. *Topics in Language Disorders,* vol. 9, no. 3, pp. 15–20.

Chittenden, E. (1991). Authentic assessment, evaluation, and documentation of student performance. In Perrone, Vito (Ed.), *Expanding student assessment,* pp. 22–31. Alexandria, VA: Association for Supervision and Curriculum Development.

Fishman, J. A. (1972). The sociology of language. In Giglioli, P. P. (Ed.), *Language and social context.* Great Britain: Penguin Books.

Haney, W. (1991). We must take care: Fitting assessments to functions. In Perrone, Vito (Ed.), *Expanding student assessment,* pp. 142–63. Alexandria, VA: Association for Supervision and Curriculum Development.

Maeroff, G. I. (1991, December). Assessing alternative assessment. *Phi Delta Kappan,* vol. 73, no. 4, pp. 272–81.

Tchudi, S. (1991). *Planning and assessing the curriculum in English language arts.* Alexandria, VA: Association for Supervision and Curriculum Development.

Part III
CREATING A CULTURE OF READING

Reading Begins in the Crib

Eleanor Thonis
Wheatland School District, California

When infants are born, they greet their new surroundings with the birth cry. This forerunner of language fills those in attendance with wonder, joy, and gratitude. The cry sets breathing in motion and begins the impressive process of taking in oxygen and clearing out carbon dioxide from the lungs. Newborns take an active role in ridding themselves of the mucous in various bodily cavities and immediately dedicate their energies to the control of their new environment and their parents. During neonates' most welcome wakeful, but quiet, time they practice using their sense organs to provide information about the world into which they have been thrust. These sensory data form the basis for understanding and interpreting an overwhelming amount of stimuli that will assault tactile, visual, auditory, olfactory, and gustatory messages as conveyed through these channels. The remarkable pilgrimage of growth begins.

This article suggests that many visual, motor, and perceptual abilities nurtured in infancy are harbingers of success as children meet the challenge of becoming literate during their schooling.

Movement

While infants are taking in the many sensations of touch, sight, sound, taste, and smell, they are making exciting discoveries about themselves. They hold their heads upright, move their arms, raise their legs, reach for objects, roll over, follow voices, and grasp toys. They continue to delight everyone with their burgeoning skills. Human learning is rooted in movement. If humans could not move, they could not learn. Infants move the tongue, the nose, the mouth, the throat, and the eyes. They use the air as they coo, babble, gurgle, and grunt. They track their eyes from right to the left, from left to right, and from top to bottom. They stop and fix their visual attention on objects that capture their interest. They move their hands, their arms, and their fingers as they develop the muscular strength to hold and to release objects that excite them. These incredibly complex movements require an integration and motor control of their eyes, hands, brains, muscles, and central nervous system.

At first, the neonate's space is highly restricted. It is comforting to be wrapped snugly in a blanket and to be held safely in the mother's arms. In time, the infant's space expands and offers new experiences beyond the confinement of the crib. This moving, changing, thriving, little human learns about a larger area of space in which discoveries are to be made. Babies find out where they are in relation to the space around them. They search for and locate the mother or caretaker and consider the distance. To understand spatial relationships, infants focus their attention on visual details, noting the mother's face or recognizing her voice. Early exploration allows for the development of spatial comprehension that will ultimately lead to an awareness of orientation and directionality.

Language Begins

The noises that envelop new infants are assorted, undifferentiated stimuli. They hear doors opening, windows closing, telephones ringing, footsteps shuffling, people talking, and other sounds. Though sounds of all kinds may reach their ears, infants do not make any distinction among these sounds. Then, infants recognize sounds made by humans and hear human speech sounds. What a lovely discovery! They begin to sort and to sift, as they hear again and again the reassuring sounds of the mother's voice. They associate that voice with the comfort, security, and warmth so essential to their survival. Mere footsteps coming down the hall are followed by changes in clothing, warm baths, food, loving arms, and hugs. The message in the mother's voice is one of tenderness and affection. They enjoy listening for this event in their day's routine. They become increasingly aware of the melody, the rhythm, the intonation, and the patterns of their mother's language.

By the age of 16 weeks, infants laugh out loud, vocalize, and babble. They are becoming independent learners. They cry; they hiccup; they yawn; they sneeze; they suck; they swallow; and they smile. They keep their caregivers highly entertained as well as astounded by their rapid growth in physical, social, and adaptive behaviors.

Language responses are limited and delightfully unintelligible. The early precursors of speech are the cooing, vocalizing, and babbling. As air goes out of the lungs over the vocal cords, infants begin cooing purely by chance when the random movements of the speech mechanism create these sounds. Theorists suggest that cooing is *not* learned behavior. Infants don't have to work at cooing; it just happens. Cooing is something that *all* infants appear to enjoy. Cooing is not considered an early attempt at communication but rather a playful activity that infants engage in and adults around them find amusing.

Babbling is another enjoyable pastime for infants. In playful practice, infants increase the number of sounds they can make. Babbling, like cooing, has no meaning. Between the third to the eighth month, babbling may slow down or may continue to absorb little ones. Infants amuse themselves in this manner, smiling and laughing at the sound of their own voice. Often adults interpret babbling as a social act, but cooing and babbling are not primarily efforts to talk to adults. These noises are not considered speech. Later, as speech does emerge, the sounds of the cooing and babbling most likely will show little relationship to the speech patterns of the language communities into which infants have been born. Despite this fact, cooing and babbling must be appreciated for the enjoyment they provide and for the verbal practice in the movement needed for expressive language. Babies have the wonderful capacity to increase the quantity and variety of sounds in an infinite number of languages.

An especially interesting characteristic of this prelanguage period is the infant's development of inflection and pitch. Adults are often very amused at the conversational tone of the infant's cooing and babbling. It is almost as if the baby is about to make an important comment that is relevant to an ongoing discussion. When adults respond with encouragement by smiling, patting, nodding, or agreeing, infants learn the social function of language. Thus, babbling can serve as a value in social growth as well.

Language and Thinking

A critical point in the development of the thinking skills of very young children is when they are capable of representational thought. This ability to think about objects that are not physically present begins at about the age of 18 months to 2 years. Prior to this stage in growth, infants do not know that objects continue to exist if they cannot see them any longer. After they are able to understand the concept of object constancy, children are then capable of using symbols to represent what is not actually present. Following this preoperational milestone, children move on to a concrete operational phase in which they begin to understand categories, classifications, and other mental operations. Children's thinking and their language advance together as they deal with concrete realities, constructing meanings and seeing relationships.

Among the many significant influences that shape children's language and thinking are the opportunities for encounters with a stimulating and supportive environment that will nurture and enhance both. Given good physical health and sensible parents, young children are growing in their pre-reading abilities and are acquiring the sensory-motor skills, the perceptual awareness, the conceptual background, the spatial orientation, and the interest in language to be successful listeners, speakers, and thinkers.

The First Language

In response to specific social and cultural environments, children attach meanings to the sounds around them. As they become aware of objects, events, and people in their homes and neighborhood, these personal realities are labeled and stored for retrieval in the speech symbols of their families and neighbors. When productive language occurs, children generate and imitate the sounds and structure of those who care for them. As children discover the power of words, they know what others are saying and can frame responses so that hearers will understand, too. These magical exchanges are possible because speakers and hearers share a mutually understood symbol system. The boundaries of language and thought expand with abundant experience and increased language opportunities. By age five, children are considered ready and able to take on the grand adventure of learning to read and write. It is reasonable to assume that these boys and girls will read the language of their families. They have enjoyed hundreds of hours of language stimulation accompanied by and made sensible through the language of the home. As children have named objects, events, and people, developed perceptual constants, recognized concepts, learned functional relationships, realized certain fixed properties, and searched for an understanding of their world, they have used the language of their home to mediate meaning. They have also labeled and stored these meanings in schemata that are available for retrieval through that home language. It follows then, to the extent school resources are available, children should read first in the language they know, the one for which they have schemata, vocabulary, and control of language structure.

When children are English speakers and are placed in an instructional program that has been designed for English-speaking students, the language of both students and program is consistent with constructs of prior knowledge and of human development. When children are not speakers of English and when there is no language and literacy program available to them in their home language, then some serious effort must be made to modify existing instruction. School districts will have difficult decisions to make. Changes in curriculum, time, staff, methods, and materials are indicated. The nature of change and its implications for improvements in teaching and in learning have to be decided at the local level. The need for change, however, is self-evident.

Appropriate Instruction

As children approach school age, they expect that going to school means learning to read and write. These tasks become the educational objectives of early childhood instruction. The question of appropriate instruction for language minority children centers on the language to be used in the classroom. Language is content, but it also carries content. If children do not understand the language of the teacher and if the teacher does not understand the language of children, both are at a very serious disadvantage in the teaching and learning efforts. Two concerns challenge schools as they plan for an effective and appropriated curriculum: (1) providing the strong, solid programs in oral and written English and (2) retaining the cultural and linguistic legacy of children. The continuing debates over the position of English in the instructional plan distract the schools and drain their energy. There is no argument. Of course, non-English speakers must acquire excellent skills and content in English. Children must have rich and relevant opportunities for becoming fluent and literate for participating fully in the English-speaking community.

For children who have come from homes where a language other than English is used, instruction should begin with their strengths. Five-year-olds are competent learners who have already taken in a great deal of information about their physical and their psychological world. They have used their senses and have interpreted their perceptions, concepts, images, sounds, and symbols at a level commensurate with their opportunities and their encounters with specific environments. They possess an orientation to the space around them and are on their way to understanding directionality. They are improving in their abilities to use the tools of the classroom—to grasp pencils and crayons, to hold paintbrushes, to manipulate other art media, to construct towers with blocks, and to follow rhythmical musical patterns. In addition, five-year-olds are developing the social skills for working in small groups, for establishing habits of listening, for following directions, and for behaving appropriately in the school setting. Many of these essential skills have grown from their very early beginnings as infants—cooing, babbling, and enjoying sociability.

When the school community consists of large numbers of children who speak the same language as in the case of Spanish, Chinese, Vietnamese, or other language groups, there are good reasons for beginning instruction in reading and writing in the home language. A rationale for this approach follows:

- Language has been acquired in the family and carries many personal feelings and memories.

- Recognition and acceptance of children's home language nurtures their self-esteem.

- It is reasonable to *read* first the language that is controlled in its oral form.

- Reading and writing skills are part of, not separate from, children's total development.

- There are many universal and common characteristics among languages that have potential for transfer to English.

- Caring, competent teachers are vital to the successful teaching of reading in *any* language.

These are but a few reasons that support an approach to literacy in the language of the home. While young children are advancing their native literacy skills, they should play in English as they listen and speak informally in enjoyable activities—poems, stories, pictures, film, cooking, games, role-playing, and other sensory-motor pursuits that build schemata to be stored and retrieved in English. Decisions to create dual language opportunities depend upon the philosophy of the school district, the support of the community, the wisdom of the administrators, the resources of the school, and, most importantly, on the professional competence of the teaching staff.

Grouping for Instruction

There are numerous questions that must be asked as the instructional plan for culturally diverse children is being considered.

One concern revolves around the best way to organize and group children. Almost everyone agrees that all children benefit from placement in heterogeneous classrooms. Children learn from their peers as well as from their teachers. Nonnative speakers of English enjoy working with native English speakers who may serve as good language models. It has been frequently noted that heterogeneity of groups alone, however, is not always a guarantee of success. Teachers express their anxieties about young children who appear drowning in a sea of unfamiliar language and lost in a storm of indecipherable print. These are the boys and girls who may be trying to interpret the two cultures and two languages of their dual experiences at home and at school. The result may be sad consequences of two poorly developed languages, neither of which is strong enough to carry the content of the curriculum. Alternatives to placing language minority children in this situation are these: (1) placement for part of the day in small groups for needed instructional support; (2) providing the opportunity for services within the classroom from an itinerant teacher; (3) grouping across grade levels where children of the same language with compatible instructional needs receive assistance; (4) tutoring from students in middle grades in junior high school; (5) team teaching by personnel, one of whom is competent in the children's language; and (6) assignment to language and literacy centers with special staff. There are also other options that may be considered after the multiple needs of students have been reviewed.

A significant factor in planning the delivery of services is the continuity of the program. Young children's schooling must be thought about in terms of immediate and long-range goals. Immediate goals and objectives should address quality instruction that will identify and use the present developmental stages and the language abilities of the children. Long-range goals and objectives should include a plan for the time and pacing of the curriculum that lies ahead. Children's advancement toward such long-range goals is likely to be successful when the plan has provided for careful articulation and communication from level to level. Unfortunately, many language minority families move from school to school or from region to region, and children may lose out when they transfer. Teachers discover gaps in children's knowledge and skills when they have had a high rate of school transiency.

For children in early childhood an appropriate curriculum is one that combines all of the best practices suited to their growth and development. Such practices cooperate with their physical need to touch, to do, to move, and to talk. They need direct contact with real people, real objects, and real events. They enjoy and learn from experiences that will answer their questions, allow them to explore, keep them safe, and satisfy their curiosity. In reaching for the (at times) elusive skills of literacy, they should have the chance to experiment with different methods of gaining control of print. Despite persuasive arguments lauding one approach over another, teachers well recognize that not all children learn in the same way. For this reason and for many others, teachers should be flexible in adapting activities for a variety of young learners and for the manner in which they learn.

Linguists comment that language is the best show that man puts on. The miracle that is called language begins with the birth cry, grows into words, expands into chains of words, and incorporates pitch, stress, and intonation in speech patterns that are comprehensible. Saint Augustine wrote in A.D. 398:

> We do not learn from mere words, that is sound and noise. Those which are not signs cannot be words. If I hear a word, I do not know whether it is a word or not until I know what it *means*. Once we establish its link with things, we come to know its *meaning*.

A primary object of instruction is one of helping children clarify and expand meanings for language that they already possess. Another purpose is one of adding new words and new meanings to children's existing repertoire of verbal skills. The dilemma facing those who plan and direct the program is the question of what language or languages are to be used. When children are facing written discourse, what written language or languages are to be presented? These are not easy questions to answer, but they are very important in terms of educational outcomes. Those persons who are responsible for curriculum decisions should be guided by these considerations:

- a developmental view of learning,
- a genuine valuing of the home language,
- a sequential continuity of program, and
- a real emphasis on standards of excellence.

The Role of Parents

Parents are their children's first teachers and continue to contribute greatly to their social, emotional, and language growth long after they have been enrolled in school. At home, parents attend to children's health needs. They provide food, rest, relaxation, play, medical care, and protection. To foster mental health, parents encourage independence, stimulate curiosity, promote responsibility, and expect success in school. Parents make certain that their children attend school regularly, review homework, participate in school festivities, and confer with school personnel.

At home, parents may read to their children and talk over what they have read. Parents encourage children's accomplishments in language and literacy, rewarding them for their efforts and sharing their success with members of the extended family. They may promote writing skills through leaving notes, reminding children of activities or chores on a message board, helping them correspond with out-of-town relatives, making grocery lists, and using writing in a variety of other exchanges of information. Perhaps one of the most productive parental actions to support language and literacy is to limit television or to share in the viewing of suitable-for-children television presentations. Parents are partners with the schools during these formative, first few years. They serve as models of readers and writers. Parents' praise and encouragement of children's efforts mean so much to them and spur them to keep on learning. Parents with books, newspapers, and magazines in the home make it possible for children to observe the important people in their lives enjoying print media.

When parents do not speak the language used in the school, it may be difficult for them to feel comfortable about visiting the classroom, volunteering on field trips, or conferring with school personnel. Every effort should be made to help these parents feel welcome and valued in the school. Teachers can express these feelings by other means than words—a smile, an outstretched hand, a cordial gesture. When conferences are scheduled, the addition of a person who can interpret is a courtesy that parents appreciate. It is also helpful to parents to offer to visit them at home or to arrange an early evening conference more convenient to their households. The hospitality of the teacher tells a great deal about the school and its program.

In summary, for all children language acquisition is the normal, expected behavior. Children of every language group follow a continuum of language that is universal, invariant, continuous, cumulative, and complex. Characteristically, children may be observed going through certain identifiable stages as they acquire language. When language that is comprehensible emerges, it is telegraphic. Later, there is a period in which more extended and elaborate forms are expressed. Language is, for young learners, embedded in context. By the time children are using language with ease and fluency, they are putting thoughts together in larger segments. The sources of language stimulation and the models are several: parents (especially the mother), relatives, siblings, teachers, friends, and television.

When children have the advantage of developing two languages, they move through these same stages of language acquisition and receive stimulation from the same sources. If the second language follows the acquisition of the first language, in contrast to children who may have grown up in a two-language household, such children bring their native language skills to the new language. It is wise to remember that these learners are children first and then are potential second language learners.

Finally, though the interests of teachers and parents of school-age children appear remote from the immediate concerns of parents and caregivers of infants, essential milestones en route to this developmental task of early and middle childhood are being met or being missed during the rapid period of infant growth. Infants are preparing for reading when they receive and differentiate among sensory stimuli. They are discovering how to interpret touch, sound, visual images, tastes, and odors. They are finding out about their body scheme, object constancy, right-left discrimination position in space, visual closure, figure-ground, and distances between objects. Each one of these explorations is part of children's sensory-motor integration ability. As infants pay attention, observe, recognize, and remember, they are growing in intelligence. Their sociability, beginning before intelligible speech, is getting them ready for sharing and participating in a group. Whether infants grow to be monolingual, bilingual, or multilingual, all of them begin their language and their literacy in the crib.

About the Author

Eleanor Wall Thonis is the district psychologist in the Wheatland, California, schools. She has taught language arts courses in the graduate and undergraduate divisions of the University of California, Davis, and California State University, Sacramento. She studied reading in early childhood under Professor Donald Durrell at Boston University and linguistics with Professor Robert Politzer at Stanford University. Her interest in the needs of language minority children has been expressed in numerous articles and books. Among her works are: *Teaching Reading to Non-English Speakers, Literacy for America's Spanish-Speaking Children,* and *The English-Spanish Connection.* Doctor Thonis has served as the past chair of the Multilingual-Multicultural Committee of the International Reading Association (1988–1990).

Suggested Reading

Butler, D., and Clay, M. M. (1982). *Reading begins at home.* Exeter, NH: Heinemann Educational Books.

Katz, L. G. (1988). *Early childhood education: What research tells us.* Bloomington, IN: Phi Delta Kappan Educational Foundation.

Thonis, E. (1983). *The English-Spanish connection.* New York: Santillana Publishing Company.

Teaching Language and Literacy in the Context of Family and Community

Ana Huerta-Macías
El Paso Community College, Texas

Elizabeth Quintero
University of Minnesota, Duluth

> [. . .] nos conosimos [sic] entre sí y cambiamos ideas y pues yo estuve muy contenta. (We got to know each other and we exchanged ideas and, well, I was very happy.)
>
> —Parent, commenting on Project FIEL, an involvement program

Introduction

While educators have known for decades that parent involvement is a contributing factor to a child's educational success, it is only recently that the dynamic impact of parents' involvement in their children's education has been documented (Careaga, 1988; Delgado-Gaitan, 1991; Epstein, 1987; Fredericks & Rasinski, 1990; Galen, 1991; Nieto, 1985; Powell, 1990; Sandoval, 1986; Simich-Dudgeon, 1987; Wells, 1986). The positive effects of parent involvement, furthermore, are so far-reaching that they extend across social lines. Epstein (1987) elaborates:

> The recent acknowledgments of the importance of parent involvement are built on research findings accumulated over two decades that show that children have an advantage in school when their parents encourage and support their school activities. . . . The evidence is clear that parental encouragement, activities, interest at home, and participation in schools and classrooms affect children's achievements, attitudes, and aspirations, even after student ability and family socioeconomic status are taken into account. Students gain in personal and academic development if their families emphasize schooling, let the children know they do, and do so continually over the school years. (pp. 119–120)

Thus, a strong parent-involvement program not only plays a significant role in the parents' own development but is also a critical factor in the schooling success of their children.

Parent Involvement— Reconceptualized

The concept of parent involvement has changed over the years and has become an important issue not only in bilingual education programs but in all educational programs. In the past, "involved" parents took on passive roles as they were called upon, for example, to give approval to bilingual education for their children, to participate in PTAs, to work as teachers' aides, to sell popcorn after school, to do the street patrol or other activities where they were not directly involved with their children's schooling. Now parents are being called on to take a more active role in the education of their children because educators and researchers are recognizing that the home environment can be a crucial factor in the acquisition of literacy and in a child's success in school and therefore in life.

Parents are now reading to, or with, their children, doing hands-on literacy-building activities with their children, writing stories with their children, and developing their own literacy and parenting skills through classes offered by schools, churches, social-service agencies, and other community organizations. Some of the programs doing these types of activities have been documented in the literature: Project PAT (Parents as Tutors), (Sandoval, 1986); Project PAL (Parents Assisting in Learning), (Garcia, 1986); Project FIEL (Family Initiative for English Literacy), (Quintero & Macías, 1991); the Pajaro Valley Experiment (Ada, 1988); the Parent

Readers Program (McIvor, 1990); Project Home Base (Goodson et al., 1991); the Family Study Institute (Goodson et al., 1991); and the Benson Early Literacy Program (Goldenberg & Gallimore, 1991). Studies of the above projects as well as other programs, furthermore, have shown that they were highly effective not only in the area of literacy development but also in the affective areas where educators reported higher levels of self-concept, for instance, on the part of the parents and students involved.

The implementation of parent involvement programs, however, has raised issues regarding the linkages between home and school, and the need to reconceptualize the process. Auerbach (1990) points out that, "Increasingly, educators are becoming aware, on the one hand, of the importance of family contributions to the literacy development of children and, on the other hand, of the enormous gaps in communication between home and school" (p. 9). Yet, such communication is needed as a bridge between family and school for effective parent involvement programs. Much has been written about the sociocultural and linguistic differences found between home and school for minority families and the importance of establishing sociocultural congruency for children to succeed in school (Delgado-Gaitan, 1991; Trueba & Spindler, 1989). However, rather than making an effort to link with the home and establish common ground, school personnel have in the past translated the differences into "deficits." Delgado-Gaitan (1991) elaborates, "Deficit perspectives depict inactive parents in the schools as incompetent, unable to help their children because they have a different language, work long hours away from home, belong to different ethnic groups, or are just not interested" (p. 6). She then goes on to describe a very successful parent involvement program in a Latino community (the Carpinteria case) which was grounded on the assumptions (among others) that all individuals have strengths and that a truly democratic society provides all people choices and opportunities to exercise their strengths.

Parent involvement, in many possible forms then, can be the logical link between home and school if it accepts and values parents as partners in education who have much to offer their children despite their level of formal education (or lack of) and respects the linguistic and cultural background of the parents and values it as an asset that the teacher can use to enhance literacy instruction in the classroom.

Research has strongly refuted the notion that poor, minority, immigrant families do not value literacy (Comer, 1984; Delgado-Gaitan, 1990; Diaz, Moll & Mehan, 1986; Goldenberg & Gallimore, 1991; Quintero & Macías, 1991). However, because of past experiences many parents have been made to feel that they are incapable of helping their children because of a lack of formal schooling, because they are illiterate or semiliterate, or because they do not speak, read, or write English fluently. While the above are seen as obstacles in parent involvement programs that utilize the "transmission" (Auerbach, 1990) or "banking" (Freire, 1985) models of education, they are not in a program that is truly participatory and that sees literacy not as something standardized and formalized but rather as the creation and communication of meaning within a context.

Sociocultural Connections

Freire and Macedo (1987) write about literacy in this sense: "The command of meaning and writing is achieved beginning with words and themes meaningful to the common experience of those becoming literate, and not with words and themes linked only to the experience of the educator" (p. 42). Recent research in the areas of literacy development and language acquisition in culturally diverse populations reaffirm developmental, holistic approaches to teaching and learning that give social context and school/home linkages great importance (Edelsky, 1990; Ferreiro & Teberosky, 1985; Goodman, Goodman & Flores, 1984; Harste, Woodward & Burke, 1984; Quintero & Macías, 1991; Rigg & Enright, 1986). Thus, it is essential that teachers and other school personnel link reading and writing activities to the home situation of the students in order to enhance literacy development. Auerbach (1989) addresses this:

> Literacy is meaningful to students to the extent that it relates to daily realities.... The teachers' role is to connect what happens inside the classroom to what happens outside so that literacy can become a meaningful tool for addressing the issues in students' lives. (p. 166)

These connections can be made by utilizing the parents as

teachers (which they are from the time their children are born) and exploiting their experiential knowledge of themselves and their children to develop literacy at home. This knowledge includes the linguistic and the sociocultural that by their very natures are woven into the fabric of everyday life.

This approach of using parents and families as mediators for literacy development is particularly important in the case of minority families. Moll (1990) elaborates on this, "We [including colleagues] believe that a meaning-centered model of reading allows bilingual students to take full advantage of their first language abilities and to surpass the limits set by their more limited knowledge of their second language.... We have made similar claims about teaching writing as communication" (p. 9). Moll goes on to describe the establishment of a social network between parents and schools and emphasizes that, "This model of reciprocal exchange provides new ways of defining the families as important resources; a novel vehicle for unused social and intellectual resources to be applied in instruction." (pp. 6–7)

Linkage Activities for Literacy Development

How then can teachers involve parents in the education of their children at home? First, the teacher can simply acknowledge and respect and refer to the fact that literacy practices and materials do exist in the homes of many working-class minority families (Chall and Snow, 1982 [cited in Auerbach, 1989]; Delgado-Gaitan, 1987 [cited in Auerbach, 1989]; Goldenberg & Gallimore, 1991; Taylor, 1983). Reading material in both English and Spanish is often found, for example, in the form of letters from family members, newspapers, magazines, flyers, advertisements, and school material. The fact, then, that literacy does exist in the home environment of many families should be recognized as a positive factor in the children's literacy development. Parents then should be encouraged to let their children participate, for example, in letter reading and writing, taking messages, making grocery lists, birthday cards, etc.

In addition, a recognition that many families possess specialized knowledge that can be shared with the classroom is significant for establishing intellectual and sociocultural networks. These "funds of knowledge" can be exploited by inviting parents to share their expertise with the class. Moll (1990) describes such a visit as it occurred in one teacher's classroom:

> Mr. T.... was a construction worker.... His visit was also very interesting. He was nervous and a little embarrassed, but after a while he seemed more relaxed. The children asked him a great number of questions. They wanted to know how to make the mix to put together bricks.... He explained the process and the children were able to see the need for mathematics because he gave the quantities in fractions. They also wanted to know how to build arches. He explained the process. (p. 11)

Thus, this networking proved to be immensely successful as a community-mediating approach to instruction.

Another example of a parent sharing her expertise with other adults and children occurred in an intergenerational literacy project (Quintero & Macías, 1991) that was implemented in the El Paso, Texas, area. The class (parents and children) was engaged in a discussion about cotton. (Cotton fields surround the rural community where the class was taking place.) One of the parents took this opportunity to share her expertise on this topic with the rest of the group, as she had been raised in a migrant family that grew and picked cotton as well as other crops. During that lesson she not only taught the group about the different stages in the growth of the cotton plant but also at one point corrected the teacher. This parent also expanded on the subject by talking about the difference between river water versus well water for growing cotton and fruits, again showing her in-depth knowledge in this area.

A similar incident that occurred at another site of the same project also serves as an example of parents sharing their knowledge with the instructor and with other parents and children. The theme of the lesson was on plants and the parents geared the discussion to the medicinal use of plants and herbs. The class was soon engaged in a lively discussion of remedies for stomachaches, insomnia, colds, and even skin rashes. Thus the participatory nature of the class had again successfully involved the parents in sharing their expertise with the class.

Parents should also be encouraged to do hands-on activities in the home as a way of developing literacy with young children. The research on young children's education tells us that active manipulation of the environment (touching, seeing, tasting, etc.) is essential for children to construct knowledge; "Children need years of play with real objects and events before they are able to understand the meaning of symbols such as letters and numbers" (Bredekamp, 1986, p. 4). We also know that social relationships play a fundamental role in the cognitive development of young children; "Language development is fundamental to learning and language development requires social interaction" (NAEYC, 1991, p. 26). Language learning can thus be enhanced in the home in parent-child interactions as language is used for real-life communication purposes.

These activities can be done by all families, including those with non-English-speaking, illiterate, and/or semiliterate parents. The following are examples of projects that parents can undertake with their children using materials typically found at home:

- Preparing a favorite family/traditional recipe
- Creating a family picture collage or a collage using magazine pictures
- Making a calendar with thematic artwork for each month
- Making objects, such as a jewelry box or an *ojo de dios* (typical Indian art using yarn in geometric shapes), using craft sticks
- Making up a song, poem, or story—perhaps about a traditional family activity
- Drawing a picture about a favorite *cuento* (tale) or family celebration

These types of projects, furthermore, can serve as a springboard to reading and writing activities. The child and/or parent, for example, can initiate an extension of these projects by writing and reading a story or poem about a collage which they made; by writing their favorite activities/celebrations for each month of the calendar year; by writing a *cuento* which has previously been handed down orally to the new generation; or by writing the instructions for making an *ojo de dios*. These types of activities provide enjoyable and meaningful literacy development for young children while encouraging them to pursue additional reading and writing experiences.

Conversations also serve as an excellent parent involvement technique for developing literacy. Educators and researchers in the area of language acquisition have long recognized that listening, speaking, reading, and writing skills are all interrelated (Krashen, 1985; Nessel & Jones, 1981; Oller, 1979). Thus, parents should be encouraged to develop conversations with their children at home not only because of linguistic gains but more importantly because they serve to link classroom topics (literature-based and other) to the personal experiences of the family, for it is this linkage which is at the core of literacy development: "Literacy is fundamentally about meaning; it results from our interaction with the world and the text. . . . Language and culture shape the meanings we attach to experience and text" (Fingeret, 1990, p. 5).

For example, if a class has been involved in a discussion of *Bringing the Rain to Kapiti Plain,* the teacher might encourage the parents to speak to their children, in English and/or Spanish, about their own experiences as children in another country (perhaps using family pictures) or a parallel experience in the family's own life where, for instance, they were in dire need of resources, or to relate to them traditional tales, or *cuentos,* from their native land.

Other examples of these connections through conversations occurred in the intergenerational family literacy project mentioned above where, for instance, a lesson on "Family Treasures" involved not only a reading of books such as *El escondite* but also children bringing treasures from home to share with the group. In one class this included an image of Our Lady of Guadalupe which had been handed down for generations, while in another class a family brought a baby's baptismal dress. In all cases the families were eager and proud to talk about these sentimental objects that formed bonds between the generations.

Additional conversational activities can be done by all families, regardless of their linguistic and sociocultural background. They can also serve as a catalyst for reading and writing activities at home and/or as part of an integrated curriculum at school. The following are some examples:

- Sharing a traditional, funny song and discussing its origin (if known) or who taught it to the child or family member
- Telling a story that an elder told the parent about life as a child
- Sharing a traditional survival skill that is often carried out intergenerationally

- Recounting a legend that traces the origins of a people's or an animal's place and purpose in life
- Sharing a traditional sequencing rhyme or proverb and explaining the content of the message
- Talking about the origins of specific cultural/family celebrations and how they were celebrated in the past when the parents were children

Another way to involve parents is by recognizing that literacy development is bidirectional; that is, not always just from parent to child but also from child to parent. A child with illiterate or semiliterate parents should be encouraged to read to his/her parents and/or siblings as a way of developing the child's own literacy. Auerbach (1989) reports on a very promising parent involvement study that was based on a model of children reading to parents:

> This study found that children who read to their parents on a regular basis made significant gains, in fact greater gains than did children receiving an equivalent amount of extra reading instruction by reading specialists at school. Particularly significant was the fact that low parental English literacy skills did not detract from the results. (p. 17)

Conclusion

An effective parent involvement program is not restricted to the classroom, or to volunteer PTA activities, or to home activities, but should very much be part of the workings of the entire school and community. This "extended," integrated support (that is, support by principals, counselors, teachers, and other school personnel as well as by community organizations) is essential in order to maintain the program as a dynamic one. It is essential that school personnel recognize that they themselves must be educated, through cross-cultural knowledge, concrete experiences, and self-reflection.

ABOUT THE AUTHORS

Ana Huerta-Macías is a research associate at the El Paso Community College. Having received her doctorate in the broad field of Applied Linguistics, her teaching and research interests have led her in the past 14 years to work and publish in the areas of teacher development, ESL, bilingualism, bilingual education, and most recently, parent involvement and family literacy. Dr. Macías, who was a codirector of Project FIEL, a bilingual family literacy project, is currently planning to undertake the direction of a new family literacy program through the Literacy Center of the El Paso Community College.

Elizabeth Quintero is an assistant professor at the University of Minnesota, Duluth. Her educational background, teaching experience, research interests, and publications combine early childhood education and bilingual education. Her dissertation research on biliteracy development of Spanish-speaking preschoolers in a Headstart program and her interests in family contexts of diverse cultural groups led to the design and implementation of Project FIEL. Dr. Quintero is now involved in teacher development for culturally diverse settings, implementing another family literacy project in collaboration with Duluth Headstart, which serves the Hmong community, and collaborating on curriculum development for early childhood programs that serve Spanish-speaking and Hmong children in St. Paul, Minnesota.

REFERENCES

Aardema, V. (1989). *Bringing the rain to Kapiti Plain.* New York: Scholastic, Inc.

Ada, A. F. (1988). The Pájaro Valley experience: Working with Spanish-speaking parents to develop children's reading and writing skills in the home through the use of children's literature. In Skutnabb-Kangas, T., and Cummins, J. (Eds.), *Minority education: From shame to struggle.* Philadelphia: Multilingual Matters.

Auerbach, E. (1990). *Making meaning, making change: A guide to participatory curriculum development for adult ESL and family literacy.* Boston: University of Massachusetts.

Auerbach, E. (1989, May). Toward a sociocontextual approach to family literacy. *Harvard Educational Review,* vol. 59, no. 2, pp. 165–81.

Bredekamp, S. (1986). *Developmentally appropriate practice in early childhood programs.* Washington, DC: National Association for the Education of Young Children.

Careaga, R. (1988). *Keeping LEP students in school: Strategies for dropout prevention* (Program information guide series, no. 7). Washington, DC: National Clearinghouse for Bilingual Education.

Comer, J. P. (1984). Home-school relationships as they affect the academic success of children. *Education and Urban Society,* vol. 16, pp. 323–37.

Delgado-Gaitan, C. (1991). Involving parents in the schools: A process of empowerment. *American Journal of Education,* pp. 20–46, Vol. 100, No. 1.

Delgado-Gaitan, C. (1990). *Literacy for empowerment: The role of parents in their children's education.* London: The Falmer Press.

Díaz, L., Moll, L., and Mehan, H. (1986). Sociocultural resources in instruction.

A context-specific approach. In *Beyond language: Social and cultural factors in schooling language minority children*. Los Angeles: California State Department of Education and California State University.

Edelsky, C. (1990, November). Whose agenda is this anyway? A response to McKenna, Robinson and Miller. *Educational Researcher*, pp. 7-11.

Epstein, J. L. (1987, February). Parent involvement: What research says to administrators. *Education and Urban Society*, vol. 19, no. 2, pp. 119-36.

Ferreiro, E., and Teberosky, A. (1985). *Literacy before schooling*. Portsmouth, NH: Heinemann.

Fingeret, A. (1990). *Let us gather blossoms under fire . . .* Paper presented at conference, Literacy for a Global Economy: A Multicultural Perspective. El Paso, TX.

Fredericks, A. D., and Rasinski, T. V. (1990, February). Working with parents: Involving the uninvolved: How to. *The Reading Teacher*, pp. 424-25.

Freire, P. (1985). *The politics of education*. S. Hadley, MA: Begin and Garvey Publishers, Inc.

Freire, P., and Macedo, D. (1987). *Reading the world and the word*. S. Hadley, MA: Begin and Garvey Publishers, Inc.

Galen, H. (1991, January). Increasing parental involvement in elementary school: The nitty-gritty of one successful program. *Young Children*, vol. 46, no. 2, pp. 18-22.

Garcia, D. (1986). Parents assisting in learning, Florida International University. In *Issues of parent involvement and literacy: Proceedings of the symposium*, pp. 93-95. Washington, DC: Trinity College.

Gerson, S. (1986). *El escondite*. Mexico City: Editorial Trillas.

Goldenberg, C., and Gallimore, R. (1991, November). Local knowledge, research knowledge, and educational change: A case study of early Spanish reading improvement. *Educational Researcher*, vol. 20, no. 8, pp. 2-13.

Goodman, K., Goodman, Y., and Flores, B. (1984). *Reading in the bilingual classroom: Literacy and biliteracy*. Washington, DC: National Clearinghouse for Bilingual Education.

Goodson, B., et al. (1991). *Working with families: Promising programs to help parents support young children's learning; Summary of findings*. Cambridge, MA: ABT Associates, Inc.

Harste, J. C., Woodward, V. A., and Burke, C. L. (1984). *Language stories and literacy lessons*. Portsmouth, NH: Heinemann.

Krashen, S. D. (1985). *Inquiries & insights*. Hayward, CA: Alemany Press.

McIvor, M. C. (1990). *Family literacy in action: A survey of successful programs*. Syracuse, NY: New Readers Press.

Moll, L. C. (1990). *Community-mediated instruction: A qualitative approach*. Paper presented at National AERA, Chicago, IL.

National Association for the Education of Young Children and the National Association of Early Childhood Specialists (NAEYC). (1991). *Guidelines for appropriate curriculum content and assessment in programs serving children ages 3 through 8: A position statement*. In *Young Children*, vol. 46, no. 3, pp. 21-38.

Nessel, D., and Jones, M. (1981). *The language experience approach to reading*. New York: Teachers College Press.

Nieto, S. (1985, Sept.–Dec.). Who's afraid of bilingual parents? *Bilingual Review*, vol. 12, no. 3, pp. 179-89.

Oller, J. W. (1979). *Language tests at school*. Great Britain: Longman.

Powell, D. R. (1990). *Families and early childhood programs*. Washington, DC: National Association for the Education of Young Children.

Quintero, E., and Macías, A. H. (1991). *Family initiative for English literacy*. (Final report, Title VII project). El Paso, TX: El Paso Community College Literacy Center.

Rigg, P., and Enright, S. (1986). *Children and ESL: Integrating perspectives*. Washington, DC: TESOL.

Sandoval, M. (1986). Parents as tutors. In *Issues of parent involvement and literacy: Proceedings of the symposium*, pp. 89-90. Washington, DC: Trinity College.

Simich-Dudgeon, C. (1987). Involving LEP parents as tutors in their children's education. *ERIC/CLL News Bulletin*, vol. 10, no. 2, pp. 3-4.

Taylor, D. (1983). *Family literacy: Young children learning to read and write*. Portsmouth, NH: Heinemann.

Trueba, H., and Spindler, G. and L. (1989). *What do anthropologists have to say about dropouts?* Bristol, PA: The Falmer Press.

Wells, G. (1986). *The meaning makers*. Portsmouth, NH: Heinemann.

Mother-Tongue Literacy as a Bridge Between Home and School Cultures

Alma Flor Ada
University of San Francisco, California

In this essay, I will address the importance of the mother tongue and its maintenance. After a brief overview of the many perspectives from which additive bilingualism (maintaining one's home language while acquiring a second one) can be defended, I will then focus on one in particular—the importance of strengthening the relationship between parents and children and children's ties to their cultural communities of origin.

Schools can never be neutral in this regard, especially in the case of language/ethnic minority and/or working-class/poor children. The conscious or unconscious practices of the school, including its approach to literacy, serve to either validate or invalidate the home culture, thus helping or hindering family relationships.

Yet once our commitment is clear, we can find simple yet powerful means to develop our students' literacy in a way that honors and strengthens their connection to their community, home culture, and language.

I will begin by reflecting on something that we often take for granted—the significance that the development of language has had on our evolution as humans. Through the creation of the symbolic system of language, we have developed our abilities to communicate our ideas, to express our feelings, to build relationships, to transmit knowledge gathered through generations, to record our past, and to plan our future.

Though communication is at the heart of language, we do not always need to have another person present in order to speak. Sometimes we speak with ourselves. As the great Spanish poet Antonio Machado said:

Quien habla solo
espera hablar a Dios un día...

He who talks to himself
hopes to talk to God someday...

And in our solitude, language often becomes a means to express the richness of the human soul, a way to turn one's feelings and emotions, one's anguishes and concerns, one's doubts and reflections into a song, a poem, a story, a novel, or a play, and thus contribute to the sum total of human culture.

Language is one of the very first elements of communication between the newborn child and the world. Even before birth, the child begins listening to the mother's voice in the womb as the sound is carried by the amniotic fluid. As a result, the newborn child has been shown to already recognize his or her own mother's voice.

We soothe babies with our words, we encourage them, we praise them, we rock them to sleep, we show our love and caring for them through our words as well as our gestures, thus creating a deep connection between the mother tongue and the young child, the young person.

Research has shown that the babbling of all human infants is identical during the first few months of life, but shortly afterwards, and long before the child is capable of pronouncing any distinguishable words, the sounds of the babbling change in response to the phonological features more common to the language or languages spoken around the infant. This occurs to the extent that a phonetician can determine the languages of the caretakers from the inflections of the infant's babbling.

Many years ago I received a valuable lesson from a very young child, a lesson that I have never forgotten. I would like to share that experience in memory of that child and of all children whose maintenance of their mother tongue is being threatened.

Back in the days when I was a young college student, one of my teachers, a Chicano nun, led a group of us who volunteered to work on Saturdays at an orphanage in a "barrio" of Denver, Colorado. Our major task was to give the children their weekly bath, but we also took time to interact and play with the children.

I developed a great love for the children, and in particular for one little three-year-old girl. As I have always loved to tell stories, I would often gather the children around me for storytelling time. While the children were all Mexican, most of them had lost their Spanish, and so I usually told the stories in English.

One Saturday afternoon, as I was telling stories with the little girl on my lap, she whispered in my ear: "Speak the other way, please, speak the other way." I realized that she was asking me to speak in Spanish, and I was surprised by her request. "Why do you want me to speak Spanish if you don't understand it?" I asked. And then, with a feeling in her voice that moves me to this day, she said: "I don't understand it, but that's the way my mother used to sound."

"That's the way my mother used to sound" has resonated in my ears ever since. Those few words taught me the lesson that no child should ever be deprived of the opportunity of knowing, developing, or enjoying the language in which her or his mother "used to sound."

It is a human, inalienable right to develop the legacy that was created through thousands of speakers:

cuántos millones de bocas
tienen pasadas
viene el ayer hasta el hoy
va hacia el mañana . . .

how many millions of mouths
have these words traveled through
in them yesterday reaches today
and journeys toward tomorrow . . .

says the poet Pedro Salinas in his eloquent poem "Verbo," written in honor of his language, our Spanish.

Unfortunately, we live in a society where frequently languages other than English are perceived as a threat instead of a richness. There is no valid rationale for this hurtful and damaging attitude. No one denies the value of a common language, nor the fact that English has historically been the common language and will continue to fill that role. What we disagree with are the false assumptions that language is an either/or choice, that in order for the nation to have a common language, individuals have to give up their own mother tongue. That is what cannot be explained nor justified, because it should be obvious that being fully bilingual is not detrimental in any way; on the contrary it can be useful and rather fun.

No one questions the importance of the full development of English skills in every child, in every young person, or in every adult in this country. Everyone needs to be able to use our common instrument of communication effectively and efficiently. Yet at the same time, there is no basis for promoting the acquisition of English at the expense of losing one's mother tongue. Instead, much research strongly concludes that the most effective route to "good" English as a second language is a strong foundation in one's first language.

The soundness of promoting additive bilingualism, or the acquisition of a second language while maintaining one's first language, can be supported from various perspectives:

- **Psycholinguistic Factors** The strong affective identification with the mother tongue is exemplified by the little child from Denver who longed to hear the language that represented "how my mother used to sound."

- **Pedagogical Reasons** A language is best learned at a young age, both because children have an innate ability for learning languages and because acquiring a language is a long process. It has been shown to take up to six or seven years to reach near-native fluency in a second language. The European curriculae have traditionally included foreign languages for children, on the pedagogical premise that one should learn a skill or a content area at the age at which one is most suited to learn it.

- **Social Reasons** Languages are natural resources. Speakers of multiple languages can be an asset for international relations, trade, cultural exchange, and enrichment of the cultural heritage of the nation.

- **Reasons of Justice** As long as some of the best universities in the country maintain foreign language requirements for admission and give credits for learning a foreign language, it should be argued that schools that allow children to lose their mother tongue are passively encouraging the loss of what would otherwise be a future academic advantage of those children.

There are, then, several aspects from which one could defend the principle of additive bilingualism. I have chosen to focus my current efforts on one aspect that I consider to be the most significant—the right of every parent to be able to fully communicate with her or his children and the need for every child to engage in meaningful communication at home.

A fundamental part of the present-day crisis in our society is the diminishment of parent-child interaction. When there is no communication between parents and children, there is no passing on of family history, no sharing of experiences that can become models for our young people, and no exchange of ideas or negotiation of meaning in a search for alternatives, for conflict resolution, or for planning and creating the future.

The greater the risks and difficulties our students face—drug abuse, early pregnancies, gang violence, as well as increasing racism, practically nonexistent social services, and severe lack of economic opportunities—the stronger the need to have meaningful parent-child interaction.

I do not believe, and I am not proposing, that schools should take over the responsibility of the family. I am saying that we cannot afford to disown the fostering of parent-child interaction since the more that we can strengthen it, the more manageable our own roles as teachers become.

Parents of language minority students usually send their children to school with great expectations. Many times these parents are convinced that their own social conditions may never change, but they hope that, by means of education, their children will be able to have a better future.

Speaking of the parents I know best, I can attest that while most Hispanic parents wish for a professional career and economic betterment for their children, their hopes do not stop there. Their dreams also include the hope that their children will "bring honor to their community," "know how to respect others, so that they in turn will be respected," "be good human beings," "be kind and generous," "be honest," "help make the world a better place," "assist other people in their communities," "contribute to society, to the world." These are all direct quotes from different parents. These same thoughts are repeated over and over again, in countless different wordings, by the Hispanic parents who I encounter in my work.

The parents believe that the schools will know how to make those dreams come true. They have full trust in the schools, which many consider as a "second home" for their children. Often, children are told that they should consider the teacher their "second mother" or their "second father."

The children who come to school from these homes often encounter the contradiction that, while their parents tell them to value the school and what the school teaches, the curriculum and the school practices do not in turn honor and respect children's parents and home environment.

Schools emphasize literacy, and rightly so. Books are presented as repositories of knowledge, as doors to all that there is to know. Most classroom activities revolve around books. Yet in the books children find in the classroom, there is often little or no recognition of themselves, their families, and their communities. And when children go home, often there are no books. Their parents do not own books, do not go to the library to borrow books, most certainly have never authored a book. How must children feel about the discrepancy between the emphasis on the value and importance of literacy they often encounter at school and the lack of literacy they encounter at home?

For many children, the explicit parental message to respect the school environment and the school's lack of respect for the home environment result in a conviction that the school culture is the "right" culture. Disconcerted about their parents, who don't seem to fit the "accepted" images proposed by school and society, students internalize the attitude that in order to belong, they must distance themselves from their families. Most often in an unconscious manner, they begin by feeling ashamed of their parents and their origin, rejecting their home language, anglicizing their names, and accepting the mores and attitudes that they perceive as superior.

They are often at grave risk of internalizing negative self-images of inferiority and defeat. It is these same students who, having become effectively alienated from their families and cultural communities, are most in danger of fulfilling their need to belong by succumbing to peer pressure, with unfortunate gang affiliations often substituting for missing family ties. Other children may react differently. Perhaps because their family and community affiliation is strong, they may never feel quite comfortable in schools, an environment that they perceive to be alien. And so they respond in a passive manner, simply awaiting the first opportunity to leave the system.

Undoubtedly, there are some children who manage to reconcile the two worlds. They maintain their admiration and appreciation for their parents, their community, and their culture, as they learn and integrate the best of the school culture, perhaps with an inner commitment to someday restore the omissions found in the school culture. Nevertheless, I am afraid that this is an enormous demand to place on children; only a few succeed at it.

What can schools do to address this issue? How can they counter the damage that they often create through unconsciously devaluing homes where literacy is not a common practice or whose culture is markedly different from that of the school?

Experience has shown me that this is not a hopeless situation. There are simple yet effective ways that teachers can affirm and include children's families and cultural backgrounds, thus strengthening the parent-child interaction of which we spoke earlier. They can do this even in situations where they do not speak the children's home language and in situations where there are many different languages spoken in the classroom.

I travel frequently. A standard question one encounters on planes is "What do you do?" If I am tired or want solitude, I answer, "a college professor," but if I want to engage in conversation, I answer instead, "an author."

The following anecdote is an example of how this prestige bestowed by print can be used to empower parents. In Windsor, California, in a parent program supported by Even Start, a first-grade boy wrote a book about a camping trip that his family had taken. There were a few pages depicting how the mother had announced that the family was going camping, how they had packed the car, and where they had gone.

A couple of lines of text on each page accompanied the boy's delightful drawings. As with all books written by the children in this program, the book was "published." The story was typed, the child's drawings were pasted onto the pages, the book was photocopied, and each parent in the program received a copy.

A few months later, on one of my visits to the program, a strong young man approached me to introduce himself. As we shook hands, he told me proudly, "I'm Mr. Lara, from 'The Lara Family Goes on Vacation.'" Every time that I share this anecdote after having shown the book in question, the audience laughs, because it is touching that a parent would choose to introduce himself as a character in his six-year-old son's story. But if we reflect on it, the anecdote points to the significance of being recognized, in print, as a protagonist.

For the last several years, I have been encouraging teachers to create in their classrooms books written by the children about themselves and their parents, family, and community.

Depending upon the age of the children, they may take questionnaires home, tape-record interviews, or simply ask their parents to discuss with them different themes related to the family experience. Subjects that teachers have succesfully experimented with include:

The Family Immigration Experience
How long has the family lived at its current location? Where did they live before? How were these places different? Who made the decision to move? What were the major difficulties encountered? The saddest moments? The happiest? In what way could things have been different?

The Family's Present Life Experiences
What are the things that they miss most from their previous life? What things do they like most about the United States? Which do they like least? What things would they like to change?

The Parents' or Relatives' Childhood Memories How was life different then? What are some things that existed in their parents' childhood that are not present now? What is present now that was not present then? What were their favorite activities? Who were their friends?

Important Moments in the Parents' Lives How did they meet? How did they decide to get married? What do they like about each other?

Names in the Family How were the parents named? Who chose their names? What do their names mean? Who chose the child's name? Is there anyone else in the family with the same name? What does the name mean?

These are only some examples. The possibilities are endless. They can relate to any aspect of the curriculum being taught. What is significant is that they transmit the message to children and to parents that their experiences are important and valued by the school.

One way to ensure the success of these activities is to have the teacher model them first. Teachers who have sent home copies of books made by themselves, sharing their own life stories and family stories, have experienced greater ease in connecting with students and their parents. The teacher's book sends the message that the teacher is also a human being, that parents, teachers, and children all share the same human condition—having a mother, a father, being part of a family.

Fear of the parents' possible illiteracy or their lack of knowledge of the English language should not be deterrents to carrying out the proposed activities. Children can interview their parents orally, copy down the parent's responses, or even tape-record them. And if the home language is not English, then it is even more important that the school validate the interaction between students and their parents in the home language.

In a bilingual classroom, books can be produced in both languages. This is, of course, optimal, as students will be developing their literacy skills in both languages. But this approach is by no means limited to bilingual classrooms. In classrooms where the teacher does not speak the students' home language or languages, students can create books in English, even though the original research may be carried out in the home language. In addition to fostering immediate parent-child interaction, the process will be promoting the acceptance and maintenance of the home language—and thus the possibility for future family integrity—while also developing valuable translating and interpreting skills on the part of the students.

Teachers doing this kind of work have made valuable discoveries. To begin with, they have discovered themselves as authors. Their students are excited to read and discuss books written by their teacher, and a closer student-teacher relationship develops as a result of shared personal experiences.

The process of sharing life stories with parents helps break down communication barriers, and parent-teacher relationships also improve and deepen. Parents are often more willing to participate in classroom activities as a result.

By incorporating knowledge of the student's home and community life, the curriculum gains greater relevance. Student interest, attention, and even attendance have improved as a result.

Some teachers' success stories have surpassed all our expectations. A Houston teacher had all of the Spanish-speaking parents contribute a story. The stories were compiled to create a class book entitled "Continuando nuestra cultura" ("Continuing Our Culture"); copies were distributed to all of the parents.

When the teacher was proudly sharing the book at a teacher's conference, it caught the eye of a representative of a major publishing house. Four of the parents have now received contracts to have their stories incorporated into a new major reading series due to appear next year.

But it is not the spectacular success stories that I want to emphasize here, inspiring as they may be. Rather, it is the cumulative effect of the continuously reiterated message to the students about the value of their parents, their language, and their culture that I believe holds the potential for bridging the gap between home and school.

Inspired by the words of one of the parents of Windsor, who, when asked for advice that he would give his children, said, "We are here to make the world a better place," other teachers are encouraging their students to ask their parents for words of advice. Parents' words, then, are featured and studied with the same kind of attention and reverence that the sayings of famous people have traditionally received.

For some time now, we have been aware of the importance of having cultural diversity in textbooks and children's books. The negative effects of the current imbalance are recognized in the following words of a migrant parent.

> Why can't I find books for my children that portray me and my family, that show our values and our way of life? Why do they discriminate against us? We farm workers do not discriminate against anyone. The work of our hands feeds all. Do they discriminate against us because our skin is burnt by the sun? Don't they know that the sun is the source of warmth, of light, of life?

As educators, we want publishers to be aware of the need to publish books that indeed tell all the stories, portray all of the people. But it is not enough to make known our demands that such books be available on the market. We also need to facilitate the creation of those books in our classrooms, where indeed every one of our students and their parents or caretakers can be protagonists and authors.

In the process, we hope that students and their parents will reclaim the strength of their voices and the power of the human gift of language. We want to help them reclaim the role of protagonists of their own life story and authors of their own reality. Together we can redefine "success" as being not an individual achievement that separates and alienates us from our communities but rather a measure of the strength of the connections we have with each other and our ability to facilitate the empowerment of our communities.

Helping Students Find Their *Voice* in Nonfiction Writing

TEAM-TEACHING PARTNERSHIPS BETWEEN DISTANT CLASSES

Dennis Sayers
New York University

Fiction and Nonfiction: The Great Divide in Teaching Literacy

Long before they come to school, children are surrounded by stories. Indeed, at every turn, they find stories. Parents regale their infant children with the rudimentary narratives found in games like "peek-a-boo"; in these rituals, the adults gradually "hand over" the storytelling role to their young listeners (Bruner, 1966). After infancy, generation after generation of youngsters have internalized the story lines woven into the traditional children's folktales, songs, and games of their cultural heritage (Simons, 1990).

For non-English-speaking children of immigrant, refugee, migrant, and sojourner parents,[1] the narratives bound up in these oral traditions are among the most important ways in which they will encounter, in a strange land, their family's cultural heritage. This is especially true among Spanish-speaking children, since Latino culture has a rich and varied folklore tradition, ranging from fables and folktales to lullabies and game songs. For some of these children, there are also the narratives of picture books and storybooks read to them by parents, relatives, and older friends, although children's books in their native language are usually hard to come by. For many more, there are the story lines of animated Saturday morning cartoon shows, television commercials, and motion pictures.

To be sure, young children of every linguistic and cultural background are not mere passive recipients of this all-pervasive "story culture." Through fantasy and improvisational dramatic play, they endlessly rework, transform, and appropriate many of the elements, characters, and plots of the stories that fascinate them (Paley, 1990). As a result, preschool children develop a deep familiarity with what has been termed "story grammar."

Story grammar is one example of the many richly elaborated schemata that children develop—schemata that, once they start formal schooling, become a multi-purpose tool for learning. Schemata are especially useful for learning to read. According to the schema theory of reading comprehension, learners of all ages organize knowledge into networks of related concepts (Noyce & Christie, 1989). As we hear or read a text, we constantly refer to these schemata.

To better understand how schemata work in the comprehension process, let us imagine the narrative of a story about a main character celebrating her birthday with a party. A young listener/reader will refer to at least two schemata as he or she attempts to comprehend this story.

First, as we have noted, there is the schema of story grammar itself, since even the youngest listener/reader has already developed sophisticated expectations about the workings of setting and plot and how characters attempt to overcome obstacles and achieve an effective resolution. Second, all children bring a complex "birthday party" schema to their reading—a schema in which the roles of the participants and the sequence of actions are clearly defined (for example, candles must be blown out before the cake may be eaten and the presents are opened). The birthday party schema structures the listener/reader's expectations of any narrative about this important ritual. Both these schemata—the story grammar and the birthday party schemata—will be very helpful to young learners as they approach our imaginary story.

However, no schema is static. For while children have many evolved schemata by the time teachers begin to work with them at school, it is important to realize that each schema is also evolving. Here, schema theory borrows a page from Piagetian developmental theories by asserting that reading comprehension takes place when we either (a) *assimilate* what we are reading into an existing schema, or (b) *accommodate* what we are reading by actually modifying the schema itself (Pappas, 1990).

According to schema theory, cultural experience also figures largely in reading comprehension (Barnitz, 1986). To return to our birthday party example, a child hearing or reading a story about a character's birthday will anticipate many of the story's elements and thus will use his or her schema to build comprehension. If, however, in the course of the story, a piñata should appear, children of Mexican and Central American heritage will easily *assimilate* into their preexisting schema this rather complicated element (which goes something like, "one by one, blindfolded party guests are spun around until they are dizzy, then they attempt to burst with a long stick a brightly colored papier-mâché animal filled with hard candies that is suspended from the ceiling"). This is an easily assimilated element because piñatas are part of their lived experience; indeed, these children would be surprised if a piñata were *not* a part of any story depicting a birthday party. But for children who have no direct experience with piñatas, a full comprehension of our imaginary story could only take place as they *accommodate* this new "piñata" element by transforming and extending their existing "birthday party" schema.

In the early years of schooling, usually from kindergarten through second or third grade, a great deal of learning is organized around fiction narratives, as teachers attempt to encourage learning by tapping into children's highly developed story schemata. This is especially true in classes that use whole-language, literature-based, or integrated language arts approaches to teaching (like those advocated in this volume). In these classes, we might say that nearly all new learning is built upon and extended through "storying."

However, around third grade, and certainly from fourth grade on, young students confront—often with a shock—a drastically different kind of writing. In Chall's (1979) terminology, students switch gears from "learning to read," which is based principally on story narratives, to "reading to learn," using the expository writing found in their social studies, science, and math textbooks, as well as in other nonfiction trade books. The familiar devices such as plot, character, and action that had helped students comprehend one story narrative after another are of absolutely no help when they encounter expository writing. This is because expository or nonfiction writing designed to convey information is structured through a large variety of more complicated organizational patterns, ranging from simple listings to complex logical relationships like cause and effect or comparing and contrasting (Horowitz, 1985; Meyer & Freedle, 1984). The difficulty is that these organizational devices are largely unfamiliar to most children, since very few youngsters have had any significant previous exposure to this type of highly formalized writing—whether in school, at home, or from living in the larger society (Englert & Hiebert, 1984; Drum, 1984).

Compared with children's easy familiarity with story forms, it is a much more daunting task that teachers confront when they seek to help students relate to expository writing. Put simply, when it comes to reading and writing, elementary students are much more accustomed to fictive modes of expression than they are to nonfiction writing. Fortunately, many innovative teaching strategies have been developed to help young readers comprehend nonfiction writing designed to convey factual information like that found in subject-area textbooks; for example, graphic organizers and pattern guides encourage students to visualize some of the important structural components of expository writing (Barnitz, 1985; Carrell, 1984; Piccolo, 1987; Slater, 1985).

In addition, the parallel reading of fiction and nonfiction materials focusing on a common theme has been shown to hold great promise for linking the familiar literary devices associated with "storying" with the less familiar organizational patterns of nonfiction writing (Crook & Lehman, 1991). Thematic units (or integrated units, as they are sometimes called) hold special promise in the bilingual literacy education of non-English-speaking hispanophone students. Thematic units offer these students multiple occasions to enrich and extend semantic associations in their mother tongue as they encounter related vocabulary and concepts across all the subject areas (language arts, creative arts, science, math, and social studies) during several weeks. This is especially important when the larger society offers so few opportunities for the reinforcement of concept development in their mother tongue. Research has indicated that strong concept and literacy development in the mother tongue is related to higher levels of English language acquisition and academic achievement in general (Cummins, 1981).

However, these promising practices—pattern guides, graphic organizers, and thematic units—focus on one part of the literacy equation, that is, on the reading comprehension of texts written in an expository mode. These "reader based" approaches need to be supplemented by teaching techniques that also encourage students to see nonfiction writing from a "writer based," or author's, point of view. In a word, students must not only become informed consumers of expository writing; they also need motivating, exciting contexts in which they may develop as competent producers of nonfiction writing. And, if they are to be prepared for the many expository texts that they will be called upon to read—with comprehension—in the upper elementary grades, they must begin to write original, personalized nonfiction early in the primary grades.

Creating an Audience for Students' Nonfiction Writing: Distance Partnerships Between Teachers

Team-teaching partnerships between distant teachers provide one such context for developing students' awareness of expository text from an "insider's," or writer's, perspective. As we shall see in the following section, distance team-teaching is a time-tested strategy that has enjoyed a wide following for nearly 70 years. But just what is it precisely?

As with other simple but powerful educational strategies, it is easier to describe what team-teaching partnerships between distant classes *are not* than it is to come up with an invariable definition of what they are.

Team-teaching partnerships between two classes are definitely *not* student-to-student pen pal projects but rather class-to-class collaborations. And while there are no hard-and-fast rules for organizing a team-teaching partnership between teachers in two schools, we can expect that in a typical partnership—as a bare minimum—two teachers will plan identical short-term projects in both their classes, and as a culminating joint activity, each teacher will exchange her or his students' work with the distant partner class.

Partner teachers generally undertake one of three types of curricular projects, which I will describe in more detail in a later section of this chapter: (1) shared student journalism and publishing; (2) comparative investigations, including dual community surveys, joint science investigations, and contrastive geography projects; and (3) both traditional and modern folklore compendia, extending from oral histories and collections of proverbs to children's rhymes and riddles, lullabies and game songs, as well as fables and folktales. But before describing these categories of curricular projects that have arisen over decades of class-to-class exchanges, it is essential to consider a deceptively simple issue: how best to begin a long-distance team-teaching partnership.

GETTING OFF TO THE RIGHT START[2]

There is a saying in English, "Well begun is half done." This is nowhere truer than in the planning and in the initiation of effective team-teaching partnerships. Three elements are especially critical in getting off to a good start. First, the commitment of both teachers is decisive. Finding a partner teacher is easily enough accomplished. Many effective partnerships begin when two teachers from neighboring districts who already know each other agree to work together or when two teachers meet at a conference and plan to engage in joint curricular projects. Other teachers prefer to contact a "Partner Teacher Clearinghouse" like ORILLAS (see below) to help locate a class in another state or country to work with.

In every case, the key word is **commitment**. Perhaps the most critical element in long-distance team-teaching is the quality of the working relationship between the two partner teachers, who must be determined to meet their mutually agreed upon goals. While a team-teaching partnership may be a simple and effective context for learning, it can only produce results if the partner teachers honor the commitment they have made to work together. When both teachers keep their commitment, there are few strategies that are more exciting and rewarding; if not, the results will be measured in the frustration and disappointment of students in both classes.

Second, before launching a team-teaching project between two classes, teachers usually find it helpful to exchange what have come to be known as "Culture Packages." Culture Packages have also been called by various other names, such as "Getting to Know You," "Let Us Introduce Ourselves," or "Our School and Our Community Packages." Whatever name is chosen, in every case the function of the Culture Package is the same: to break the ice and establish a common point of reference between distant classes by exchanging a group "self-portrait." Culture Packages are envelopes or small boxes filled with student autobiographies, maps, photographs, audio and videotapes, student artwork, and other memorabilia from the school and the community such as postcards, school newspapers, and exemplary student work. As school and community "self-portraits" are shared, partner classes begin to compare and contrast their communities and world views, which are so often taken for granted. In this way, critical thinking skills are developed that are rooted in students' daily lives, their families, their school, and their community.

The day that a Culture Package arrives is an exciting day in any partner class. As a rule, everything else stops in the classroom as the teacher and students prepare to discover the contents of the Culture Package. Yet students' natural enthusiasm when opening the package can be channeled by teachers to further magnify the learning experience. This takes careful timing and a commitment by the ORILLAS teachers to provide relevant and timely feedback to one another. For example, it is usually best if the two teachers agree to mail the Culture Packages on the same date, rather than one class sending a package and then waiting for the partner class to send theirs (a "waiting game" that is certain to prove frustrating). Also, the sending class can help the receiving class maximize the impact of the Culture Package by including a detailed "packing slip." This packing slip can add a fascinating dimension to receiving a Culture Package. On the packing slip the sending teacher should indicate his/her class's rationale for selecting each item; for instance, the sending class might include these annotations for the receiving class:

> **ITEM:** Map. WHY WE THOUGHT YOU WOULD BE INTERESTED: If you look carefully at this illustrated map of San Diego, you'll see that we've marked the location of our school with an *X*. Barrio Logan is just a few miles from Balboa Park, whose museums are a favorite destination for school field trips.
>
> **ITEM:** Photographs of the students. WHY WE THOUGHT YOU WOULD BE INTERESTED: In this album you'll find a photo of each of the students in our class. Each student brought in a photo from home so that you can see where they live, a vacation they took, or other family members.

ITEM: Audiocassette. WHY WE THOUGHT YOU WOULD BE INTERESTED: This audiotape is really an oral "group letter" describing a typical day at our school. As a class we discussed what we wanted to tell you, planned out in what order the students would speak, practiced our speeches, and THEN recorded it. We wanted it to sound nice, like a radio show!

ITEM: Videotape. WHY WE THOUGHT YOU WOULD BE INTERESTED: We created this video to illustrate the "games project" we started in our class last week. We began by asking students to write instructions for favorite games. Then we made this video to show how the games are actually played. We've also included the written instructions so you can try to play the games, too.

ITEM: School newspaper. WHY WE THOUGHT YOU WOULD BE INTERESTED: Six of the students in our class are also in the journalism club and worked on this edition of the school newspaper. The editorial about the school dress code was written by Gustavo and addresses an issue that has been very controversial here. A group of parents has been trying to discourage gang activity by getting the school to adopt uniforms.

The receiving teacher can use this packing slip to shape her or his class's discussion as the contents of the Culture Package are revealed, item by item.

The first impulse upon opening a Culture Package is to immediately display its contents on a classroom bulletin board. However, before exhibiting the Culture Package, it is very helpful for the receiving teacher to take a few moments and jot down notes of her/his students' reactions to the items in the Culture Package. The teacher can ask students to discuss such key topics as "What we liked best or found most interesting about the package you sent us," "Questions we have after receiving your package," and "Things about your class, your school, and your community that we would like to know more about"—all topics of tremendous interest to the sending class. It is very important to mail these questions and comments by return post immediately to the distant partner class. The receiving teacher's notes will offer invaluable feedback to the students who sent the Culture Package and will stimulate these students to develop a more critical awareness of their school and community.

Third, after exchanging Culture Packages, it is important to begin immediately on a team-teaching project that extends the curriculum in both your classes and that can be completed by a specified date, usually before the end of each semester. The most effective team-teaching projects are those that make sense in *both* classes. Of course, it is inevitable that each partner teacher will have different curricular goals; for example, one teacher may have a social studies unit on families while her partner might have a math/science unit on mapping. Yet these teachers can plan a common activity in such a way that both their curricular goals are achieved and extended. For example, students in both classes could ask parents for their birthplaces and could then translate this information according to a common format such as:

My name is Waleed Graham. I was born at latitude 43 degrees North (43°N), longitude 73 degrees West (73°W). My mother was born at 43°N, 73°W. My father was born at 31°N, 80°W. Here is some more information about my family tree:

My mother's mother's birthplace was 34°N, 57°W.

My mother's father's birthplace was 43°N, 73°W.

My father's mother's birthplace was 31°N, 73°W.

My father's father's birthplace was 31°N, 55°W.

The partner classes could then exchange the paragraphs they have written. Such an activity could lead to interesting and provocative discussions in both partner classes on immigration and family mobility. The key point in this example is that both teachers have designed a "doable" team-teaching project in a way that complements, extends, and enriches each of their preexisting curricular units.

THREE OF THE MOST COMMON TEAM-TEACHING PROJECTS

Examples of team-teaching projects include shared student journalism, comparative community surveys, dual local geography projects, and parallel folklore and oral history studies in which students interact in new ways with their families, relatives, and the elders of their community.

CREATING
A CULTURE OF
READING

1. **Shared Student Publications** Classroom journalism and publishing are among the most common team-teaching projects. This is probably because student newspapers and magazines are a flexible format into which virtually any type of writing growing out of a curricular project can "fit." Also, everyone in a student journalism project has clearly defined roles. Students are "reporters" when they write articles for local newsletters; "editors" while revising and polishing their writing; and "correspondents" when they send finished articles for inclusion in the school newspaper produced by their distant partner class. In some cases, two partner classes decide to plan and publish a single newsletter by establishing a "joint editorial board." Students from both classes form a panel to make the innumerable decisions that go into a successful journalistic product, ranging from the title of the newspaper and the topics that reporters will cover in both classes to the final stages of production involving artwork, layout, and printing. This project can be enriched by inviting reporters and editors from community newspapers to offer professional advice to students and by organizing field trips to local newspaper offices.

2. **Comparative Investigations** The second type of team-teaching project can take many forms, but one of the most popular and illustrative is the "comparative community survey." Here, the partner classes pick a theme of common interest. This theme is usually a controversial one that confronts and challenges the students' respective communities (for example, homelessness, drug abuse, deforestation, or the depletion of the ozone layer). The classes nominate and together evaluate various items for inclusion in a joint community survey that taps public opinion on their chosen theme. Items are selected that provide both quantifiable data and open-ended reactions. When the survey is completed, the partner class teachers help students to analyze the results and to craft a report on their community's stance toward the controversial theme. These reports are then shared between partner classes. The spirit of the comparative community survey is to "Think Globally and Act Locally," and the project often leads to joint community actions initiated by teachers and students.

    The goal of this activity, like other comparative investigations, is to develop students' critical inquiry skills. As community "self-portraits" are shared, partner classes begin to compare and contrast their communities and world views, so often taken for granted. This same impulse drives other team-teaching projects that fall under this category, such as joint science investigations and contrastive geography projects.

3. **Folklore Compendiums and Oral Histories** In the third category of team-teaching projects are collections of folklore and community narratives. These projects can involve numerous distant classes, not only two partner classes, since the more wide-ranging and diverse the participation, the richer the final product. There is no lack of folklore material to investigate locally and then to share, compare, and contrast with a faraway partner class or with dozens of other classes in the ORILLAS network: proverbs and the fables with which they are often associated; children's word games, riddles, and rhymes; traditional folktales; even lullabies and folksongs. An especially important outcome of folklore studies is that students come to view their parents and relatives as vital sources of valued cultural knowledge. Folklore studies often lead to more sophisticated oral history projects, in which students conduct more extensive, formal interviews with their peers or elders on themes relating to community history.

The Origins of Distance Team-Teaching Partnerships

The beginnings of distance team-teaching partnerships could not have been more humble or inauspicious. Célestin Freinet began his 46-year career as an elementary school teacher in 1920 at a one-room rural schoolhouse in the French Maritime Alps. Yet by the time of his death in 1966, Freinet coordinated the largest long-distance team-teaching network ever formed—involving 10,000 schools in 33 nations—and

169

had developed an approach to teaching that continues to shape the practice of educators throughout Europe and Latin America and in many African and Asian nations (Lee, 1983; Sayers, 1990).

Freinet saw "mass media" as the greatest threat to children's education. Mass media, in Freinet's thinking, was a broad term that referred to any reformulation of an experience that attempted to substitute an *interpretation* of the original experience for a direct encounter with the experience itself; thus, for Freinet mass media was polymorphous, ranging from textbooks and fixed curricula to broadcast media and motion pictures. The danger of mass media was that it caused a profound "psychic disequilibrium" between children and their surroundings. "With our mass media we think we have attained new insight into life that seems to go beyond and make superfluous actual experience" (C. Freinet, 1974, p. 28). Freinet argued that balanced psychological development in children is possible only through interaction, both socially with peers and adults and physically with the environment. "We understand that neither external science, nor verbalisms, nor imagery can replace this necessary engagement" (C. Freinet, 1974, p. 28).

Freinet felt that, by providing a social context designed to encourage interaction and engagement with physical reality, teachers can play a decisive role in helping students achieve a more balanced personality development.

> Our fundamental concern, at every level, should be to bring children back to the true life of their surroundings, to confront them with the elements, to have them experience the elementary laws which govern their relationship with everything in their environment . . . so that, strengthened by this firm engagement, they may resist the distortions fostered by the mass media. (C. Freinet, 1974, pp. 89–90)

To this end, he developed three complementary teaching techniques that encouraged students to engage with their classmates, families, and community members while disengaging from the plethora of "secondhand" imagery generated by the mass media.

The first technique Freinet developed was the "learning walk." Weather permitting, students would join him in exploratory walks through the town. During these walks, they would gather information and impressions about community life that formed the basis for subsequent classroom activities in reading and writing, science, and math. As a regular follow-up activity to these walks, the students authored, as a group, what Freinet called "free texts." At first, these writings were merely collected in a folder. But soon Freinet introduced his second technique: classroom printing, which helped the students place even more value on their writing. His elementary students became expert at producing hundreds of typeset copies of their writings for their families and friends.

But the birth of long-distance teaching partnerships can be precisely dated with the introduction of the third of Freinet's techniques. Freinet met Réné Daniel, a colleague from a neighboring province who became interested in Freinet's techniques, and they agreed to exchange Culture Packages as well as writings their students had authored and printed. Freinet's diary records the arrival of the first Culture Package with the single entry: "October 28, 1924; we are no longer alone" (E. Freinet, 1975, p. 45).

For Freinet, long-distance exchanges were not an end in themselves; rather, partnerships between faraway classes served as the indispensable precursor to a more profound and active engagement by the learner in understanding and in transforming social realities much closer to home. Indeed, in Freinet's view long-distance learning partnerships create a context—we might even say a *pretext*—for students to collaborate more intensively and productively with people in their own classroom and community, as well as with students, parents, and teachers from a distant community.

> When we live very close to our surroundings and to people, we eventually come not to see them. . . . But thanks to the questions which emanate from afar, our eyes are opened; we question, we investigate, we explore more deeply in order to respond with precise verifications to the inexhaustible curiosity of our correspondents, based on a natural motivation. This gradually leads to an awareness of our entire geographic, historic, and human environment. (Gervilliers, Berteloot & Lemery, 1977, pp. 29–30)

Through this activity, students come to replace an unquestioning view of their world with a more objective, conscious, and critical perspective.

As students attempt to respond to the surprising questions of their faraway collaborators, they become involved in a process of reflective *distancing* from the reality that surrounds them.

The child, because she needs to describe them, develops a consciousness of the conditions of her life, of the life of her town or her neighborhood, even of her province. She had been living too close to these conditions and through interscholastic exchanges *she has distanced herself from them in order to better comprehend the conditions of her life.* . . . We must take advantage of this impulse of curiosity, this new vision, these instances of discovery. (Gervilliers, Berteloot & Lemery, 1977, p. 31, emphasis added)

Yet distancing is not the only outcome; students also discover multiple opportunities for purposeful *engagement* with their day-to-day reality. According to Freinet, reflective distancing leads to social action: "Interscholastic networks . . . are conducive to a true cultural formation, offering to each individual several possibilities of action over his surroundings, and causing a profound engagement with human beings and with things past, present and future" (Gervilliers et al., 1977, p. 15). Thus, a two-fold process of *reflective distancing* and *purposeful engagement* with the physical and social world in which students live are the hallmarks of Freinet's writings on the educational potential of long-distance teaching partnerships.

We may now begin to appreciate the usefulness of Freinet's ideas and techniques for helping young students expand their literacy skills beyond story narratives into the complex skills of writing and reading nonfiction, expository writings. As Freinet put it, class-to-class collaborations create a learning context that ensures that "spontaneous written expressions will be, at one and the same time, (a) an expansion of the child's personality and (b) an occasion for acquiring, broadening and defining a range of topics: language arts, the sciences, history, geography, ethics, etc. while linking them to the child's interests" (E. Freinet, 1975, p. 94). Through learning partnerships between distant classes, two important goals are attained. First, students directly experience the people and the environment that condition their daily lives and reflect upon this encounter, thus reversing the "psychic disequilibrium" caused by the pervasive influence of mass media. Second, students acquire, broaden, and define—all from an insider's writer-based perspective—the subject-area knowledge that forms the basis of all expository writing. We will examine these implications in greater detail in the last section of this chapter.

ORILLAS: A Multilingual Long-Distance Team-Teaching Network

The times—and communications technology—may have changed since Freinet's day, but the activities that take place in teacher partnership networks have remained much the same. While teachers in Freinet's network utilized the national postal services as their principal line of communication, contemporary educators have added several other high-technology communication media to their regular mail exchanges. For example, a large percentage of the educators who participate in the ORILLAS teacher partnership network, which the author has helped coordinate since 1985, make use of electronic mail and computer-based conferencing to plan and implement joint educational projects between distant classes and to "electronically publish" their students' collaborative work.

ORILLAS team-teaching partnerships are multilingual (in French, Haitian Creole, English, Portuguese, Spanish, and American and French Canadian Sign Languages) and multinational (with about 120 schools, principally in Puerto Rico, Quebec, and the United States, but also in English-speaking Canada, Costa Rica, France, Japan, and Mexico). DeVillar and Faltis in *Computers and Cultural Diversity* (1991) judged ORILLAS "certainly one of the more, if not the most, innovative and pedagogically complete computer-supported writing projects involving students across distances" (p. 116).

Despite the newer technologies, activities in ORILLAS are surprisingly similar to Freinet's original scheme. Now, as then, teacher partnerships (a) begin with a commitment between two teachers, (b) are inaugurated with an exchange of Culture Packages, and (c) culminate in some identical curricular activity in both classes, which is then shared with distant partner "classmates." Yet as times have changed, so have teacher partnership networks. ORILLAS, in particular, has responded to the evolving challenges of schooling in our ever more interdependent world by exploring new issues of intercultural communication.

Especially intriguing are the numerous ORILLAS partnerships that link classes from a wide range of backgrounds in culture and language, for most ORILLAS exchanges are either conducted in two languages or involve bicultural students. Four types of partnerships merit special mention: namely, class-to-class collaborations concerned with bilingual education, foreign language education, multicultural education, and reducing prejudice.

PARTNERSHIPS INVOLVING STUDENTS IN BILINGUAL EDUCATION PROGRAMS

ORILLAS Case Partnership #1: A 4th-grade bilingual education classroom in New Haven, Connecticut, with students of Puerto Rican heritage paired with a partner class in Caguas, Puerto Rico.

In another generation, it was common for non-English speaking children of immigrant, refugee, migrant, and sojourner parents to be placed in all-English classrooms where they understood nothing of what their teacher or classmates were saying. Most often these students were given seatwork "until they caught up." In fact, large numbers fell behind and dropped out of school. Luckily for some of these students who were forced to drop out, there were many unskilled and semiskilled jobs that were then available in the manufacturing sector of the economy. Times have changed; while there are fewer minority language children who are placed in "sink or swim" classrooms, our society's service economy now offers drastically fewer opportunities to the inevitable school dropouts that result from this abusive practice. Bilingual education programs seek to help minority language students stay in school and not fall behind in their subject-area studies by adopting the mother tongue of the students as the language of instruction; at the same time, the students study English as a second language.

The most effective bilingual programs are also concerned to develop bilingual literacy, that is, literacy in the mother tongue and in the majority language of the society—which, in a U.S. context would be English. This two-fold goal is not viewed as contradictory or divisive but as mutually reinforcing. As noted earlier, research has shown that high levels of literacy in the mother tongue result in skills that are transferred to reading and writing in the second language (Cummins, 1981). Moreover, by maintaining students' skills in their mother tongue, bilingual programs help parents play a key role as partners with teachers in their children's education; absent bilingual programs, parents are more likely to "lose touch" with their children during the crucial adolescent years (Ada, 1988; Skuttnab-Kangas, 1984). And, of course, fully bilingual students have skills that give them clear advantages in today's job market.

Yet for these students whose home language is not the society's dominant language, there are many obstacles to developing and maintaining mother tongue literacy. This is because, in most cases, the minority language receives comparatively little reinforcement in the wider society beyond the home and the school. We can see this most clearly by comparing the language experience of two children as they begin their first day of formal schooling, one who speaks the society's majority language (that is, in the North American context, English) and the other from a minority language background. The majority language child will have been exposed to countless encounters with "environmental print" in English, ranging from supermarket packaging to street signs and mass media such as television. Naturally, the minority language child has as rich an oral language base as the English-speaking child. However, the minority language child will have had a great deal less exposure to environmental print in his or her mother tongue.

Once these two children are in school, their respective teachers face very different challenges in developing students' native-language literacy skills. The teacher of the majority language student can develop literacy through genuine reading and writing activities directed toward the wider society, such as articles for school newspapers or letters to cultural organizations, businesses, and governmental agencies. On the other hand, the teacher of the minority language student has a much more restricted "readership" for her student's literacy products, often limited to herself, other classmates of that language background, and a relatively small circle of parents.

For bilingual program students, teacher partnerships like ORILLAS can play an important, indeed a decisive, role in the development of mother tongue literacy. Suddenly, a context is created that increases the readership for these students' native language nonfiction writings many times over. For example, ORILLAS has established numerous partnerships between Puerto Rican students enrolled in bilingual programs in the United States and distant colleagues in

Puerto Rico. While working on joint curricular projects, the U.S. bilingual program students interact extensively *through writing* with "partner classmates" in Puerto Rico who are highly competent models of fluent Spanish-language usage. Thus, by making possible daily contact, via computers and other technologies, with fellow students from the countries of their parents' birth, teacher partnerships like ORILLAS can work to foster full bilingual literacy among language-minority students.

FOREIGN LANGUAGE EDUCATION PARTNERSHIPS

ORILLAS Case Partnership #2: An elementary French as a foreign language class in northern Maine paired with a class in the French-speaking province of Quebec.

ORILLAS Case Partnership #3: An upper elementary Spanish as a foreign language class in Los Angeles paired with a bilingual education (Spanish-English) class in New York City.

Recently, there has been a resurgence of interest in foreign language education in elementary schools (FLES). In part, this renewed interest is the result of the growing awareness that the ability to speak (at least) two languages is fast becoming a requirement in business, the helping professions, and government. Students in North American schools have a long way to go in this regard. There are 10,000 Chinese studying English for every student of Chinese in the United States; in general, North American students are notoriously underprepared in foreign languages (Crawford, 1989).

Congress authorizes funding yearly to promote foreign language instruction, and every indication suggests this is a costly endeavor. It is estimated that the Department of Defense spends $12,000 to provide a single student a year-long course in Korean, resulting in a lower level of Korean language skills than a 5-year-old child brings to school (Campbell & Lindholm, 1987). Meanwhile, as Senator Paul Simon has pointed out, the United States has incredibly rich linguistic resources that it has done little to develop; he writes:

> One of every fifty Americans is foreign-born. We are the fourth largest Spanish-speaking country in the world. Yet almost nothing is being done to preserve the language skills we now have or to use this rich linguistic resource to train people in the use of a language other than English. (Simon, 1980, p. 27)

Ironically, the U.S. government also spends millions to fund a particular type of bilingual program (namely, Transitional Bilingual Programs) that is designed to replace the native language skills that students have acquired at home with English language skills; most graduates of these misnomered "bilingual" programs have lost or will soon lose their abilities in the language of their homes (Crawford, 1989, p. 164). As Crawford notes, while one government agency funds a number of extremely costly efforts to teach foreign language skills, another office allocates monies that, in effect, eradicate the country's already existing linguistic and cultural natural resources.

Since foreign language proficiency takes so long to develop, it makes sense (a) to begin fostering these skills through well-designed FLES programs as early as possible; moreover, as Senator Simon suggests, it makes further sense (b) to preserve our linguistic resources *as well as* (c) to tap the already existing language skills we have in our communities in order to more efficiently develop foreign language proficiency among new learners. ORILLAS team-teaching partnerships respond to all three of these imperatives.

The challenge for FLES programs has always centered on how to develop second language proficiency without excessive reliance on formal, grammatical study of the target language. ORILLAS responds to this challenge by providing young foreign language learners a context in which they can interact—again, through nonfiction writing focused on their lives and their communities—with distant classmates who are competent speakers of the target language. With its stress on interaction through writing (and on the reading of genuine writings), this approach stands traditional foreign language pedagogy on its head.

Most foreign language teachers are trained to develop separately and in sequence the four language skills of listening, speaking, reading, and writing. Although it comes last in the traditional scheme of foreign language teaching, writing—in the context of long-distance team-teaching partnerships—holds special advantages for foreign language learners. Written text, unlike spoken conversations, "holds still" so that the foreign language learner can take the time necessary to elaborate and revise his or her developing comprehension of its meaning. Moreover, by responding *in writing* to a written text in the target language, the learner is encouraged to employ structures and vocabulary usage that were modeled in the writing of his or her distant interlocutor.

As noted above in Case #2, ORILLAS has established effective foreign language learning partnerships between classes in the United States and native French-speaking classes in Quebec; additionally, there have been partnerships between U.S. classes and Spanish-speaking classes in several countries. Spanish or French become the "coin of the realm" for the foreign language learners as they complete curricular projects and then share their work with their partner classmates. But ORILLAS class-to-class collaborations have also encouraged exchanges between foreign language learners and another important group of competent models of target language skills that too rarely interact with "mainstream" students: namely, language minority students in bilingual education programs in U.S. schools, as illustrated in Case #3. Clearly, these special kinds of exchanges are mutually beneficial: the foreign language students are exposed to highly competent speakers of the target language, while the minority language students become more aware of the value of their linguistic heritage in the eyes of other students, and thus learn to take pride in their native language competence.

PARTNERSHIPS FOCUSED ON MULTICULTURAL EDUCATION

ORILLAS Case Partnership #4:
A fifth-grade class in Brooklyn, New York, with English-speaking students from a range of home language backgrounds and nationalities (including children whose parents are English-dialect speakers from the West Indies, Haitian Creole speakers, Cantonese Chinese speakers, speakers of Korean, and Spanish speakers from the Dominican Republic and Puerto Rico) paired with a class in Rio Piedras, Puerto Rico.

Recently, many state departments of education and numerous urban school districts have reexamined their social studies curriculum with a view toward providing students a more accurate reflection of the full range of historical players—Native American, African American, and numerous immigrant groups from *every* continent—who have contributed to the cultural diversity of American life. These efforts, which have also influenced multimillion dollar state and local textbook adoption decisions, have received much attention in the press, where multicultural education has been either praised for its attention to historical accuracy (West, 1992) or roundly condemned for calling into question the accepted verities of traditional historical narratives that have focused on the European roots of the U.S. political and social system (Schlesinger, 1992).

Multicultural education has become a priority issue among educational policymakers for at least two reasons. First, in the last two decades considerable progress has been made in terms of historical scholarship. Newer methods of doing historical research have caused historians to rethink traditional interpretations of the past; moreover, scholars in the women's and ethnic studies departments that were established at many universities during the last 20 years have begun to uncover and publish important documentary evidence that supports a broader-based approach to American studies.

Second, the demographics of the student population in the nation's schools has undergone a rapid transformation in the last two decades. Not only has the traditional "majority-minority" distinction been rendered obsolete in dozens of key urban centers—where Americans of European descent are now a minority and one or more "minority groups," such as Asian, African American, Latino, and other immigrant groups, have become the majority—but the schools of California have already passed the "minority as majority" watershed mark and will soon be followed by school systems in New York, Texas, and Florida, together with countless other urban centers around the country. Educational policymakers are increasingly realizing that the effectiveness of the school systems they administer, both at the state and local level, will be measured in terms of how well the schools prepare *all students*, whether from minority or majority backgrounds, to assume productive roles in today's rapidly evolving world. Even at the national level, more and more Americans understand that a productive multicultural workforce, indeed, a workforce that is both literate *and* technologically competent, is the only guarantee of security later in life for the growing number of older citizens in an increasingly "graying" America.

ORILLAS responds to these pressing realities in several ways. For school systems with no multicultural curriculum in place, long-distance partnerships can provide students an invaluable contact with other cultural groups that will enrich their understanding of other cultures. Where a school district has already implemented a multicultural curriculum, working with a partner class can help bring the curricular units to life. In either case, the very fact of having a partnership with a distant class encourages local students to look more closely at their own community and at the multiple perspectives that may be found right before their eyes, within their own class, school, and neighborhoods. As these students use nonfiction writing to complete projects with their partner classmates, they will develop important insights into how reading and writing can mediate intercultural communication. And if they also use word processors to polish their writing and share their projects using computer-based communications systems, these students will also be building important technological skills as they engage in multicultural learning.

IMPROVING INTERGROUP RELATIONSHIPS AND REDUCING PREJUDICE

ORILLAS Case Partnership #5: An exchange between a class of Japanese-speaking students at a woman's college in Kyoto, Japan, and English-speaking future elementary school teachers taking a social studies teaching methodologies course in New York City.

ORILLAS Case Partnership #6: A collaboration between a class of French-speaking high school students in Quebec and a group of Spanish-speaking secondary students in Carolina, Puerto Rico.

Interestingly, some ORILLAS classes have actually used their *lack* of familiarity with the language of their partner class as a springboard for increased multicultural learning at a local level. For example, if a class does not understand the Spanish writing that they are receiving from their partner class, one effective response is to seek out local resources—whether fellow classmates or schoolmates, parents or community members—who can help translate into English, both linguistically and culturally, what the distant class has sent. In this example, the desire to understand another distant culture acts as a catalyst that activates face-to-face communication with "cultural informants" in the local community. Most important, not only has the message from faraway translated but, in the eyes of the students and their teacher, the status of the local informants has been raised. This can be an extremely important outcome in a community with a history of prejudice toward members of a specific cultural group.

There are other ways in which long-distance partnerships between teachers can work to improve intergroup relationships. More and more teachers are faced with the daunting challenge of incorporating children from a "minority" background into a class that is composed primarily of "majority" or "mainstream" students. Very often, the minority students are accorded a lower status by their classmates, and often the academic achievement of the minority students "fulfills the prophecy" of the lowered expectations of those around them. A particularly effective strategy for a teacher with such a class would be to establish a team-teaching partnership with a teacher who has students from the same cultural background as the minority students. In this type of customized partnership, the local minority students become cultural and linguistic experts who are especially qualified to help their classmates understand the strange but exciting messages they are receiving from their distant partner class. There is strong evidence that this type of partnership improves not only the majority students' attitudes toward their minority classmates but also serves to raise the self-esteem of the minority students themselves (Sayers, in press).

Conclusion: Schema Theory, Revisited

This chapter began with a discussion of the schema theory of reading comprehension. Schema theory is concerned with how an *individual* comprehends a written text through a dual process of assimilating new information to an existing schema (a structured codification of prior knowledge) and of accommodating new information by modifying an existing schema. Special mention was made of a particular schema—the "story grammar" that every child develops prior to entering school—that helps individual young readers comprehend fiction writings.

In effect, the team-teaching partnerships we have been discussing in this chapter work to develop students' literacy skills with nonfiction writing by encouraging the *social* construction of schema, building on *individual* schema as they evolve but extending and strengthening them through social interaction. Here,

Freinet's writings may prove helpful to us in fashioning a new version of schema theory that can account for the kind of literacy development that regularly occurs in long-distance team-teaching partnerships.

Much like schema theory itself, the exchange of texts between faraway classes was an integral, complementary component of a two-part process of literacy development. The learning of reading skills in Freinet's approach grows out of the interplay between students' greater familiarity with their own highly contextualized, locally-produced texts and their desire to understand the more decontextualized, unfamiliar texts that they receive from distant "partner classes."

> If on the one hand the child... creates new texts to satisfy his need for self-expression, utilizing words and expressions without worrying himself about the technicalities of syllables and letters, then on the other hand the practice of partnerships between classes places reading in an entirely different context. When the task becomes to decipher a written page [from a partner class], there is a totally different motivation, but equally personalized.... This is the moment in which the child really moves into reading comprehension and becomes aware of it as a process. Familiar words are immediately discovered and ones that have never been seen are analyzed perspicaciously. (Balesse & Freinet, 1973, pp. 64–65)

In other words, as local students worked in groups on curricular projects rooted in their own familiar realities, they were using their literacy skills to *assimilate* facts about their everyday lives into a common, socially constructed schema, which they then shared with their partner class. *Accommodation* occurred later when these same students received a similar curricular project from their partner classmates. The unfamiliar texts provoked their curiosity in a way that powerfully motivated strenuous efforts at further learning, ranging from simple language mechanics to alien vocabulary and complex comprehension issues. Indeed, for Freinet, the ability to comprehend writings from distant students formed a key aspect of his dual criteria for measuring achievement in literacy skills: "To our way of thinking, our students know how to read when they can easily read all the works they and their classmates have written, and when they can read passably well the texts sent from their correspondents" (Balesse & Freinet, 1973, p. 68).

Thus, team-teaching partnerships between distant classes hold great potential for helping students develop high levels of literacy with factual, descriptive, expository, and nonfiction written texts. Certainly this is the lesson to be learned from Freinet's decades of experience:

> Wherever this powerful teaching device of interscholastic partnerships is introduced, it becomes immediately evident to what extent this natural technique is superior to the artificial contrivances which are arrayed in order to provoke the interest and work necessary to assure the acquisition of the essential academic skills. (Gervilliers et al., 1977, p. 23)

Moreover, as was seen in the discussion of the ORILLAS team-teaching network, these distance collaborations are also promising for the insight they provide into effective intercultural communication and bilingual learning, competencies that are becoming more and more important with each passing school year.

Notes

1. The term "sojourner" refers to the large number of students who are involved with their families in what have been termed "circular" or "binational" migrations between two nations. Many sojourner students are found in Puerto Rican, Mexican, and Dominican communities, both in the United States and in their countries of origin.
2. Many of the suggested activities described in this section are drawn, in edited form, from orientation materials authored or coauthored by Kristin Brown, Enid Figueroa, and Dennis Sayers, coordinators of the ORILLAS teacher partnership network.

About the Author

Dennis Sayers is a professor of Bilingual Education at New York University. He has worked in bilingual, TESOL, and teacher education since 1973 and received his doctorate from the Harvard Graduate School of Education. In 1985 he, Kristin Brown (elsewhere in this book), and Enid Figueroa of the University of Puerto Rico founded ORILLAS, an international computer-based network of long distance team-teaching partnerships. The goal of ORILLAS is to strengthen cultural pride among linguistic minority students by making possible daily contact—via computers and other technologies—with fellow students from the countries of their parents' birth, thus fostering full bilingualism. Dr. Sayers' research interests include: biliteracy development; "circular" or binational migration; the reduction of prejudice toward minority students through collaborative learning activities; classroom questioning and intercultural inquiry; and the pedagogical theories of Célestin Freinet. These issues are the subject of a forthcoming book with Jim Cummins, *Brave New Schools: Cultural Illiteracy and the Politics of Exclusion*.

REFERENCES

Ada, A. F. (1988). Creative reading: A relevant methodology for language minority children. In Malave, L. M. (Ed.), *NABE '87. Theory, research and application: Selected papers*. Buffalo: State University of New York.

Balesse, L., and Freinet, C. (1973). *La lectura en la escuela por medio de la imprenta* (F. Beltran, Trans.). Barcelona: Editorial Laia. (Original work published 1961 as *La lecture par l'imprimerie a l'ecole* [Reading through printing in schools].)

Barnitz, J. G. (1986). Toward understanding the effects of cross-cultural schemata and discourse structure on second language reading comprehension. *Journal of Reading Behavior*, vol. 18, no. 1, pp. 95–116.

Barnitz, J. G. (1985). *Reading development of nonnative speakers of English: Research and instruction*. Language in Education Series, ERIC Clearinghouse on Language and Linguistics. Washington, DC: Center for Applied Linguistics and Harcourt Brace Jovanovich. (Also available on microfiche, ED 256 182.)

Bruner, J. (1966). *Toward a theory of instruction*. New York: W. W. Norton.

Campbell, R., and Lindholm, K. (1987). Conservation of language resources. *Educational Report Series, no. 8*. Los Angeles: University of California, CLEAR.

Carrell, P. L. (1984). Schema theory and ESL reading: Classroom implications and applications. *Modern Language Journal*, vol. 68, pp. 332–43.

Chall, J. (1979). The great debate: Ten years later, with a modest proposal for reading stages. In Resnick, L., and Weaver, P. (Eds.), *Theory and practice of early reading*. Hillsdale, NJ: Erlbaum.

Crawford, J. (1989). *Bilingual education: History, politics, theory and practice*. Trenton, NJ: Crane Publishing Company.

Crook, P., and Lehman, B. (1991). Themes for two voices: Children's fiction and nonfiction as "whole literature." *Language Arts*, vol. 68, pp. 34–41.

Cummins, J. (1981). The role of primary language development in promoting educational success for language minority students. In *Schooling and language minority students: A theoretical framework*. Los Angeles: Evaluation, Dissemination and Assessment Center, California State University.

DeVillar, R., and Faltis, C. (1991). *Computers and cultural diversity: Restructuring for school success*. Albany, NY: State University of New York Press.

Drum, P. A. (1984). Children's understanding of passages. In Flood, J. (Ed.), *Promoting reading comprehension*, pp. 61–78. Newark, DE: International Reading Association.

Englert, C., and Hiebert, E. (1984). Children's developing awareness of text structure in expository materials. *Journal of Educational Psychology*, vol. 76, pp. 65–74.

Freinet, C. (1974). *Las técnicas audiovisuales* (J. Colome, Trans.). Barcelona: Editorial Laia. (Original work published 1963 as *Les techniques audiovisuelles* [Audiovisual techniques].)

Freinet, E. (1975). *Nacimiento de una pedagogía popular: Historia de una escuela moderna* (Pere Vilanova, Trans.) Barcelona: Editorial Laia. (Original work published 1969 as *Naissance d'une pedagogie populaire* [Birth of a popular pedagogy].)

Gervilliers, D., Berteloot, C., and Lemery, J. (1977). *Las correspondencias escolares* (Editorial Laia, Trans.). Barcelona: Editorial Laia. (Original work published 1968 as *Les correspondances scolaires* [Interscholastic correspondence].)

Horowitz, R. (1985). Text patterns: Part I. *The Reading Teacher*, vol. 28, pp. 448–54.

Lee, W. B. (1983). Célestin Freinet, the unknown reformer. *Educational Forum*, vol. 48, no. 1, pp. 97–114.

Meyer, B. J., and Freedle, R. O. (1984). Effects of discourse type on recall. *American Educational Research Journal*, vol. 21, pp. 121–43.

Noyce, R., and Christie, J. F. (1989). *Integrating reading and writing instruction in grades K-8*. Boston: Allyn and Bacon.

Paley, V. G. (1990). *The boy who would be a helicopter*. Cambridge, MA: Harvard University Press.

Pappas, C., et al. (1990). *An integrated language perspective for teaching in elementary school*. White Plains, NY: Longman's.

Piccolo, J. A. (1987). Expository text structure: Teaching and learning strategies. *The Reading Teacher*, vol. 40, pp. 838–47.

Sayers, D. (in press). Bilingual team-teaching partnerships over long distances: A technology-mediated context for intra-group language attitude change. In Faltis, C., and DeVillar, R. (Eds.), *Cultural diversity in schools: From rhetoric to practice*. Albany, NY: State University of New York Press.

Sayers, D. (1990). *Interscholastic correspondence exchanges in Célestin Freinet's Modern School Movement: Implications for computer-mediated student writing networks*. Keynote address, October 17, 1990. First North American Freinet Congress, St. Catharines, Ontario.

Schlesinger, A., Jr. (1992). *The disuniting of America*. New York: Norton.

Simon, P. (1980). *The tongue-tied American: Confronting the foreign language crisis*. New York: Continuum.

Simons, E. (1990). *Student worlds, student words: Teaching writing through folklore*. Portsmouth, NH: Boynton/Cook.

Skutnabb-Kangas, T. (1984). *Bilingualism or not: The education of minorities*. Clevedon, England: Multilingual Matters Ltd.

Slater, W. (1985). Teaching expository text structure with structural organizers. *Journal of Reading*, vol. 28, pp. 712–19.

West, C. (1992) Diverse new world. In Berman, P. (Ed.), *Debating P.C.: The controversy over political correctness on college campuses*. New York: Laurel/Dell.

Balancing the Tools of Technology with Our Own Humanity:

The Use of Technology in Building Partnerships and Communities

Kristin Brown
Project ORILLAS, New York University

The Voices of Bilingual Educators

"Personalmente no puedo ni debo estar marginada frente a toda esta tecnología, pero aun pienso que de ninguna manera podemos pretender que todo esto pueda reemplazar en alguna forma el contacto humano entre los maestros, los alumnos y la comunidad." [Personally, I can't and shouldn't remain alienated when confronted by all this technology, yet I still think that in no way should we imagine that all this can replace human contact between teachers, their students, and the community.]
—*Elsa Mayorga-Cruson*

"I must begin by stating that I am leery of introducing certain aspects of technology in the classroom too soon. . . . I hesitate about introducing computers to children before they have had the exposure to more natural ways of learning, discovering, and expressing themselves." —*Marco Berger*

"I believe the most relevant issue at hand is balancing the tools of technology with our own humanness. . . . Are we using the end of creating students competent in futuristic technology to determine the focus of our teaching? Or are we looking at using technology to teach creative and critically based questioning of the educational and social process itself?" —*Nancy Jean Smith*

These are the voices of bilingual teachers enrolled in a graduate seminar on teaching Spanish literacy in the bilingual whole language classroom. Their voices serve as an invitation for all bilingual educators to consider the role of technology in our classrooms. To what extent do your views reflect those expressed above? The comments made by these teachers convey a strong sense of responsibility for preparing the language minority students in their classes to succeed in an increasingly technological world. Yet they also reveal a number of concerns. The teachers are interested in using technology but want to do so in a way that is consistent with their goals of encouraging students to actively and critically examine and question the world around them, all the while interacting with and learning from one another and the community in which they live.

Teachers are constantly reminded that technology skills will be essential in the world in which students will find themselves when they leave school. Bilingual teachers, in particular, feel this pressure to stay abreast of the changing times; statistics show that bilingual classrooms are lagging seriously behind in technology use. Low-income and ethnic minority students tend not to have the same access to computers as do their middle-income, nonminority counterparts; when minority groups or students with special learning difficulties do get access, they are more likely to be assigned to drill and practice rather than to problem-solving activities (Mehan, Moll & Riel, 1985). For immigrant students from minority language backgrounds, access to computers is especially limited. These traditionally underserved students are much less likely to learn with computers since only 22 percent of regular classroom teachers who teach limited English proficient students use computers compared to 50 percent of all other regular classroom teachers (Roberts & staff, 1988). Bilingual educators are anxious to bridge this equity gap.

Technology, however, has had negative effects both in schools and in the larger society. Of this there is little doubt. At home children spend large numbers of hours sitting passively in front of the television. The images they receive from mass media have to a large extent replaced not only the reading of books but interactions with others and engagement with the world around them. In schools a great deal of money has been spent on acquiring educational technologies. Yet in many cases the technologies remain idle for much of the school day and when they are used they are often employed for educationally trivial purposes or to transmit facts to students who are placed in the role of passive learners. Although the research literature frequently refers to the "power of educational computing," the reality is that many computers in schools are being used as little more than electronic workbooks.

The unfulfilled promises associated with technology use have left bilingual teachers with mixed feelings. The presence of technology in our lives is not going to go away and cannot be ignored. Yet initial efforts to incorporate computers and other technologies into the classroom have not been impressive. Bilingual teachers, such as those whose voices were heard at the beginning of this chapter, find disappointingly little evidence that the use of technology will support them in their efforts. They worry that overreliance on technology will undermine their efforts to make their classroom a humane place where the voice of each child is heard—where the emphasis is not on acquiring knowledge but creating it and using it to examine and change the world around them. How to justify the greater use of machines that have traditionally placed the student in a passive role?

There is a seductive quality about technology, something enticing in the promise that there is always something better just around the corner. Whatever solutions to educational problems that technology might hold, however, are unlikely to come in the form of a better machine that operates faster and has more features than machines of the past. Nor is it likely that a single solution will be appropriate for all students, just as standardized curriculum and standardized testing are inappropriate. On the contrary, the wisest and most powerful uses of technology are likely to come from sound pedagogical principles and from a knowledge of the language minority students in our classroom and their communities. The most important factors in exploring what those uses might be are not related to technical expertise but rather to trusting our instincts as humane teachers.

Three examples follow that illustrate the directions that progressive bilingual educators have taken in using technology in three distinct settings. These were selected to suggest a range of possible uses for technologies. The student populations portrayed are different, as are the technologies employed. In no case, however, was the technology used to teach or transmit skills in a traditional sense. Instead, the technologies are being used as communication tools; not simply to record and transmit words and voices but to create contexts, communities, and partnerships in which people traditionally silenced found a voice, contexts that encourage critical questioning. Each educator sought to develop uses which made sense in terms of the goals and participants in the project. In each case they were concerned about teaching students with emerging language skills. In every instance they were working with minority language populations and were concerned about the development of voice. These educators viewed literacy not just as the ability to read and write but rather as communicative competence in a variety of social settings.

Visits to Three Schools

Portrait #1: The Pajaro Valley Literacy Project and Alma Flor Ada's Creative Reading Steps: Enhancing critical reflection with videotape technology.

The Pajaro Valley Literacy Project is now widely known among educators interested in adult literacy and parent involvement in the schools. In this project Spanish-speaking parents—many with little schooling—not only learned how to develop their children's reading and writing skills through the use of children's literature but, in many cases, began to write themselves and eventually became recognized as community leaders. This innovative project received awards in 1990 as an exemplary bilingual education program from the California Association for Bilingual Education (CABE), the California State PTA, and has been recognized by California Tomorrow as a model project. As such, it has been implemented at numerous school sites.

This project was judged highly successful not only because it promoted literacy skills but also because it advanced goals that relate specifically to parent empowerment. The bilingual educators who worked with Alma Flor Ada, a professor at the University of San Francisco and an award-winning children's book author, to plan the Pajaro project had several motives for selecting the topic of children's literature. In addition to serving as a context for parents and their children to develop reading and writing skills, children's literature was also a theme that would not seem intimidating to parents, while providing opportunities for dialogue.

The decision to structure each session to promote dialogue among the parents had its roots in the work of Paulo Freire, the Brazilian scholar and adult educator, whose influential ideas will be discussed later in this section and whose work in the area of adult literacy had demonstrated the power of group dialogue among adults with emerging literacy skills. In the children's literature class, after each book was read, parents discussed the stories using a set of questions developed by Dr. Ada designed to encourage participants to relate each story to their own lives, to discuss alternative solutions to problems raised in the text, and finally to consider taking actions that would enrich and improve their own lives.

Using educational technology with the parents was not a part of the original design of the program. However, when over 60 Spanish-speaking parents gathered at the school library for the first meeting the project facilitators realized the interest was strong and that the process would be worth documenting. To this end, a video camera was set up to record the sessions. Because the project facilitators intended to use the videos for evaluation purposes, they were careful to record each two hour session and to include on the video all three phases of each meeting, the presentation of the books by the group leaders, the following discussion circles in which parents related the themes presented in the books to their own lives, and the open dialogue in which parents shared their concerns and read the books they had written with their children during the previous week.

After a few meetings, the facilitators began to notice changes taking place among the parents, such as greater confidence and willingness to speak in front of a group, and were glad that they had records of this process for their archives. However, it wasn't until these videos were available for parents to take home with them on a check-out system that the recordings began to play a bigger role in the project.

Indeed, the impact of this educational technology was unexpected and surprised everyone involved. One evening an eight-year-old boy who accompanied his mother to class volunteered to read to the group one of the books previously discussed. With a practiced hand he turned the pages of the book and with a confident voice and the eye contact of an experienced storyteller, he read the story to the roomful of adults. So impressed was the group with the storyteller's art and feeling with which the young boy read the book that they broke into applause. As the boy was being congratulated for his storytelling skills, he revealed that at his home the family had watched seven times the video of the session in which that book had been originally read.

In this way, the concepts presented were reinforced along with the model of how a story can be read or told. Yet this does not fully explain the impact of the videos on the community. The videotapes provided the children of Watsonville with the opportunity of seeing their parents reading aloud the stories created by their children. Alma Flor Ada explains, "The children have felt double pride, both in seeing their parents on the screen and in hearing their own stories being read aloud. This might explain why not only elementary school children but high schoolers as well have shown great interest in writing stories every month" (Ada, 1988, p. 233). The technology had made it possible for the children and parents to see themselves in new roles as active producers and interpreters of their own writings.

The number of families taking home the videos grew. The parents explained to the facilitators that instead of renting commercial videos they would check out the videos of the children's literature class and play them on the weekends for family and friends. For the families this became an evening's entertainment and they reported having a great time seeing themselves on the television, talking about how much they enjoyed the class, pointing out their friends, and critiquing their own performances as they read books to the group.

From time to time segments from these tapes were reshown during the meetings and discussed. According to Alma Flor Ada, "This allowed the parents to re-experience the process and analyze the dialogue further" (p. 233). Gradually, the amount of time at the meeting devoted to discussion among the parents grew longer. In this forum, parents not only described how they had used the books at home during the week with their children but also raised other social and political issues that were on their minds. Common concerns emerged from these discussions including the importance of bilingual education, the parents' pride in their culture, discipline issues, ways to help children succeed in school, problems such as drug use, and cultural differences between the U.S. and Mexico. One tape, for example, captures Mr. Andrade (who later became a "voice for his community," according to one of the teachers) describing the discouragement he felt upon coming to the U.S. and how great the contrast was between his village in Mexico, where everyone knows and greets one another, and his present town where, when he sees another person, he wonders if that person might harm him.

As the school year progressed the parents became less timid and gradually took on leadership roles, first in the meetings and later in their schools and community. During the evening literature sessions the parents asked to assume responsibility for leading the book discussion circles. One of the facilitators commented, "Mrs. Moran from Calabasas School spoke so clearly and strongly. She later became school site president. And Mr. Ramírez later presented at the state and national migrant conference." The parents, no longer intimidated by the school system, sat on committees and school site councils at their children's schools. As one father explained, "In these meetings we have learned to talk without being embarrassed or shy; it is very important to get rid of our inhibitions, because it is very difficult to talk in public." These parents, who had now honed their skills for speaking in front of a group and gained confidence at the parent meetings, had become leaders and policymakers in their community.

The videos, originally intended only for use by the teachers for documentation purposes, became a highly significant part of the whole project. It is important to note that the role the videotapes played in this project differed sharply from that of most video use in schools. In contrast to educational videos, whose purpose is to introduce new facts and concepts and to bring into the classroom scenes from the outside world, here the video is used to capture images of the participants themselves in the process of learning and engaging in dialogue to create knowledge together. Encouraging the participants to reflect more critically on their own learning provides them greater insight into their own experiences as learners, while giving them greater confidence to act upon these insights.

The idea that it is important for those involved to reflect on the process of learning through dialogue is one promoted strongly by Paulo Freire. He believes that a key moment in the process of critical reflection—reflection where the group begins to analyze their reality in a critical way and with an eye toward transforming that reality—occurs when participants step back, view themselves from a distance and gain a new perspective, reflecting on the very process in which they are engaged. These videotapes served as a catalyst for critical reflection among the Pajaro Valley parents.

We should not find it surprising that audiovisual technology also played a significant role in Paulo Freire's literacy campaigns in fostering this reflective distancing. Indeed, Freire used slides in his literacy campaign to promote dialogue and critical reflection among preliterate adults in Brazil. The first slides in the series contain familiar, everyday scenes from the communities of the participants. As a group, the participants in the dialogue circles discuss their roles in the communities in which they live and begin to see them in a new way. Freire (1970/1988) explains that:

> [when a] representation is projected as a slide, the learners effect an operation basic to the act of knowing: *they gain distance from the knowable object* [emphasis added]. This experience is undergone as well by the educators, so that educators and learners together can reflect critically on the knowable object which mediates between them. (p. 15)

In the last slide that Freire used in his literacy campaigns the image that the group discusses is the picture of themselves engaged in group discussion. Thus the adult learners begin to see the meaning and value of dialogue and critical reflection in a group context. As Cynthia Brown has written in *Literacy in 30 Hours: Paulo Freire's Process in Northeast Brazil* (1987):

> [The last slide] enables the group to develop its critical consciousness—to look at itself and reflect on its own activity. This picture shows a circle of culture functioning; participants can easily identify it as representing themselves. . . . The function of the circle of culture is examined by everyone—what the experience has meant, what dialogue is, and what it means to raise one's consciousness. By the time the group had reached this tenth picture, participants had regained enormous confidence in themselves, pride in their culture, and desire to learn to read. (pp. 224–25)

In a strikingly similar fashion, video technology played a key role in the Pajaro Valley project and in ways that surprised all the parents, children, and teachers involved. It became an educational technology that helped everyone in this community education project gain a new perspective on themselves as active learners capable of effecting change in their communities.

Portrait #2: La Escuela Abelardo Díaz Morales and the International ORILLAS Proverbs Project: Using telecommunications to conduct folklore investigations in the Spanish-speaking world.

La Escuela Abelardo Díaz Morales, named after a famous Puerto Rican educator, is an elementary school in Caguas, Puerto Rico. The students at this school are proud of their computer lab, the walls of which never fail to catch the eye of the visitor. On these bulletin boards are photographs of students and their teachers, flags of Mexico and California, illustrated maps, richly colored student artwork, a collection of Yaqui legends from the Southwest, and several issues of the student-produced newspaper "Cemi." These bulletin boards trace the history of this school's participation in Project Orillas. Each year since 1986, the computer writing teacher, Rosita Hernández, has engaged in a long-distance team-teaching exchange with a teacher in another class.

De Orilla a Orilla (From Shore to Shore), ORILLAS for short, is an international, multilingual network for bilingual, foreign language, and ESL teachers and other educators interested in cross-cultural learning. This project, codirected by the author, may be succinctly described as a computer-based collaborative teaching network for classroom practitioners. ORILLA's three-fold goal has been to use various classroom technologies to (1) increase both the native and English language proficiency of ethnic and linguistic minority students, (2) to improve both their academic achievement and their self-esteem, and (3) to promote positive intergroup relations between majority and linguistic minority students. To accomplish these ends, ORILLAS has employed an educational networking model first developed by the French pedagogue Celestin Freinet in 1924 (see companion chapter in this volume by Dennis Sayers). Following Freinet's model, ORILLAS is *not* a student-to-student pen-pal project but rather a class-to-class collaboration designed by partner teachers who have been matched according to common teaching interests and their students' grade level.

The first year Rosita participated in the project, her partner class was from San Diego, the next year from Arizona, and the following year from Tijuana. For the last two years she has been collaborating with a bilingual teacher in Connecticut, Arturo Solis. The interests of the students in Rosita's class, the themes her students are studying in their other classes, and the interests and curriculum of the partner teacher all play a role in making the decisions about what projects to collaborate on. This year, her class and Arturo's introduced the communities of Caguas and New Haven to each other by exchanging student-produced slide/tape shows in which the students in each class nominated important sites and situations in their communities to be photographed and then narrated a text telling about each slide into a tape recorder. Next, using word processing and telecommunications, their students collaborated on a joint newspaper, with a team from each class forming the editorial board to make the decisions about what to include in the final publication. To coordinate their own collaborative "works-in-progress," Rosita and Arturo use electronic mail to stay in frequent contact and to transmit their students' work. The computer network has also made it possible for them to stay in touch with the wider group of ORILLAS teachers and to participate in ORILLAS group projects, including a survey of endangered species, an international human rights project, and an intergenerational folklore investigation of childhood games.

Several times a week, often at morning recess, Rosita logs on to the computer network to see if there are messages waiting for her from her partner class. "You have three new messages" the computer announced one Monday. The first was from Arturo explaining that the final copy of the newspaper, produced jointly by their classes, was in the mail. Her students would be excited. After reading the electronic mail that had been sent to her personally, Rosita checked the bulletin board section, the section where teachers or coordinators can post messages or announcements to be seen by all the ORILLAS participants. The other two new messages were from the project coordinators, one in Spanish and one in English, announcing the ORILLAS group project for the upcoming semester: a proverbs contest. She knew that not only other teachers from Puerto Rico, but teachers from French Canada, from many parts of the United States, from Mexico and maybe a few from Central America would come across this message too. This could prove to be interesting. She left another quick note for Arturo—remember to check the announcements—and logged off so she could print out the proverbs announcement and read it more carefully before sharing it with her fourth graders.

"Tell us again what the categories are," the class asked after Rosita read them the message. "I know a proverb," one student began eagerly, " 'Dime con quién andas' [tell me who your friends are] . . ." ". . . 'y te diré quién eres' [and I will tell you who you are]," the rest of the class chimed in. "But let's try to think of some with animals," they added. "How about, 'Perro que no camina, no encuentra hueso' [A dog that doesn't walk around won't find a bone]. That's what my uncle says to my father who he thinks should sell his house here and move to New York to look for a full-time job." "I know what your father could tell your uncle," another student replies, " 'Pájaro en mano vale cien volando' " [A bird in the hand is worth two in the bush]. "Who's going to write these down?" By the end of the period the class had typed in on the computer a list of 32 proverbs, 9 of which included the names of animals. As the class period ended they discussed where to get more. "I'll ask my teacher," announced one student. "I'll ask my grandmother," said another.

The next time the computer writing class met, everyone brought in proverbs to share, even the students who rarely turned in homework on time. Over the next few weeks the list grew as students collected proverbs from parents, older brothers and sisters, grandparents living at home, neighbors, and other nearby relatives. It was during the school's spring break, however, the week of "Semana

Santa" when families travel to other parts of the island to visit friends and relatives, that the list grew the most dramatically. Just before the vacation, Rosita printed out for each student a copy of the animal proverbs collected up to that point. When the students arrived back at school the following week their lists

---

Announcing: International Proverbs Project

from Kristin Brown, Dennis Sayers, and Enid Figueroa
ORILLAS Coordinators

ORILLAS is sponsoring a multilingual proverbs contest. We invite your students to participate in one or more of the following categories:

- **BEST DRAWING** illustrating one of the following proverbs: "Those who live in glass houses should not throw stones" or "It takes all kinds to make the world go around."

- **BEST ORIGINAL FABLE.** Students pick a proverb, write an original story illustrating that proverb, then give the proverb at the end of the story as the "punchline."

- **GREATEST NUMBER OF "ANIMAL" PROVERBS SUBMITTED BY A SINGLE CLASS.** Example, "A barking dog never bites." Helpful hint: Ask the parents and relatives of your students to help out!

- **GREATEST NUMBER OF CONTRADICTORY PROVERBS SUBMITTED BY A SINGLE CLASS.** Example, "There's no place like home" contradicts "The grass is greener on the other side of the fence."

- **BEST ORIGINAL ESSAY ON "WHAT'S WRONG WITH THIS PROVERB."** Pick a proverb you don't agree with and write an essay explaining what is wrong with the views it projects. Not all proverbs are wise; some of them say terrible things about others. For example, the sexist proverb "A woman's place is in the home" suggests that women should only do housework. Other proverbs are racist, ageist, or ridicule people with handicaps.

The contest is open to students of all grades and speakers of all languages. By identifying proverbs whose social, moral, or political views are obsolete, by searching for modern examples to illustrate noble or wise proverbs, and by exploring under what circumstances seemingly contradictory proverbs are true, we can all help define the "collective wisdom" of the twentieth century.

At the end of the semester each participating class will receive a booklet containing selected student essays, photocopies of the drawings, and a list of all the proverbs collected. We look forward to hearing from you. To participate in the contest or contribute to the collection, write to KBROWN.

---

were well-worn and greatly extended. "Exactly a hundred animal proverbs!" they exclaimed when they had finished adding the new proverbs to the old. It was time, they decided, to send one copy of the list off to the project coordinators and another to Mr. Solis's class.

"We'd like to read some of your stories," they wrote to their partner class, "Did any of the students write fables about animal proverbs?" Arturo had described in an earlier message how his class had decided to do a unit on fables, first reading fables in Spanish and English written by Samaniego, Aesop, and La Fontaine, then writing their own fables based on the proverbs they had collected. Arturo wrote back, "Yes, Jessica wrote a fable about an animal proverb which she has ready to send to you. She dedicates this story to her own grandfather who helps her with her math and reading homework."

El mismo perro pero con diferente collar.

Había una vez una maestra llamada Ms. Caraballo. Estaba enseñando a sus estudiantes de 3.ᵉʳ grado cómo multiplicar. Ella les enseñaba todo lo necesario a sus alumnos.

"Bueno estudiantes", dijo Ms. Caraballo. "¿Cuánto es 2 × 3?" Sólo una estudiante levantó su mano y dijo, "seis". Todos los estudiantes entendieron eso, menos Pedro.

"Maestra", dijo Pedro, "yo no sé cómo hacer eso".

"Bueno Pedro", dijo Ms. Caraballo amablemente. "Esto es como si tú dijeras 3 + 3, pero en otra forma. Como si dijeras 3 + 3 + 3 que es lo mismo que 3 × 3, que es igual que 9, pero en otra forma".

"Ahora ya entiendo", dijo Pedro. "Es como mi abuelo me dijo del refrán—'el mismo perro pero con diferente collar'."

[The same dog but with a different collar.

Once there was a teacher named Ms. Caraballo. She was teaching her third-grade students to multiply. She taught her students everything they needed to know.

"OK, students," said Ms. Caraballo, "how much is 2 × 3?" Only one student raised her hand and said "six." All the students understood this, except Pedro.

"Teacher," said Pedro, "I don't know how to do that."

"Well, Pedro," said Ms. Caraballo in a friendly way, "it is like saying 3 + 3 but in a different form. Just as 3 + 3 + 3, 3 × 3, and 9 are all different ways of saying the same thing."

"Now I understand," said Pedro, "it's just like the proverb my grandfather taught me—'The same dog but with a different collar.' "]

Arturo added, "Mónica, who just moved here from Puerto Rico, would also like to share her story with you. She hopes that Daymari, Yazmín, Víctor, and any of the other students in your class who have lived at one time in the U.S. will write back to us and tell us which of these two proverbs they agree with."

A kilómetro dividido viene el olvido. Las distancias hacen que el amor crezca.

Había una vez dos niños que crecieron juntos, una niña y un niño. Siempre jugaban juntos, caminaban juntos, nadaban juntos y se iban a la escuela juntos. Un día los papás del niño se fueron a Nueva York y la niña se quedó en Puerto Rico. Cuando estaban tan lejos se dieron cuenta que se extrañaban y se querían. Entonces la mamá le dice a la niña, "olvídate de ese niño, aquí hay muchos otros niños, búscate un amigo aquí, pues 'A kilómetro dividido viene el olvido'." Pero la niña le decía que no y que ella y él siempre se recordaban uno del otro porque 'Las distancias hacen que el amor crezca'.

[Out of sight, out of mind. Absence makes the heart grow fonder.

Once there were two children who grew up together, a girl and a boy. They always played together, walked together, swam together, and went to school together. One day the boy and his parents moved to New York and the girl stayed in Puerto Rico. When they were so far apart they realized how much they missed each other and cared for each other. The mother said to the girl, "Forget about that boy, there are many others here, 'Out of sight, out of mind.' " But the girl told her mother no, that she and he would always remember each other because 'Absence makes the heart grow fonder.' "]

CREATING A CULTURE OF READING

At the beginning of May, a package arrived in the mail at the school with not just one book of proverbs but two. So many animal proverbs had been collected by the students in Puerto Rico, Mexico, and the United States that they filled a volume of their own. Rosita's students counted them (630 animal proverbs in Spanish), noting with pleasure when they found their own among them. They also found in the package a large envelope and inside, an award certificate. The students at La Escuela Abelardo Díaz Morales had collected more animal proverbs than any other class. The students found a prominent place on the bulletin board to display the certificate, and Rosita made photocopies of the two books so that the students would be able to check out the books and share them with their families.

The second volume of the proverbs book, containing the fables, essays, and drawings that were submitted by the participating classes, illustrates the different ways the project evolved in different classrooms. Some interesting writing came from students who wrote about proverbs they don't agree with. Proverbs are controversial by nature because it is impossible to separate them from the social fabric in which they have developed and exist. Cervantes recognized this when he called proverbs, "short sentences drawn from long experience." In the following examples, students from New York draw on their own experiences as they critique proverbs they feel are unfair:

Buen indio pero sólo muerto.

Yo no estoy de acuerdo con esto, definitivamente no, porque esto quiere decir que los indios no son buenos. Pues esto no es así, solamente en la tele es que se ven los indios malos, pero también se ven los indios buenos. Es verdad que hay indios buenos y que viven unas vidas tranquilas y útiles. Mi maestra dice que también este refrán se le aplica a otras razas de gente que sea diferentes a la nuestra. Pues si es así, pues en todas razas de gente hay buenas y malas. Yo soy de Puerto Rico y sí hay buenos y malos entre nosotros.

[The only good Indian is a dead Indian.

I do not agree with this, definitely not, because this says that Indians are no good. But this is not the case, only on the TV do you see bad Indians, but you also see good Indians. It is true that there are good Indians and that they live peaceful and useful lives. My teacher says that this proverb also applies to other races of people that are different from our own. This is true; in every race there are both good people and bad. I am from Puerto Rico and it is true that there are good people and bad among us.]

Students from all the regions represented in this project were critical of proverbs they found to be sexist. The least popular proverb among bilingual students in the United States was:

El lugar de la mujer es en el hogar.

Yo Martha Prudente no estoy de acuerdo en que la mujer esté en el hogar. Eso era el pensamiento de los tiempos antiguos. Así era como mis padres pensaban pero yo no porque soy rebelde. Sí, yo voy a tener un hogar pero si quiero trabajar voy a trabajar. Y pienso ser enfermera antes de casarme y después yo sigo trabajando en mi carrera.

[A woman's place is in the home.

I, Martha Prudente, do not agree that a woman's place is in the home. This kind of thinking is old-fashioned. This is how my parents thought, but not me because I am a rebel. Yes, I will have a home but if I want to work I will work. I hope to be a nurse before I get married and afterwards continue working in my career.]

Older family members and grandparents had contributed so much to the proverbs project that this was also an unpopular proverb:

Perro viejo no aprende.

Yo no estoy de acuerdo con eso porque yo conozco gente mayor o de edad que sí aprenden y sí tienen la mente muy clara. Mi abuelo tiene un amigo en Santo Domingo que sabe muchas cosas. Él sabe tanto como para enseñar a otras personas mucho más jovenes.

[You can't teach an old dog new tricks.

I do not agree with this because I know older people who do learn and who have a very sharp mind. My grandfather has a friend in Santo Domingo who knows many things. He knows so many things that he can teach much younger people.]

The contest described above stems from a long-standing and continuing interest on the part of ORILLAS teachers in using folklore in the classroom. The teachers involved in the project concluded that proverbs provide an excellent vehicle for students to share cultural and linguistic knowledge:

◆ Proverbs are universal.

◆ The families of students are involved, encouraging oral histories.

◆ Analyzing proverbs encourages discussion, critical thinking, and a deromanticized appreciation of culture.

◆ Language minority students in the United States build links to their (in some cases, disappearing) culture and take pride in their rich proverbial heritage.

◆ Students studying Spanish as a second language gain from the cultural knowledge embodied in proverbs.

◆ Young students can participate as the amount of text to be shared is small and easily entered in the computer.

◆ Proverbs can encourage much longer writings, such as opinion statements or modern fables.

◆ Categorizing proverbs by themes can be done with a data base facilitating cross-cultural comparisons.

◆ Collecting proverbs is a provocative, yet discrete, task—it's rich, but has a concrete product as an outcome.

In this project, telecommuncations made it possible for bilingual students from diverse regions to collaborate on a wide-ranging investigation of proverbs and to create materials that classroom teachers can use to stimulate reading and writing and that can be shared with families and communities as a reminder of the rich oral heritage in the Spanish-speaking world. Folklore collections of all kinds are useful in building bridges between schools and families and the wider community of Spanish speakers.

Portrait #3: Sherman School Parent/Child Computer Class and Project Orillas: Strategies for using computers to promote collaborative learning in a heterogeneous class.

Sherman Elementary is located in Barrio Sherman in San Diego, California, in a neighborhood principally composed of Latino, African American, Cambodian, and Euro-American communities. During the 1989–1990 school year, ethnic and linguistic minority parents and their children from this school participated in an ORILLAS telecommunications exchange with other groups of parents and children from Denver, Colorado, and from Caguas, Puerto Rico. While most ORILLAS partnerships take place between school-age children, this example describes the experiences of a group that included both parents and children. I selected this example because of the particularly wide range of ages, languages, and literacy skills of the participants. It is important to note that the changing dynamics in the Sherman class are similar to those that take place in a bilingual class where there are students with varying degrees of Spanish and English proficiency (Sayers, in press, article for Faltis & DeVillar).

At the start of the 1989–1990 school year, Sherman School announced an after-school computer course for both parents and their children. All parents, regardless of their linguistic or academic backgrounds, would be welcome. Both the teacher of this literacy class, Lourdes Bouras, and the school contact person, Laura Parks-Sierra, had worked extensively with students in the ORILLAS Project in previous years and had discovered the effectiveness both of using computers with a variety of communication activities and of having students work in teams.

The design of the parent-child literacy course would be similar to the approach they had already used in ORILLAS: local partners would work on the computer, learning to use it both as a writing tool (word processing) and as a communication tool (telecommunications). Next, the many partners who made up the Sherman School literacy course would form another kind of partnership with distant "partner classes," using electronic mail. Finally, what they wrote would eventually be published locally in a newsletter distributed in the community. The only difference between previous ORILLAS' projects and this literacy course would be that this time the local partnerships would be made of a parent and his or her child.

The "computer" course was announced at school to all second to sixth grade students and on the first night of the class dozens of parents appeared. Several confided that they were tired after long days at work and of caring for families and might not have left the house except for the insistence of their children for whom computer time is a favorite activity. However, by the end of the evening many commented that they were intrigued with the prospect of learning how to use a computer with their children, particularly the idea of communicating with other parents and children in far-off places like Colorado and Puerto Rico.

At the outset there were some difficulties just in learning to use word processing and other software. Explanations to the group seemed labored: the teacher was fluent in Spanish and in English, but English speakers initially expressed some impatience at having to wait during translations, at the time thus "wasted" or "taken" from more important, computer-related tasks. Parents were at very different levels of English proficiency. Moreover, Ms. Bouras reported her sense that during initial computer projects, whoever was at the keyboard assumed control, creating barriers for others to join in as full participants.

Yet once communications from the distant parent groups began to arrive, some interesting changes seemed to take place in parents' and students' attitudes, both toward engaging in computer-based collaborations and toward language use. The teacher and school contact person insist that parents and students began to see the computer as a tool for communication. In this regard, it was clear that everyone felt more comfortable with the new technology, since communication was something that all understood and felt competent at. The group, faced with the task of representing and describing San Diego in response to the initial questions of the distant groups, became more cohesive.

To help introduce themselves to their partner groups in Colorado and Puerto Rico, the Sherman School parents and children decided to make and send a "cultural package" that featured a book to which everyone could contribute, regardless of their level of literacy in their mother tongue or in English. For example, the Cambodian family in which parents could not speak, read, or write in English brought in the most pictures, hand-drawn sketches, and magazine articles. Together, parents and their children elaborated a clear picture of the book they wanted to send; the parents and children worked in teams to create the different sections and then shared their writing and the pictures they had gathered with the rest of the group. By the time the parents had helped one another, the children had helped their parents, and all the text had been typed in and printed out using the computer; the cultural package book had become a "seamless" group product where the individuality usually expressed in the concept of "authorship" had become unimportant.

Moreover, the status of the Spanish speakers changed when the majority of the text began arriving in Spanish. As the group logged on to the electronic mail system to read messages from Colorado and Puerto Rico, parents and children pulled their chairs as close as possible to the computer to read the text as it came across the screen. Suddenly, proficiency in Spanish became highly prized as the texts which everyone in the course was so interested in reading scrolled by in Spanish. English speakers now saw the importance of devoting time to translation, even insisting that translation be done carefully to ensure that everyone understood the messages. English-speaking parents, who previously had worked on their own, sought seats next to Spanish speakers and were active in assuring that the teacher had translated every detail (at times, double-checking with their local bilingual/bicultural "expert"). In Ms. Parks-Sierra's words, "These discussions really seemed to bring the group together."

Thus the concept of teamwork was expanding. To be sure, all teams did not function identically. Some parents and their children "shared" equally all stages of writing (prewriting, drafting, and revising and editing) and translating (from their home language to English and back). Other teams divided the writing task in a variety of effective ways, with some parents playing the key role of topic "definers" in the home language while their children, who sat at the keyboard, acted as language interpreters and "refiners" in English.

Dear Parents and Children,

Our names are Keovong, Maria, and Eam. I am Keovong the one that is typing because I am good at typing. I was born in Philippines and my parents are from Cambodia. My mom come to computer class. My mom is writing in Cambodian and someone will translate it in English or Spanish. My dad used to come with me to the computer. Many of my people had died in Cambodia. My land has been taken by the bad people. But now I am far away from my home land and I am safe in San Diego. . . .

Your new friend,

Keovong Sar [October 1990]

This was just the first stage in the "sequence of nested collaborations." Next there would be closer collaboration between linguistic minority groups, as parents and children translated for one another and began to share their differing cultural and linguistic skills.

CREATING A CULTURE OF READING

Unlike previous courses for parents sponsored by the Sherman School, attendance in the parent-child computer course justified continuing the class for the entire academic year. Parents and children attributed this, in large part, to the communications with the faraway parent groups and the parents' continuing interest in what the distant partner classes would write. By the end of the year, the Sherman School parents and children had created numerous collaborative publications including:

◆ A bilingual booklet of parent-teacher conference guidelines distributed to all of Sherman School's parents and teachers.

◆ Bilingual books, including a parent-child guidebook to San Diego for the Sherman School library's permanent collection, and for the Puerto Rico and Colorado parent groups, describing interesting places for families to visit in San Diego.

◆ An international *refranero,* or book of proverbs, for which parents consulted with their extended families to create lists of proverbs (and how they are used).

◆ An international collection of articles on self-esteem and technology, for which the Sherman School computer class worked with university professors, psychologists, teachers, and other parents and children from North America and South America.

◆ A community newspaper—the product of collaboration with teachers and administrators and children at Sherman School.

As parents saw the many resources and talents of the members of the group and realized how much they could accomplish if they just pooled their efforts in a way that hadn't happened in the past, they came to see that other parents would be interested in what they had to say. They gained confidence in their ability to publish a newspaper and they realized that together they had the potential to effect change in the community through their voices. Literacy skills emerged without having been "taught" in these long-distance partnerships where the emphasis was on collective group-to-group participation.

REFLECTIONS ON THE VISITS

These are all stories about technology use, yet they are also stories about the building of partnerships and communities, stories of people committed to learning together, both within classrooms and across distances. The educators in these classrooms found ways to create dialogues in which the lives and the concerns of each of the students emerged and could be woven together to form the basis for the curriculum and which encouraged students to reflect on the process of learning and what it means in their lives.

It is largely because of the commitment of these bilingual educators to tailor the curriculum to the unique characteristics and experiences of their students that one classroom may seem to the observer quite different from the next. For example, the coordinators of the Pajaro Valley project found that videotapes, with their capacity to capture images and record voices of the participants, were ideally suited for their community-based work with adults. In contrast, when the teachers at Sherman School focused on word processing and telecommunications, they were selecting a written medium for communication. Although many of the participants in their project, like those in the Pajaro Valley project, had only emerging written language skills, this choice of technology was extremely effective in bringing together members of the heterogeneous group into the teams where their literacy and communication skills were nurtured. In the example of the proverbs project, word processing and telecommunications were again employed but for a different purpose. While in the Sherman School computer class, teachers were concerned with developing written skills; in the proverbs project, on the other hand, teachers used technology to help students rediscover and revive disappearing oral traditions.

While in each of these classrooms, technology use evolved in unique ways, an interesting pattern emerges when the examples are examined collectively. In every case, as noted earlier, the educators were concerned both with creating authentic contexts for dialogue and providing opportunities for critical reflection. What role does technology play in promoting dialogue and reflection? In the Pajaro Valley project, the opportunity for parents to meet together in the school library where they could read books and discuss not only children's literature but their own lives, provided the context for dialogue. Videotapes later served the important purpose of fostering the process of critical reflection that had begun in the group. This process was described by Freire as "reflective distancing," that is, the process of gaining sufficient distance from one's immediate reality in order to better understand it.

A closer examination of the other two examples, however, shows a different yet equally intriguing form of "reflective distancing" at work. In both the Sherman School computer class and Puerto Rican proverbs projects, the groups corresponded with distant classes. These partnerships between classes can also provide a meaningful context for dialogue. As students raise questions for the distant group and respond to the questions the partner class sends them, they begin to see their own lives in a new way. First, students come to know their own communities better as they seek to describe those communities for their partners. Then, as they come to see their own world through the eyes of the distant class, they gain distance from the reality which surrounds them, another example of the process of reflective distancing. Thus, there are built-in opportunities in class-to-class exchanges for the kind of productive distancing that leads to critical reflection.

There are, however, other challenges in sustaining dialogue in these long-distance partnerships. For a true dialogue to develop between distant classes—an exchange where students raise genuine questions and respond sincerely to what the other group sends—students must feel engaged and committed. This is where technology can play an important role. With the use of telecommunications, where texts are exchanged over the telephone lines, the turn-around time is minimal, eliminating the long wait associated with exchanges through the mail. The texts then take on a lively conversational quality. In addition, when photographs, audiotapes, and videotapes are exchanged the classes come to know each other and become truly interested in how other students think and perceive the world. In the words of the children who engage in these partnerships, technology helps make the distant partners more "real" and more "human."

These examples help illustrate the dual role technology can play in promoting dialogue and critical reflection in the classrooms of bilingual educators. In face-to-face dialogue, technologies can be instrumental in creating the distance necessarily for critical reflection. In exchanges between distant classes, technologies can help establish the kinds of personal relationships that foster authentic dialogue.

Implications for Bilingual Educators: Principles for Guiding Decision Making About Technology Use

In each of the previous three examples, the educators involved developed uses for technology that were highly effective in their particular settings. These detailed portraits illustrate the extent to which the decisions made by these educators responded to the needs and interests of the participants in their projects. They also reveal how uses for technology were discovered serendipitously. In the Pajaro Valley project, videotapes were first intended for evaluation purposes and the decision to share them with the parents was made after the project began. At Sherman School, having students work on writing and "communication" projects together at the computer became a focus of the project only after other kinds of sharing at the computer were shown to be less successful. In Puerto Rico, participation in the computer writing network was originally seen as a way to build students' written skills and to learn about life in other countries. In fact, the network provided unexpected opportunities for students to explore more deeply the rich oral traditions in their own families and communities.

These experiences, very different from one another but all effective in building both oral and written language skills, suggest that lists of recommended technologies or catalogs of proposed activities are not useful without a constant focus on the different paths educators might take in adopting technologies in their classrooms. The examples help convey the subtleties of the decisions educators make and suggest the inappropriateness of standardized approaches. What may be most useful are broad principles for technology use. The following basic principles were derived from the writings of Paulo Freire, Celestin Freinet, Mario Lodi (an Italian follower of Freinet), Alma Flor Ada, and other progressive educators and are supported by current research on language acquisition, the writing process, and collaborative learning.

I. *Look for technologies over which you can get control, especially communications technologies.*

Find ways to use technologies as tools for creating knowledge in social contexts. Tool applications might involve producing and filming original plays with a videotape recorder, using audiocassette recorders for intergenerational interviews, writing with a word processor, doing research with data bases, or mounting joint projects with distant classes through telecommunications. In particular, look for communications technologies, technologies that will allow your students to capture, record, and share their own words and worlds.

In searching for tools that will be useful in your classroom do not overlook the potential uses of old or "out-of-date" machines such as overhead projectors, thermofax machines, or slide projectors that may be gathering dust on the shelves at your school. Consider using technologies that are not usually found in classrooms, such as fax machines, to exchange student artwork and illustrated poems with other classes or to consult with local business or community organizations. Finally, getting control over technology may mean not using the machines with the materials or software that come with them. A ditto machine does not have to be used for worksheets; a roomful of expensive drill and practice software may be less useful than a single public domain word processing program with Spanish fonts.

II. *Look for technologies that will allow students to publish their writing.*

When students' writing is read, appreciated, and responded to by others, the student authors see the importance of their words and are motivated to continue writing. The books students write can be photocopied so that copies can be placed not only in the classroom and school libraries but also sent home with the students. There are also a variety of printing technologies that make it possible for every class to produce a periodical publication. This might take the form of a newspaper, a magazine, or a series of books to be shared with other classes.

Desktop publishing software makes it easy for students to assume responsibility of a newspaper project from beginning to end and to print out a professional-looking newspaper that can then be photocopied and distributed to the community. Such specialized software, however, is not necessary. Word processing and a classroom printer make an ideal combination, or if computers are not available, a typewriter and a thermofax machine or photocopy machine can be used. Student control of the process and frequency of publication will in most cases be the most important factors.

Classroom journalism projects can be enriched by organizing field trips to local newspaper offices and by arranging to stay in touch with the newspaper staff. Using speakerphones, fax machines, or telecommunications software and a modem, students can discuss editorial decisions and questions about the publishing process with reporters and editors from local bilingual newspapers. Keep in mind that peer editing and responding can also be a rich source of feedback during the writing process. Classroom printers and school duplicating machines make it easy for students to make multiple copies of their writing to share with classmates during the composing process.

III. *Look for technologies that will allow you to record oral language.*

Encourage your students to create "oral texts." Young children love to tell stories and to retell the stories they have been told at home and school. With technologies such as audiotape and videotape that make it possible to record and replay oral language, students can share their ideas and stories with a wider audience of friends, family, and distant audiences. In this way, students gain a sense of what it means to become an author even at a very early age.

A good way to begin is to have a tape recorder running as the students tell about a drawing they have created or a photograph of themselves engaged in a favorite activity with their family. The words of the student can be transcribed into a book by an upper-grade student volunteer. Another possibility is to have students' first presentations to a large group be a drawing or series of drawings that they have created on overhead transparencies, along with a tape recording of their voices. In this way they can put their best work in front of the class, rerecording if they are not happy with the first version. In one class, newly arrived immigrant students told their stories by creating filmstrips with a series of illustrations and an accompanying tape. When their stories were projected in front of the group, the young authors could sit with the audience and experience for themselves the impact of their own words.

Encourage students to use audio- and videotape recorders to bring the voices of the community into the school. Technologies that record voices are useful not only as a bridge between oral and written language but also as a bridge between the school and the community. These technologies hold great potential for helping to make the reality of the students present at all times in the school setting and to represent the different cultures of the students in our classrooms and schools.

Together, students and their families can create compendiums of folklore and collections of community narratives. Folklore compendiums can include collections of proverbs, children's rhymes and riddles, fables and folktales, and lullabies and songs. These collections are really inter-generational studies, since students often "go straight to the source" by consulting with parents, grandparents, and other relatives in their extended families. Comparative oral histories take a slightly different approach. To complete these projects, students (armed with tape recorders and notebooks) arrange to interview key community figures on agreed-upon themes, such as "what was school like for parents and grandparents?" or other topics relating to local community heritage. Oral histories can be an excellent vehicle for students to study the important themes of history, change, and conflict in their own communities.

IV. *Encourage students to work collaboratively to create group texts.*

There are many benefits to be gained from collaborative learning projects. Working together to create an article for a classroom newspaper or a story to send to distant friends can be helpful for emerging writers. When students work collaboratively on a project there are a number of valuable outcomes: (a) the many talents and differing perspectives of the contributors are reflected in a richer final product that is satisfying to all involved; (b) the division of labor, if carefully organized, provides opportunities for students to demonstrate their strengths to their peers; (c) students who are shy about producing on their own can contribute where they feel most comfortable; (d) the need to plan out loud will make clear to all involved the stages of the composing process.

Group productions need not be limited to written texts. In addition to the opportunities audio and video technologies provide, new developments in interactive multimedia, where computer technologies can be used to combine graphics and text with video and audio sequences, hold great potential for group work. A sixth-grade class used interactive multimedia to create a presentation of the "baile folklórico" of Mexico. One team used computer graphics to create a map of Mexico with each region labeled. Another team learned the dances from several regions and created costumes. A third team videotaped their classmates performing the dance and assembled all the pieces. Another elementary class plans to create a multimedia presentation using HyperCard to rewrite the history of their city from the perspective of the immigrant groups who have settled there, using videotaped and audiotaped interviews with members of the community. They have digitized old photographs and are writing a text and creating a map of the different neighborhoods.

V. *Encourage students to use technology in responding creatively and critically to the books they read.*

Creative expression can have a valuable role in any reading program. All stories lend themselves to some sort of dramatic expression. Students might write a script and act out a play based on the book. The performance might then be videotaped for the classroom lending library. The idea of creating different versions of a text has a special meaning in light of new views on reading. Reading is coming to be seen not as extracting the author's meaning from the text but instead relating it to the reader's own life. "Within this creative conception of reading, the essential element is not what the text says, but what the text comes to mean to the reader once he or she has processed it from his or her own experience and thus critically reinterpreted the text" (Ada & Zubizarreta, 1989, p. 11). For example, students might use audiotapes to create a "radio show" with editorial comments from the perspectives of the different characters in the story. Or students might use videotape to act out two different versions of the story to relate and contrast their own experiences with the reality presented by the book.

VI. *Use technology to promote critical reflection.*

A question raised by one of the bilingual teachers at the beginning of this chapter asked how we might use technology to teach creative and critically based questioning of the educational and social process. This kind of awareness entails not simply looking outward but also looking inward at our own goals and asking ourselves what we want to learn and what we are learning. As teachers we can encourage students to keep records of their own learning through journals.

It is important, however, not only to think in terms of individual progress but also in terms of group progress toward the collective goals of the class. Recording students' voices, words, actions, and thoughts can encourage them to discuss their experiences both at school and in the community. Students might keep a record of what they as a group are accomplishing and want to accomplish. Keep a camera in class. One of the students might take the role of "resident photographer" in charge of documenting the project. Encourage students to create an album in which they write the text telling what happened and what they learned. Talk about projects the class engages in as having a beginning (identify how that interest came from the lives of the students), a middle, and a future (discuss what steps are being taken and what further questions have arisen).

The emphasis is now on portfolio assessment. These portfolios can have a number of purposes; one is to share with families to let them see them progress and see changes that are taking place. As you think about how best to display the strengths of the each student, consider using audiotapes to record a student reading or recounting a favorite story. You might also include a videotape with the student acting out a play with friends or teaching a minilesson to the class. One school encourages the students to each keep their own computer disk or to create a folder on the computer's hard disk that can serve as an "electronic portfolio" for the writing they consider to have been most significant in their development as a writer.

VII. *Use technology to engage your students in dialogue with another class: long-distance team-teaching partnerships.*

When you create a long-distance team-teaching partnership with a distant class you provide students a motivating context for communication as well as a context for interactive inquiry. If your students correspond with a group of native Spanish speakers there will be valuable opportunities to strengthen Spanish language skills. As described earlier, technology can play the important role of "amplifying the volume" to ensure that the distant class has a strong presence in your classroom: (a) telecommunications facilitates a rapid turn-around time for messages so that a sense of dialogue is created between the two classes and sustained; and (b) photographs, audiotapes, and videotapes help students get to know one another.

Of all the principles mentioned, perhaps this one holds the most promise. It is a broad activity within which many of the other strategies described can have a role. In almost every instance, the value of the other strategies can be enhanced by involving a partner class. There is another reason, however, that this strategy holds tremendous potential for our work. Team-teaching partnerships are not only partnerships between children; they are partnerships between teachers.

This section on principles began with a comment about how some of the most powerful uses of technology in the examples had been discovered along the way and that the educators involved, because they were observant and reflective teachers, had adjusted their plans to take advantage of the technologies they had introduced into the classroom in new and unanticipated ways. In so doing, they discovered new uses for these tools. Celestin Freinet, who created the largest interscholastic network ever formed, described the context provided by interscholastic exchanges as that of a scientific laboratory in which teachers can discard the rigidities of fixed curricula and the latest teaching methods in fashion. "The introduction of new tools in the public schools and their optimum performance will be greatly facilitated by the human network that links each school with many others: interscholastic exchanges" (Freinet 1967/1975, p. 168). Interscholastic exchanges allow teachers to collaborate in the development of new techniques with their colleagues and thus remain vital as learners of teaching.

Concluding Remarks

The words of Paulo Freire offer an interesting commentary on the concerns of the teachers quoted at the beginning of the chapter:

> Critically viewed, technology is nothing more nor less than a natural phase of the creative process which engaged man from the moment he forged his first tool and began to transform the world for its humanization (Freire, 1970/88, p. 50).

The three projects examined in this chapter suggest that there is nothing inherent in technology that limits its use to the ways in which it has predominantly been used in the past. It is time to wipe the slate clean. Indeed, there may be situations in which technological tools are uniquely suited to help us in the task of engaging students and encouraging them to question critically the world in which we live.

About the Author

Kristin Brown is a bilingual educator and specialist in the use of telecommunications to promote biliteracy development and cross-cultural learning. She has worked in the field of bilingual and multicultural education since 1977, first as a bilingual elementary level teacher and then as a teacher educator at San Diego State University. Currently she is studying in the Doctoral Program for International and Multicultural Education at the University of San Francisco where she is coordinating a binational research project on circular migration. In 1985, Kristin, along with Dennis Sayers (see this volume) and Enid Figueroa of the University of Puerto Rico, founded ORILLAS, an international computer-based network of long-distance team-teaching partnerships. Kristin works closely with the participating teachers to investigate such issues as the use of folklore to share cultural and linguistic knowledge, the development of collaborative learning techniques to promote positive intergroup relations among ethnic and linguistic minority students, and the use of telecommunications to develop bilingual literacy skills in parent and community groups.

References

Ada, A. F. (1988). The Pájaro Valley experience: Working with Spanish-speaking parents to develop children's reading and writing skills through the use of children's literature. In Skutnabb-Kangas, T., and Cummins, J. (Eds.), *Minority education: From shame to struggle*. Clevedon, England: Multilingual Matters Ltd.

Ada, A. F., and Zubizarreta, R. (1989). *Language arts through children's literature*. San Francisco: Children's Book Press.

Berger, M. (1992). *Technology in the classroom!!??* University of San Francisco. Unpublished manuscript.

Brown, C. (1987). Literacy in 30 hours: Paulo Freire's process in Northeast Brazil. In Freire, P. (Ed.), *For the classroom: A sourcebook for liberatory teaching*. Portsmouth, NH: Heinemann.

Freinet, E. (1967/1975). *Nacimiento de una pedagogía popular*. Barcelona: Editorial Laia.

Freire, P. (1970/1988). Cultural action for freedom. *Harvard Educational Review*. Cambridge, MA.

Mayorga-Cruson, E. *La tecnología en la clase*. University of San Francisco. Unpublished manuscript.

Mehan, H., Moll, L., and Riel, M. (1985). *Computers in classrooms: A quasi-experiment in guided change*. (NIE Report 6-83-0027). La Jolla, CA: Interactive Technology Laboratory.

Roberts, L., and staff (1988). *Power on! New tools for teaching and learning*. Washington, DC: U.S. Government Printing Office.

Sayers, D. (in press). Bilingual team-teaching partnerships over long distances: A technology-mediated context for intra-group language attitude change. In Faltis, C., and DeVillar, R. (Eds.), *Cultural diversity in schools: From rhetoric to practice*. Albany, NY: State University of New York Press.

Smith, N. J. *Technology*. University of San Francisco. Unpublished manuscript.

The Principal's Role in Promoting BILINGUAL *Literacy*

María Luisa González
New Mexico State University

Cynthia Risner-Schiller
Las Cruces Public Schools, New Mexico

Elba-María Stell
El Paso Independent School District, Texas

The literature-based approach to promoting bilingual literacy is a movement away from traditional basal-focused instruction. The movement has as its cornerstone the use of literature in Spanish to acquire and develop reading and writing simultaneously. It is founded on solid theory and research in literacy development. This approach features reading and writing together with speaking and listening to foster meaningful communication.

Although many bilingual teachers have been implementing approaches similar to the one described, such an approach will not have true and continuing impact until it becomes a schoolwide effort. This can only be accomplished under the leadership of the principal. It is the principal who will facilitate the implementation of this model and assure its integration in a bilingual setting. In order to do this a principal must cultivate teacher partnerships, strengthen teacher commitment, and enlist support from children, parents, the central office, and the community-at-large within the school. The principal must accept that the key players are the bilingual teachers, students, and parents. Beyond the school context the principal extends her/his role of advocate for bilingual education by inviting central office staff and the community-at-large to become partners in the literature-based approach to bilingual literacy.

THE PRINCIPAL'S ROLE IN LITERATURE-BASED INSTRUCTION

It is the principal who sets the tone in building the program by creating a team effort that involves all the different partnerships: teachers and other school staff, children, parents, the central office, and the community. The principal fosters a feeling of ownership by creating an atmosphere that embraces the students' and parents' culture and language. By incorporating a literature-based program that includes this culture and language, the principal is able to renew interest in learning for students and parents, thus facilitating literacy development.

The principal, together with the staff, must find creative ways to assess the program. The principal must assist in redirecting, when necessary, any policy or procedure that may create obstacles to the success of the program, such as scheduling, grouping, and use of facilities, equipment, or materials. It is critical that the principal believe that the teaching/learning experience can be drastically improved in his/her school through the use of literature-based instruction (Brandt, 1987).

Principals must become highly knowledgeable about the research, theory, and practices associated with this model within bilingual education. Research shows that teachers are more receptive to the training that they receive when principals are also participants. When principals expect teachers to implement a literature-based approach in their classrooms but are unable to explain what it is or answer any of their questions, teachers become discouraged and resentful (Heald-Taylor, 1989). Research by Heald-Taylor (1989) demonstrates that the successful implementation of any new curriculum depends on the support teachers receive from principals.

The role of advocate will be evidenced as the principal deals with concerned parents, financial constraints, and teacher evaluations. It is up to the principal to deal with concerned parents in explaining how bilingual education is in their child's best interest. The principal needs to include parents in meetings, discussion groups, and in training sessions related to the use of a literature-based approach in bilingual education. It is essential that she/he keep abreast of current practice and continue to educate herself/himself through professional readings and conference attendance. In some situations principals may need to become creative in financing to be able to supply classrooms with quality reading materials. In other situations principals may need to use alternative methods of evaluating teachers because observation instruments may not accurately portray what is occurring in a literature-based classroom.

CULTIVATING TEACHER PARTNERSHIPS

Shanklin and Rhodes (1989) write that if principals want teachers to move toward the implementation of literature-based instruction, they must surround teachers with the same supportive climate they expect teachers to provide for their students. First and foremost, bilingual teachers must be encouraged to take risks. The authors of this chapter maintain that implementing new tasks is risky not only because the teacher will be trying new approaches but also because the teacher doesn't know how the supervisor is going to respond and evaluate. The principal must be supportive of teachers as they take the risk of going beyond teaching easily measured objectives to educating children to be competent and avid readers in two languages (Winograd & Greenlee, 1986).

Teachers must also feel free to question and participate in the implementation of decisions. Questions are important because they indicate that the teachers are beginning to consider the possibility of teaching literacy skills in a different context with a different emphasis. Questions such as the following can be used to stimulate staff discussion or guide staff research:

- How will teachers cover all the objectives included in state or national standardized tests?
- How can teachers and principals assess student progress?
- How will principals evaluate bilingual teachers?

Principals should not be concerned if the questions have a negative tone because initially teachers are likely to feel overwhelmed and uncertain about what is expected of them (Heald-Taylor, 1989). This skepticism is healthy because it is evidence that teachers as professionals are formulating judgments of what is in the best interest of their students (Shanklin & Rhodes, 1989). Heald-Taylor (1989) cautions principals to be wary of thrusting literature-based instruction on teachers without involving them in any of the related decisions because not doing so is likely to breed resentment. Teachers should be allowed to determine whether they wish to make great changes immediately or gradually ease into literature-based instruction (Shanklin & Rhodes, 1989).

If principals want teachers to trust children to learn through literature-based instruction, they must trust teachers to teach using this approach. Principals must be willing to relinquish some of their control if they want teachers to do the same. The fear that the adoption of a more humanistic approach such as literature-based instruction will lead to lower standards must be addressed (Smith, 1992).

In addition, teachers must be provided with the resources necessary for implementation (Shanklin & Rhodes, 1989). A variety of quality reading material in Spanish is necessary for a bilingual literature-based program. Professional reading materials for bilingual teachers to augment their own knowledge about this model are imperative. Teachers must understand the theory, research, and philosophy that support it. Principals must also be willing to provide consultative resources when necessary to further their understanding of literacy development as well as that of their teachers (Heald-Taylor, 1989).

Principals establish the climate for this undertaking in a variety of ways. For example, a principal, together with her/his faculty, may elect to visit several exemplary bilingual education literature-based programs. As the principal becomes convinced that the successful implementation of a literature-based approach in bilingual education is possible, the teachers become convinced as well. Once all are convinced, enthusiasm spreads and the principal begins to purchase professional reading materials to assist the staff in making the transition.

Another method may be to send a well-respected bilingual teacher to literacy conferences. Upon returning this individual would share the acquired information with the remainder of the staff. Depending on the faculty and its professional needs, a principal may choose to move more slowly toward establishing the environment for a literature-based program by sharing and discussing articles with teachers. As part of a carefully planned implementation of literature-based instruction, the principal may administer the Concern Based Adoption Model Questionnaire. The questionnaire is used to determine whether teachers are in the awareness, information, or management stage. The information from this questionnaire can be used to plan inservices before any steps are taken toward implementation.

STRENGTHENING TEACHER COMMITMENT

Maintaining and strengthening teacher commitment is accomplished through meaningful staff development. Staff development is essential to the successful implementation of literature-based instruction. Neubert and Bratton (1987) concluded, after examining the research of Showers, that the most effective training components are:

1. study of the theory underlying the method;
2. observation of the method demonstrated by experts;
3. practice of the method with feedback; and
4. coaching in the real teaching situation.

The study of the underlying theory of literature-based instruction can be accomplished in a variety of ways. Shanklin and Rhodes (1989) recommend monthly meetings to discuss recent research and theory. They emphasize the importance of teachers reflecting on the application of theory to their own teaching by studying videotapes and developing action research projects. While presentations by experts can help with the understanding of theory, this vehicle of staff development must be coupled with practice or coaching because merely using presentations by experts results in a 5 percent implementation rate, while presentations by experts coupled with practice and coaching result in a 95 percent implementation rate (Shanklin & Rhodes, 1989).

It is wise to schedule many informal sessions where teachers lead the theory discussions. During these meetings, bilingual teachers can explore their own questions and concerns (Heald-Taylor, 1989). They can also share the ways in which they are conducting reading and writing instruction. Additionally, teachers can use this time for problem solving to enable them to become confident in their decision-making abilities. By allowing teachers to assume the leadership role in these discussion meetings, their ownership of this model will grow (Shanklin & Rhodes, 1989).

The remaining components of staff development are observation of the method demonstrated by experts, practice of the method with feedback, and coaching in the real situation. An effective approach to training that incorporates all three of these components features the coach teaching with the teachers as they implement new models of instruction (Neubert & Bratton, 1987). This enables teachers to see how the experts teach and respond in the same environment in which they work and receive feedback and coaching as they apply new models in their classrooms. For this arrangement to be most effective:

- the teacher must perceive the coach as more knowledgeable than she/he is;
- the coach must demonstrate success in the classroom;
- the coach must support and encourage the teacher's efforts in implementation;
- the coach must realize that the ownership of the lesson, students, and the classroom is maintained by the regular teacher; and
- the coach must be accessible to the teacher for planning and conferencing.

Heald-Taylor (1989) has suggested that principals work in classrooms with teachers whenever possible to support literature-based instruction. If principals meet the above criteria, working in the classroom could serve the dual functions of providing support and coaching. Because of the individual needs of the different teachers on a campus, the time a principal spends in each classroom will vary.

McEvoy (1987) wrote of the importance of "commonplace occurrences" in staff development. Principals can use informal communication and monitoring to stimulate and reinforce teachers' professional development. She identified these six successful subtle techniques for staff development:

- informing teachers of professional development opportunities and following up personally with those most likely to benefit or be interested;
- disseminating articles and books to individual teachers or the entire faculty;
- focusing staff attention on a specific theme by discussing it with teachers and asking questions frequently regarding progress in its implementation;
- soliciting teachers' opinions to identify their concerns and issues as well as recognize teachers as professionals and colleagues;
- encouraging experimentation through a supportive attitude and recognizing individual teachers' accomplishments by talking about these accomplishments to parents, other teachers, and community members as well as facilitating teacher exchanges.

McEvoy (1987) believes there are many advantages to these commonplace occurrences, or informal supervision. While researchers have criticized the brief, broken, and spontaneous nature of principals' communications, these characteristics may be what make the substance of these conversations more appealing and acceptable to teachers. These quick exchanges may convey a principal's message of concern and support in a nonthreatening manner. While many principals maintain that their daily routine prevents them from supporting innovations, these contacts fit well into the fullest of schedules.

Principals can continue to promote staff development in different ways. A school may select a major focus to study for a year, such as whole language in the context of bilingual education. The principal, together with staff, may arrange for presentations on the specific topic with local bilingual education professors and select pertinent books to read and share in a study group format. Schools may choose to invite bilingual teachers using literature-based instruction from another school to conduct their inservice sessions for the first semester. During the second semester they may break into study groups according to the results of their needs assessments. Principals are encouraged to share professional readings with teachers, sending as many as possible to workshops and conferences, working in classrooms, and masterfully using commonplace day-to-day interactions. Faculty participation in planning for staff development enhances its effectiveness.

Even when successful staff development is implemented, 100 percent faculty support of literature-based instruction in bilingual education is not guaranteed. Schools may be divided into camps with those who are amenable to the approach and those who are solidly against it. Teachers who continue resisting the approach after every effort has been made to convince them of its benefits should be assisted in finding a school more suitable to their personal needs and style. Principals may find that, once literature-based instruction in bilingual education is adopted by the school, the very experienced bilingual teachers are either rejuvenated by the model or choose to retire rather than change.

ENLISTING CHILDREN'S SUPPORT

The success of any educational program rests in the hands of the children. It is therefore even of more consequence to enlist the support of bilingual children in creating a literacy-centered atmosphere in the school. Children must become full-fledged members in the teaching/learning process involving bilingual literacy. In reality, this membership must become ownership for the program belongs to them. The principal must keep this orientation and focus on the child. It is ironic that many educators become so "possessed" by a movement that they often lose sight of the main constituent—the child.

Research shows that for any instructional program to be effective, the principal must become an integral force in its development, becoming a role model for both teachers and students (González, in press). As a leader of instructional leaders (teachers) (Schlechty, 1990) and a leader of readers (children) the principal acts as the cohesive element in pursuing a biliterate school community. Successful strategies that may assist principals in student involvement with literature-based instruction are:

- communicating with students on a daily basis regarding the importance of reading in Spanish and English;
- discussing what books they have read or are currently reading;
- creating readers' clubs in Spanish and in English for all the adults of the school community as well as the children;
- taking an active role by reading to children in both languages;
- supporting faculty in their efforts to invite bilingual authors;
- modeling enjoyment of reading;
- recognizing all children as authors;
- reinforcing student and teacher efforts formally and informally; and
- monitoring and discussing student progress with teachers and students as well.

Personal contact on the part of the principal validates the importance of literacy to the student. This validation assists in making students full participants in their own literacy development. With full participation, students become enthusiastic supporters of their own learning.

ESTABLISHING PARTNERSHIPS WITH PARENTS

For any literature-based program to succeed, the support and active participation of parents are absolutely necessary. It is critical for schools to understand that parents seek partnership with the schools instead of patronage (Lindle, 1989). Principals are often tempted to tell parents what the school has planned for their children; however, this strategy is not likely to yield optimal results. It is the role of the principal to orchestrate planning sessions involving both parents and teachers. The school staff is responsible at these planning sessions for sharing the philosophy, research, theory, and assessment of the literature-based program in bilingual education. Parents are responsible for sharing what they know about their children as well as their concerns about the education of their children.

For parents to openly communicate and become involved in the school, it is critical that the principal, with the help of other staff members, establish a nonthreatening environment (González, 1991). Research concerning parents' expectations affirms that they want a "personal touch" in lieu of an air of professionalism (Lindle, 1989).

Involvement with parents cannot be limited to the initial planning sessions. It must be an ongoing process throughout the education of their children. The following suggestions may be useful in maintaining the partnership and commitment of parents.

- The principal can encourage teachers to use parent volunteers in actual instruction so that parents feel that their time is wisely used and children receive the additional individual attention they require.

- The principal can be responsible for organizing and implementing the training sessions in English and Spanish for parent volunteers to maximize their effectiveness.

- The principal can continue to organize parent-staff planning meetings throughout the program. These ongoing meetings should focus on new developments in the field, student progress, parental concerns, and program modification based on these sources of information.

- The principal must communicate to parents that they are truly valued and welcomed in the school. Socials and award ceremonies can recognize parental contributions. The principal's availability when parents want to talk also goes a long way in saying, "I value your contributions and opinions."

- The principal can write monthly school-wide newsletters for parents as well as the community-at-large. Topics for the newsletter can include acknowledgements of assistance the school has received, current needs of the school in terms of tangible items as well as volunteers, examples of students' progress, and a calendar of activities as well as new information regarding literature-based instruction. It is vitally important that this newsletter be written in both English and Spanish for all parents to read.

Establishing a partnership with parents is essential for student success in bilingual education. When students see the school and their parents working together, it strengthens their sense of belonging to the educational system and furthers their learning.

ENLISTING CENTRAL OFFICE SUPPORT

From the beginning the principal must educate central office personnel about literature-based instruction in bilingual education. Their support and commitment can spell success or failure for this initiative. Their positive inclusion throughout the development of this approach can greatly facilitate its acceptance as well as its dissemination. Principals, as biliteracy advocates, must frequently visit the central office to share the successes of their bilingual students. In turn, central office personnel should be invited to school on an ongoing basis and be made to feel like integral partners in support of the program. They should be included in parent night activities, school functions, and frequent, informal visits during the school day. This will make them better aware of the challenge of teaching limited English proficient students literacy and keep them in tune with the latest in classroom practices. Central office personnel, through observation and personal contact, will experience firsthand how successful students can be with literature-based instruction.

The following suggestions may prove useful in strengthening the partnership between the central office and individual schools.

- Central office personnel (COPS) are invited to assist as reading partners in individual classrooms. By staggering their lunch schedules, COPS will be able to volunteer on set days of the week to work with students either on a small group or individual basis. During this time they can read to students or provide an extra pair of hands for whatever arises.
- COPS can serve as pen pal partners by reading and responding to student letters sent through the school mail.
- COPS can provide display areas for student literacy projects. Parents and children should be invited to view their work on display.

It is the responsibility of the building principal to keep the central office informed regarding the progress of the school biliteracy program. The information should be broader than mere paperwork and formal documentation. Every effort should be made to create a viable central office biliteracy partnership with the schools.

ENLISTING THE SUPPORT OF THE COMMUNITY-AT-LARGE

The demands on the school staff in a literature-based bilingual program may be greater in terms of time and individual attention each child should be given. Therefore, it is necessary to establish partnerships with local community groups. Community groups should include church organizations, business and service groups, as well as individual volunteers (González, 1992). In order to initiate this type of involvement, the principal may find it necessary to make presentations to these groups. To maintain the true interest of the community, it is important that community members be engaged in meaningful activities beyond the bake-sale level of commitment.

These activities can involve assisting children on an individual or group basis. Care must be taken in ensuring that all volunteers in any school activity be properly trained to know what is proper school procedure as well as the nuts and bolts of promoting biliteracy development in students.

The benefits of including community people in the biliteracy partnership are multiple. The additional contact time that students receive is invaluable toward creating a positive literary experience. Increased community understanding of the school and its roles can lead to valuable political support. By increasing the interaction between the community and students in the teaching and learning process, the problems associated with school isolation are diminished. Increased goodwill is established when the principal and staff promote community biliteracy partnerships.

SUMMARY

The principal's acceptance of and commitment to a literature-based approach in bilingual education is an essential element for its successful implementation on a schoolwide basis. The principal's leadership is the key that links teacher, children, parents, the community-at-large, and the central office staff. First and foremost, the principal must create the supportive climate for teachers so that they in turn will provide it for children.

It is here that the principal can be the role model, not only for teachers, but for children and parents as well. The principal must empower teachers and parents in order for teachers and parents to do the same. From the beginning, both must be included in planning and decision making in everything that involves the education of children. If the environment is nonthreatening, not only will children be willing to take risks, but so will teachers and staff. If within such an environment children and parents see their culture and language as a vital and viable part of the literature-based approach in bilingual education, they will then accept it and work in partnership with the school.

The success of a literature-based approach in bilingual education requires much more substance on the part of the principal than mere enthusiasm. The principal must become very knowledgeable in the research and practice of the literature-based approach to biliteracy. The principal must become an instructional leader in the true sense of the term. To lead in this fashion, the principal must apply all things—finances, policy, procedures, program assessment, and even teacher evaluations—in the service of the bilingual education program.

In this way, the student is best given an opportunity to acquire literacy in both languages. The principal is the catalyst who brings the people and the resources together for the successful implementation of a literature-based program in bilingual education.

ABOUT THE AUTHORS

María Luisa González is associate professor of Educational Management and Development at New Mexico State University in Las Cruces. Her publications include articles in national journals on at-risk children. She serves on the National Advisory Board for the Education of Homeless Children and is a member of New Mexico's 21st Century Commission on Education. Currently, she is director of the New Mexico Center for Rural Education. She is executive director for the New Mexico ASCD affiliate.

Cynthia Risner-Schiller is a Master Teacher for the Las Cruces Public Schools. She facilitated the reading adoption process for the Las Cruces Schools and provides frequent in-service for local teachers in the area of literacy and language acquisition. She currently serves on the State of New Mexico Performance Based Assessment Task Force and the Las Cruces Public Schools' America 2000 Task Force.

Elba-María Stell is a bilingual teacher with the El Paso Independent School District. She has been a teacher for 20 years and is very involved in the writing of curriculum and staff development in her district. In 1992 she was named Campus Teacher of the Year and in 1984 she was recognized as Bilingual Teacher of the Year by the Southwest Association for Bilingual Education. She has an M.A. in Education from the University of Texas at El Paso.

REFERENCES

Brandt, R. (1987). On teachers coaching teachers: A conversation with Bruce Joyce. *Educational Leadership,* vol. 44, pp. 12–17.

González, M. L. (1992). Educational climate for the homeless. In Stronge, J. H. (Ed.), *Educating homeless children and adolescents: Evaluating policy and practice,* Newbury Park, CA: Sage Publications.

González, M. L. (1991). School-community partnerships and the homeless. *Educational Leadership,* vol. 49, no. 1, pp. 23–24.

Heald-Taylor, G. (1989). *The administrator's guide to whole language.* New York: Richard C. Owens Publishers, Inc.

Lindle, J. C. (1989). What do parents want from principals and teachers? *Educational Leadership,* vol. 47, no. 2, pp. 12–14.

McEvoy, B. (1987). Everyday acts: How principals influence development of their staffs. *Educational Leadership,* vol. 44, pp. 73–77.

Neubert, G. A., and Bratton, E. C. (1987). Team coaching: Staff development side by side. *Educational Leadership,* vol. 45, pp. 29–32.

Schlechty, P. C. (1990). *Schools for the 21st century: Leadership imperatives for educational reform.* San Francisco: Jossey-Bass, Inc., Publishers.

Shanklin, N. L., and Rhodes, L. K. (1989). Transforming literacy instruction. *Educational Leadership,* vol. 46, pp. 59–62.

Smith, F. (1992). Learning to read: The never-ending debate. *Phi Delta Kappan,* 73 (6), pp. 432–441.

Winograd, P., and Greenlee, M. (1986). Students need a balanced reading program. *Educational Leadership,* vol. 43, pp. 16–21.

Part IV
PROMOTING BILITERACY

PROMOTING
BILITERACY

Effective Transitioning Strategies:
ARE WE ASKING THE RIGHT QUESTIONS?

Lilia I. Bartolomé
Harvard University

Introduction

Much of the current discussion regarding linguistic minority academic achievement in our schools stresses the topic of successful or effective teaching strategies. The term *teaching strategies* refers to an educational plan or a series of activities/lessons designed to obtain a specific goal or result. However, before we can discuss these strategies—transitioning strategies in particular—and their effectiveness or ineffectiveness, it is necessary to discuss their perceived effectiveness within the larger sociocultural context. We must consider why, on the one hand, these strategies are warranted, and on the other hand, why these strategies are deemed effective in a given sociocultural context.

In his letter to North American educators, Paulo Freire (1987) warns against uncritically importing and exporting strategies and methods with no regard for sociocultural contexts. He states that teachers must possess content area knowledge *and* political clarity to be able to effectively create, adopt, and modify teaching strategies that simultaneously respect and challenge the learner. It is critical that educators become so well versed in the theory of their specializations that they own their knowledge. This ownership imbues the educators with confidence while translating theory that enables them simultaneously to consider the population being served and the sociocultural context in which learning is expected to take place. It is equally critical that teachers comprehend that their role as educators is not politically neutral. In negating the political nature of their work, teachers maintain the status quo and their students' subordinate status (status that reflects their group's subordinate political and economic status in the larger society). Conversely, teachers can become conscious of and subsequently challenge the role of educational institutions and their own roles as educators in maintaining a system that often serves to silence students from subordinate groups.

Teachers must remember that schools, similar to other institutions in society, are influenced by perceptions of socioeconomic status (SES), race/ethnicity, language, or gender. They must begin to question how these perceptions influence classroom dynamics. It is especially important for teachers who work with students from subordinate groups to recognize historical (and current) attributions of low status to members of low SES linguistic minority populations and the subsequent mistreatment/underservicing of such populations in the schools.

So, while it is certainly important to identify effective instructional strategies, it is not sufficient to narrow and restrict our focus to instructional issues solely related to teaching methods and activities. This discussion must be broadened to reveal the deeply entrenched deficit orientation toward "difference" (e.g., social class, race/ethnicity, language, gender) in our schools. We must also ask how this view has affected our perceptions of linguistic minority students and shaped our approaches for teaching them.

In this paper I will also argue that by taking this comprehensive approach to analyzing language arts teaching strategies identified as effective within a particular sociocultural reality, we can shift our focus from the strategy itself to more fundamental pedagogical features common *across* strategies. These student-centered features are known by educators to constitute good teaching for any population. More important, in the case of linguistic minority students, they serve to offset potentially unequal relations and discriminatory structures and practices in the classroom. Without underestimating the importance of teachers' knowledge of methodology, such focus is neither sufficient nor a substitute for comprehensive and critical understanding of pedagogy and the teacher's role in its implementation—*especially* as it relates to students from subordinate populations.

For this reason, I will caution readers against the general tendency to reduce complex educational issues (those that reflect greater social, political, and economic realities) to mere "magical" methods and techniques designed to remediate perceived student cognitive and linguistic deficiencies. I will conclude by proposing what Macedo (in press) calls an antimethods pedagogy that refuses to be enslaved by the rigidity of models and methodological paradigms. An antimethods pedagogy should be informed by a critical understanding of the sociocultural context that guides our practices so as to free us from the beaten path of methodological certainties and specialisms.

This is a pedagogical process that requires both action and reflection. Using it, instead of importing or exporting effective strategies, teachers are required to re-create and reinvent those effective approaches, taking into consideration the sociocultural limitations *and* possibilities.

Our Legacy: A Deficit Orientation and Unequal Relations in the Classroom

Teaching strategies are neither designed nor implemented in a vacuum. Design, selection, and use of particular teaching approaches and strategies arise from perceptions about learning and learners. It is especially important, when discussing learners from subordinate populations, that we deal candidly with our deeply rooted and traditional deficit orientation toward difference. The most pedagogically advanced strategies prove ineffective in the hands of educators who implicitly or explicitly subscribe to a belief system that renders linguistic minority students, at best, culturally disadvantaged and in need of fixing (if we could only identify the right recipe!) or, at worst, culturally or genetically deficient and beyond fixing. Despite the fact that alternative models are utilized to explain the academic failure of certain linguistic minority groups—academic failure described as historical, pervasive, and disproportionate—the fact remains that our views of difference are deficit based and deeply imprinted in our individual and collective psyches (Flores, 1982; Menchaca & Valencia, 1990; Valencia, 1986, 1991).

The deficit model has the longest history of any model discussed in the education literature. Valencia (1986) traces its evolution over three centuries.

Also known in the literature as the "social pathology" model or the "cultural deprivation" model, the deficit approach explains disproportionate academic problems among low status students as largely being due to pathologies or deficits in their sociocultural background (e.g., cognitive and linguistic deficiencies, low self-esteem, poor motivation). . . . To improve the educability of such students, programs such as compensatory education and parent-child intervention have been proposed. (p. 3)

The deficit model of instruction and learning has been critiqued by numerous researchers as ethnocentric and invalid (Boykin, 1983; Díaz, Moll & Mehan, 1986; Flores, 1982; Sue & Padilla, 1986; Trueba, 1989; Walker, 1987). Mehan (1992) correctly maintains that new lines of research offer alternative models that "shift the source of school failure away from the characteristics of the failing child, their families, their cultures and toward more general societal processes, including schooling" (p. 2). Unfortunately, these alternative models often give rise to a kinder and liberal yet more concealed version of the deficit model. Despite the use of less ethnocentric models to explain the academic standing of linguistic minority students, I believe that our deficit orientation toward difference, especially as it relates to low socioeconomic groups, is very deeply ingrained in the ethos of our most prominent institutions, especially schools, and in compensatory programs such as bilingual education. Yet the study of structural factors within the schools has triggered research yielding valuable insights into the asymmetrical and unequal relations and how they are manifested between teachers and students from subordinate groups.

The number of studies that examine unequal power relations in the classroom have increased in recent years. Unequal and discriminatory treatment of students based on their socioeconomic status, race/ethnicity, language use, and gender have been empirically demonstrated. Findings range from teacher preference for Anglo students to bilingual teachers' preference for lighter-skinned Latino students to teachers' negative perceptions of working-class parents compared to middle-class parents and finally to unequal teaching and assessment practices in schools serving working-class and more affluent populations (Anyon, 1988; Bloom, 1991; Lareau, 1990; U.S. Commission on Civil Rights, 1973). Especially indicative of our inability to deal honestly with our deficit orientation is the fact that the teachers in these studies—teachers from all ethnic groups—were themselves unaware of the active role they played in the differential and unequal treatment of their students.

Furthermore, many research studies that examined culturally congruent and incongruent teaching approaches actually describe the negotiation of power relations in classrooms where teachers unwittingly impose participation structures upon students from subordinate linguistic minority groups (Au & Mason, 1983; Heath, 1983; Mohatt & Erickson, 1981; Philips, 1972). These studies, in essence, capture the successful negotiation of power relations that resulted in higher student academic achievement and teacher effectiveness. Unfortunately, interpretations and practical applications of this research have focused on the *cultural* congruence of the approaches. I emphasize the term *cultural* because in these studies the term is used in a restricted sense devoid of its dynamic, ideological, and political dimensions. According to Giroux (1985), "Culture is the representation of lived experiences, material artifacts and practices *forged within the unequal and dialectical relations* [emphasis added] that different groups establish in a given society at a particular point in historical time" (p. xxi). I utilize this definition of *culture* because, without identifying the political dimensions of culture and subsequent unequal status attributed to members of different cultural groups, the reader may conclude that teaching methods simply need to be culturally congruent to be effective—without recognizing that not all cultural groups are viewed and treated as equally legitimate in classrooms.

Given the sociocultural realities in the above studies, the specific teaching strategies may not be what made the difference. It could well be that the teacher's effort to "share the power," treating students as equal participants in their own learning and, in the process, discarding (consciously or unconsciously held) deficit views of the students, made the difference. Utilizing a variety of strategies and techniques, students were allowed to interact with teachers in egalitarian and meaningful ways. Teachers also learned to recognize, value, utilize, and build upon students' previously acquired knowledge and skills. In essence, these strategies succeeded in creating a comfort zone so students could exhibit their knowledge and skills and ultimately empower themselves to succeed in an academic setting. McDermott's (1977) classic research reminds us that numerous teaching approaches and strategies can be effectively utilized so long as trusting relations between teacher and students are established and power relations are mutually set and agreed upon.

It is against this backdrop that teachers can begin to interrogate the unspoken yet prevalent deficit orientation used to hide SES, race/ethnicity, linguistic, and gender inequities present in American classrooms. And it is against this backdrop that we turn our discussion to bilingual education and its persistent mirroring of a deficit view of linguistic minority students.

Bilingual Education, the Deficit Model, and the Practice of Transitioning

Despite the fact that current bilingual education models emerged from an enrichment two-way bilingual program designed to serve Cuban refugees in Dade County, Florida, in 1963, government intervention changed the program's focus when it was applied to low SES Mexican-American and Puerto Rican student populations. Crawford (1989) explains that the focus shifted

> from an enrichment model aimed at developing fluency in

two languages to a remedial effort designed to help "disadvantaged" children overcome the "handicap" of not speaking English. From its outset, federal aid to bilingual education was regarded as a "poverty program," rather than an innovative approach to language instruction. (p. 29)

The belief that students from subordinate linguistic minority groups have language problems is very much present in the origins of bilingual education. Flores, Cousin, and Díaz (1991) point out:

> One of the most pervasive and pernicious myths about [language minority] children is that they have a language deficit. This myth is not reserved just for bilingual and non-English-speaking students; it is also commonly held about African-American and other minority students [as well as English dominant linguistic minority students]. (p. 9)

In addition, these students are perceived as lacking valuable life experiences necessary for academic success. The consequent belief is that these deficits, in turn, cause learning problems. Bilingual education is then viewed as a compensatory program designed to remediate students' language problems, referring to their limited English proficiency. Educators often fail to interrogate the deficit model, which may constitute the *real* problem to the extent that it disconfirms rather than confirms linguistic minority native language experiences.

Currently, the Federal government identifies two needs of limited English proficient students: (a) to develop their English proficiency so that they can fully benefit from instruction in English, and (b) to enhance their academic progress in all subject areas (U.S. Department of Education, 1991). The U.S. Department of Education lists three general program types capable of teaching limited English proficient students English language skills necessary for success in school: transitional bilingual education; two-way, or developmental, bilingual education; and special alternative instructional programs. Only the first two programs utilize the student's native language for academic and instructional purposes. Special alternative instructional programs are "designed to provide structured English language instruction and special instructional services that will allow a limited English proficient child to achieve competence in the English language and to meet grade promotion and graduation standards" (p. 17). Of the three programs, transitional bilingual programs represent the largest percentage of programs currently funded by the Federal government (U.S. Department of Education, 1991).

Broadly defined, transitional bilingual education programs allow the use of limited English proficient students' native language in academic settings while they acquire the English language proficiency necessary to transition into English-only settings. Crawford (1989) criticizes the ambiguity of transitional bilingual education as it relates to native language use:

> The definition of transitional bilingual education is broad, requiring only that some amount of native language and culture be used, along with ESL instruction. Programs may stress native-language development, including initial literacy, or they may provide students with nothing more than the translation services of bilingual aides. Contrary to public perceptions, studies have shown that English is the medium of instruction from 72 to 92 percent of the time in transitional bilingual education programs. (p. 175)

Spener (1988) adds that what too often occurs in transitional bilingual education is that "programs provide only a limited period of native-language instruction and do not guarantee English mastery. Thus, these programs often prevent children from attaining fluency in either their native language or in English" (p. 133).

Nevertheless, the common assumption is that students exiting bilingual classrooms and entering "regular" or English-only classrooms necessarily possess native language literacy skills and will therefore transfer or apply these (presumed) skills to their English academic work. The problem is not so much with the assumption that skills transfer from one language to another. A number of recent studies suggest that cross-lingual transfer does occur (Avelar-La Salle, 1991; Clarke, 1988; Faltis, 1983; Hernández, 1991; Reyes, 1987; Zhang, 1990). The difficulty lies in the assumption that students are indeed being taught native language literacy skills.

In addition, we need to question the hidden objective embedded in the transitioning model that requires that limited English proficient students discontinue the use of their native language as they increase their fluency in English. Again, this subtractive view of bilingualism mirrors our deeply rooted deficit and assimilative orientation that often devalues students' native language. In other words, Freire's (1987) requirement that teachers possess political clarity regarding the sociocultural material conditions within which transition takes place will enable them to see the inherent contradiction of the educational language policy. We can accept the native language as long as it is used only minimally and temporarily, that is, until it is replaced with English. Is it not ironic that while we discourage the maintenance of linguistic minority students' native language throughout their education, we require mainstream English-speaking students to study a foreign language as a prerequisite for college—where many continue their foreign language studies for some years.

Even if we accept the underlying deficit notion of transitional bilingual education, we need to question how it is possible to expect students to transfer or apply native language literacy skills to English literacy tasks when, in reality, they have had little opportunity to develop these skills in their native language in school. All too often, students are held accountable and penalized for not possessing the very native language literacy skills that the school has failed to develop in the first place. In situations such as these, we must call into question the assumption that students are allowed to develop native language literacy skills so the transfer of skills really *can* occur. Does shuttling students from so-called bilingual classrooms where English is the medium of instruction from 72 to 92 percent of the time to classrooms where it is the *sole* medium of instruction constitute transitioning, or does it constitute receiving more of the same English-only instruction?

To discuss effective transitioning strategies, it is necessary to contextualize them within the ideal model of bilingual education. That model promotes the development of native language literacy skills beyond basic decoding and encoding skills and teaches English as a second language literacy skills in an additive fashion with native language literacy skills. Building on the assumption that the ideal model is possible, we can then discuss teaching strategies identified as effective for preparing students to learn literacy skills in both the native language and English.

The Politics of Student-Centered Teaching

Numerous teaching strategies and approaches promise to facilitate transfer of native language literacy skills to an English as a second language context. Well-known approaches and strategies such as cooperative learning, language experience, process writing, and whole language activities can be used to create learning environments where students cease to be treated as objects (Pérez & Torres-Guzmán, 1992). In successful applications of these approaches and strategies, students are treated with respect and viewed as active and capable subjects in their own learning.

Student-centered teaching strategies can take many forms. One may well ask, is it not merely common sense to promote approaches and strategies that recognize, utilize, and build on students' existing knowledge bases? Yes, it is. However, it is important to recognize, as part of our effort to increase our political clarity, that these practices have *not* typified classroom instruction to students from subordinate populations. Cummins (1989) reminds us of the need for emancipatory pedagogical practices instead of dehumanizing "banking" notions of learning, where subordinate students are viewed and treated as empty receptacles in need of filling. The practice of learning from and valuing student language and life experiences *often* occurs in classrooms where students speak a language variety and possess cultural capital that more closely matches the mainstream (Anyon, 1988; Lareau, 1990). Unfortunately, this practice is not a given with student populations traditionally perceived as deficient and lacking. Student-centered teaching strategies in the latter context require teachers consciously to discard deficit notions and genuinely value and utilize students' existing knowledge bases in their teaching. Furthermore, these teachers must remain open to the fact that they will learn from their students. Learning is not a one-way undertaking.

We recognize that no language variety or set of life experiences is inherently superior, yet our social values reflect our preferences for certain language varieties and life experiences over others. Student-centered teaching strategies such as cooperative learning, language experience, process writing, and whole language activities can help to offset or neutralize our deficit-based failure to recognize subordinate student strengths. Our tendency to disconfirm these strengths occurs whenever we forget that learning only occurs when prior knowledge is accessed and linked to new information.

Jones, Palincsar, Ogle, and Carr (1987) explain that learning *is* linking new information to prior knowledge. Prior knowledge is stored in memory in the form of knowledge frameworks. New information is understood and stored by calling up the appropriate knowledge framework and integrating the new information. Acknowledging and utilizing existing student language and knowledge makes good pedagogical sense. The process also constitutes a humanizing experience for students traditionally *de*humanized and disempowered in the schools. I believe that strategies identified as effective in the literature have the potential to offset that reductive education where "the educator as *the one who knows* transfers existing knowledge to the learner as *the one who does not know*" (Freire, 1985, p. 114).

Creating learning environments that incorporate student language and life experiences in no way negates teachers' responsibility for providing students with particular academic content knowledge and skills. It is important not to confuse academic rigor with rigidity that stifles and silences students. The teacher is the authority, with all the resulting responsibilities that that entails; however, it is not necessary for the teacher to become authoritarian in order to challenge students intellectually. Education can be a process in which teacher and students mutually participate in the intellectually and exciting undertaking we call learning. Students *can* become active subjects in their own learning instead of passive objects waiting to be filled with facts and figures by the teacher.

As mentioned earlier, a number of student-centered teaching strategies possess the potential to transform students into active subjects and participants in their own learning. However, for the purposes of illustration, I will briefly discuss one approach currently identified as promising for both English-speaking "mainstream" students and linguistic minority students in upper elementary grades. I will highlight some key features of the strategy and explain its potential to empower teachers and students; in other words, its potential to humanize the educational process. The approach is referred to in the literature as "strategic teaching."

Strategic Teaching and the Potential for Teacher and Student Empowerment

Strategic teaching refers to an instructional model that explicitly teaches students learning strategies that enable them consciously to monitor their own learning; this is accomplished through the development of reflective, cognitive monitoring, and metacognitive skills (Jones et al., 1987). The goal is to prepare independent and metacognitively aware students. Examples of learning strategies include teaching various text structures (i.e., stories and reports) through frames and graphic organizers. *Frames* are sets of questions that help students understand a given topic. Readers monitor their understanding of a text by asking questions, making predictions, and testing their predictions as they read. Before reading, frames serve as an advance organizer to activate prior knowledge and facilitate understanding. Frames can be used by the reader during reading to monitor self-learning. They can also be used after a reading lesson to summarize and integrate newly acquired information.

Graphic organizers are visual maps that represent text structures and organizational patterns used in texts and in student writing. Ideally, graphic organizers reflect both the content and text structure. Graphic organizers include semantic maps, chains, and concept hierarchies and assist the student to visualize the rhetorical structure of the text. Jones et al. (1987) explain that frames and graphic organizers can be "powerful tools to help the student locate, select, sequence, integrate and restructure information—both from the perspective of understanding and from the perspective of producing information in written responses" (p. 38).

PROMOTING BILITERACY

Although much of the research on strategic teaching focuses on English monolingual mainstream students, recent efforts to study bilingual and limited-English-proficient linguistic minority students' use of these strategies show similar success. This literature shows that strategic teaching improved students' reading comprehension and conscious use of effective learning strategies in the native language (Avelar-La Salle, 1991; Chamot, 1983; Hernández, 1991; O'Malley & Chamot, 1990; Reyes, 1987). Furthermore, these studies show that students, despite limited English proficiency, are able to transfer or apply their knowledge of specific learning strategies and text structure to English reading texts. For example, Hernández (1990) reports that sixth-grade limited English proficient students learned in the native language (Spanish) to generate hypotheses, summarize, and make predictions about readings. He reports:

> Students were able to demonstrate use of comprehension strategies even when they could not decode the English text aloud. When asked in Spanish about English texts, the students were able to generate questions, summarize stories, and predict future events in Spanish. (p. 101)

Avelar-La Salle's (1991) study of third- and fourth-grade bilingual students shows that strategic teaching in the native language of three expository text structures commonly found in elementary social studies and science texts (topical net, matrix, and hierarchy) improved comprehension of these types of texts in both Spanish and English.

Such explicit and strategic teaching is most important in the upper elementary grades, when bilingual students are expected to focus on English literacy skills development. Beginning at about third grade, students also face literacy demands distinct from those encountered in earlier grades. Chall (1983) describes the change in literacy demands in terms of stages of readings. She explains that at a stage three of reading, students cease to "learn to read" and begin "reading to learn." Students in third and fourth grade are introduced to content area subjects such as social studies, science, and health. In addition, students are introduced to expository texts (reports). This change in texts, text structures and in the functions of reading (reading for information) calls for teaching strategies that will prepare students to comprehend various expository texts (e.g., cause/effect, compare/contrast) utilized across the curriculum.

Strategic teaching holds great promise for preparing linguistic minority students to face the new literacy challenges in the upper grades. As mentioned earlier, the primary goal of strategic instruction is to foster learner independence. This goal in and of itself is laudable. However, the characteristics of strategic instruction that I find most promising grow out of the premise that teachers and students must actively interact and negotiate meaning in order to reach a goal. To assist students in becoming independent, reflective, and empowered learners, Jones, Palincsar, Ogle, and Carr (1987) recommend that teachers follow this instructional sequence:

1. Teachers access and assess current student knowledge about pertinent content and learning strategies via think-aloud and other prereading brainstorming activities. During this phase of instruction, teachers learn about their students' existing knowledge bases as well as students' questions and concerns regarding their own learning.

2. As a result of the above informal assessment, teachers explicitly explain the new content and strategies to students. After considering students' existing knowledge bases and questions, the teacher and student link the new content and strategies with prior knowledge and skills. The teacher and students identify and discuss the target strategy or strategies (declarative knowledge), how they should employ the strategy or strategies (procedural information), and in what context they should employ the strategy (conditional information).

3. Teachers model the new strategy or strategies so that students have the opportunity to witness the thought processes and behaviors involved in the employment of the strategy. For example, in reciprocal teaching, teachers initially model for students the process of formulating questions that will assist students to monitor their own learning during reading.

4. Teachers scaffold the instruction and provide students the time to practice and demonstrate their use of the strategy or strategies. Scaffolding is "a

process that enables a child or novice to solve a problem, carry out a task, or achieve a goal which is beyond his unassisted efforts" (Wood, Bruner & Ross in Jones et al., 1987, p. 55).

5. The teacher apprentices students and provides extensive support of their efforts. This support is temporary; teachers gradually reduce their support so that students assume sole responsibility and become independent learners.

6. Teachers relate strategy instruction to motivation so students recognize the significant role they play in their own learning and academic success. By providing students with experiences in which they see the successful results of strategic learning, it is possible to change students' expectations for success and failure and help them sustain strategy use (modified from Jones et al., 1987).

Throughout the strategic learning process, students are empowered in learning contexts in which teachers allow them to speak from their own vantage points. Before teachers attempt to instruct students in new content or learning strategies, efforts are made to access prior knowledge so as to link it with new information. In allowing students to present and discuss their prior knowledge and experiences, the teacher legitimizes and treats as valuable student language and cultural experiences usually ignored in classrooms. If students are allowed to speak on what they know best, then they are, in a sense, treated as experts—experts who are expected to refine their knowledge bases with the additional new content and strategy information presented by the teacher.

Teachers empower themselves in the process. To carry out this recommended sequence of instruction, teachers must be knowledgeable in both the subject area and the necessary learning strategies for successful learning to occur within that particular subject area or discipline. O'Malley & Chamot (1990) describe teacher empowerment in this type of teaching:

> Teaching becomes an active and decision-making process in which the teacher is constantly assessing what students already know, what they need to know, and how to provide for successful learning. This requires that teachers not only be good managers but also have an extensive knowledge base about their subject and about teaching learning strategies. . . . Teachers act as models and demonstrate mental processes and learning strategies by thinking aloud to their students. (p. 188)

Teachers are often empowered in the process of implementing strategic instruction because they must become experts in the subject areas they teach as well as in the key learning strategies that will facilitate students' acquisition of the subject matter. In addition, teachers must constantly monitor their students' existing knowledge bases as well as their growing mastery of the new content and learning strategy knowledge.

Furthermore, teachers play a significant role in creating learning contexts in which students are able to empower themselves. Teachers act as cultural brokers of sorts when they introduce students not only to the culture of the classroom but to particular subjects and also prepare students to behave as "insiders" in the particular subject or discipline. Gee (1989) reminds us of the social nature of teaching and learning. He contends that for students to do well in school, they must undergo an apprenticeship into the subject's or discipline's discourse. That apprenticeship includes acquisition of particular content matter, ways of organizing content, and ways of using language (oral and written). Gee adds that these discourses are not mastered solely through teacher-centered and directed instruction but by "enculturation or apprenticeship into social practices through scaffolded and supported interaction with people who have already mastered the discourse" (p. 7).

Models of instruction such as strategic teaching can promote such an apprenticeship. In the process of apprenticing linguistic minority students, teachers must interact in meaningful ways with students. This human interaction often familiarizes individuals from different SES and race/ethnic groups and creates mutual respect instead of the antagonism that so frequently occurs between teachers and their students from subordinate groups. In this learning environment, teachers and students learn from each other. The strategies serve, then, not to fix the student but to humanize the learning environment. Teachers are forced to challenge implicitly or explicitly held deficit attitudes and beliefs about their students and the cultural groups to which they belong.

A Humanizing Pedagogy: Going Beyond Teaching Strategies

As discussed earlier, numerous teaching strategies possess the potential to humanize the learning process. It is urgent that teachers break free from lock-step methodologies so they may utilize any number of strategies or features of strategies to serve their students more effectively. When I recall a special education teacher's experience related in a bilingualism-and-literacy course I taught, I am reminded of the humanizing effects of teaching strategies that, similar to strategic teaching, allow teachers to listen and learn from their students. This teacher, for most of her career, had been required to assess her students through a variety of close-ended instruments and then to remediate their diagnosed "weaknesses" with discrete skills instruction. The assessment instruments provided little information to explain why the student either answered a question correctly or incorrectly, and they often confirmed perceived student academic and cognitive weaknesses. The fragmented discrete skills approach to instruction restricts the teacher's access to existing student knowledge and experiences not specifically elicited by the academic tasks. Needless to say, this teacher knew very little about her students other than her deficit descriptions of them.

As a requirement for my course, she was asked to focus on one limited English proficient special education student over the semester. She observed the student in a number of formal and informal contexts, and she engaged him in a number of open-ended tasks. The tasks included allowing him to write entire texts such as stories and poems (despite diagnosed limited English proficiency) and to engage in "think-alouds" during reading. Through these open-ended activities, the teacher learned about her student's English writing ability, his life experiences and world views, and his reading meaning-making strategies. Consequently, the teacher constructed an instructional plan much better suited to her student's academic needs and interests; even more important, she underwent a humanizing process that allowed her to recognize the varied and valuable life experiences and knowledge her student brought into the classroom. This teacher was admirably candid when she shared her initial negative and stereotypic views of the student and their radical transformation. Initially, she had formed an erroneous notion of her student's personality, world view, academic ability, motivation, and academic potential on the basis on his Puerto Rican ethnicity, low-SES background, limited English proficiency, and moderately learning-disabled label. Because of the restricted and closed nature of earlier assessment and instruction, the teacher had never received information about her student that challenged her negative perceptions. Listening to her student and reading his poetry and stories, she discovered his loving and sunny personality and learned his personal history. In the process, she discovered and challenged her deficit orientation. The following excerpt exemplifies the power of the student voice for humanizing teachers.

My Father

I love my father very much. I will never forget what my father has done for me and my brothers and sisters. When we first came from Puerto Rico we didn't have food to eat and we were very poor. My father had to work three jobs to put food and milk on the table. Those were hard times, and my father worked so hard that we hardly saw him. But even when I didn't see him, I always knew he loved me very much. I will always be grateful to my father. We are not so poor now and so he works only one job. But I will never forget what my father did for me. I will also work to help my father have a better life when I grow up. I love my father very much.

The process of learning about her student's rich and multifaceted background enabled this teacher to move beyond the rigid methodology that required her to distance herself from the student and confirm the deficit model she unconsciously adhered to. In this case, the meaningful teacher-student interaction humanized instruction by expanding horizons through which the student demonstrated human qualities, dreams, desires, and capacities that close-ended tests and instruction never capture. The specific teaching strategies utilized, in and of themselves, may not be the significant factors. The actual strengths of strategies depend, first and foremost, on the degree to which they embrace a humanizing pedagogy that values the students' background knowledge, culture, and life experiences.

Teaching strategies are means to an end, that is, humanizing education to promote academic success for students historically mistreated and underserved by the schools. A teaching strategy is a vehicle to a greater goal. A number of vehicles exist that may or may not lead to a humanizing pedagogy, depending on the sociocultural reality in which teachers and students operate. Teachers need to examine critically these promising teaching strategies and appropriate the aspects of those strategies that work best in their particular learning environments. Too often, teachers uncritically adopt "the latest in methodology" and blame students (once again) when the method proves ineffective.

Methods, teaching strategies, and techniques are not panaceas. For this reason, I believe that we cannot reduce transitioning success to a specific strategy or methodological paradigm. More important than strategies are the teacher's political clarity and critical understanding of the need to create pedagogical structures that eliminate the asymmetrical power relations that subordinate linguistic minority students (Freire & Macedo, 1987). As the strategic teaching approach demonstrates, features that lead to a process in which students are treated with dignity and respect make all the difference. In other words, these teaching strategies provide conditions which enable subordinate students to move from their usual object position to subject positions. I am convinced that the transitioning from object to subject position produces more far-reaching effects than transitioning from the native language to English. In fact, if the former transitioning occurs, the latter will present little difficulty.

I believe that educators, particularly bilingual teachers, would be far more effective if they critically understood the complex interrelationship of sociocultural factors shaping the educational context within which they are expected to transition students. The teachers' high level of criticity would empower them to develop the necessary pedagogical structures that cease to view and treat limited English proficient students as lacking, or as having language problems. Teachers could develop pedagogies to enhance those native language skills necessary for application to English language settings. Otherwise, these educators could easily fall into what Macedo (in press) calls an entrapment pedagogy; that is, "a pedagogy that requires of students what it does not give them" (p. 6). An uncritical acceptance of the transitioning model could very well lead to such entrapment. Finally, I would urge educators to understand that, above all, the critical issue is the degree to which we hold the moral conviction that we must humanize transitioning linguistic minority students into the English-only mainstream by eliminating the hostility that often greets these students. This process would require what Macedo (in press) suggests, the "antimethods pedagogy" that

> would reject the mechanization of intellectualism. . . . The antimethods pedagogy challenges teachers to work toward reappropriation of [the] endangered dignity [of both teacher and student] and toward reclaiming our humanity. The antimethods pedagogy adheres to the eloquence of Antonio Machado's poem, "Caminante, no hay caminos. Se hace el camino al andar." (Traveler, there are no roads. The road is created as we walk it [together].) (p. 8)

ABOUT THE AUTHOR

Dr. Bartolomé is currently Assistant Professor of Education at the Harvard Graduate School of Education in Teaching, Curriculum and Learning Environments, and Human Development and Psychology. She has prepared preservice and elementary teachers in bilingual, English as a second language, and multicultural education. She has taught and teaches courses in bilingualism and literacy and multicultural education. Research interests include oral and written language acquisition patterns of bilingual and other linguistic minority students and cross-cultural literacy practices in home and school contexts. Dr. Bartolomé is interested in applying research findings to improving classroom instruction and teacher training practices.

REFERENCES

Anyon, J. (1988). Social class and the hidden curriculum of work. In Gress, J. R. (Ed.), *Curriculum: An introduction to the field*, pp. 366–89. Berkeley, CA: McCutchan.

Au, K. H., and Mason, J. M. (1983). Cultural congruence in classroom participation structures: Achieving a balance of rights. *Discourse Processes*, vol. 6, pp. 145–68.

Avelar-La Salle, R. (1991). *The effect of metacognitive instruction on the transfer of expository comprehension skills: The interlingual and crosslingual cases*. Unpublished doctoral dissertation, Stanford University.

Bloom, G. M. (1991). *The effects of speech style and skin color on bilingual teaching candidates' and bilingual teachers' attitudes toward Mexican American pupils*. Unpublished doctoral dissertation, Stanford University.

Boykin, A. W. (1983). The academic performance of Afro-American Children. In Spence, J. T. (Ed.), *Achievement and achievement motives: Psychological and sociological approaches*, (pp. 322-69). San Francisco: W. H. Freeman.

Chall, J. (1983). *Stages of reading development*. New York: McGraw-Hill.

Chamot, A. U. (1983). How to plan to transfer curriculum from bilingual to mainstream instruction. *Focus*, vol. 12, Washington, DC: National Clearinghouse for Bilingual Education.

Clarke, M. A. (1988). The short circuit hypothesis of ESL reading—Or when language competence interferes with reading performance. In Carrell, P. L., Devine, J., and Eskey, D. E. (Eds.), *Interactive approaches to second language reading*, pp. 114-24. New York: Cambridge University Press.

Crawford, J. (1989). *Bilingual education: History, politics, theory and practice*. Trenton, NJ: Crane.

Cummins, J. (1989). *Empowering minority students*. Sacramento: California Association for Bilingual Education.

Díaz, S., Moll, L. C., and Mehan, H. (1986). Sociocultural resources in instruction: A context-specific approach. In *Beyond language: Social and cultural factors in schooling language minority students*, pp. 187-230. Los Angeles: California State University; Evaluation, Dissemination and Assessment Center.

Faltis, C. J. (1983). *Transfer of beginning reading skills from Spanish to English among Spanish-speaking children in second grade bilingual classrooms*. Unpublished doctoral dissertation, Stanford University.

Flores, B. M. (1982). *Language interference or influence: Toward a theory for Hispanic bilingualism*. Unpublished doctoral dissertation, University of Arizona at Tucson.

Flores, B., Cousin, P. T., and Diaz, E. (1991). Critiquing and transforming the deficit myths about learning, language and culture. *Language Arts*, vol. 68, no. 5, pp. 369-79.

Freire, P. (1987). Letter to North-American teachers. In Shor, I. (Ed.), *Freire for the classroom*, pp. 211-14. Portsmouth, NJ: Boynton/Cook.

Freire, P. (1985). *The politics of education: Culture, power and liberation*. South Hadley, MA: Bergin & Garvey.

Freire, P., and Macedo, D. (1987). *Literacy: Reading the word and the world*. South Hadley, MA: Bergin & Garvey.

Gee, J. P. (1989). Literacy, discourse, and linguistics: Introduction. *Journal of Education*, vol. 171, no. 1, pp. 5-17.

Giroux, H. (1985). Introduction. In Freire, P., *The politics of education: Culture, power and liberation*, pp. xi-xxv. South Hadley, MA.: Bergin & Garvey.

Heath, S. B. (1983). *Ways with words*. New York: Cambridge University Press.

Hernández, J. S. (1991). Assisted performance in reading comprehension strategies with non-English proficient students. *The Journal of Educational Issues of Language Minority Students*, vol. 8, pp. 91-112.

Jones, B. F., Palincsar, A. S., Ogle, D. S., and Carr, E. G. (1987). *Strategic teaching and learning: Cognitive instruction in the content areas*. Alexandria, VA: Association for Supervision and Curriculum Development in cooperation with the Central Regional Educational Laboratory.

Lareau, A. (1990). *Home advantage: Social class and parental intervention in elementary education*. New York: Falmer Press.

Macedo, D. (in press). Preface. In McLaren P., Lankshear, C. (Eds.), *Conscientization and resistance*. New York: Routledge.

McDermott, R. P. (1977). Social relations as contexts for learning in school. *Harvard Education Review*, vol. 47, no. 2.

Mehan, H. (1992). Understanding inequality in schools: The contribution of interpretive studies. *Sociology of Education*, 65 (1).

Menchaca, M., and Valencia, R. (1990). Anglo-Saxon ideologies in the 1920s–1930s: Their impact on the segregation of Mexican students in California. *Anthropology and Education Quarterly*, vol. 21, pp. 222-45.

Mohatt, G. V., and Erickson, F. (1981). Cultural differences in teaching styles in an Odawa school: A sociolinguistic approach. In Trueba, H., Guthrie, X., and Au, K. H. (Eds.), *Culture and the bilingual classroom: Studies in classroom ethnography*. Rowley, MA: Newbury.

O'Malley, J., and Chamot, A. U. (1990). *Learning strategies in second language acquisition*. New York: Cambridge University Press.

Pérez, B., and Torres-Guzmán, M. E. (1992). *Learning in two worlds: An integrated Spanish/English biliteracy approach*. New York: Longman.

Philips, S. U. (1972). Participant structures and communication competence: Warm Springs children in community and classroom. In Cazden, C., John, V., Hymes, D. (Eds.), *Functions of language in the classroom*. New York: Teachers College, Columbia University.

Reyes, M. (1987). Comprehension of content area passages: A study of Spanish/English readers in the third and fourth grade. In Goldman, S. R., and Trueba, H. T. (Eds.), *Becoming literate in English as a second language*, pp. 107-26. Norwood, NJ: Ablex.

Spener, D. (1988). Transitional bilingual education and the socialization of immigrants. *Harvard Education Review*, vol. 58, no. 2, pp. 133-53.

Sue, S., and Padilla, A. (1986). Ethnic minority issues in the U.S.: Challenges for the educational system. In *Beyond language: Social and cultural factors in schooling language minority students*. Los Angeles: California State University; Evaluation, Dissemination and Assessment Center.

Trueba, H. T. (1989). Sociocultural integration of minorities and minority school achievement. In *Raising silent voices: Educating the linguistic minorities for the 21st century*. New York: Newbury House.

U.S. Commission on Civil Rights (1973). *Teachers and students: Report V: Mexican-American study: Differences in teacher interaction with Mexican-American and Anglo students*. Washington, DC: U.S. Government Printing Office.

U.S. Department of Education (1991). *The condition of bilingual education in the nation: A report to the congress and the president*. Washington, D.C.: U.S. Government Printing Office.

Valencia, R. (1991). *Chicano school failure and success: Research and policy agendas for the 1990s*. New York: Falmer Press.

Valencia, R. (1986, November 25). *Minority academic underachievement: Conceptual and theoretical considerations for understanding the achievement problems of Chicano students*. Paper presented to the Chicano Faculty Seminar, Stanford University.

Walker, C. L. (1987). Hispanic achievement: Old views and new perspectives. In Trueba, H. T. (Ed.), *Success or failure: Learning and the language minority student*. New York: Newbury House.

Zhang, X. (1990). *Language transfer in the writing of Spanish speaking ESL learners: Toward a new concept*. Paper presented at the Fall Conference of the Three Rivers Association of Teachers of English to Speakers of Other Languages. (ERIC Document Reproduction Service No. ED 329 129.)

Promoting Biliteracy

Issues in Promoting English Literacy in Students Acquiring English

Kathy Escamilla
University of Colorado

NOTE: This article is meant to help bilingual teachers avoid the pitfalls of early transition. It is also meant to help mainstream English teachers who often receive bilingual children as they are transferred out of bilingual classrooms. After reading this article, teachers may wish to share it with their principals and mainstream colleagues.

Introduction

There are currently around 5.3 million school-aged children in the United States who enter school speaking a language other than English (Lyons, 1991). This population has grown from 3.6 million in 1980 and it is projected to grow by another 35 percent (or to over 7 million) between now and the year 2000 (Lyons, 1991). The rapid growth of students who do not speak English natively has necessitated the development and implementation of various educational programs to serve these students. Most commonly these students have been referred to in the literature as limited English proficient (LEP). However, this label symbolizes a deficit view of these children with a narrow focus on what they do not yet do well (speak English). This paper, in an effort to create a more positive label for these children, will refer to them as Students Acquiring English (SAE).

Educational programs for SAE students range from programs that make little use of the student's native language (such as ESL programs and/or immersion) to those that make some use of a student's native language (transitional bilingual education) to those that make extensive use of a students' native language (maintenance or late-exit bilingual programs). It is important to note that 95 percent of the funded programs for students who do not speak English proficiently are for ESL programs and Transitional Bilingual Education Programs (Lyons, 1991). Further, even late-exit bilingual programs rarely exist past sixth grade.

The rapid growth of SAE children in U.S. schools has created a severe shortage of certified bilingual/ESL teachers. A current estimate of this shortage places the number of teachers needed at 119,710 and the number available at 50,000, creating a shortage of about 69,000 teachers (Macías, 1989). It is important to note that university teacher preparation programs are not graduating enough bilingual/ESL teachers to meet this need in the near future (Macías, 1989).

These data are important for several reasons. First, the great shortage of certified bilingual teachers most certainly means that there are many teachers with no formal training who are teaching SAE children. Further, the rapid growth of the numbers of SAE children added to the almost exclusive implementation of early-exit bilingual programs implies that most SAE children will be transferred to all English classrooms early in their educational years. It is most likely that these transitioned students will wind up in classrooms with teachers who speak only English and who have no formal training in how to teach SAE children. This shortage further encourages the implementation of early-exit bilingual programs as districts often do not have the qualified staff to expand programs into the upper elementary grades.

Considering the above, it is interesting to note that the majority of research on the teaching of SAE children has involved looking at these children in the context of bilingual/ESL classrooms (see García, 1988; Ramírez, Yuen & Ramey, 1991; Tikunoff, 1983). However, very little has been written about how to help SAE children after they have been exited from bilingual/ESL programs (for an exception, see Hamayan & Perlman, 1990).

Further, few districts have in-service and/or training programs for mainstream teachers receiving SAE children and few universities mandate this type of course work as a part of a teacher preparation program for mainstream teachers. Given that the mainstream teaching population is 95 percent white (Macías, 1989), it is not likely that these teachers will have had extensive experiences with students who are culturally and linguistically diverse. Finally, few districts have communication mechanisms to encourage teacher collaboration between bilingual/ESL and monolingual English programs.

In view of the above, it is imperative that schools and universities begin to explore ways to support monolingual English teachers who daily receive SAE children into their classrooms. It is important to help bilingual teachers understand the concerns related to premature transition into English literacy. Limited resources create situations where bilingual teachers feel great pressure to transfer students from native language reading to reading in English. The purpose of this article is to discuss issues and considerations related to the development of literacy and biliteracy in SAE children.

The article will begin with a review of those aspects of literacy that are thought to be universal. Universal literacy concepts are important as they constitute those concepts, strategies, and skills that are common to every language and that do not need to be learned a second time by SAE students. The remainder of the article will focus on multiliteracies that will need to be developed if SAE children are to be successful readers of two languages.

Both bilingual and mainstream teachers have a great responsibility for the development of multiliteracies in SAE children. However, they may not have the preparation time or support to orchestrate this learning effectively.

Universal Aspects of Literacy

There is a large and ever-growing body of literature that documents the positive effects of native language literacy on the development of literacy in a second language (Cummins, 1989; Huddleson, 1987; Krashen & Biber, 1988; Medina, 1988). The more proficient students are in their native language, the higher the proficiency they can attain in second language literacy (Cummins, 1981; Escamilla, 1987; Troike, 1978; Willig, 1985).

It is thought that proficient L1 readers are more likely to become proficient L2 readers because they transfer reading strategies and concepts from the first language to the second language reading situation. It is further thought that these concepts transfer because certain aspects of literacy are universal. Universal concepts do not need to be relearned in the second language.

In a review of the research in reading and writing in bilingual education and English as a Second Language, Rodríguez (1988) identified four general aspects of literacy that are universal. Briefly summarized, these universal literacy concepts include the following: (1) social and pragmatic; (2) semantic; (3) syntactic; and (4) orthographic/graphaphonic.

Thonis (1981, 1983) identified two categories of universal literacy concepts. These are language-general concepts that will transfer from one language to another no matter what two languages are involved. The second are language-specific concepts that transfer from one language to another if the two languages have similar orthographic systems (e.g., Spanish/English and Italian/Spanish).

The pragmatic concepts, as defined by Rodríguez (1988), consider students' self-perceptions within social and cultural contexts. Students who are literate in a first language see themselves as literate. As literate people, they approach the second language literacy situation with cognitive strategies that enable them to interact with print. If they have high degrees of native language literacy, they feel that they are capable of learning to read in a second language and therefore approach the second language learning situation with motivation and confidence (Thonis, 1983). Further, first language literacy experiences in formal settings (schools) develop academic skills such as study habits, concentration, task completion, and a knowledge of the culture of the classroom that greatly facilitate the development of literacy in the second language (Rodríguez, 1988). Perhaps the most important potential for transfer involves student attitudes toward reading. Students who find first language reading to be stimulating and pleasurable and who see reading as fun will bring this attitude to the second language learning situation.

The semantic dimension of literacy is universal in that students who are literate in their first language have learned to interact with printed material (Rodríguez, 1988). Further, they know that literacy is communicative and that there is meaning attached to the printed word. Finally, prior knowledge in academic areas that has been learned in the first language transfers to the second language so that concepts don't have to be relearned.

To illustrate the above, a student who has learned about the respiratory system in Spanish most likely learned the concepts about the system as well as the vocabulary, and how to read the words that symbolize these concepts. As these students learn to read in English, they bring with them the prior knowledge of the respiratory system which need not be relearned. This prior knowledge will transfer and they will simply need to learn the English system for communicating these already familiar concepts.

The third universal aspect of literacy is related to syntactic notions and language grammar. Literate students know that literacy is structured around certain discourse rules (Rodríguez, 1988). While they may not yet know the grammar of English, their knowledge that language has structure, and that it is rule-governed and predictable, provides a universal knowledge of "grammarness" that greatly facilitates literacy development in other languages.

Finally, literate students have a knowledge of the orthographic (writing) system of their language as well as the graphaphonic (sound/symbol) system of their language. They know that reading/writing is symbolic (Rodríguez, 1988). The general knowledge that written systems are symbolic and communicate messages is universal and can be applied to all languages.

It is important that teachers of SAE students know that students who have high levels of literacy in their native language have acquired universal literacy concepts that transfer to reading in English. Teachers will not need to reteach these skills.

It is equally important to discuss that there are some aspects of literacy that are *not* universal. If students are to become truly biliterate, they will need to develop multiliteracies. Multiliteracies relate to the differences in aspects of literacy that exist between languages (Rodríguez, 1988). These differences include schematic knowledge of cultural concepts and discourse forms.

And it is important that teachers of SAE children understand both the universal aspects of literacy and the aspects of literacy that vary from language to language. For students who are not literate in their native language and/or who have low levels of literacy in their native language, teachers will need to develop both universal literacy concepts and multiliteracy concepts. As previously stated, for students who are literate, mainstream teachers will more likely need to focus on the development of multiliteracies. The remainder of this paper will discuss the multiliteracies that mainstream teachers need to consider as they develop biliteracy in SAE children.

Aspects of Multiliteracy: The Development of a Schema for English Text

As SAE students begin to read in English, teachers may assume that their reading program should be similar to that of native English speakers. As a result, they may focus their efforts on teaching reading strategies that students already possess at the expense of developing the multiliteracies that are needed to become biliterate. Studies conducted by Moll and Díaz (1985) and Padrón (1985) conclude that English reading instruction for SAE students must be differentiated from reading for monolingual English students.

Moll and Díaz (1985) conducted an ethnographic study with Spanish-speaking students learning to read in English. In this study, they found that teachers who were teaching English reading to SAE students were spending a great deal of time having students read aloud and pronounce words correctly. English reading lessons focused almost exclusively on decoding and included very little instruction that would help students comprehend or interact with what they were reading.

Padrón (1985) conducted a similar study where English reading teachers were teaching cognitive strategies to students who were literate in Spanish. Cognitive strategies included such things as recalling what they had read, summarizing, locating information, using context clues, and generalizing. She concluded that, for proficient readers of Spanish, instruction in cognitive skills in English did not improve their comprehension in English as they already had cognitive strategies but lacked knowledge of the structure of English.

As a first step, then, instruction should shift away from oral reading and learning to "say the words correctly" toward a focus of helping students interact with English text.

Further, guiding students to interact with text should *not* be confused with teaching comprehension skills (such as recalling and locating information). English reading students may, in fact, read the words and correctly answer the questions without any idea about what the text means.

To illustrate how this might happen, consider the following passage. Read it and answer the questions.

> The procedure is actually quite simple. First, you arrange things into different groups. Of course, one pile may be sufficient depending on how much there is to do. If you have to go somewhere else due to lack of facilities that is the next step. Otherwise, you are pretty well set. It is important not to overdo things. That is, it is better to do too few things at once than too many. In the short run, this may not seem important, but complications can easily arise. A mistake can be expensive as well. At first the whole procedure will seem complicated. Soon, however, it will become just another facet of life. It is difficult to foresee any end to the necessity for this task in the immediate future, but then one can never tell. After the procedure is completed, one arranges the materials into different groups again. Then they can be put into their appropriate places. Eventually, they will be used once more and the whole cycle will then have to be repeated. However, this is part of life.
> (Bradsford & Johnson, 1973, p. 400)

Comprehension Questions

1. What happens if you make a mistake?

2. What should you do first?

3. Why are the groups necessary?

4. Why is it important to know this procedure?

5. What happens if you have no facilities?

In the above passage, it is quite possible that you read all the words and answered all the questions correctly. In a typical reading class, by simply reading your answers to the questions, we might assume that you had, in fact, understood the passage. Further, you may have used reading strategies, such as going back to the reading, to help you answer the questions.

In spite of this, most people, although they can answer the questions, find the passage to be difficult. It probably would not have helped to have you read the passage aloud. However, if you had been told that the passage was about washing clothes before you read it, it might have been a little easier to understand.

Reread the passage. You will most likely find that the words and phrases take on a new meaning. This is because you utilized what psycholinguists refer to as "schema" to interpret the words as you read them. The schema about laundry that you used the second time you read the passage enabled you to interact with

PROMOTING BILITERACY

the passage in a way that was more meaningful than when you were not able to use your schema.

With regard to SAE children learning English, we often confuse ability to "read the words" and "answer the questions" with ability to meaningfully interact with the text.

Despite high levels of native language literacy, many SAE children, because of a lack of prior knowledge and experience with the U.S. cultures, may not have yet developed the schema necessary to meaningfully interact with many of the English language texts they will be called upon to read.

To illustrate the above situation, study the cartoon below. Note that this cartoon has exactly eleven words and most SAE children in English classrooms would be able to read the words easily. Further, if you asked them what the message of the cartoon is, they would most likely answer that the cartoon is about cheating.

However, if you study the cartoon a little more closely you will discover that, in order to truly interact with it, you must have much greater knowledge than a simple ability to read the words.

Make a list of the background experiences and/or schema that you need to be able to interact with the message. Further, aside from your knowledge, list the perceptions and/or attitudes you would need to have in order to agree or disagree with the message.

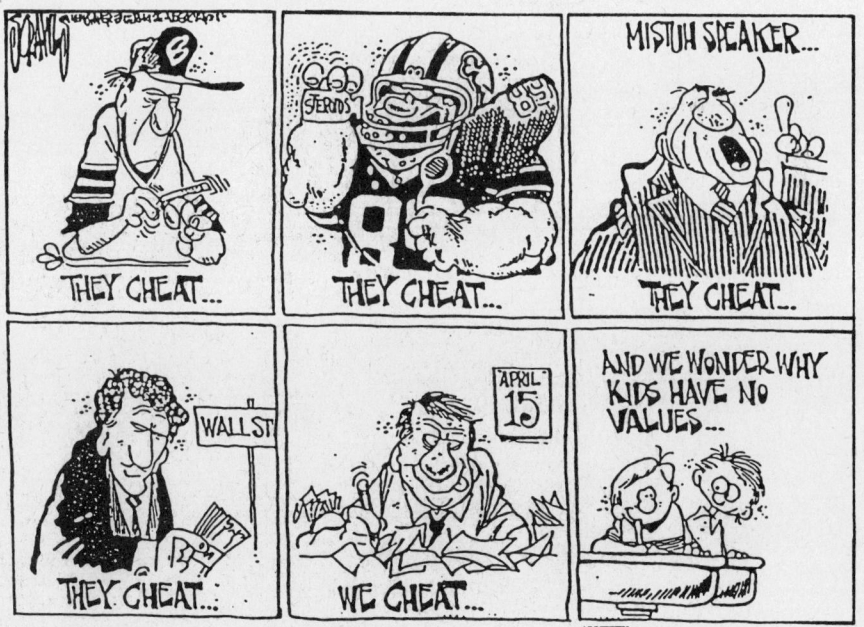

SCRAWLS reprinted by permission of NEA, Inc.

From the above it becomes apparent that the reader must know much more than how to "read the words" in order to comprehend the message. For example, the reader would have to know that filing baseballs and the use of steroids in football are illegal and therefore use of them while playing is considered to be cheating. They would further need to know that these activities often occur in U.S. sporting events. They would need to know that the third frame represents the political system that is sometimes less than honest and that Wall Street is a specific place in New York City that represents the business interests of our country. Further, Wall Street has faced several scandals recently with regard to a phenomenon called "insider trading." In addition, they would need to know that April 15 is the day taxes are due in the United States and that some Americans do not pay all of their taxes. Nowhere in the cartoon is any of the above explicitly stated, and yet it is crucial to understanding the message.

Moreover, insufficient prior knowledge will not only interfere with a student's ability to comprehend the message, but will also interfere with meaningful interaction with text that builds new schema.

For example, in an effort to get students to express their opinions a teacher may ask, "Do you agree with this cartoon?" SAE students with only surface level knowledge of the cartoon may say, "Yes, no one should cheat." Deeper knowledge, however, might lead to a richer discussion about whether or not all baseball players, etc., cheat and/or whether adult cheating in fact influences children, etc.

The above, rather lengthy discussion, is meant to illustrate that an important consideration in the development of multiliteracies is the need to build in students a schema that will enable them to meaningfully interact with English text. Teachers of SAE children should not assume that knowledge which may be common for native-English-speaking children will also be common to SAE children, for these children may not have prior knowledge or may have conflicting prior knowledge.

Escamilla (1992) summarizes the following anecdotes to illustrate conflicting schema:

A sixth-grade teacher asked her TLC students to practice reading "Cinderella" in English so that they could read it to the first grade. When she asked the students where Cinderella was going, one answered, "to a ball game like football or baseball."

A seventh-grade teacher decided to use Dickens' *A Christmas Carol* as a shared reading experience to expose her TLC students to English classics. As she read the passage to them where Tiny Tim used his "muffler" to keep warm, one student said, "I thought you said they didn't have cars back then?" It took her a while to realize that the student only knew the word muffler as a part of a car.

A school psychologist was asked to test a TLC student who was suspected of having a learning disability. The boy had moved from Mexico to a rural area of Colorado. When the psychologist asked him to name the seasons, he listed, "deer season, duck season, and fishing season."

These examples serve to illustrate the need to develop multiple schemata in SAE students learning to read in English. The role of the teacher in helping to develop this schema cannot be overemphasized. Schema building is a significant aspect of literacy in any language; however, language-specific schema is especially crucial to the building of multiliteracies.

The Development of Multicultural Understanding

The development of multiliteracies also requires a knowledge of cultural notions that are embedded in literacy events. Barnitz (1985) explains that cultural knowledge requires the ability to "read between the lines" to interact with text.

PROMOTING BILITERACY

Several examples of how culture influences text interpretation are included in the following paragraphs. Escamilla (1992) asked forty third-grade students to read a paragraph, and then answer two comprehension questions about the passage. All forty students speak English and read the passage without difficulty. All forty students attend the same elementary school in a working-class neighborhood near Denver, Colorado. Twenty of the children were monolingual English Anglos and twenty were Hispanics who had varying degrees of ability in Spanish. The paragraph contained the following information:

The López family lived in the middle of a barrio. There were ten members in their family—six girls, two boys and their parents. They were poor, and having such a big family created hardships and problems. (Steck-Vaughn, "The López Family," 1976)

After reading the paragraph, students were asked to answer the following questions:

1. What is a barrio?

2. What created hardships in the López family?

With regard to the first question, 18 out of 20 Hispanic students responded that a *barrio* is a "neighborhood where people speak Spanish." They also identified relatives who live in a barrio (e.g., grandparents, aunts, uncles, cousins). The majority of Anglo students, on the other hand, also identified a barrio as a neighborhood, but their responses classified a barrio as a "dangerous neighborhood" where "gangs" live, and people "do drugs." The word barrio was not defined for students in the passage and each student had to use prior knowledge and experience to answer the question. Student responses indicate that their cultural experiences may have greatly influenced their responses. Embedded in these responses is not only varying knowledge of what a barrio is but an attitude of the desirability of living in a barrio.

Responses to the second question also varied according to ethnic group. The majority of Hispanic students responded that hardships in the López family were created because they were "poor" or had "no money." The majority of Anglo students, on the other hand, responded that the hardships in the López family were caused by the fact that the family "had too many children."

It is interesting to note that in traditional Hispanic families, large families are thought to be a blessing. This value is not necessarily held by middle-class Anglo families. Therefore, the variation in student responses to the passage may have been related to different cultural values.

All student responses to both questions can be considered to be "correct" as the questions required interpretation and inference to which there is no specific "right" or "wrong" answer. However, it is interesting to note that answers given to both questions were similar among Hispanic students and among Anglo students. However, Hispanic and Anglo responses differed greatly from each other. As we encourage students to interact with text, it is imperative that we understand how cultural differences may affect their interpretations of text meaning.

Steffensen et al. (1979) conducted a similar study with high school students from the United States and India. In this study both groups of students were asked to read a story about an American wedding and an Indian wedding. As with Lipson (1983), comprehension for both groups was higher when they read about the wedding from their own culture. Further, each group misinterpreted events from the other culture. For example, in the American wedding, the bride wore her grandmother's dress. The Indians reading this inferred that the bride must have been poor because they could not afford a new wedding dress. A passage from the Indian wedding stated that the couple was going to Northern India after the wedding. The Americans reading this passage inferred that the couple would be honeymooning in Northern India. In fact, the couple was going to live with his parents, which is an Indian custom.

Results of these studies have important implications for teachers of SAE students. First, there a mismatch between the materials that SAE children are often asked to read in English and their home or cultural experiences. This mismatch creates situations in which it appears as if SAE children are *not* comprehending what they read. This apparent lack of comprehension, however, should not be interpreted as a *reading problem*. It is rather an indication that the student is unfamiliar with the context of the text. It is important that teachers be able to identify text that is culturally familiar to students and not assume that they have the cultural knowledge to "read between the lines."

Second, the field of reading has been moving away from asking recall and low-level comprehension questions to encouraging teachers to engage students in comprehension tasks that involve higher-level inference skills such as analysis, synthesis, and evaluation. In order for SAE students to infer meaning and interact with texts, teachers will have to help them become familiar with cultural content that may be new to them.

Teachers of SAE students must help to develop these multiliteracies by helping students to understand and recognize cultural differences and by building a knowledge of the dominant U.S. culture. At the same time, it is also important for teachers to try and identify literature, written in English, that is culturally familiar to their students, and that they may have already read in Spanish. In this way teachers can use student strengths (e.g., their knowledge of their own culture) to help them develop literacy in English.

Language Discourse Differences: Language Logic

Aside from the schema and cultural differences between languages, it is important for teachers to understand that there are significant differences in text structure and discourse across languages. SAE students learning to read in English will expect discourse to be patterned according to the conventions and constraints of their native language (Barnitz, 1985). For example, English discourse written forms are represented in a linear structure. The story grammar in English narrative prose is hierarchically represented and stories progress from point A to point B in a linear fashion. For the Asian American and Native American students who are literate in their native language, thought patterns are circular and narrative prose styles may, therefore, focus on a different story grammar (Barnitz, 1985). While Spanish and other Romance languages, along with Russian and other Slovak languages, also have a linear structure, the story grammar allows for a great deal of digression (digression is even more acceptable in Russian and Slovak languages than in Spanish). Further, Semitic languages such as Hebrew and Arabic are repetitive in nature.

PROMOTING BILITERACY

Kaplan (1970) visually illustrates how discourse structures vary according to language, and Collier (1991) adds sample discourse events to illustrate these differences. Both the visual and narrative representations of these discourse differences are presented below.

English—In English, the story line would focus on "getting to the point" and the discourse event might sound like, "I need a pair of shoes. I'm going to the store. I'll buy running shoes."

Semitic—Semitic languages have been described as taking "two steps forward and one step back" in their discourse structure. An example of this may be, "I need shoes, I'll go to the store. I need shoes, I should measure my feet. I need shoes, my old ones are worn out, etc." While the story line advances here, there is clearly a great deal of repetition that would not be found in a similar event told in English.

Asian/Native American—As stated before, these languages have a circular logic in such a way that discourse is structured around a topic many times without directly stating the topic. In fact, for speakers of these languages, being too direct is considered to be rude. An example of this structure is as follows, "In the winter the ground is cold and frozen. In the summer it is hot and there are sand burrs. Your feet can get frostbite or burns. You need shoes." Note that this example talks around the subject of needing shoes but not directly to it.

Spanish/Romance Languages—While these languages, like English, have linear logic, they allow for a great deal of digression that would be considered superfluous in English. For example: "I need a pair of shoes. I'll get some running shoes. You know my sister, she got some running shoes a while ago at J. C. Penney's. They gave her blisters, but they were cheap. Maybe we should go to Penney's to look for shoes."

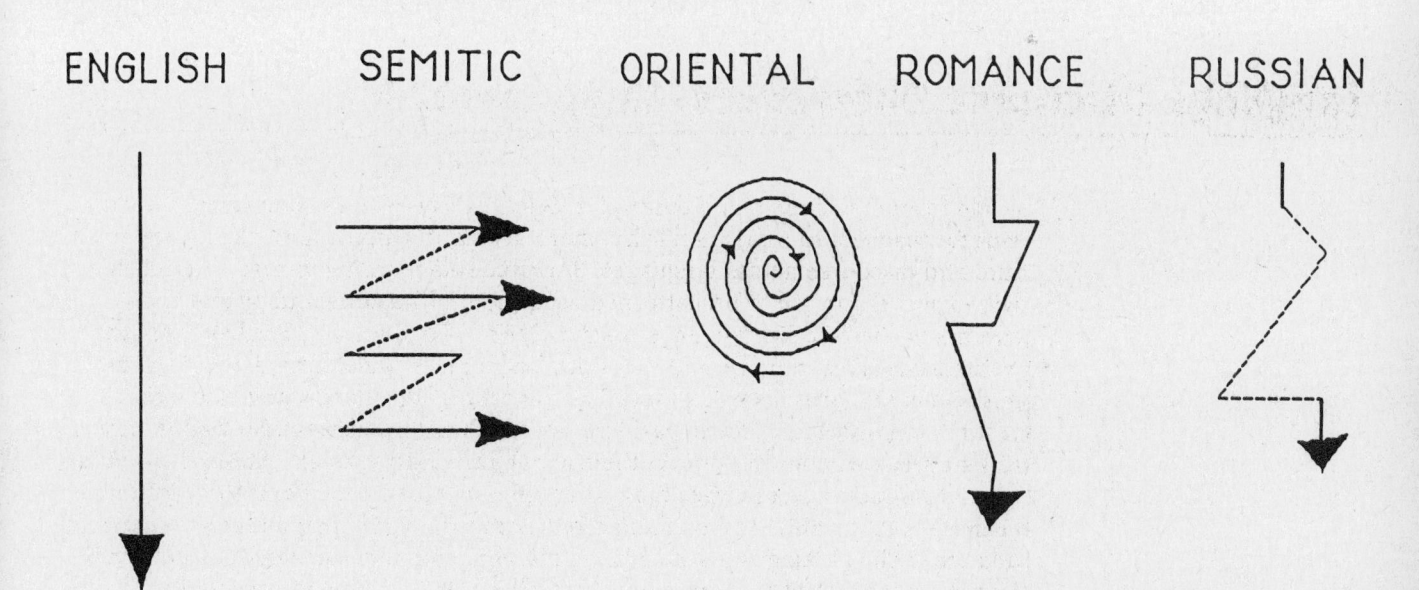

ENGLISH   SEMITIC   ORIENTAL   ROMANCE   RUSSIAN

Russian/Slovak—As with the Romance languages and English, Russian and Slovak languages are linear. However, the discourse structure allows for even greater digression than in the Romance languages. Consider this example, "I need a pair of shoes. You know, back in Czechoslovakia they have the worst factories. All their goods are worthless and the communists have ruined everything. You can't get a decent pair of shoes there. I'm glad to buy shoes here."

The above examples are meant to demonstrate how structure and logic vary across languages. These differences affect the way texts are written, and therefore will affect the ways in which SAE readers interact with English text. Teaching strategies must be aimed accordingly to promote the SAE child's awareness of discourse text pattern differences and the specific pattern of English. Further, the teacher must also guide the child to understand differences in semantic and lexical features of English.

Language Discourse Differences: Forms and Functions

Escamilla and Garza (1981) conducted a study that analyzed comprehension questions included in three widely used third-grade basal readers. The purpose of the study was to ascertain which language forms and functions were most critical for SAE children to understand in order to be able to successfully participate in reading instruction conducted exclusively in English. They then compared what the basal readers expected to what three commonly used oral ESL programs taught and to what was tested on three commonly used language assessment tests. Results indicated that there is almost no match between what ESL programs teach, what the tests assess, and what is expected in English reading programs.

These results are significant for several reasons. First, even though SAE students have been through oral ESL programs and may speak English, they may not yet have acquired all of the language forms needed to successfully interpret comprehension questions in English reading programs.

As teachers are encouraged to use higher-level questioning strategies as a part of reading instruction, the language forms needed to successfully interpret comprehension type questions get more difficult.

The following discussion provides a brief outline of the types of language forms that Escamilla and Garza found to be essential for interpreting comprehension questions in English texts. Again, these forms were rarely taught and never tested in formal ESL programs.

Idioms—English idioms are widely used in basal readers. Examples include: "Grandma had to use elbow grease to get the old table clean"; "John found out that the shoe was on the other foot when the children made fun of him"; "The Wrights lost their father in the winter of 1865." Interpretation of idioms requires that students know the collective meaning of a phrase which requires greater knowledge than knowing the meaning of each separate word.

Tag Verbs—Tag verbs in English are verbs that change their meaning when one or more tag words are added. For example, the verb to run has one meaning but the verb to run down (as in to run down a list or to run down someone) gives the verb a totally different meaning. While literal uses of verbs are taught in ESL programs, their idiomatic forms are seldom taught, but often used in basal readers. Examples of this include:

to make	to make believe
to mix	to mix up (get mixed up)
to stand	to stand up for/against
to wear	to wear out

Common comprehension questions using these structures include, "Why did Charlie get mixed up about the picnic plans?" or "Make believe that you were Billy. What would you do?" Clearly, students must understand the difference between literal verbs and tag verbs if they are to successfully interpret the questions.

Alternative Questions—Reading comprehension questions commonly ask students to make choices. For example, "Would you rather be like Jim or Sam in the story?" "Would you rather be a cat or a dog? Write a story about it." These either/or questions are important to encourage students to get involved with text, however, they are rarely taught in ESL. Consequently, SAE students may only hear and interpret one part of the question and assume the question is a yes/no or other type of question.

Modals—English modals are critical forms in reading comprehension especially in interpreting inference and other higher-level questions. Modal words include *would, could, should, might,* and *will.* Typical questions include, "What do you think Carlos might find in the country?" "Could this story have really happened?" "What would you do if you were Bill?" "Do you think the fox will starve?" A lack of understanding of modals and questions using modals will severely limit a student's ability to participate in a reading group discussion.

Conditionals—Related to the above, a common structure for asking reading comprehension questions is the conditional structure using modals. Examples of these structures include: "What would have happened if the story had been about a horse instead of a dog?" "If you were Tommy, what would you have done?" "If you were Jill which wish would you have wished for?" This linguistic form represents the type of creative question that teachers are being encouraged to use in their instructional programs. It is, therefore, likely to be used with even greater frequency by teachers, which makes comprehension of the form even more crucial for SAE students.

Teachers of SAE children should analyze text prior to instruction from the standpoint of identifying structures and/or forms with which SAE children may not be familiar. They will then need to help clarify these structures for the children.

Summary

To summarize all of the issues discussed above, it is necessary to underscore once again the notion that English literacy instruction for second language learners *should not* be the same as for native English speakers. Students who are literate in their first language have universal literacy concepts that transfer to a second language. These universal concepts include notions of sound/symbol relations, the symbolic nature of reading/writing, and that literacy is communication. Further, literate students transfer attitudes, study habits, and motivation to second language reading tasks.

Literate students have concepts about print and cognitive skills such as the ability to generalize and recall information. These skills will not need to be relearned by students, and it is important that teachers do not focus literacy instruction on teaching strategies that students already possess.

Moreover, SAE children must become biliterate if they are to function effectively in schools and society. Literacy in English is a significant goal in bilingual education and one in which mainstream as well as bilingual teachers play an important role. It is imperative, therefore, that all teachers acquire knowledge related to language differences and the appropriate strategies to assist SAE children to become confident biliterate students and lifelong learners.

About the Author

Kathy Escamilla is a specialist in multicultural education. She is a Research Associate at the BUENO Center for Multicultural Education at the University of Colorado at Boulder, Colorado, and was formerly an Assistant Professor in Education at the University of Arizona. Her many publications include articles on Reading Recovery in Spanish (Descubriendo la lectura) and studies in the acquisition of bilingualism and biliteracy. Kathy Escamilla was Chairperson for the National Association for Bilingual Education's National Conference in 1990.

References

Barnitz, J. G. (1985). *Reading development of non-native speakers of English: Research and instruction.* Monograph of the Center for Applied Linguistics. Washington DC: ERIC Clearinghouse. ED no. 256182.

Bradsford, J. D., and Johnson, M. K. (1973). Considerations of some problems of comprehension. In Chase, W. C. (Ed.), *Visual information processing.* New York: Academic Press.

Collier, C. (1991, Aug.). *Cognitive learning styles, strategies, and language differences.* Paper presented at the BUENO Center, University of Colorado, Trainer of Trainers Summer Institute. Vail, CO.

Cummins, J. (1989). *Empowering minority students.* Sacramento, CA: California Association for Bilingual Education.

Cummins, J. (1981). The role of primary language development in promoting educational success for language minority students. In *Schooling and language minority students: A theoretical framework.* Los Angeles: California State University; Evaluation, Dissemination and Assessment Center.

Escamilla, K. (1992, Feb.). *Reading as a cultural event.* Paper presented at the Colorado Association for Bilingual Education (CABE) Conference. Northglenn, CO.

Escamilla, K. (1987). *The relationship of native language reading achievement and oral English proficiency to future achievement in reading English as a second language.* Unpublished doctoral dissertation, University of California, Los Angeles.

Escamilla, K., and Garza, S. A. (1981, May). *Are you sure your students are ready to read in English?* Paper presented at the National Association for Bilingual Education (NABE) Conference, Boston, MA.

García, E. (1988). *Effective schooling for language minority students.* Occasional papers in bilingual education. Washington, DC: National Clearinghouse for Bilingual Education.

Hamayan, E., and Perlman, R. (1990). *Helping language minority students after they exit from bilingual/ESL programs: A handbook for teachers.* Washington, DC: National Clearinghouse for Bilingual Education.

Huddleson, S. (1987). The role of native language literacy in the education of language minority children. *Language Arts,* vol. 64, no. 8, pp. 827–41.

Kaplan, R. (1970). Cultural thought patterns in inter-cultural education. *Language Learning,* vol. 16, no. 1.

Krashen, S., and Biber, D. (1988). *On course: Bilingual education's success in California.* Sacramento: California Association for Bilingual Education.

Lipson, M. (1983). The influence of religious affiliation on children's memory for text information. *Reading Research Quarterly,* vol. 18, no. 4, pp. 448–57.

The López Family (1976). Austin, TX: Steck-Vaughn.

Lyons, J. (1991, May). View from Washington: Trends and projections. *NABE News,* vol. 14, no. 6, p. 19.

Macías, R. (1989). *Bilingual teacher supply and demand in the United States.* Los Angeles: USC Center for Multilingual/Multicultural Research and the Tomás Rivera Center.

Medina, M. (1988, April). *Native language proficiency and Spanish achievement in an eight year maintenance bilingual education program.* Paper presented at the annual meeting of the National Association for Bilingual Education Conference, Houston, TX.

Moll, L., and Díaz, S. (1985). Ethnographic pedagogy: Promoting effective bilingual instruction. In García, E., and Padilla, R. (Eds.), *Advances in bilingual education research,* pp. 127–49. Tucson, AZ: University of Arizona Press.

Padrón, Y. N. (1985). *Utilizing cognitive reading strategies to improve English reading comprehension of Spanish-speaking bilingual students.* Unpublished doctoral dissertation, University of Houston.

Ramírez, D. J., Yuen, S. D., and Ramey, D. R. (1991). *Executive summary, final report: Longitudinal study of structured English immersion strategy, early-exit and late-exit transitional bilingual programs for language minority children,* contract no. 300-87-0156. San Mateo, CA: Aquirre International.

Rodríguez, A. (1988). Research in reading and writing in bilingual education and English as a second language. In Ambert, A. (Ed.), *Bilingual education and English as a second language: A research handbook 1986-87,* pp. 62–117. New York: Garland Pub.

Steffensen, M., Joag-Dav, C., and Anderson, R. (1979). A cross-culture perspective on reading comprehension. *Reading Research Quarterly,* vol. 15, no. 1, pp. 10–29.

Thonis, E. (1983). *The English-Spanish connection.* Northvale, NJ: Santillana Publishing Company.

Thonis, E. (1981). Reading instruction for language minority students. In *Schooling and language minority students: A theoretical framework,* pp. 147–81. Los Angeles, CA: California State University, Dissemination and Assessment Center for Bilingual Education.

Tikunoff, W. (1983). *Applying significant bilingual instructional features in the classroom.* Rosslyn, VA: Interamerica Research Associates.

Troike, R. (1978). Research evidence for the effectiveness of bilingual education. *Bilingual Education Paper Series,* vol. 2, no. 5. Los Angeles, CA: California State University, National Dissemination and Assessment Center.

Willig, A. C. (1985). A meta-analysis of selected studies on the effectiveness of bilingual education. *Review of Educational Research,* vol. 55, no. 3, pp. 269–317.

Biliteracy From the Students' Points of View

Toni Griego Jones
University of Wisconsin—Milwaukee

This paper addresses a factor in biliteracy development that is not usually singled out as a part of reading instruction. It is, however, every bit as important as methodology, reading materials, or instructional paradigms. The neglected factor is the mind-set of children regarding the development of two languages, specifically Spanish and English in bilingual programs in American public schools.

Teachers know that children's attitudes and perceptions are at the core of their motivation to learn. For second language learners, attitudinal and motivational factors are particularly critical since learning a new language is not just a matter of acquiring new information. Learning a new language necessitates a personal entry into a new cultural group as well (Dulay, Burt & Krashen, 1982; Delgado-Gaitan & Trueba, 1992; Wong-Fillmore, 1991; Ramírez, 1985). Language acquisition is very complex as students are forced to adopt new cultural norms of social interaction of the target group as well as a new linguistic code. Students' attitudes about their native language group, about the target language group, and about their relationships with both groups influence their willingness to learn the new language. Spanish-speaking children must come to grips with their feelings about their minority status and with how they are perceived by the majority language group. Society's attitudes toward minority languages are closely linked to feelings about the ethnic groups themselves. Language, being one of the more visible manifestations of any cultural group, has often been the lightning rod that attracts the prejudice and discrimination that is directed at minority ethnic or racial groups. Negative perceptions of the majority society are internalized by children, and minority students often feel ashamed of their language and angry toward the larger society (Ramírez, 1985; Skutnabb-Kangas & Cummins, 1988). English-speaking students in bilingual settings must also deal with attitudes they have acquired regarding the minority group/language and their relative power status. In short, students' feelings about their native and second languages can't be separated from their feelings about self. These feelings need to be understood in order to maximimize learning and literacy development in any and all languages.

Teachers involved in the development of biliterate individuals, then, must concern themselves with information about attitudes held by their students toward the two languages in their lives. What do children in bilingual classrooms understand about biliteracy development, and what are their attitudes toward each language involved in the bilingual setting? What do children think each language is for and how do they feel about developing their native language and learning a new one? Since most bilingual classrooms use Spanish and English, the questions can be even more specific. How do Spanish-speaking children feel about becoming literate in Spanish and learning English as a second language? Others may want biliteracy for them, but what do the children themselves want?

Discussions of biliteracy have usually been limited to language minority students, but, in order to produce realistic, natural opportunities for biliteracy development in public schools, discourse should begin to encompass speakers of the majority language as well. What do English-speaking children who are part of bilingual classrooms understand about learning two languages? What are their attitudes toward becoming literate in a minority language as well as that of the mainstream?

Relatively few bilingual programs enroll English-speaking students, so the majority of students in bilingual classrooms are Spanish speakers who are limited in their English skills. Since this is the case, "biliteracy" development has most often meant adding English while attempting to develop Spanish to some degree. A core practice in all bilingual classsrooms is the use of the native language for instruction in content areas and, in most cases, for initial reading instruction as well. Research and experience tell us that developing literacy skills in a child's native language is the most effective and efficient way of empowering students to learn all subjects, to become skilled in cognitive and linguistic processes, and to eventually acquire a second language (Cummins, 1988; Krashen & Biber, 1988). Hence the attention to using Spanish in bilingual classrooms.

Bilingual educators by and large understand the pedagogical importance of using a student's native language for instruction. They work hard at finding Spanish reading materials and learning strategies for teaching literacy skills in Spanish. Secure in their belief that the use of Spanish benefits students, bilingual teachers are sometimes surprised when they encounter children who are ambivalent or openly resist using Spanish in school, preferring to use English even when they are limited in their ability to do so. A common concern raised in my experience in bilingual teacher preparation is the frustration teachers feel when they have fulfilled requirements for bilingual certification, only to find that Spanish-dominant students sometimes shy away from using Spanish and often resent being placed in Spanish reading groups. Others have also noted this classroom behavior (Commins, 1989; Nieto, 1992; Ramírez, 1985).

Kindergartner's Perceptions of Spanish and English

The importance of attending to children's perceptions of Spanish and English was highlighted for me several years ago by interviews I conducted with kindergartners entering a brand new Two-Way bilingual program. Although years of teaching in elementary bilingual classrooms had taught me not to assume that Spanish-dominant children would be overjoyed at the opportunity to read in Spanish, findings from the interviews concerned me. I had always believed that it was the transitional orientation of most bilingual programs that caused the students' rush to English. Two-Way programs, on the other hand, are committed to biliterate development and emphasize development of *both* languages. I expected, then, that children in a Two-Way program would have a different attitude toward the development of both languages. However, descriptions children gave of their reading and writing efforts revealed that even in this setting, where both languages were equally valued, Spanish speakers and English speakers alike perceived English to be the more "legitimate" school language.

Interviews with children focused on their emerging literacy skills and were tape-recorded in December 1988 and again in May 1989. Reading behaviors were documented and writing samples were analyzed. Children described their own writing, telling what they wrote about and how they felt about it. They answered questions about the language they were writing in, and the language(s) used in their descriptions were also noted. The most interesting findings, however, were the perceptions students had of the relative status and function of Spanish and English.

For example, English was used by all students even when children were Spanish dominant and limited in their ability to use English. All native Spanish speakers used a mixture of Spanish and English words and phrases to describe what they had written, using English whenever they were able. Two Spanish-dominant students answered questions stated in Spanish with English responses and indicated that their journals were written in English even though their narratives describing them were in Spanish. They described the writing as English but they did not have enough proficiency in English to actually use it in telling what they wrote about. One "bilingual" student did not initially use Spanish in the interviews although he was clearly more comfortable in Spanish. Only one native English speaker volunteered Spanish in her description and did use a string of Spanish words to tell about her writing. She invented Spanish sounding words and used all the Spanish words she knew in an effort to "speak Spanish." The other two English speakers did not volunteer any attempts at Spanish. The first interviews were done while students were still in the early stages of literacy development as they were beginning to read and write. Their inclination to use English did not change over the course of the year, even after they had been immersed in literacy activities in both languages.

The descriptions of those students who were further along in the development of literacy described Spanish and English as being basically the same in function (communication)—they "just look different." They articulated a clear concept of what language is for—"to ask questions and to tell things." These were students who were identifying and pointing to letters and words as they read, and they were incorporating letters and words in scribbles and pictures. Many of their written letters and words were identifiable as Spanish. In spite of seeing the two languages as basically the same, however, they somehow perceived English to be the language they were supposed to write in eventually.

Children's apparent preference for English was undoubtedly due to many factors, factors inside and outside of the classroom. The point was that even though school personnel and parents had committed themselves to biliterate development of students and had gone through great pains to establish their Two-Way bilingual school, they were temporarily confounded by the children's—even Spanish-dominant children's—orientation toward English. The perception of English as the preferred school language was something they had not expected. Children regarded Spanish as "okay" to use but seemed to view it as a vehicle they leaned on as they worked to become proficient in English.

Although the number of students interviewed in this study was very small (three Spanish-dominant children, four bilingual, and three English-dominant children), the finding caused school personnel to examine their assumptions about children's readiness to develop both languages. They realized that they did not know what students in their school really thought about learning and developing Spanish. If these were the views of the youngest children just entering a school that promoted biliteracy, what did children in the upper grades who had been in traditional bilingual or "English only" schools think? Parents enrolled their children with the intention of having them learn two languages, but what did the children themselves understand about the eventual goal?

Teachers in the school subsequently developed strategies that consciously attended to upgrading students' perceptions of Spanish as a language for literacy development. For example, they separated languages for instruction by alternating days of instruction. A pair of teachers, one English-speaking and one Spanish-speaking, alternated their groups of children, but only taught in their dominant language, thereby ensuring that Spanish had equal time and status and was used for all academic and literacy learning tasks. They recruited more Spanish-dominant students so that the classrooms would be balanced in numbers of each language group. The school lobbied for more Spanish language materials, including children's literature in Spanish and content-area materials. Most importantly, though, the awareness and sensitivity of the kindergarten teacher to students' perceptions and attitudes was increased and she incorporated her knowledge of these attitudes in her daily lesson planning, making sure that activities addressed this affective objective as well as skills and knowledge.

Influences on Students' Attitudes

How can we explain the apparent contradiction in students turning away from something that is proven to be the most effective tool teachers can use in educating them? Language-minority students' ambivalence about their native language can be explained in part by others' views of them. Students receive messages about their worth and value and subsequently about their language, from a variety of sources—home and family, community, schools, and the larger society. The United States is one of the most monolingual societies in the world and language use is strongly associated with political power. English is the acknowledged dominant language, with various ethnic groups struggling to retain the right to use their languages. Proficiency in English, or even willingness to speak English and abandon other native languages, is strongly identified with being American (Andersson & Boyer, 1978; Castellanos, 1985; Crawford, 1989; Hakuta, 1986; Nieto, 1992; Scarcella, 1990). American society has had a long, intense history of negative and neutral attitude cycles toward non-English languages. Today we are in a cycle of negativity that spawns movements such as Official English and withdraws support from bilingual education. Increased immigration (especially from Spanish-speaking countries), contributes to fears and apprehension among mainstream English speakers that English will loose its dominant position. The relative decline in the economic power of the United States and loss of jobs to foreign countries also fuels animosity toward non–English speakers. The animosity and negative feelings of the majority society are felt by language-minority children, and they carry those feelings with them to the mainstream society's schools.

The reasons for our history and our current state of xenophobia are beyond the scope of this paper but are well documented in the sources cited. The important point here is that children (and their parents and teachers) internalize the attitudes of society and develop self-concepts and concepts of others based on the messages they receive. Had our history been different, had linguistic diversity been valued instead of alternately being attacked or ignored, language-minority children might be prized in today's schools instead of viewed as deficient.

Another way of looking at resistance to using the native language is to describe it in terms of a "pull" toward English. One unfortunate reason that students are pulled toward English and alienated from their native language is simply because that is the orientation of many bilingual programs. The majority of bilingual programs have a transitional focus and are evaluated on how quickly they can transfer students into English-only classroom settings. Indeed, the use of Spanish in bilingual classrooms is often only justified or permitted because it is the most efficient and effective tool for learning English, rather than something that should be developed in its own right. This orientation results in having students who enter school with the potential for full biliteracy leaving school without literacy skills in their native language. Unfortunately, much of the native language loss experienced by Spanish speakers and their subsequent failure to achieve full biliteracy may be due to the focus on developing English and concurrent lack of attention to developing Spanish in bilingual classrooms.

Only a few school districts have bilingual programs that are committed to achieving full biliteracy. Some, such as Developmental, Maintenance, and Two-Way programs, do have full biliteracy as a goal and have successfully achieved biliteracy for some of their students (Collier, 1989). However, as indicated in the interviews with kindergartners, even in those programs that do emphasize native language development and seek to develop truly bilingual students, there may be cause to think that the balance is tipped in favor of greater development in English. The "buy-in" to biliteracy isn't automatic on the part of students. We have very little accurate data on how successful programs have been in reaching the goal of developing biliterate individuals. Most research and evaluation has been focused only on measuring achievement in English proficiency. Those students who do achieve biliteracy do not generally have that achievement measured and reported.

In order to understand students' attitudes, we must put the goal of biliteracy in perspective and know what we are up against when we expect students to become biliterate. Societal values that work against the development of non-English languages are powerful forces, causing children and bilingual programs alike to promote English and back away from other native languages. The implication of the discussion above is that there is more to developing biliteracy than teacher qualifications and effective instructional strategies and books in both languages. The success of biliterate development also depends on students' attitudes and their understandings of biliteracy and what it means for them.

Assessing Students' Attitudes and Understandings

The first step in understanding students' views about biliteracy is to formally or informally assess those views. In discussing children's viewpoints, I include two constructs: (1) attitude and (2) understandings of language and its function. Attitudes are difficult to define and even more difficult to assess because they cannot be observed or measured directly. Their existence must be inferred from their consequences. While there isn't complete agreement among social scientists about the definition of *attitude*, there is substantial agreement that *affect for or against* is a critical component of the attitude concept (Mueller, 1986). There is an evaluative aspect to attitude. The definition could be restated as "a like or dislike of a psychological object." Sociolinguists have also used the term *language attitude* to define this same evaluative reaction or feeling toward language.

The role that attitude plays in determining human behavior makes it critical that teachers be aware of students' attitudes and make use of the knowledge they have about those attitudes. Mueller describes the importance of attitude in human interactions this way:

> Attitudes constitute an immensely important component in the human psyche. They strongly influence all of our decisions: the friends we pick, the jobs we take, the movies we see, the foods we eat, the spouses we marry, the clothes we buy, and the houses we live in. We choose the things we choose, to a large extent, because we like them. (p. 7)

I submit that children also choose the languages they use because they "like" them, that is, their affect toward them is positive. Therefore, part of our job in developing biliteracy becomes one of helping students learn to like their native language and to like their second language. Their affect for or against either will affect their behavior, i.e., language choice.

Since most formal methods of assessing attitudes are probably not feasible for teachers in classrooms, teachers could more readily use informal ways of assessing children's attitudes. For example, keeping in mind the idea of *affect for or against* as a critical component of attitude, interviews with students about their reading and writing, about their home language, about how they feel about using each language could help determine affect for or against the use of each language in general, and for specific academic- or school-related functions in particular. What is a student's affect toward using each language to convey information about subjects such as science or math? As long as students think of Spanish as primarily for home and social activities, they won't develop it for academic purposes. If they are to become biliterate they need to begin to choose Spanish as a language for the more "academic" tasks.

By proactively planning activities that use Spanish in an academic context, we can counteract the negative views learned from society about Spanish not being an acceptable language for school. A problem might be that in our efforts to value children's home language and to make them feel comfortable in school, we unconsciously limit the use of Spanish to more affective situations rather than "cognitive" ones.

The second part of what we need to assess, children's understandings, includes what students actually *know* about each language and how it is used at home, in their communities, in school, and in the larger society. This encompasses their knowledge of the political, social, and power relationships among speakers of the various language groups. For example, do they know why their parents may encourage them "to speak English as much as they can"? Do they know why the teacher speaks two languages, or maybe one language better than the other? Do they understand the historical context for English being the dominant language in this country or do they just assume that is the natural order of things? Do they know that Spanish and English are major languages in the rest of the world, and where they are used? Knowledge and new information always mediate attitudes and perceptions of reality.

Without adding to what teachers already have to do in the classroom, informal interviews, observations, and recording information noted could yield useful information about an important aspect in planning for biliterate development. Students' attitudes and understandings of dual language development are important variables that have generally been systematically overlooked in development of programs designed to foster biliteracy, specifically in reading and writing. This is an area that we don't know. Most educators' energy has been spent researching *how* students learn native and second languages, on learning about the process and products, but not on why. Although it is important to study the cognitive and linguistic processes involved in learning languages, we may be missing an important part of planning for biliteracy if we don't consciously assess and address students' perceptions of what they are doing in learning two languages and why. Without conscious attention to attitudes, we are operating on assumptions about students' motivation to learn two languages. Approaches to teaching reading such as Whole Language and the Language Experience Approach indirectly address the effect in learning, but we are making assumptions about where students are in their desire to learn two languages if we do not assess them. We may be projecting our attitudes and values onto students and expecting that they are in tune with them. Instruction may be more effective if we focus attention on understanding attitudes toward language. Further, we can't assume that our particular students in our particular classrooms think and understand the way everyone else does. Across the country children are in very different circumstances.

It seems that bilingual educators have been so pressed to develop effective programs—programs that work—that we have focused on "how to" and assumed that children have clarified their understanding of what we are up to. There is a need to make assessment and sensitivity to linguistic attitudes a more formal part of reading and writing instruction. We can counteract negative messages they are receiving from other areas of their lives and utilize positive attitudes toward their respective languages.

About the Author

Toni Griego Jones is Assistant Professor in the Department of Curriculum and Instruction at the University of Wisconsin-Milwaukee. She directs the Bilingual Teacher Certification Program for their School of Education. She teaches classes in bilingual education, urban education, and language assessment in addition to conducting evaluations of reform efforts in public schools. Prior to teaching at the university, she was a bilingual classroom teacher and administrator in the Denver Public Schools and taught ESL to adults. Research interests and publications are in the areas of educational reform, as it relates to Hispanic student populations and bilingual teacher preparation. Dr. Griego Jones received her Ph.D. from the University of Colorado, Boulder, in 1988.

References

Andersson, T., and Boyer, M. (1978). *Bilingual schooling in the United States*. Austin, TX: National Educational Laboratory Publishers, Inc.

Castellanos, D. (1985). *The best of two worlds*. Trenton, NJ: New Jersey State Department of Education.

Collier, V. P. (1989, March). *Academic achievement, attitudes, and occupations among graduates of two-way bilingual classes*. Paper presented at the annual meeting of the American Educational Research Association, San Francisco, CA.

Commins, N. L. (1989). Language and affect: bilingual students at home and at school. *Language Arts*, vol. 66, pp. 29–43.

Crawford, J. (1989). *Bilingual education: History, politics, theory and practice*. Trenton, NJ: Crane Publishing Co., Inc.

Cummins, J. (1988). From multicultural to anti-racist education: An analysis of programmes and policies in Ontario. In Skutnabb-Kangas, T., and Cummins, J. (Eds.), *Minority education: From shame to struggle*. Philadelphia: Multilingual Matters Ltd.

Delgado-Gaitan, C., and Trueba, H. (1992). *Crossing cultural borders*. New York: The Falmer Press.

Dulay, H., Burt, M., and Krashen, S. (1982). *Language two*. New York: Oxford University Press.

Hakuta, K. (1986). *Mirror of language*. New York: Basic Books, Inc.

Krashen, S., and Biber, D. (1988). *On course, bilingual education's success in California*. Sacramento: California Association for Bilingual Education.

Mueller, D. J. (1986). *Measuring social attitudes*. New York: Teachers College, Columbia University.

Nieto, S. (1992). *Affirming diversity*. New York: Longman Publishing Group.

Ramírez, A. G. (1985). *Bilingualism through schooling: Cross-cultural education for minority and majority students*. Albany: State University of New York Press.

Scarcella, R. (1990). *Teaching language minority students in the multicultural classroom*. Englewood Cliffs, NJ: Prentice-Hall, Inc.

Skutnabb-Kangas, T., and Cummins, J. (1988). *Minority education: From shame to struggle*. Philadelphia: Multilingual Matters Ltd.

Wong-Fillmore, L. (1991). The care and education of America's young children: Obstacles and opportunities. In Kagan, S. L. (Ed.), *The 90th yearbook of the national society for the study of education*. The National Society for the Study of Education. Chicago: University of Chicago Press.

COOPERATIVE LEARNING STRATEGIES:
Bilingual Classroom Applications

Josefina Villamil Tinajero and Margarita E. Calderón
The University of Texas at El Paso

Rachel Hertz-Lazarowitz
The University of Haifa, Israel

Introduction

The purpose of this article is to provide teachers with ideas on how to utilize cooperative learning strategies to enhance their daily instruction of the Language Arts in bilingual classrooms. The focus is on the use of basal reader texts. Basal readers are one of the primary tools used by teachers for teaching reading and writing. The article provides the background for teachers to realize that with some restructuring of the activities they have traditionally planned for themselves and for their children, they can incorporate interactive-cooperative learning strategies in their bilingual classrooms.

The article first describes briefly the significance of cooperative learning in the development of both the first and second language. Accordingly, some research findings on the benefits of cooperative learning are presented. Second, the article provides teachers with practical suggestions on how to integrate cooperative learning strategies using their basal readers. This is done by presenting seventeen cooperative learning structures and examples of how to apply them to reading instruction. Introducing cooperative learning to classrooms requires a restructuring of the classroom as to teacher and student roles. Thus the third part offers suggestions for designing a cooperative classroom. Hopefully, the reader of this article will be able to utilize simple cooperative learning structures successfully in her/his teaching while using the basal reading program.

Cooperative Learning for Bilingual Students

Instruction for students acquiring English (SAEs) is a complex process. These students must be taught to read and write in their native language, transitioned into the second language, and finally mainstreamed into the monolingual English curriculum (Cummins, 1989). Effective interaction and communication among and between students and among and between students and the teacher seems essential to the accomplishment of these tasks. Cooperative learning offers the tools to enhance this type of communication and interaction (Calderón, 1989; Calderón, Hertz-Lazarowitz & Tinajero, 1991).

Cooperative learning is an educational movement in U.S. schools. The essential elements of cooperative learning include structured learning in small groups of two to six students, with face-to-face interactive discourse about the learning content. Learning tasks are designed to maximize student effective and participatory learning. By assigning tasks to individuals and the group, the group learning processes are geared to maximize individual accountability. There are various schools of thought within the cooperative movement. However, all of them share a structured group process by which students are engaged in a cooperative learning context that enhances their academic, social, and affective development. (See Cohen & De Avila, 1983; Johnson & Johnson, 1991; Slavin, 1990, 1983.)

Cooperative learning for bilingual students has been found: (1) to support interaction and thus the development and use of the first language in ways that support cognitive development and increased second language skills; (2) to increase the frequency and variety of second language practice through different types of interaction; (3) to provide opportunities to integrate language with content instruction; (4) to provide inclusion of a greater variety of curricular materials to stimulate language use as well as concept learning; and (5) to provide opportunities for students to act as resources for each other and thereby assume a more active role in learning (Calderón, Tinajero & Hertz-Lazarowitz, 1992; McGroarty, 1989).

BENEFITS OF COOPERATIVE LEARNING FOR FIRST AND SECOND LANGUAGE INSTRUCTION

Cooperative learning consists of a myriad of teaching strategies that develop social and academic communication skills. Cooperative learning strategies such as Paired Reading, Team Writing, and Team Products allow students to regain reading and writing in their first language almost immediately. Students quickly realize that they all have something to contribute and that their ideas are valued and encouraged by peers and teacher (Calderón, 1989; Calderón, Tinajero, Hertz-Lazarowitz, 1992).

For students acquiring English, cooperative learning strategies offer a natural approach (Krashen, 1981), rich with language experiences that integrate speaking, listening, reading, and writing. The activities tap the students' cultural backgrounds and make these experiences meaningful, relevant, and interesting for them. When these activities are structured for ESL instruction, they can help students develop proficiency in English efficiently and effectively.

Simple cooperative learning activities such as Roundtable, Numbered Heads Together, and Concept Cards can be used to develop concepts and vocabulary in a fun and meaningful way. Moreover, communicative competence is more likely to occur when students learn to work in teams.

Implementing even simple cooperative strategies with the primary language basal readers and later on integrating them with a quality transitional program, such as the Macmillan Transitional Reading Program (Tinajero & Long, 1989), enables students to develop high levels of proficiency in both languages. By merging the basal reader's activities with cooperative learning strategies students begin reading and writing in their primary language and learn to work effectively in groups. When it is time to transition, students will have already learned the cooperative structures and can then concentrate on second language acquisition. Then they can enjoy their stories, get creative with writing in the second language, and feel proud of their daily products and successes (Calderón, 1989; Tinajero & Calderón, 1988).

Implementing Cooperative Learning in the Basal Language Arts Classroom

CREATING THE CLIMATE FOR A COOPERATIVE CLASSROOM

Johnson and Johnson (1991) identify three modes of learning and teaching in our schools: competitive, individualistic, and cooperative. According to this terminology, students in most classrooms compete with other classmates on resources such as the teacher's attention, social status, and grades. Daily experiences of testing, grading, and being exposed to teachers' questions put students in a competitive mode. In each of these situations there are a couple of "good" students who win learning rewards, and many "losers" who don't make it and will not get the rewards that the classroom setting offers. Most of the classrooms have only a couple of good students who constantly participate and answer teachers' questions and get A's on their tests. Many other students are considered losers in these competitive classrooms. Research has shown that as early as the first months in first grade, students can identify who is doing well in the classroom and who is not (Good & Brophy, 1987).

Consequently, in the competitive mode type of teaching/learning many students lose their desire to learn and participate. School life becomes frustrating for them and they withdraw from academic engagement. In the individualistic mode of teaching/learning teachers try to avoid the competitive mode by assigning students many individual learning tasks, thus minimizing social and academic comparisons between strong and weak students. While in the former competitive mode, students experience the "sink or swim" approach; in the individual type of learning, students lack the feeling for the social context of the classroom and classroom cohesiveness is low (Hertz-Lazarowitz, 1992).

The third mode is the cooperative one. In this type of classroom, students work in teams while interacting in their learning. Principles of positive interaction, division of work, positive interdependence, individual accountability, and group products are integrated into the learning experience of the students and the teachers. The slogan "You swim, I swim, we are together," captures the essence of the cooperative class.

Undoubtedly, there is a place for competitive, individualistic, and cooperative modes in the learning experiences in our classrooms. However, research shows that most of our teaching/learning takes place in either competitive or individualistic modes of learning and very little cooperation exists in the classroom (Hertz-Lazarowitz, Baird, Webb and Lazarowitz, R., 1984; Kohn, 1986; Weinstein, 1991).

In order for a teacher to introduce cooperation as a legitimate mode in the classroom, norms and rules for a cooperative classroom should be defined, practiced, and implemented for students and teachers alike.

Before starting any group activity the teacher must negotiate social norms with the students. First, the teacher can suggest a couple of social norms such as "Be Positive" or "No Put Downs." The teacher can then ask the students to put their heads together. Working in groups, students can then come up with one social norm they feel should be established in the classroom. Thus, the groups contribute more social norms to the list. These norms are discussed and posted as the social rules of the classroom. At the end of each week, the students review their behavior according to the norms. Then they put their heads together again to eliminate those norms no longer needed and to come up with new ones. After three or four weeks of applying this process, a climate of cooperation is established. Usually children come up with norms such as: "Be Positive," "No Put Downs," "Listen to Each Other," "Everyone Contributes," "Take Turns," "Have Fun But Stay on Task" (Hertz-Lazarowitz & Calderón, in press).

COOPERATIVE LEARNING STRATEGIES

This section presents 17 cooperative strategies. Most of them are simple strategies and can be integrated in most reading and writing lessons. This section begins by introducing pair work and suggests that teachers move gradually to groups of three and four. Some of the strategies suggested here were developed by the authors of this article. Others represent modifications of structures suggested in the literature (Cohen, 1987; Gibbs, 1987; Hertz-Lazarowitz & Fuchs, 1987; Johnson, Johnson & Holubec, 1991).

1. Paired Reading

The teacher instructs the children to sit side by side or ear to ear and to take turns reading a selection. Children alternate reading sentences or paragraphs (Calderón, Tinajero & Hertz-Lazarowitz, 1992; Stevens et al., 1987).

2. Turn to Your Neighbor and (Say/Write/Draw)

During or after reading a basal reader selection, the teacher instructs the children to turn to their neighbor and to ask questions regarding what they have read. For example, after the children read, in pairs, a couple of paragraphs from the story "Mi primera maestra," children may turn to their neighbor and ask, "Where is the bus going?" or "Who is on the bus?" Children can infer their answers from the very first picture that accompanies the text. Other examples of activities that create interaction among kids are:

a. Tell your neighbor what paragraph you liked best in the story and why.

b. Show your neighbor the sentence you wrote about a particular vocabulary word and check each other's sentences.

c. Discuss with your neighbor question number one at the end of the story: *Antes de que se abriera la escuela, ¿dónde estudiaban los niños del rancho?*

d. Discuss with your neighbor what you want to write about: *A la hora de recreo, ¿cómo ayudaban los niños a construir la escuela?*

3. Brainstorming in Groups

Brainstorming can be used in different stages of working in the reading selection. The teacher can suggest a theme or present a question. Working in groups, the children can brainstorm as many answers, ideas, or facts about a particular topic as they can. For example, after reading the story, "La cotorra que no quería decir Cataño," the teacher asks children to brainstorm all the things they have learned about parrots. Children brainstorm for a few minutes, add their personal knowledge about parrots, and then list their ideas on chart paper. In one third-grade bilingual class, the children compiled the following list about parrots after reading the story.

Las cotorras . . .
   son aves de muchos colores
   se encuentran en lugares cálidos
   tienen pico grueso y duro
   hacen mucha bulla
   son amigables
   son animales domésticos
   son cariñosos
   aprenden a hablar
   no entienden lo que dicen
   viven en lugares con mucha vegetación o montañosos
   son de tres pulgadas a tres pies de largo
   también viven en casas

4. Think/Pair/Share

After reading a story, the teacher instructs the children to complete one of a variety of activities which requires them to elaborate on the story. For example, after reading a story such as "Colorín":

a. Students think about a new title for the story and write it down individually. They then pair up with a partner and share their ideas.

b. Students think about the main idea of the story, write it down individually, and then pair and share.

c. Students think about a new ending to a story. Next, they pair with another student and share their new ending orally. Then they share their new endings with another pair of students or with the whole class.

d. In preparation for a story retell activity, students brainstorm the main ideas or events of the story and then list them on chart paper. For example, in the story "Colorín" one group of bilingual children brainstormed the following main ideas in preparation for retelling the story to their neighbor.

"Colorín"

1. *Nace Colorín.*
2. *Ve unas patas por todas partes.*
3. *Necesita ayuda y su mamá le ayuda a pararse.*
4. *Colorín vive con su familia.*
5. *De repente sale un león.*
6. *La mamá elefante llama a los otros elefantes.*
7. *Todos protejen a Colorín y el león se va.*
8. *La mamá le enseña muchas cosas a Colorín.*
9. *Le enseña a usar la trompa.*
10. *Colorín crece cada día.*

5. Havruta (Camaraderie)

In pairs one child takes the role of the teacher and explains different story elements to his or her partner who takes the role of the learner. For the next selection they reverse the roles and the learner becomes the teacher and vice versa (Hertz-Lazarowitz & Fuchs, 1987).

6. Heads Together

Working in groups of two or four, children consult among each other for a short time to answer a question posed by the teacher. The children reach consensus as a group and one child in each group reports the answer.

For example, while reading the story, "¿Qué hay para el almuerzo?" the teacher instructs children to do the following: *"Comparen lo que necesitan en sus casas con lo que necesitan los animales para vivir en el zoológico."* The children then work in groups of four to complete the answer to the question. One child from each group is then called upon to answer the question.

7. Numbered Heads Together

In this strategy, groups of four children first select their team name. Then each child in the group is assigned a number (1, 2, 3, 4). Groups discuss a given question related to the selection just read for two minutes. Students make sure that everyone in the group is prepared to answer the question. The teacher then randomly picks a number and a team name out of the "hat." That person answers for the group. Then that team name and number go back into the hat and the teacher selects another one. For example, as children work on the story "On the Run" in their transitional reading book, *Stepping Stones* (Tinajero & Long, 1989), the teacher instructs the children to discuss the following questions:

a. What does Shadow like to eat?

b. Give reasons why no one likes Shadow.

c. Why do you think Shadow goes after things that look good to eat?

d. How do you think Shadow feels about the very, very large man that sells jam?

8. Learning Buddies

Three to four students meet frequently during the reading of a selection to:

a. clarify information;

b. review answers to questions;

c. review for tests;

d. practice spelling or vocabulary words.

9. Round Table

Students sit in a small circle. Only one paper and pencil are used. After one student writes a response, the paper and pencil are passed to the student on his/her right. The next student writes a response and passes the paper and pencil to the right. They continue this process until the teacher calls time out. This strategy can be used for:

a. brainstorming adjectives to describe a particular character;

b. writing words that come to mind when they hear a word like *camping*, knowing that this is a key word in the upcoming basal selection;

c. writing one word or sentence to describe their feelings after they have finished reading a selection.

10. Write Around

This strategy is basically the same as round table except that all students have their own paper and pencil. For example:

a. Children retell a story just read and then edit each other's work. Each student's paper goes around the table for all children to edit.

b. Children create their own stories based on the story they just read. Their story goes around the table for all children to edit.

c. Children summarize stories. Each child writes the first line of the summary. The paper goes around the table and each child adds a line. The group ends up with four summaries.

d. Freewriting a creative story. All students start with an open-ended sentence, finish that sentence, and pass it on. They keep adding to each other's stories until they wind up with four separate stories. The group then selects one story and together they write an ending. As an example, Aaron Resendez, a second grader in a bilingual classroom wrote the following creative piece after reading "El pequeño cohete":

El pequeño cohete

Había una vez una fiesta. Llegó un pequeño cohete. Salieron muchas personas. Una de las personas se metió la mano al bolsillo y sacó un cuchillo y hizo un madriguero y sacó la magia y se fueron al espacio. Después yegaron [sic] a Pluto y trajiero [sic] más personas a la fiesta.

11. Character Mapping

Students work in groups of four to complete a graphic organizer called a character map. Students choose a character from the story that they have just read and identify basic traits or attributes for that character. Students then make a picture of the character and, using a spoking technique, come up with four to six words to describe the character. They also write a short explanation for each of the descriptive words. Emergent writers can use drawings to illustrate their maps. The children then share their maps with the rest of the class (Tinajero & Long, 1989). For example, after reading the story "El pequeño cohete," a group of four second-grade children in Irma Calderón's class prepared the following map (see Figure 1) to describe Zoila, the main character in the story. The story is about a little girl named Zoila who dreams about a firecracker that becomes a rocket. The rocket takes her into space. Once completed, the children's map was full of colorful drawings of Zoila, rockets, stars, houses, trees, and flowers.

12. Story Mapping

After reading a story, the children work in groups of four to map the story. The map includes the title of the selection, the setting, the main characters, the main idea, the events, and the ending or conclusion. Each group then presents their map to the rest of the class. For example, a group of third-grade bilingual children completed the following story map (see Figure 2) for the story "La cotorra que no quería decir Cataño," a story that takes place in Cataño, Puerto Rico. In this story when Yuba fails in all his efforts to teach his parrot to say "Cataño," the name of the town they live in, he strikes a bargain with Don Casimiro, a rich poultry breeder who offers to buy her—he can keep the parrot if he gets her to say "Cataño." Eventually, the parrot does say "Cataño," but only after destroying the breeder's coop. At the end, Yuba and his parrot are reunited.

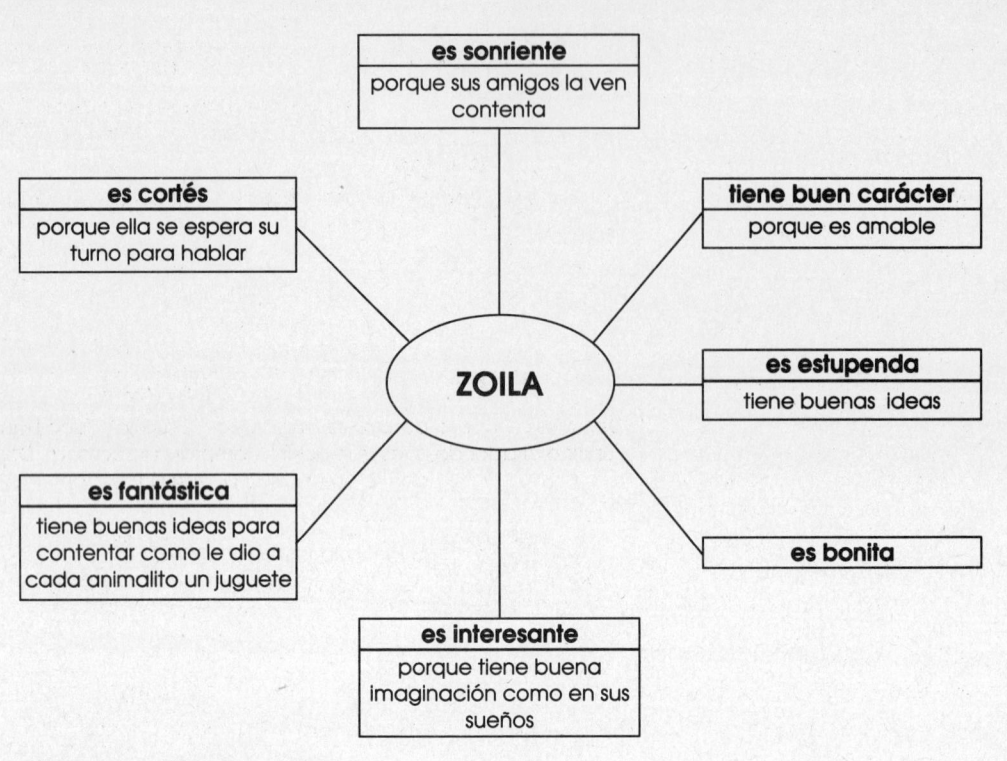

```
           es sonriente
        porque sus amigos la ven
              contenta


   es cortés                          tiene buen carácter
porque ella se espera su                porque es amable
   turno para hablar


                                          es estupenda
                    ZOILA                tiene buenas ideas


   es fantástica
tiene buenas ideas para                      es bonita
contentar como le dio a
cada animalito un juguete

           es interesante
        porque tiene buena
      imaginación como en sus
              sueños
```

Figure 1 *Character Map*

13. Story Retell

After the story mapping activity, students do a Story Retell activity. This activity is a highly interactive one, providing students with the opportunity to work closely with a partner. Here students sit with a partner, face to face, and take turns retelling the story with as much fidelity and detail as possible. Partners learn to probe or cue one another as they take turns telling the story and helping the storyteller. Before students do this activity on their own, teachers are encouraged to role-play the Story Retell activity with several students, paying special attention to probing and cuing strategies so that the retelling is as accurate and as complete as possible. Next, pairs of students are asked to role-play while the teacher provides guidance and feedback on the interaction. The teacher then goes around the room helping students practice with their partners. Afterward, students discuss with their partners what they liked about the story. Volunteer storytellers can then go up to the podium and tell their stories to the whole class. This helps the storytellers fine-tune their speech skills and also model for other students the art of storytelling (Stevens et al., 1987).

14. Jigsaw (Aronson, Blaney, Stephan, Sikes, and Snapp, 1978)

This strategy calls for the reading of the selection to be divided into four parts. Each student in a group is made responsible for reading one part of the story and presenting it to the group. In this way, the jigsaw puzzle parts become a whole. This technique is most effective with pattern stories where each part is self-standing. In another example, using vocabulary words or spelling words, the teacher cuts one list into four pieces. Students learn their own words and then teach them to their group mates. The test is given individually and includes all the words. In this way children create interdependence and are motivated to teach and learn all the words.

(Title)
La cotorra que no quería decir "Cataño"

(Setting)
Cataño-un pueblo en Puerto Rico

(Characters)
- la cotorra
- Yuba, marinero retirado, y dueño de la cotorra
- don Casimiro, un rico criador de aves que quiere comprar la cotorra

(Main Idea)
Después de que la cotorra se niega decir "Cataño", Yuba hace un trato con Don Casimiro, un rico criador de aves que quiere comprar a la cotorra. Don Casimiro se puede quedar con la cotorra si lo puede hacer que diga "Cataño".

(Event 1)
Yuba no puede hacer a la cotorra que diga "Cataño".

(Event 2)
Yuba hace un trato con Don Casimiro.

(Event 3)
Al fin la cotorra dice "Cataño" pero destruye el gallinero.

(Ending)
Don Casimiro le devuelva la cotorra a Yuba, el dueño. Yuba y cotorra están muy contentos.

Figure 2 *Story Map*

15. Tea Party

For this strategy, the class is first divided into two groups. The groups form two concentric circles in the middle of the room and face each other. Students in the outer (or inner) circle get a list of questions related to a selection just read. Each pair of students then answers the question jointly. Students are given one or two minutes to answer the question. After they answer the first question, the students in the outer circle move one step to the right. They now face a new partner and a new question. Each pair of students now answers the second question. Students continue to move to other partners until they answer all the questions. There are other variations for using this strategy. For example, the inner circle is given the definition of the words while the outer circle is given the vocabulary words.

16. Team Investigation (Hertz-Lazarowitz & Calderón, 1992; Sharan & Hertz-Lazarowitz, 1980)

Some reading selections lend themselves to team investigation. After reading and discussing a story, children can select a topic of interest they want to investigate further. For example, one transitional class read the selection "Mary Poppins" and learned about tea parties in England. The class decided to do further investigation on the custom of tea parties in different countries. Thus, each team selected a country and they did additional in-depth reading. Each group prepared a presentation in which they shared their knowledge with the rest of the class (Hertz-Lazarowitz, 1990). Another example is team investigation related to science. After reading the story "El pequeño cohete" the children in a bilingual class decided to conduct further research on astronauts. Another group chose to further investigate the solar system. In another class, the children decided to investigate a variety of geography topics after reading the story "El gato que vuela."

17. Team Books

In groups, children write creative stories that are based on certain elements of a story just read. After prewriting, writing, revising, and editing their stories, each team makes a creative book to publish their story. The books can be shape books, accordian books, pop-up books, or any type of creative book made with construction paper, color makers, and masking tape. Artifacts or magazine cutouts can be used to embellish the books. For example, after reading the story "Un zoológico fabuloso" the children took certain elements from the original story to write their own version of the story. They produced a large book made out of construction paper with many illustrations that they had pasted on each page. Their own version of the story was as follows:

Page 1: *Hugo va al zoológico con el dinero que le dio el hada.*

Page 2: *Hugo ve a Hipolito, el hipopótamo. Hipolito está en el agua pero no se ahoga.*

Page 3: *Hugo ve aves fabulosas. Hugo ve un elefante también. Hugo dice que todos los animales son fabulosos.*

Page 4: *Hugo se compra un helado y se va a la casa.*

In some classrooms where teachers implemented the above cooperative learning structures, students became very enthusiastic as they interacted with classmates using these strategies. The following comments were written by bilingual children who wrote about "What do I like about cooperative learning?"

Edgar S., a third grader, wrote: "What I like about cooperative learning is that we get to read in partners better than reading by yourself. If you are discussing the questions [to a story] all by yourself for sure that you won't get good sentences. And if you discuss them with your partner, you will get very, very good sentences."

Carlos S., another third grader, wrote: "I like to read with my partner because we learn more. When you are going to get to UTEP [the local university] or Del Valle [a nearby local high school], I'm going to get smart."

Rick C., a third grader, said: "I like everything about reading. But my best part is when we get in a group and discuss because we get to talk and work as a group."

Albert L., another third grader, said: "I like to work with my group so we can get the right answers. And I like to stand up when the teacher tells me to answer the question. My group is so good with me because when I don't know the answer to the question that my teacher tells me they get to help me so I can answer that question."

How a Good Cooperative Classroom Functions

The cooperative classroom looks and sounds very different from a traditional classroom in which children sit in rows doing their own individual work. In cooperative bilingual classrooms, students work on tasks planned by either the teacher or the children themselves. In cooperative classrooms, children work together, consult with one another, and teach one another while being creative. Children check for one another's understanding, and often elaborate about content and ideas. In the process of such learning, children help and assist one another. A visitor to a cooperative classroom will sense immediately the excitement and interaction that takes place in the classroom (Calderón, Hertz-Lazarowitz

& Tinajero, 1992; Hertz-Lazarowitz & Davidson, 1990; Hertz-Lazarowitz & Schachar, 1990; Hertz-Lazarowitz, 1992).

Because talking for learning is legitimized and encouraged in cooperative classrooms, children, and particularly children acquiring English, express themselves in both English and Spanish in a natural way. Duran (1990) and Hertz-Lazarowitz (1990) have shown that students can help each other to progress according to their developmental level and restructure their verbal expression in a way that enhances their language development. This is particularly important in bilingual classrooms, where students have widely varying proficiencies in both Spanish and English. Observation in cooperative classrooms revealed that children with varying levels of proficiency, including those with no English proficiency, participated actively and expressed their ideas in Spanish. Often an English-speaking student would translate what the Spanish-speaking students said, from Spanish to English. The group then integrated the Spanish-speaking student's ideas into the group product in English. The fact that students use both languages in their discussions about the reading selections and then phrase their discussion as a final group product in one language contributes a great deal to the social self-esteem and academic competence of all students (Calderón, Tinajero & Hertz-Lazarowitz, 1992).

The role of the teacher in the cooperative classroom shifts dramatically. The teacher becomes a supporter, a facilitator, and a monitor of group activities. Often the teacher conferences with groups of children or listens to their talk. When the teacher is this close to the learning process, she/he hears the voice of learning in the children's talk and is more capable of providing specific feedback. As a result, the teacher's instructional routine is more personalized and becomes one-to-one or one-to-group tutoring (Hertz-Lazarowitz & Shachar, 1990).

The physical and social-academic organization of the cooperative classroom creates a climate that is friendly, warm, and inviting for learning and communication. This is not fulfilled by simply putting children in groups. It is accomplished by putting children to work as a community of group learners.

Conclusion

This article has provided teachers with a variety of ideas for integrating cooperative learning strategies to daily reading and writing activities using basal readers.

Teachers who use cooperative learning with their basals have many success stories to share—even when they introduce only one cooperative strategy a day. Some of the teachers report on children who have really blossomed. New discoveries of children's abilities, academic successes, and enhancement of self-esteem have taken place as teachers have introduced group work. When cooperative learning is implemented, the social climate of the classroom becomes more positive and children learn to get along with one another. Children make more friends. Teachers also share their reflections and perspectives on their own teaching, maintaining that cooperative learning revitalized their teaching.

It is important to emphasize that interweaving cooperative activities should be done gradually and while teachers continue to receive additional training in cooperative learning. Teachers should continue, however, to use other strategies that have been particularly effective for them while introducing cooperative structures. For example, whole language practices appear to be effective and complementary to cooperative learning strategies.

Cooperative learning strategies are beneficial to students of all ages and all levels of language proficiency. Students from diverse backgrounds can participate actively and contribute their knowledge in reading, writing, and other communications. Students feel safe and comfortable as they become literate in both their first and second languages.

About the Authors

Josefina Villamil Tinajero is currently Associate Professor of Bilingual Education and Director of the Mother-Daughter Program at the University of Texas at El Paso. She is a fellow of the Kellogg National Fellowship Program and past president of the Texas Council of Reading and the Bilingual Child. Dr. Tinajero is an author of several reading programs published by Macmillan/McGraw-Hill School Publishing Company: *Mil maravillas, Campanitas de oro, Transitional Reading Program, A New View, The Write Idea,* and *Cuentamundos*. Currently, she serves as associate editor of *The Journal of Educational Issues of Language Minority Students* and on the editorial board of *Teacher Education and Practice*. She has also served on the editorial board of *The Reading Teacher*. Dr. Tinajero has prepared elementary teachers in bilingual, ESL, and reading and has been a consultant for numerous school districts throughout the United States. Currently, she is conducting research on the effects of cooperative learning on language minority students and on literacy and the transfer of learning.

Margarita Calderón is currently at the University of Texas at El Paso as Associate Professor in the Department of Educational Leadership and as Director of the Teachers' Learning Community Center, which brings teachers, principals, and students together to study Cooperative Learning and ways of building communities of learners at El Paso and Juárez schools. She is also conducting several research projects: a five-year study of cooperative learning in bilingual settings, a study of effective staff development program designs, and one on schoolwide implementation of cooperative learning and teacher support systems. She is the originator of the Multilingual Trainer of Trainers Institutes (MTTI) model for staff development. She conducts yearly MTTI institutes for state departments of Education in the United States, México, and Pacific Rim countries.

Rachel Hertz-Lazarowitz, Ph.D., is a professor of educational psychology at Haifa University in Israel. She has published extensively in the area of cooperative learning and group investigation. Dr. Hertz-Lazarowitz is currently conducting research with the Ysleta Independent School District in El Paso, Texas, on cooperative learning in bilingual settings.

Note: Teachers interested in more information on cooperative learning can refer to: IASCE, the International Association for the Study of Cooperation in Education, *Cooperative Learning Magazine*, PO Box 1582, Santa Cruz, CA 95061-1582.

References

Aronson, E., Stephan, C., Sikes, J., Blaney, N., and Snapp, M. (1978). *The jigsaw classroom*. Beverly Hills, CA: Sage Publications.

Calderón, M. (1989). Cooperative learning for LEP students. *Newsletter of the Intercultural Development Research Association*, vol. 16, no. 9, pp. 1–7.

Calderón, M., Hertz-Lazarowitz, R., and Tinajero, J. (1992). *Bilingual students in CIRC (Cooperative Integrated Reading and Composition)*. Unpublished manuscript.

Calderón, M., Hertz-Lazarowitz, R., and Tinajero, J. (1991). Adapting CIRC to multiethnic and bilingual classrooms. *Cooperative Learning Magazine*, vol. 12, no. 1, pp. 17-20.

Calderón, M., Tinajero, J., and Hertz-Lazarowitz, R. (1992). Adopting cooperative integrated reading and composition to meet the needs of bilingual students. *The Journal of Educational Issues of Language Minority Students*, vol. 10, pp. 79-106.

Cohen, E. G. (1987) *Designing group work: Strategies for the heterogeneous classroom*. New York: Teachers College Press.

Cohen, E. G., and de Avila, E. (1983). *Learning to think in math and science: Improving local education for minority children*. A final report to the Walter F. Johnson Foundation. Stanford, CA: Stanford University.

Cummins, J. (1989). *Empowering minority students*. California Association for Bilingual Education.

Duran, R., and Duran, J. (1990). *Teaching the discourse of cooperation*. Paper presented at the American Research Association, April 16-20. Boston, MA.

Gibbs, J. (1987). *Tribes*. Santa Rosa, CA: Center Source Publications.

Good, T. L., and Brophy, J. E. (1987). *Looking in classrooms* (4th ed.). New York: Harper and Row.

Hertz-Lazarowitz, R. (1992). Understanding students interaction behavior: Looking at six mirrors of the classroom. In Hertz-Lazarowitz, R., and Miller, N. (Eds.), *Interaction in cooperative groups: Theoretical anatomy of group learning*. New York: Cambridge University Press.

Hertz-Lazarowitz, R. (1990). *Observation of classroom interaction in CIRC*. Report no. 3, University of Texas at El Paso.

Hertz-Lazarowitz, R., Baird, H., Webb, C., and Lazarowitz, R. (1984). Student-student interaction in science classrooms: A naturalistic study. *Science Education*, vol. 68, no. 5, pp. 603-19.

Hertz-Lazarowitz, R., and Calderón, M. (in press). Implementing cooperative learning in elementary schools: The facilitative voice. In Sharan, S. (Ed.), *The handbook of cooperative learning*. New York: Praeger.

Hertz-Lazarowitz, R., and Calderón, M. (1992). *Investigation group magnifies cooperative learning*. El Paso: MTTI.

Hertz-Lazarowitz, R., and Davidson, J. (1990). *Six mirrors of the classroom: An integrative model of the classroom*. Unpublished manuscript. Haifa University, Israel.

Hertz-Lazarowitz, R., and Fuchs, I. (1987). *Cooperative learning in the classroom*. Haifa, Israel: Haifa Ach Publishers (Hebrew).

Hertz-Lazarowitz, R., and Shachar, H. (1990). Teachers' verbal behavior in cooperative and whole-class instruction. In Sharan, S. (Ed.), *Cooperative learning: Theory and research*, pp. 77-95. New York: Praeger Publishing Co.

Johnson, D. W., and Johnson, F. (1991). *Joining together: Group theory and group skills* (4th ed.). Englewood Cliffs, NJ: Prentice-Hall.

Johnson, D. W., Johnson, F., and Holubec, E. G. (1991). *Circles of learning: Cooperation in the classroom* (rev. ed.). Edina, MN: Interaction Book Co.

Kohn, A. (1986). *No contest: The case against competition*. Boston: Houghton Mifflin.

Krashen, S. (1981). Bilingual education and second language acquisition theory. In California State Department of Education (Eds.), *Schooling and language minority students: A theoretical framework*, pp. 51-82. CA: Office of Bilingual Education.

McGroarty, M. (1989, Winter). The benefits of cooperative learning arrangements in second language instruction. *NABE Journal*.

Sharan, S., and Hertz-Lazarowitz, R. (1980). A group investigation method of cooperative learning in the classroom. In Sharan, S., et al. (Eds.), *Cooperation in education*, pp. 14-46. Provo, Utah: BYU Press.

Slavin, R. E. (1990). *Cooperative learning: Theory, research and practice*. Englewood Cliffs, NJ: Prentice-Hall.

Slavin, R. E. (1983). *Cooperative learning*. New York: Longman.

Stevens, R. J., Madden, N., Slavin, R. E., and Farnish, A. M. (1987). Cooperative integrated reading and composition: Two field experiments. *Reading Research Quarterly*, vol. 32, pp. 453-54.

Tinajero, J., and Calderón, M. (1988). Language experience approach plus. *Journal of Educational Issues of Language Minority Students*, vol. 2, pp. 31-45.

Tinajero, J., and Long, S. (1989) *Macmillan transitional reading program*. New York: Macmillan Publishing Company.

Weinstein, C. S. (1991). The classroom as a social context for learning. *Annual Review of Psychology*, vol. 42, pp. 493-25.

Enhancing the Skills of Emergent Writers Acquiring English

Josefina Villamil Tinajero
The University of Texas at El Paso

Ana Huerta-Macías
El Paso Community College, Texas

Introduction

The above statement by Frank Smith begins an essay on misconceptions or myths about the nature of writing that have too often been harbored in classrooms and that have thus kept children from developing their potential as writers. Smith (1983) adds, "writing as children are expected to learn and to practice it in many classes is a highly unnatural activity." (p. 81)

Minority children, particularly, have been the victims of misconceptions not only about the development of writing but also about writing in a second language. This has been true, for example, in still too-familiar instances where we find that language minority children have been relegated to doing an endless array of grammar, spelling, and vocabulary exercises, designed to "increase" their proficiency in English, before they are allowed to engage in more natural writing activities such as story or poetry writing.

> **Every child who can talk has the capacity to learn to write and also to seize upon the possibilities of written language with enthusiasm.**
>
> —Smith, 1983 (p. 81)

Increasingly, however, the research on second language acquisition has addressed issues related to the teaching of writing to students acquiring English (SAEs). This article first will focus briefly on this research with respect to the nature of the process of learning to write in the second language and will secondly suggest a variety of activities and strategies that have been found to be effective in supporting the natural development of writing and second language acquisition. Third, the assessment of students' writing will be discussed and sample scales will be presented.

Emergent Literacy in the Second Language

Krashen and Biber (1988) suggests that students *acquire* rather than *learn* a language in a natural progression of stages. As language is acquired, literacy in the new language develops. That is, current research suggests that the second language is acquired in the same manner as the first language and that it is acquired most effectively in a highly interactive, total communication environment. Furthermore, because the processes of listening, speaking, reading, and writing are interrelated and interdependent, when children develop their oral language, as through conversations and through reading and listening to stories, they are in effect also developing their written communication skills.

Writing, then, develops along with the other communication skills in the second language as students interact with others and engage in meaningful and purposeful tasks. SAEs can and should be encouraged to compose in the second language as they move along a developmental pathway toward "mastery" in the second language. Research (Hudelson, 1986) has demonstrated that second language learners can and do create different texts for different purposes including expressive writing, poetic writing, and transactional writing where the purpose is to convey information to the reader. Hudelson elaborates:

> Examination of the written products of child second language learners make it clear that they make use of whatever knowledge they have of the systems of English at a given point in time, and they use this knowledge to hypothesize about how to write in English. (p. 26)

Texts produced by SAEs look very much like those produced by young native speakers as they move along a developmental pathway towards conventional print. Second language learners, like young native speakers of English, use some or all of the same strategies as they move along this pathway:

◆ Drawing

◆ Scribbling

◆ Randomly chosen letters (The child uses letters, but there is no relationship between the letters chosen and the sounds in the words that are written.)

◆ Words copied from environmental print

◆ Invented spelling (Only one or two of the sounds heard in words are represented by print.)

◆ Transitional spelling (Features of conventional spelling, such as silent letters or doubling of consonants, begin to appear.)

◆ Conventional spelling (Martínez & Teale, 1993)

As SAEs move along the developmental pathway toward conventional print, they simultaneously move through a similar pathway toward nativelike fluency in the second language. Their writing often reflects elements from their native language. As children begin to use more sophisticated writing strategies (e.g., invented spellings) and concentrate on using nativelike written language, the content and organization of their stories and journal entries may appear to become less sophisticated for a period of time. This is to be expected and is part of the natural process of acquiring a second language and moving toward conventional print. SAEs, that is, make use of what they know about their native language and apply it to English—not always producing "Standard English." This is not cause for concern, however, but rather indicates active learning (O'Neil, 1992) on the part of children as they struggle to "construct" knowledge about the second language. The risk taking involved in the composing process is a central and positive step in children's writing development in English, for as Harste, Woodward, and Burke (1984) write, "Without risk there can be no exploration or discovery of the generative potential of literacy" (p. 132). As children get more control over sound-symbol relationships and develop their English language proficiency, they will again be able to attend more closely to what it is they want to say and to whom they want to say it (Martínez & Teale, 1993).

Edelsky (1986), in her research with children writing in a bilingual program, writes that growth in writing does not occur in a linear way but in successive reorganizations as students create, apply, revise, and abandon hypotheses about writing, using knowledge from the first and second languages. This process includes "errors" in spelling and syntax, as well as occasional code-switching or language alternation in the composing process. These are all normal and part of the second language acquisition process as students engage in writing. The following writing samples belong to bilingual children who are moving toward conventional print and nativelike fluency in English. (See Figures 1, 2, and 3.)

> Ones ver was a little turtle
> vet lef an a little box.
> Ji was veri sad cas ji dirn Jad
> tings tu lrei en omos ji was
> goan tu dai. But ji bont dai cas a
> posan queif plants to the turtle.
> Sav ji bont dai cas dai queif
> plants to the turtle.
> Bes wai ji dirin dai.
> Sau ji live hapi al the bai.

Figure 1 *Once there was a little turtle who lived on a little box. He was very sad cause he didn't have things to play and almost he was going to die. But he bought the casa* [house] *a person give plants to the turtle. Save him one day cause they gave plants to the turtle. Because with him didn't die. So he live happy all the day.*

> One supana time deors was a
> liro two boys. The first one wanted
> estey en tibal et the nadre one
> wanted to estey et besbal
> bat the dad nat ef mani
> to gif him so boy gat sum
> work et Big 8 den the boy
> hat mani to go to the
> esprsplex to play besbal
> fo evroi.

Figure 2 *Once upon a time there was a little two boys. The first one wanted stay in teeball and another one wanted stay in baseball. But the dad not have money to give him so boy got some work at Big 8 then the boy had money to go to the sportsplex to play baseball forever.*

This writing will more closely resemble conventional English writing as students are increasingly exposed to standard print in English and are immersed in a classroom environment that allows and encourages them to engage freely in interesting, relevant, and meaningful writing activities. The classroom context, therefore, can have a tremendous impact on children's development as writers (Hudelson, 1986, 1988).

One way to create a positive classroom context is to encourage students to use their background knowledge and experiences as a springboard for writing. They should be encouraged to write about experiences that are real and important to them. This might include, for example, writing about cultural traditions, personal experiences, or family celebrations. Literacy practices that exist in the homes of children should be acknowledged, respected, and also used as foundations for further literacy development. Children, for instance, should be encouraged to write letters to their friends or relatives, to help with writing grocery lists, to write telephone messages for their parents, and to label or write captions in the family picture album.

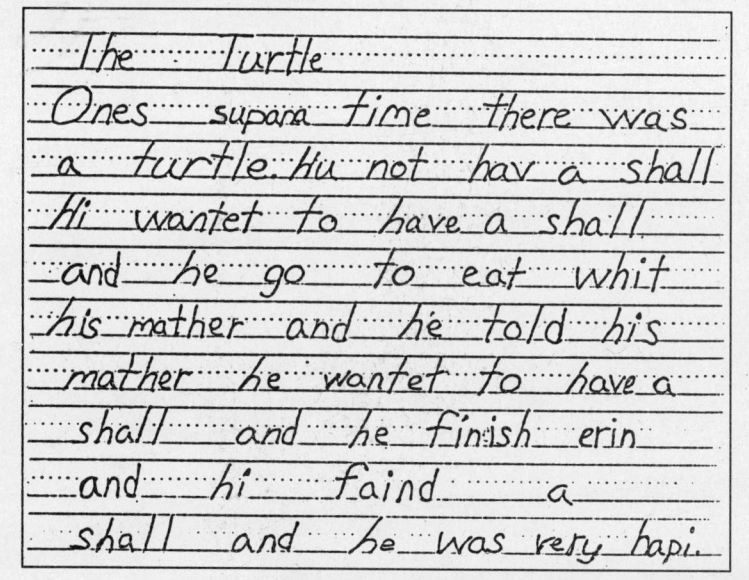

Figure 3 *Once upon time there was a turtle. He not have a shell. He wanted to have a shell and he go to eat with his mother and he told his mother he wanted to have a shell and he finish eating and he found a shell and he was very happy.*

Classroom Activities That Support Emergent Writing and Language Acquisition

Teachers often ask for practical ideas to support emergent writers who are simultaneously acquiring English. We have identified a number of activities that are particularly helpful in encouraging these students to "emerge" as writers. The activities enhance the natural development of writing and at the same time support second language acquisition. As is evident, these activities are similar to those used with first language learners. For writing development, the use of similar activities for first and second language learners is supported by current research that documents that both groups exhibit similar processes in writing development (Edelsky, 1986; Hudelson, 1986). As second language learners develop control over the language, their writing gradually begins to approximate Standard English. Hudelson's (1988) idea is that students can profitably engage in reading and writing activities in the second language even before they have gained full control over the phonological, syntactic, and semantic systems of spoken English. Reading and writing in the second language supports language development and provides valuable second language practice.

USING LITERATURE TO NURTURE CHILDREN'S WRITING

Krashen (1985) emphasizes that "reading exposure may be the primary means of developing reading comprehension, writing style, and more sophisticated vocabulary and grammar" (p. 90). Reading exposure is also central in igniting children's writing. Central to these efforts are rich literature experiences that serve as powerful models of good writing. Martínez and Teale (1993) maintain that literature nurtures children's own original story writing: "Sometimes a storyline or story theme will serve as an invitation for the child to write about a similar experience. At other times, after reading a story with a distinctive predictable pattern, children may choose to use the same story pattern to organize their own writing" (p. 13).

An excellent way to provide SAEs with rich literature experiences is to conduct shared readings with books that contain repetitive language and/or predictable outcomes. Big Books are particularly effective for group study. Shared reading activities establish a low-anxiety environment essential to language acquisition, while the repetitive characteristics of the text facilitate the natural acquisition of vocabulary, pronunciation, and language structures. Repeated readings help children to read more efficiently, gain confidence, practice using their reading skills, and increase their sight vocabulary. The reading and rereading of stories allow students to hear and practice, in an informal setting, the rhythm and structure of English. Thus, for students acquiring English, these books are excellent for cultivating language and facilitating language acquisition (Graves, 1983). Pattern and predictable books are especially powerful models of good writing for students acquiring English. Teachers can use them as springboards to writing.

USING STORY PATTERNS AS SPRINGBOARDS TO WRITING

As children recite and participate in shared reading activities using rhymes, poems, songs, and pattern stories, they learn new language patterns and vocabulary. That is, through repeated readings, students internalize a large number of language patterns found in the literature. They then borrow these underlying structures and use them to express their own thoughts and ideas. For example, in *The Bear Went Over the Mountain* the students first internalize the repetitive sentence pattern, "The bear went over the mountain," through repeated readings. This pattern then becomes part of the students' existing language repertoire which they later access to express their own thoughts and ideas.

The possibilities for teachers to use the original sentence pattern, "The bear went over the mountain," to help children create new patterns are endless. For example, the teacher can work with students as they use this sentence pattern from the rhyme to write about: "The ant went over the ant hill"; "The dinosaur went over the tree"; or "The dragon went over the moon." Working in groups or as a whole class with the teacher, the children then write their own creative rhymes. A group of bilingual second graders we worked with created their own rhyme as follows:

The bug went over the flower,
The bug went over the flower,
The bug went over the flower,
And what do you think he saw?

He saw a spider in the bushes,
He saw a spider in the bushes,
He saw a spider in the bushes,
And what do you think he saw? etc.

Suppose that another group wished to create their own scary story, as was the case in the same second-grade class. Using the repetitive sentence frame, "The bear went over the mountain," the teacher encouraged one group of students to write about "The monster went over the tree house" while another group wrote about "The dragon went over the front porch."

USING STORY STRUCTURES AS SPRINGBOARDS TO WRITING

Another way of using pattern books as springboards to writing is by encouraging children to use the sequence and structure of an original story to create and organize their own writing (Tinajero & Long, 1989). For example, after reading "The Beginning of Night" and having some discussion, the children are asked to identify the main events of a story just read. They dictate those events using a plot summary format for the story. The teacher records their ideas on chart paper or on the chalkboard. Taking dictation from children provides a model of the processes and concepts of writing. For example, in one second-grade bilingual class the children first summarized the original story, "The Beginning of Night," as follows:

The Beginning of Night

Long ago, there was no night.
The moon was always very bright.
The people worked all the time.
The people never rested.
The sun and the moon talked.
They decided to create the night.
The people rested at night.
Now people work only during the day.

Next, the teacher guided the children as they planned their own story based on the sequence and structure of the original story. Using the brainstorming technique, the children first suggested a number of ideas for their story: the beginning of day, the beginning of the sun, the beginning of the stars, the beginning of colors. They finally arrived at a consensus on "The Beginning of the Sun." The teacher then placed the original story next to the chart paper on which the new story was to be developed. In this way, it was easy for the children to use the structure of the original story as a model for developing their own story. In the same second-grade bilingual class, the children's own summary of their story plot looked like this:

The Beginning of the Sun

Long ago, there was no sun.
It was very cold.
There were no plants or birds.
The people were always cold.
The earth talked to a mountain.
The mountain became a volcano and turned into a sun.
The people were warm.
Plants grew, birds sang.

Using the plot summary as a guide, the teacher then worked with the children to write their first draft of the story. The next day the children edited and published their story as a class using the Big Book format.

Thus, teachers can capitalize on the linguistic structures found in pattern stories to launch children into English writing. In this way, children with limited English vocabularies can latch on to those structures that they have heard and suddenly find their former limited vocabularies taking on new dimensions. The pattern stories make it possible for children of either rich or limited vocabulary to find challenge in the new creations that come about as they innovate on the structures found in these books. Poems, rhymes, songs, and fairy tales all serve as models for children to imitate in their own writing.

Flores et al. (1985) maintain that pattern books and literature pieces with interesting and repetitive structures are excellent sources for students to use successfully in their early attempts at writing. Boyle and Peregoy (1990) agree, stating that second language learners need this level of support until they are ready to experiment with their own patterns. In the meantime, the patterns offer scaffolds for students until they develop sufficient proficiency in the second language.

JOURNAL WRITING

The journal is a place where children can record their thoughts, feelings, and reactions to a story that they have just listened to or read (Martínez & Teale, 1993). It is also a place where students acquiring English can express themselves about topics that are meaningful and purposeful to them, using their first or second language. For example, students can copy memorable phrases or words from selections they read or note ideas for writing. Flores et al. (1985) maintain that "journal writing is an informal instructional strategy that provides both teacher and students with a vehicle where literacy can be practiced and met with great satisfaction. It should be one of the first writing activities" (p. 7).

Journal writing is another instructional strategy that provides students acquiring English with the opportunity to develop fluency in a meaningful context. It also encourages risk taking because it is a nonthreatening literacy activity in which the children know they can experiment with the second language as they strive to communicate their thoughts in written form. Journal writing thus provides students with the opportunity for independent writing that is characteristic of an emergent literacy perspective (Strickland & Morrow, 1990).

Journals also provide teachers with the opportunity to learn about each child's interests, concerns, and ideas and to assess each child's developing literacy skills and his/her transition into the second language. It also provides teachers with the opportunity to model conventions of writing for students in the context of authentic use (Flores et al., 1985).

Journals take a variety of forms and have different purposes: individual journals, buddy journals, and dialogue journals. All are excellent activities; at times, journals are used simply for students to write their personal thoughts. At other times, as with dialogue journals, they can be used to teach new vocabulary, punctuation, spelling, language complexity, and rhetorical development with a focus on content and what is important to students.

Although journals can take a variety of forms, the most commonly used seems to be the dialogue journal. Dialogue journals can be very effective with second language learners. With dialogue journals, individual students regularly write entries to their teachers on a variety of topics selected by themselves or suggested by the teacher. The teacher then responds using an appropriate level of writing. The response often contains questions designed to generate more writing on the part of the student. The focus, furthermore, is on content rather than form, although the teacher may take note of error patterns and address them in later lessons (Peyton, 1987). Above (see Figure 4) is a journal entry from a third-grade bilingual student.

Figure 4 *Journal Entry*

DIARIES

The diary, like the journal, also provides students with an opportunity to write independently. Unlike dialogue journals, however, diaries are not interactive. The teacher does not take an active role as a participant in a dialogue (although she/he may read an entry and respond if requested to do so by the student), but the student essentially writes for herself/himself in a diary. Nonetheless, the writing is still authentic, personal, meaningful, and thus serves to develop the student's literacy.

Diaries may be personal or may focus on a content area. In the personal diary a student writes about anything that is of importance or interest in her/his life. In a content diary, a student writes about what she/he is learning in an academic area. This may, for example, take the form of a narrative on some events learned about in a history class and/or it may take the form of a progress report in a science experiment. The diary need not be totally private. If the student chooses, particular entries may be shared with the class (Hamayan, 1989).

STORY MAPPING

A story map is a special type of visual used to organize the ideas and events of a story. Story mapping can serve as an excellent prewriting activity.

As a prewriting activity, students can use the story map to plan and organize their thoughts and ideas before they begin to write (Tinajero & Long, 1989). Story mapping can also be designed as an open-ended activity. The ending of a story, for example, can be omitted and students can be asked to create their own ending to a story. Story maps can also be used to help students organize their ideas as they prepare to retell a story orally or in writing. A group of third-graders developed the following map in preparation for retelling a story they had just read, "Who's in Rabbit's House?" (see Figure 5). Using the map, students then wrote their story as a group, edited it, and then published it in Big Book format.

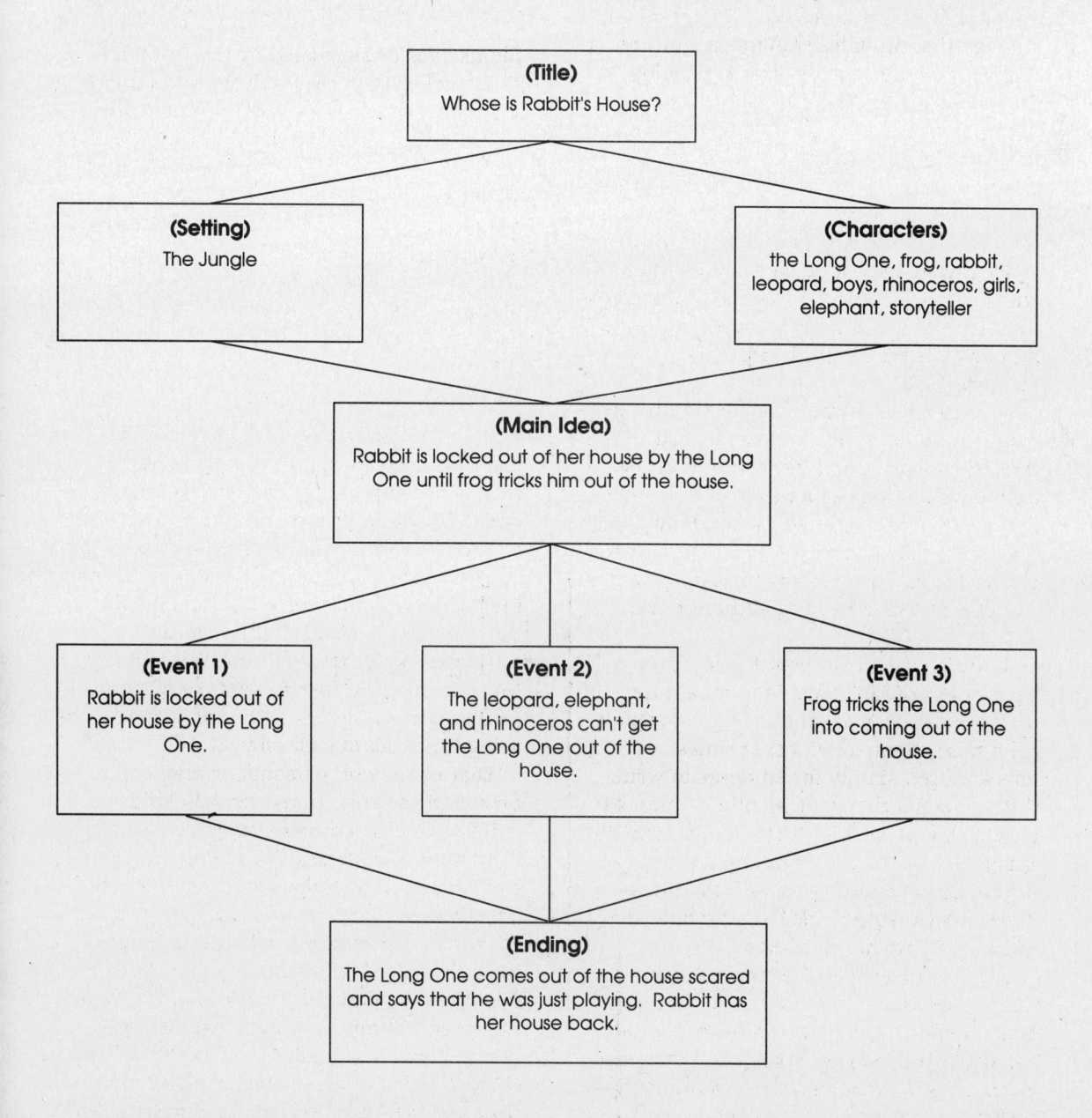

(Title)
Whose is Rabbit's House?

(Setting)
The Jungle

(Characters)
the Long One, frog, rabbit, leopard, boys, rhinoceros, girls, elephant, storyteller

(Main Idea)
Rabbit is locked out of her house by the Long One until frog tricks him out of the house.

(Event 1)
Rabbit is locked out of her house by the Long One.

(Event 2)
The leopard, elephant, and rhinoceros can't get the Long One out of the house.

(Event 3)
Frog tricks the Long One into coming out of the house.

(Ending)
The Long One comes out of the house scared and says that he was just playing. Rabbit has her house back.

Figure 5 *Story Map*

CHARACTER MAPPING

A character map is a special type of visual used to describe a character or characters. Character mapping can also serve as an excellent prewriting activity.

As a prewriting activity, students can use the character map to plan and organize their thoughts and ideas. For example, students can use the character map to brainstorm ideas before writing a descriptive paragraph about a particular character in a story. Students first choose a character from the story and identify basic traits or attributes. Students then make a picture of the character and, using a spoking technique, come up with four to six words to describe the character. They also write a short explanation for each of the descriptive words. Emergent writers can use drawings to illustrate their descriptive words. For example, after reading the book *The Bear Went Over the Mountain*, a group of third-grade bilingual students prepared this map in preparation for writing a descriptive paragraph about the bear in the story.

Based on the prewriting activity, the students then developed a descriptive paragraph about the bear that reflected the character map they had prepared.

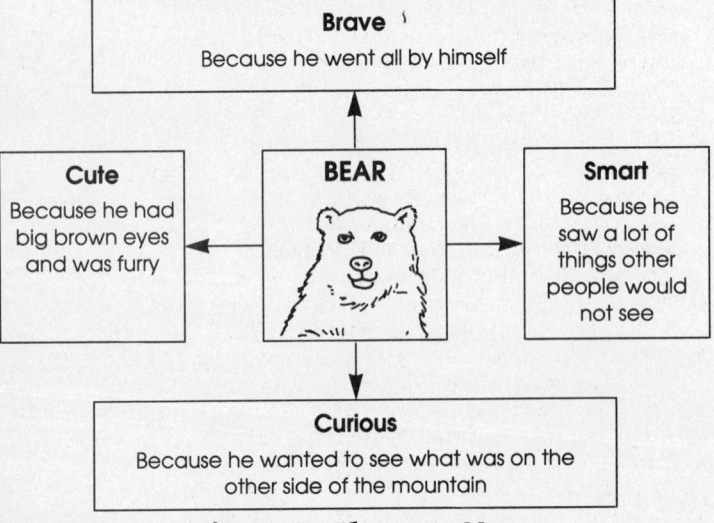

Brave
Because he went all by himself

Cute
Because he had big brown eyes and was furry

BEAR

Smart
Because he saw a lot of things other people would not see

Curious
Because he wanted to see what was on the other side of the mountain

Figure 6 *Character Map*

LANGUAGE EXPERIENCE CHARTS

Language experience charts introduce writing as a pleasurable and meaningful experience. Students learn to read and write using familiar material—their own. Through dictation, children see that their spoken language can be put into print and read by someone else. They realize that what they experience and think about may be verbalized, what they say can be written down, and what has been written can be read by others or by themselves. As children's confidence increases, so does their knowledge about written language. These activities build a natural bridge to more formal experiences with print (Strickland & Morrow, 1990). Moreover, the repeated readings of story charts provide students with the natural written forms and sound-symbol correspondences of the English language. And because the reading of storybooks is very often a part of language activities, students are continuously exposed to new vocabulary and language patterns, which they assimilate into their own dictations and journal entries.

PUBLISHING

Edelsky (1986) writes that what happens to a piece of writing during and after it is written has a significant impact on children's motivation and self-confidence in writing. Therefore, honoring student writing is part of the developmental process. Students can publish and edit their own texts and share them with peers, parents, and children, or they can display them in the library.

Publishing, moreover, can take on several different shapes. Students' writing may be published in book form (with cutout shapes, for example), in scrolls that may be displayed on bulletin boards, in school newsletters, or in a local newspaper.

These texts can also be used as a catalyst for parent involvement activities. A PTA or Chapter I group, for example, could have a literature sharing night for families, allowing the students to read and/or display their short stories, poems, or essays. Another schoolwide activity could be Saturday morning parent-child literacy groups in which the parents assist their children with literacy building, developmentally appropriate activities that are then displayed as family projects.

In sum, the techniques that can be used to enhance the writing skills of SAEs need not be different from those that are used with monolingual English-speaking students. Of significance is that the teacher recognize that some of the characteristics in the students' writing reflect an application of their knowledge of literacy in their native language to English. Thus, these types of "errors" are constructive, and the teacher should acknowledge them as such while also taking the opportunity to model appropriate English in those instances where the students have used nonconventional forms of English. Finally, the strategies used to enhance the skills of emergent writers who are learning English should be meaningful, relevant, and developmentally appropriate for the students.

About the Authors

Josefina Villamil Tinajero is currently Associate Professor of Bilingual Education and Director of the Mother-Daughter Program at the University of Texas at El Paso. She is a fellow of the Kellogg National Fellowship Program and past president of the Texas Council of Reading and the Bilingual Child. Dr. Tinajero is an author of several reading programs published by Macmillan/McGraw-Hill School Publishing Company: *Mil maravillas, Campanitas de oro, Transitional Reading Program, A New View, The Write Idea*, and *Cuentamundos*. Currently, she serves as associate editor of *The Journal of Educational Issues of Language Minority Students* and on the editorial board of *Teacher Education and Practice*. She has also served on the editorial board of *The Reading Teacher*. Dr. Tinajero has prepared elementary teachers in bilingual, ESL, and reading and has been a consultant for numerous school districts throughout the United States. Currently, she is conducting research on the effects of cooperative learning on language minority students and on literacy and the transfer of learning.

Ana Huerta-Macías is a research associate at El Paso Community College. Having received her doctorate in the broad field of Applied Linguistics, her teaching and research interests have led her in the past 14 years to work and publish in the areas of teacher development, ESL, bilingualism, bilingual education, and most recently, parent involvement and family literacy. Dr. Macías, who was a codirector of Project FIEL, a bilingual family literacy project, is currently planning to undertake the direction of a new family literacy program through the Literacy Center of the El Paso Community College.

References

Boyle, O. F., and Peregoy, S. F. (1990). Literacy scaffolds: Strategies for first- and second-language readers and writers. *The Reading Teacher*, vol. 44, no. 3, pp. 194–200.

Edelsky, C. (1986). *Writing in a bilingual program: Había una vez*. Norwood, NJ: Ablex Publishing Corp.

Flores, B., et al. (1985). *Bilingual holistic instructional strategies*. Unpublished manuscript.

Graves, D. H. (1983). *Writing: Teachers and children at work*. Portsmouth, NH: Heinemann Educational Books.

Hamayan, E. V. (1989, summer). *Teaching writing to potentially English proficient students using whole language approaches* (Program information guide series). Washington, DC: NCBE.

Harste, J. C., Woodward, V. A., and Burke, C. L. (1984). *Language stories and literacy lessons*. Exeter, NH: Heinemann Educational Books.

Hudelson, S. (1988). Children's writing in ESL. *ERIC Digest*. ERIC Clearinghouse on Language and Linguistics. Washington, DC: Center for Applied Linguistics.

Hudelson, S. (1986). ESL children's writing: What we've learned, what we're learning. In P. Rigg, and D. S. Enright (Eds.), *Children and ESL: Integrating perspectives*. Washington, DC: TESOL.

Krashen, S. (1985). *Inquiries and insights*. Hayward, CA: Alemany Press.

Krashen, S., and Biber, D. (1988). On course: *Bilingual education's success in California*. Sacramento, CA: California Association for Bilingual Education.

Martinez, M., and Teale, W. (1993) *A new view: Teacher's planning guide*. New York: Macmillan/McGraw-Hill Publishing Company.

O'Neil, J. (1992, March). Constructivism posits new conception of learning. *Update*, vol. 34, no. 3, pp. 2–8.

Peyton, J. K. (1987, April). Dialogue journal writing with limited English proficient (LEP) students. *Q&A*. ERIC Clearinghouse on Language and Linguistics. Washington, DC: Center for Applied Linguistics.

Smith, F. (1983). *Essays into literacy*. Portsmouth, NH: Heinemann Educational Books.

Strickland, D., and Morrow, L. M. (1990, February). The daily journal: Using language experience strategies in an emergent literacy curriculum. *The Reading Teacher*.

Tinajero, J., and Long, S. (1989). *Stepping stones teacher's guide: Macmillan's transitional reading program*. New York: Macmillan Publishing Company.

Content Area Instruction FOR Students Acquiring English

Carrol Moran
Educational Consultant

Abstract

Content area instruction for students acquiring English must be sensitive to the cultural and linguistic background of the student. Basic program models are discussed that should be chosen based on the characteristics of the student population and staff capabilities. The program model will determine to a great extent the amount of primary language developed during content area instruction. Regardless of the program model chosen, the following elements will create a more effective approach to content area instruction in primary or second language.

(1) Curriculum is grounded in the knowledge and experience the student brings to the classroom. (2) Organizational strategies are provided—tools that fit a concept into the bigger picture as well as to organize bits of information within the context or the topic. (3) Acquisition of academic language is facilitated through focusing on new vocabulary and concepts and providing interaction with the language and concepts in relaxed, informal ways. (4) Synthesis of new information occurs immediately after processing, and reporting or sharing is encouraged through a variety of modes of expression. (5) Students reflect on the process of how they learned as well as what they learned. This will increase the probability of transfer of the learning to new situations.

Throughout the discussion of these important elements I have woven in practical teaching strategies that incorporate the above elements in social studies, science, and math, drawn from authentic teaching situations.

Introduction

If you've ever entered a movie late, rendering you unable to make sense of the scenes before you, the importance of background knowledge information is clear. If you've been caught in a conversation between two computer hackers comparing megabytes, you know the "dumb" feeling a lack of vocabulary or language proficiency can create.

This is the experience of many students acquiring English in content area classes. Even with basic English communication skills, students are often at a loss to make sense of the information. They often lack both the academic language (Cummins, 1981) and the schemata, or maps, to make sense of the material. Many times they don't know what the bigger picture is that a concept fits into, nor do they see how it relates to their lives.

There are a variety of approaches developed by teachers and researchers to help students acquiring English achieve success in content curriculum. The basic program models outlined here provide the frame in which content curriculum is taught to students acquiring English. Local demographics and policies determine which model is used, which in turn determines the extent to which primary language is utilized. I will discuss some strengths and weaknesses of the basic models. Then I'll lay out the basic elements of instruction that benefit all students regardless of the program. These elements are the ones that connect new learning to the known and give road maps and guideposts to students to help them understand where the curriculum "is going." I will intersperse specific activities that incorporate the effective elements discussed. Finally I'll offer a brief checklist for teachers to utilize in self-assessing content area lessons.

Program Models

In the context of bilingual programs there are a variety of program models for making use of the primary language while developing English. The determining factors in the teaching situation that should determine the type of program used (local politics and policies not withstanding) include student and staff characteristics such as: ethnicity, language proficiency, degree of literacy in each language, number of students of any one language background, etc. The program model chosen in turn will determine the extent to which primary language is developed.

In programs with sufficient bilingual staff an alternate day, or alternate week, program may be instituted. With this approach, generally literacy is taught in homogeneous groups according to the strengths of students, and the content area instruction is in heterogeneous groups that switch language on a daily/weekly basis between the first and the second language.

The advantage to such an approach is that children continue to develop cognitive academic language in the primary language at the same time, beginning to build vocabulary in English. Sometimes, however, students don't see the connection between the academic language and concepts in their primary language and the vocabulary in English. This is a bridge that is often missed for students. In a study of the advantages of a primary language on a student's learning of a third language (Swain & Lapkin, 1991) where both the primary language (Italian or Spanish) and the third language (French) were Romance languages, students generally did not make use of cognates between the languages to acquire meaning. Swain suggests that perhaps this needs to be taught. Discussions that explicitly focus attention on the similarity of the languages could help students to more readily transfer meaning from one language to another (Moran & Calfee, in press).

Immersion programs, such as those in Montreal, Canada, place students of the language of prestige (in this model, English) into a classroom where all teaching is done in French. All students in the class are beginning the language together. Content areas are taught in French. Literacy in English is introduced in the third or fourth grade. This model has proven itself effective in producing balanced bilinguals who outperform their monolingual peers on some tests of cognition (Peale & Lambert, 1962). Unfortunately, the Immersion Model is sometimes misinterpreted and programs are set up that place minority language children in English-only programs competing with native English speakers and the title "Immersion Program" is misused on "submersion," also known as "sink-or-swim," models (Cummins, 1981).

Dual-language programs are an adaptation of the French Immersion Model from Canada. In Dual-language programs English-speaking students are immersed in the minority language (Spanish) alongside native speakers. Instruction in literacy as well as content areas is in the minority language for the first three years. English is gradually introduced (Lindholm, 1990). This approach has proven successful at grounding minority language students in content area concepts in their own language as well as preparing them to move into English in the intermediate grades. Majority language students appear to do as well or better than their peers in English-only programs in both literacy and content area work (Lindholm, 1990).

A team-teaching model is often used in bilingual programs where monolingual English-speaking teachers are incorporated into the program, providing a majority-language as well as a minority-language model for students. In these models, content area subjects may be taught in the student's dominant language or may vary according to the topic. Team teaching may also be used to allow teachers to build their strength in one or two subject areas rather than teach all subjects in the elementary schools. One teacher might teach all the science, another all the social studies. Or, a modified teaming approach may be used that allows flexibility for teachers to move between homogenous and mixed language grouping. For example, three teachers might teach a unit on geology. One teacher might focus on plate tectonics, and a short lecture or movie may require homogeneous language grouping. Students may then be heterogeneously grouped to build volcanoes or make plaster-of-paris fossils and process the learning from the direct teaching experience.

A concurrent approach is still utilized in some bilingual classrooms. This is basically translating back and forth between the two languages. The purpose of this kind of instruction is to keep all students involved. The drawbacks to this model is that students tend to listen only to their dominant language and so are not encouraged to build their second language. In addition, it can be tedious to bilingual students to hear everything twice.

A preview-review approach may also be used in content area instruction. A lesson is previewed in one language. The introduction—an explanation of what is going to be taught—is given in language "A." Then the lesson itself is conducted in language "B." Then the lesson is discussed and comprehension checks are done in language "A" to be sure that all students understand what is being taught. This pattern may be consistent with language "B" always being the language of instruction or it may switch back and forth as in the alternate day/week model.

When bilingual staff is not available in the language of the child, there are a number of models used by schools. Whatever the model, some form of a "Sheltered English" approach is generally followed. "Sheltered English" is a form of instruction all in English that relies on the following strategies to create comprehensible input for students acquiring English: (a) Speech is modified by using shorter, less complex sentences, slowing the pace, and using nonverbal cues such as gestures and facial expressions or repetition and paraphrasing to convey meaning. (b) Visuals including props, pictures, projected images, etc., are used with specific pointing to provide a clear reference. The drawback to Sheltered English is that often the name is used where the principles are not applied. When the principles are applied, it is sometimes a watered-down approach to the content, so that students acquiring English are not gaining the academic skills and knowledge to succeed.

Essential Elements of Content Area Instruction

Whatever the configuration of students or the program models used for teaching students acquiring English, there are a number of elements of content area instruction that will provide effective instruction for students acquiring English. Integrated throughout all of these principles must be a linguistic and cultural sensitivity toward the student, subtle focus on language strategies when appropriate, and alternative means of expression. Incorporating the following elements into instruction will make content area classes more effective for students acquiring English.

(1) Curriculum is grounded in the knowledge and experience the student brings to the classroom (Díaz, Moll & Mehan, 1986; Heath, 1983; Maria, 1989). It is important to find out what the student knows about the topic and find some bridge to connect the curriculum to his/her life.
(2) Organizational strategies are provided, tools that fit a concept into the bigger picture as well as to organize bits of information within the context or the topic (Calfee, 1981; Hernández, 1989).
(3) Acquisition of academic language is facilitated by focusing on new vocabulary and concepts and providing interaction with the language and concepts in relaxed, informal ways. Let students learn from each other (Reyes, 1991; Hudelson, 1989).
(4) Synthesis of new information occurs right after processing and reporting or sharing is encouraged through a variety of modes of expression. It doesn't have to be a written report. (5) Students reflect on the process of how they learned as well as what they learned. This will increase the probability of transfer of the learning to new situations.

All pieces are interwoven in effective instruction. Interaction, for example, can be involved in all phases of instruction. Organizational tools are utilized at every level of the process but are given a separate section in this text to emphasize the variety of tools available. Suggestions for supporting language development and alternative modes of expression are woven throughout the text. The following matrix exemplifies how the interweaving of the elements occurs throughout the instructional process.

Making Connections— Building Background

On my first day of chemistry in high school I sat memorizing the chart of chemical elements. As soon as I would learn five, I would forget three of them. I remember thinking, "What does this have to do with my life?" If anyone had informed me that chemistry can explain how bread rises, or meat tenderizes, or how plastic is made, I would have been fascinated. As it was I dropped chemistry. This is what happens to many students acquiring English, with school in general, and particularly with science, social studies, and math. They have no sense of how these topics fit into their lives. Combined with the challenging language, the motivation is often not strong enough to succeed.

In introducing a topic we need to bring out what students know about that topic. "If there is a gap, teachers should avoid the temptation to fill it by simply supplying the information; background knowledge cannot simply be presented to children who lack it, although this may seem efficient" (Maria, 1989, p. 299). There are a variety of ways to bridge the gap. Some people start with a large sheet of butcher paper on which they write, "What do you know? What do you want to know?" Others create a semantic map with the topic in the middle, having students brainstorm about the topic (Pearson & Johnson, 1978). A five-minute "quick-write" is a way to have students think about what they know. Students acquiring English may write in their own language or pair with another student to write in English. A "think-pair-share" encourages students to think quietly for a short time, then pair with a peer and talk, and paraphrase and share what their peer said (Kagan, 1989). Sometimes this knowledge check will demonstrate that more background building is necessary before students can get involved in a topic.

In social studies some concepts are rather vague for students. For example, "discrimination" or "majority rule" may need to be experienced before a discussion can take place to draw out a student's prior knowledge or experience. A simulation, where students actually experience briefly the concept (Hernández, 1989) can provide such experience. Giving real experiences through field trips or hands-on activities is another way to connect children's experience with new concepts. Narrative text—stories, biographies, historical fiction, etc.—can also bridge the distance between personal experience and historical events or even scientific concepts (Wong & Calfee, 1988).

If the selection of topics to be studied is negotiated with students, they can choose topics that have inherent interest for them. When students are involved in choosing topics that relate to their lives, they will be able to engage in their own forms of social science or ethnographic research on the topic.

Figure 1

Sources of Information	Language Support	Tools of Organization	Expression Presentation
Connections Where do students get the information they bring to school? Parents, community	Visuals, props, gestures	Diagram of a chain of events in the learning process	Quick-write Pair share

Interaction
 Break up information:
    Cooperative groups
    Paired work
    Collaborative work
	Shorter text, labeled props, mixed language groups	Assigned student roles	Checklist of group interaction
			 Sharing group procedures

Synthesis Explain charts Analysis of information Report back within group	Word lists: transitions, comparatives	Hierarchy, student-made pictures	Posters, skits, explain pictures Write-up of work
Reflection Rethinking the process of how we learned what we know	Sentence frames: We used to think . . . but now we think . . . Transition terms: *first, then, finally*	Venn diagram	Groups share thinking processes and process of accomplishing tasks with the class

In *Ways with Words*, Heath (1983) describes a science class of fifth graders (mainly African American boys reading below the second-grade level) who became ethnographers researching local folk theories and methods of agriculture. Students were told to find at least two sources of information, one oral and one written, to validate their work. They interviewed community people, read newspapers, and so on, to gain information about agriculture in their community.

> Learners in this science classroom had become ethnographers of a sort; in so doing, they had improved their knowledge of science. In addition, they had learned to talk about ways of obtaining and verifying information; terms such as *sources*, *check out* (the sense of *verify*), *summarize*, and *translate* had become part of their vocabulary. They had come to recognize, use, and produce knowledge about the skills of inquiring, compiling, sorting, and refining information. They had not only made use of inquiry and discovery method skills discussed in science and social studies methods texts; they had acquired the language to talk about these skills. (Heath, 1983, p. 320)

A group of Latino students in Arizona were introduced to social science inquiry techniques (Díaz, Moll & Mehan, 1986) when they created their own surveys to inquire about the language attitudes and practices of people in their community. They used the information they found as a basis for writing expository text. Their ownership of the writing project was evident from their choice of topic, creation of interviews, and feedback from the community. Writing became a meaningful activity.

When students become ethnographers within their own community, they bridge the gap between home and school. Their learning validates and integrates both home life and academic life. Academic skills are learned incidentally amidst involvement in the project. Ethnographic work can begin as simply as making homework assignments relate a topic to the home. In math, for instance, when children are first learning multiplication or division, they can interview family and community members to find out when these skills are used in their home or community. This information can be used to create word problems that come out of their own lives—using names of people they know, involving happenings in their own community. In social studies, when a particular aspect of history is studied, students can find out where their parents, relatives, or ancestors were and what they might have been doing during the time the event took place. Particularly when studying broad concepts such as liberty, injustice, and freedom, students will ground their knowledge by discovering what these terms mean to their own families. This kind of ethnographic work can be done on a daily basis and enrich class discussions to the benefit and sometimes enlightenment of all students as well as teachers; at the same time the content becomes grounded in the student's life. In addition students learn to formulate questions, validate sources, organize information and express that information through writing or explaining what they learned.

Creating these connections between what students bring to the learning and the new learning allows students to begin to construct conceptual understandings, which then become the basis for the inquiry work. According to the Conceptual Change Perspective of Science, which grew out of cognitive science studies of learning and knowing in knowledge-rich domains:

> This web of knowledge, or the individual's conceptual ecology (Posner et al., 1982), only becomes useful and meaningful to students when it is integrated with the learner's own personal knowledge and experiences with natural phenomena. Students come to science classes with as many ideas and explanations about natural phenomena. Their ideas are experience-based and often stand in stark contrast to the scientific explanations studied in school. A central goal of science teaching is to help students *change* their intuitive, everyday ways of explaining the world around them—to incorporate scientific concepts and ways of thinking into their personal frameworks. (Roth, 1989, p. 19)

Organizational Structures and Tools

To avoid the feeling of having entered in the middle of a movie, when a new topic is introduced, it is important to put topics in a larger context so they can be seen as part of the whole. If it is a historical event, it needs to be placed in its chronological or social context. If it's a scientific experiment, its evolution or application needs to be understood. In addition some way of breaking down the topic or organizing the information for comparison or understanding will improve comprehension. Schema building is a powerful verbal learning tactic (Derry, 1988). Schema building is done by showing organizational structures through diagrams known as "graphic organizers" to organize thinking as well as reading and writing. The following graphic organizers can be used successfully from kindergarten onward. They can be introduced as whole-class activities, incorporated into small group work, and later used by pairs and individuals for organizing information.

A semantic map (Pearson & Johnson, 1978), as described earlier, is a simple way for students to brainstorm ideas in a group or on their own. Brainstorming can begin as a whole-class project with small groups or partners adding to the semantic map as new ideas occur. Other organizational tools can then be introduced to work from the semantic map or to organize information from texts.

A matrix is a powerful organizing tool to make comparisons. A matrix is often the format of tables in social studies books. Students acquiring English may need help as to how to read the tables. Practice creating prose out of the tables by reading across as a group. Writing down the words needed to make sense out of the tables will help students acquiring English. It allows students to see relationships between aspects of a topic. It also is an excellent way to build vocabulary around a topic. As the matrix is used to compare or contrast, finer distinctions are made in word meanings and the topic gives the student a "mental file folder" in which to store this new vocabulary. Any matrix of different peoples, for example, might list elements of culture down the side for comparison (see Figure 2) and list the different cultures being studied across the top.

In science this same matrix can be used to compare attributes of different plants or animal species. Students can bring in fruits, vegetables, leaves, or other plants. As a group the class can brainstorm the most salient attributes (e.g., have seeds, grow above ground). The possible attributes can be listed down the side and the names of the fruit (or other object) can be placed across the top. Students can then decide which categories fit each of the fruit and place an *x* for the ones that work. As they work together they are not only building labels for the objects but the aspects of each object as well. In math the matrix is very powerful in solving logic problems. This is a simple tool for problem solving that is often not taught until a student is studying for college placement exams. It can easily be used with third or fourth graders in cooperative groups.

Venn diagrams are very useful in comparing any two things, groups, different points of view, different books, or different objects. The two overlapping circles allow a student to see readily what is different about each group, and where the overlap occurs is what is the same about them.

A branching tree (Figure 3) is another important structure for helping students problem solve as well as for understanding how certain kinds of text are organized (Calfee, 1981). A branching tree begins where "two roads diverge in a yellow woods" or at any point of two possible choices. It then branches out into the consequences of either of those choices. In studying the American Revolution, for example, you could discuss what the dilemma might have been for a colonist—stay with England or become independent. Then look at what might have been the consequences of each of those decisions and which might bring up a new dilemma. For example, loyalists may want to return to England or fight against their neighbors.

Figure 2 *Matrix*

Regional Group	Housing & Shelter	Food Source	Clothing	Tools
Plains Indians	Tepees	Buffalo	Deerskin Buffalo robes	Bows and arrows Travois and stone knives
Coastal Indians	Tule Huts	Seafood Acorns, berries	As needed, deerskin, rush skirts, and rabbit capes	Baskets, grinding stones
Southwestern Indians	Pueblos Adobe	Fry bread Corn and other vegetables	As needed, skins, blankets, and other adornments	Baskets Grinding Pots stones Dig sticks

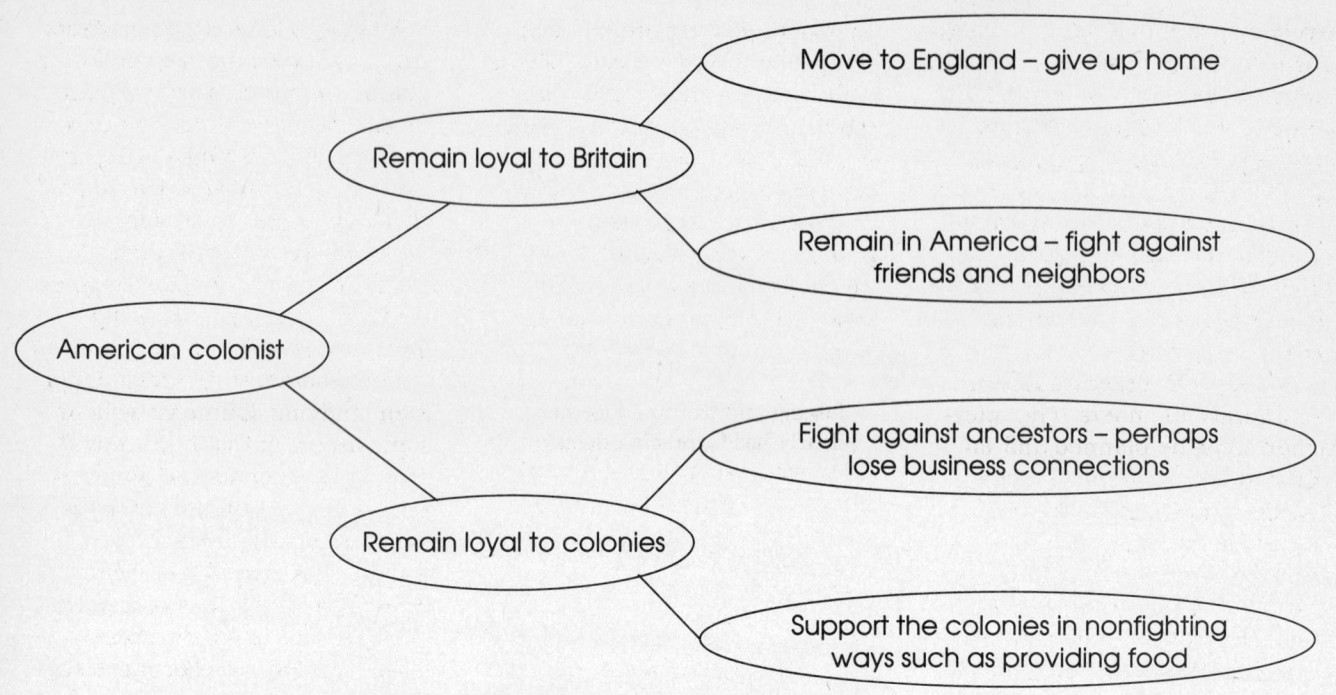

Figure 3 *The Branching Tree*

Branching tree diagram:
- American colonist
  - Remain loyal to Britain
    - Move to England – give up home
    - Remain in America – fight against friends and neighbors
  - Remain loyal to colonies
    - Fight against ancestors – perhaps lose business connections
    - Support the colonies in nonfighting ways such as providing food

The branching tree is a tool that students can use in thinking through decisions in their own lives, such as involvement in drugs, staying in school, etc. In addition to being a powerful problem-solving tool, it can be a useful linguistic tool for helping students utilize and understand complex grammar related to their lives. If a student draws a branching tree of a decision from his/her own life, even using simple pictures rather than words to convey the dilemma, a discussion can ensue and the student will have the opportunity to learn to express such experiences in sophisticated grammar, e.g., "If I had gone with that gang, I would have been arrested." Moving from prose to a diagram such as the branching tree and back to prose again is useful in organizing and thinking through ideas as well as building language skills.

Another powerful organizing tool is the chain of causality. Cause and effect are sometimes hard for students to discuss or to pick up in their reading. If students are guided to pick out important events and write them in sequenced boxes, they can then look at each box and decide if it caused the following event. Did "A" cause "B" or did it just precede "B"? It is a simple but powerful way to analyze both historical and scientific events. Organizing information from a text helps to organize our thinking. Organized thinking leads to organized writing. This chain of causality can become a lifelong skill for student growth.

In addition to helping in the background-building, connection-making stage of a lesson and the processing of information, organizing structures can help keep groups on task and provide an easy means for a group to divide up a chore. If a group decides a matrix will best organize the information, each student may be responsible for one of the rows or one of the columns on the matrix. When it is time to report back information, the organizing structure can be used to help organize the report or provide the notes to talk from. Working in groups is facilitated by the use of organizational tools, and such interactive processing is an important aspect of content area instruction for students acquiring English.

Interactive Processing

We learn to talk by talking, listening, and participating in conversations. There is a growing body of research to attest to the benefit of small-group work (Cohen, 1986; Kagan, 1989; Lotan & Benton, 1990; Taylor, 1982). If a classroom is quiet, students are not developing language. On the other hand, noise alone does not mean that students are acquiring language and concepts as effectively as possible. Creating experiences for students to interact in constructive ways is essential for content area classrooms where students are acquiring language (Reyes, 1991; Hudelson, 1989). Interaction may be with the whole group, small heterogeneous groups (homogeneous groups may be beneficial for limited purposes), pairing of students or mixing with other classes or community members. The interaction must be planned and facilitated with students' language abilities and growth in mind.

Students working in small groups to produce skits or plays to portray a historical event will remember more of the content than if they simply read about it. Also, the process of negotiating roles and creating meanings of text or events during theatrical group work provides tremendous opportunity for developing language (Wolfe, 1992). Content area vocabulary will increase significantly in such a process.

If reading material is divided up among small groups, students acquiring English have a smaller chunk of text to read. This allows a greater opportunity for successful participation in the group and greater potential for learning the content, for example, if a chapter on the American colonies is divided up assigning one colony to each group to create a skit or mural or poster for the class. All students spend less time plowing through text and more time negotiating, analyzing, and synthesizing information to share with the class. The productions by each group give the whole class access to the content. Nothing is lost and a great deal of participation, language, and concept development is gained. In a study done on nine bilingual classrooms, grades two through four, looking at cooperative groups using a math/science program, Cohen found:

> Talking and working together clearly has favorable effects on learning, especially conceptual learning. In this study, children who were seen as highly problematic by their teachers showed excellent learning gains. The sharpest learning gains were made by fully bilingual children and by developmentally precocious children whose pretest scores were below the state norms on CTBS. (Cohen, 1984, p. 186)

Cohen also cautioned against the negative effects of heterogeneous grouping without teacher intervention. Status characteristics present in the class at large come to play in any group: "Higher status students will have higher rates of participation and influence" (1984, p. 186). Cohen suggests that status characteristics in the class will be played out in the group. Status may be attributed to attractiveness, reading ability, athletic ability, race, gender, etc. She notes that teachers can mitigate these effects or actually change the status of members of the class through a variety of strategies.

Strategies for mitigating status might include choosing the lower status students to be trained on certain aspects of a task or to be given certain responsibilities that carry status. It might also mean choosing topics or tasks for which lower-status students would have greater knowledge or expertise. For example, if the lower-status group in the class are the Southeast Asian students, then studying Southeast Asia or some aspect of that culture will give these students the opportunity to be the experts. If Hispanic girls seem to have lower status in math activities, then train them on the use of a new manipulative and have them train their groups. (For more suggestions on creating successful groups, see *Designing Groupwork*, Cohen, E. G., 1986).

Interaction doesn't have to mean groups. Heterogeneous pairs of students can work effectively together on a project learning to negotiate plans and meanings. My fourth and fifth graders planned trips across the country. They were given a budget and the task of planning a two-week trip. Their job was to decide where they were going each day, how much they would spend on food, transportation, lodging, and activities. They plotted the trip on maps, calculated gas mileage, researched points of interest and drew pictures of what they would see. At one point two boys came running back from the office where they had gone to call a travel agent,

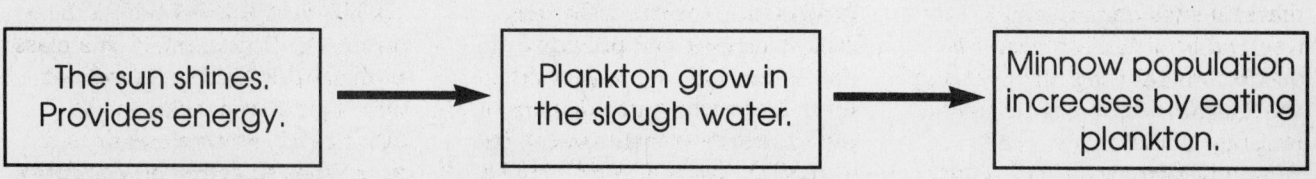

| The sun shines. Provides energy. | → | Plankton grow in the slough water. | → | Minnow population increases by eating plankton. |

Figure 4 *The Chain of Causality*

"Guess what! There's a special to Arizona; we can go round-trip for under $200." These boys were so engaged in their project that it had become real to them. One of these boys researched in English, the other in Spanish. They pooled their information and created a report that they gave in both Spanish and English.

Synthesize the Content: What Did We Learn?

I once taught a unit on African folktales. We had done extensive background building on Africa and its peoples. After reading eight different folktales, in the midst of producing plays or stick puppet theater on four of the tales, I asked the class one day in a quick-write to tell me what a folktale was. I realized from their responses that they didn't have a clue beyond its being a story. I was expecting them to distill the essence of folktales from reading and participating in them. They clearly weren't capable of doing this without some tools.

The purpose of synthesis is to think through the content that has been digested and make some sense out of it, see the patterns, find what it adds to our understanding of the world, and how it changes our conceptual understandings (Roth, 1989). This may be done by a group, in pairs, or individually. However it is done, students will need specific tools and guidance to get started. In a study of four classrooms teaching a six-to-eight-week unit on photosynthesis, which consisted mainly of interactive activities, "eighty-nine percent of the students in the study failed to grasp the central concept of the unit: that plants get their energy-containing food only by making it internally out of carbon dioxide and water" (Roth, Smith & Anderson, 1983, in Roth, 1989, p. 19).

To remedy this dilemma on our folktales unit we brainstormed what these stories seemed to have in common. After some discussion (and extensive thinking and rereading) we came up with a list of elements we thought they had in common: (a) They came from oral traditions in different parts of Africa. (b) They had characters who acted like people. (c) They had a moral or message to the story. (d) They gave us some information about the people who created the story. (We decided to call this world view.) (e) They were entertaining.

We created a matrix with these elements across the top, and the stories we had read down the side. We started with the stories being performed, and each of the four groups analyzed the story they were performing. Working in pairs within the groups, students drew a picture and wrote a paragraph explaining how a particular characteristic was true for their play. For example, one student wrote: "We learn from the folktale of 'Anansi and the Spiders' that stories are very important to the people of Africa and that stories are for everyone not just one person." The pictures and paragraphs were pasted onto a large wall matrix. We then could compare both across stories and across elements to validate our explanation of African folktales. In addition, the students shared the characteristics of their story orally when they introduced the performance of the play or puppet show.

We analyzed more stories for our matrix. The students then wrote their first essay on what folktales were. They were encouraged to use their fellow students' work on the matrix as sources. We practiced how to turn the elements listed at the top into topic sentences and how to provide support for the topic sentence by choosing examples from several different folktales. I posted lists of transition phrases such as: "for example," "in addition," and "finally" on the wall and we practiced how to use them in an essay. All students acquiring English (after six months in English reading) were able to write excellent three-to-four-page essays on "Why you should read folktales" or "What folktales are." This is the kind of scaffolded expository writing that builds success in second language writers.

Another way to scaffold writing for purposes of synthesis is to help students use available formats to synthesize their information. There are a number of repetitive formats in "patterned stories" that allow students to pick up the pattern and imitate it in their own writing. Using well written trade books as models of writing can get a reluctant writer started. An example of a simple format that can help students

Whether group work is done in a large group, small groups, or pairs, it is important that students analyze their findings and pull them together to report information back to the larger group. The analysis and synthesis of an activity is what makes the difference between "fun activities" and "fun learning experiences."

conceptualize their ideas is the English folktale, "The House That Jack Built." There are many popular versions of this story. The simplest one I have heard is as follows:

> This is the house that Jack built. This is the cheese that stayed in the house that Jack built. This is the rat that ate the cheese that stayed in the house that Jack built. [The story continues until the last line sums up the entire story.] This is the priest that married the boy and the girl, the boy that kissed the girl that milked the cow that tossed the dog that chased the cat that caught the rat that ate the cheese that stayed in the house that Jack built.

This story format has been used by many teachers over the years in both social studies and science. The following is an example of how a fourth-grade class used the format to recount their scientific knowledge and observations on a field trip to a nearby slough area. I will share just the last line which sums up of the pattern story, "The Sun That Shines on Elkhorn Slough":

> This is the sun that shines on the great hawk that grasped the little rabbit that nibbled the grass that grew in the dirt that formed with the help of micro-organisms, the micro-organisms that decomposed the dead seal that floated past the leopard shark that swallowed the minnows that ate the plankton that get energy from the sun that shines on Elkhorn Slough. (Alianza Bilingual School, Ms. Petritz)

This kind of synthesis of content provides a product that all students can take home with them and share with their families. Another way to synthesize content that also provides a great language learning opportunity is to create a "museum" or "fair" to show off the learning that students have done. Students can work in pairs or groups to gather artifacts of an era or to create science experiments or solve complex applied math problems. Once everything has been gathered and studied, students can create a short talk to share with students from other classes as they wander through the museum or fair to see the display. This allows students to practice their short speech for a purpose and repeat it over several times for different classes. The elevated adrenaline of a performance and the repetition ingrain the speech in the long-term memory.

Over the years I have observed many teachers doing exciting and interesting group activities. Unfortunately, the synthesis needed to move from an exciting activity to a learning experience is often lacking. Students need the tools to organize the information gained from their activities and to synthesize this information. Graphic organizers and adaptable formats help students to bring together the information they are learning and to process it in a way that they can make sense out of it.

Reflecting on the Process

Reflection on the process, on how we learned what we learned, can be done in journals, diaries, or five-minute quick-writes (students write everything they can think of in a five-minute period without worrying about punctuation and spelling). It can also be done by students sharing their products with another class and explaining to the class the process by which the product came about. The importance of this step is that it provides the metacognitive understanding of the process. Metacognition, or knowing what we know and how we know it, helps us to transfer knowledge to new situations.

To continue the example of the essays on African folktales, when the essays were written students were so proud of them (and so were we) that we decided they should share them in other classes. They were practice-reading the essays when someone stopped by and asked how they had done such wonderful work. To my chagrin none of them could explain the process. I realized that if they didn't remember how they had done it they would not be able to do it again. We discussed this problem and decided that rather than just read their essays, they would take the matrix to other classes and explain, step by step, how they had written the essays. (Now we had a purpose for going back over the process.)

We spent several class periods going back over the steps and practicing how to share these steps with another class. They then went off as teachers to explain expository essay writing using a matrix as an organizing tool to the other fourth and fifth grade. This served not only as reflection and metacognition on their part but also as staff development for other teachers and the introduction of a process to other students. It was well worth the extra few days spent to finish off the unit.

The reflective process can take a variety of forms. Quick-writes about a problem-solving process provide fast feedback as to what students remember about the process. Student math journals provide an excellent opportunity for individuals to write about how their cooperative group solved a particular math problem. A math journal is kept by students after their problem solving to reflect on the process and experience of what they have done. They are encouraged to draw pictures of the problem and write step by step how it was solved. A class journal or log of an ongoing science project can be kept to see what each "scientist" has observed or what procedures were performed on the project. Having one group share its process with another group, or pairs form into groups of four to share how a problem was solved or which procedures were used on a science experiment are alternatives to providing reflection on the process.

There is always the lament, "There's not enough time to do all this," but time can be divided in many ways. Language arts can be combined with content areas to allow more time to spend on synthesis and reflection (which are language arts). Time for students acquiring English can be wasted trying to cover too many topics, read too much material, and move on too quickly. Limiting the number of topics covered and dividing material to be shared in highly engaging inter-active activities that culminate with synthesis of the content learned and reflection on the process will be much more cost-effective in terms of time spent.

In Summary

There are many ways to approach the teaching of content to students acquiring English. It is preferable to provide instruction in the primary language as well as in English, and there are a variety of models to be adapted for that purpose that should be determined by the characteristics of students as well as the availability of staff. Whatever program model is chosen, there are basic elements of effective content area instruction that are summarized on the following checklist to help teachers and administrators think through content area lesson planning.

- **Connections**
  How have students been involved in the selection of topics? Will the number of topics allow in-depth study? Have students contributed as sources of knowledge on the topic? Is the context and necessary background developed?

- **Organizational Tools**
  Do students have the big picture, where the topic fits in the whole? Have we broken the topic into sizable chunks to study? Are students able to utilize a graphic organizer to make sense of information from a variety of sources? Can students move from the text to the graphic organizer and from the graphic organizer to prose?

- **Interactive Processing**
  Are students talking and interacting with peers most of the time? Do we utilize a variety of effective grouping strategies? Does status within the group vary and do all students participate in the groups?

- **Synthesis of Content**
  Have students discussed and expressed what they learned? Have there been alternative ways to express the learning?

- **Reflection on the Strategies and the Processing**
  Have students reflected on how they accomplished their goals? Can they apply their learning process in a new situation?

About the Author

Carrol Moran is an educational consultant specializing in bilingual education (for Spanish and Portuguese speakers) and second language literacy. She has worked in education for 20 years, teaching preschool through college levels. During her 14 years with the Pajaro Valley School District in Watsonville, California, she worked as a classroom teacher, reading and language specialist, and resource and mentor teacher.

Carrol is the author of several books, including: *The Keys to the Classroom: A Teacher's Guide to the First Month of School*; *The Bridge: Spanish to English*, a guide to teaching literacy in a bilingual setting; and *Colors of the Earthquake,* a rhyming book illustrated by children about the Loma Prieta earthquake. In addition she has written curriculum for kindergarten through eighth grade in math, social studies, science, and language arts and writes adaptations of curriculum for students acquiring English for major textbook publishing companies. Presently, Carrol is a Title VII Fellow in Stanford's doctoral program in Language, Literacy and Culture.

REFERENCES

Calfee, R. (1981). *The book*. Unpublished Project READ training manual. Stanford University.

Cohen, E. G. (1986). *Designing groupwork: Strategies for the heterogeneous classroom*. New York: Teachers College Press, Columbia University.

Cohen, E. G. (1984). Talking and working together: Status, interaction and learning. In Peterson, P., Wilkinson, L. C., and Hallinan, M. (Eds.), *The social context of instruction*. New York: Academic Press.

Cummins, J. (1981). The role of primary language development in promoting educational success for language minority students. In *Schooling and language minority students: A theoretical framework*. Los Angeles: California State University; Evaluation, Dissemination and Assessment Center.

Derry, S. (1988, January). Putting learning strategies to work. *Educational Leadership*.

Díaz, S., Moll, L., and Mehan, H. (1986). Sociocultural resources in instruction: A context-specific approach. In *Beyond language: social and cultural factors in schooling language minority students,* developed by Bilingual Education Office, California State Department of Education. Los Angeles: California State University; Evaluation, Dissemination and Assessment Center.

Heath, S. (1983). *Ways with words*. Cambridge: Cambridge University Press.

Hernández, H. (1989). Development of a multicultural curriculum. In *Multicultural education: A teacher's guide to content and process*. Columbus, OH: Merrill Publishing Company.

Hudelson, S. (1989). Teaching English through content-area activities. In Riggs, P., and Allen, V. G. (Eds.), *When they don't all speak English*. National Council of Teachers of English.

Kagan, S. (1989). *Cooperative learning resources for teachers*. San Juan Capistrano, CA: Resources for Teachers.

Lindholm, K. (1990, December). *Promoting bilingualism and academic achievement among English and Spanish speaking children*. Unpublished paper presented at Stanford University.

Lotan, R., and Benton, J. (1990). Finding out about complex instruction: Teaching math and science in heterogeneous classrooms. In Davidson, N. (Ed.), *Cooperative learning in mathematics: A handbook for teachers*. Menlo Park, CA: Addison-Wesley.

Maria, K. (1989, January). Developing disadvantaged children's background knowledge interactively. *The Reading Teacher*.

Moran, C., and Calfee, R. C. (in press). Comprehending orthography social construction of letter-sound systems in monolingual and bilingual programs. *Reading and Writing: An Interdisciplinary Journal*.

Peal, E., and Lambert, W. E. (1962). The relation to bilingualism and intelligence. *Psychological Monographs: General and Applied*, vol. 76 (Nov. 27), no. 564.

Pearson, P. D., and Johnson, D. (1978). *Teaching reading comprehension*. New York: Holt, Rinehart and Winston.

Posner, G. J., Strike, K. A., Hewson, P. W., and Gertzog, W. A. (1982). Accommodation of a scientific conception: Toward a theory of conceptual change. In *Science Education, 66 (2), pp. 211–27*.

Reyes, M. (1991). Instructional strategies for second-language learners in the content areas. *Journal of Reading*, vol. 35, no. 2.

Roth, K. (1989, winter). Science education: It's not enough to "do" or "relate." *American Educator*.

Swain, M., and Lapkin, S. (1991). Additive bilingualism and French immersion education: The roles of language proficiency and literacy. In Reynolds, A. G. (Ed.), *Bilingualism, multiculturalism, and second language learning*. The McGill Conference in Honor of Wallace E. Lambert. Hillsdale, NJ: Lawrence Erlbaum.

Taylor, B. P. (1982). In search of real reality. *TESOL Quarterly*, vol. 16, no. 1.

Wolfe, S. (1992). *Learning to act/acting to learn: Language and learning in the theatre or the classroom*. Unpublished doctoral dissertation, Stanford University.

Wong, I., and Calfee, R. (1988). *Trade books: A viable supplement to textbooks in earth science*. Paper presented at AERA, New Orleans.

Developing Biliteracy *in a* Two-Way Immersion Program

**Jennifer Martínez and Julie A. Moore-O'Brien,
with assistance from Ginger Dale and María Juárez-Cruz**
Windsor School District, California

Walking down the corridor toward my classroom one spring morning, something on the playground caught my attention. The March breeze carried the faint sounds of children singing and chanting in Spanish. I stopped and stood mesmerized as I watched 12 or 15 of my first-grade students actively engaged in a game of jump rope. I listened intently to the rhythmic chants of rhymes and poems we had been reciting and reading in class for the past several weeks. I gazed down the line of children awaiting their turns and saw a jumble of blond, brown, and black hair blowing wildly in the breeze. I listened to them encourage each other, criticize each other and argue over turns, as all six-year-olds do. What made this particular scene so unique was the fact that the conversations were entirely in Spanish; yet only about a third of the children were native speakers of Spanish.

It's not to say that their utterances were error free. I heard shouts of "¡Yo quieres más turnos!" (¡Yo quiero más turnos!—I want more turns!) "¡Yo no brincas mucho!" (¡Yo no brinco mucho!—I don't jump much!) or "¡Ayúdenme! ¡Yo no sabo jump." (¡Ayúdenme! ¡Yo no sé brincar!—Help me! I don't know how to jump!). However, none of these typical second language learner errors interfered with the negotiation of meaning. In fact no one even acknowledged their miscues. The conversations, the chanting, and the arguing flowed as freely as in any children's game. It wasn't long before several second graders from the English-only class next door abandoned their own game of jump rope and filed into line with the younger children. When the turn came for the first second grader to jump, one of my students ordered, "Say it in English. She's not in the Spanish class." The children changed gears without a thought and began chanting "Cinderella." When the second child prepared to jump she requested, "Say something in Spanish for me. It sounds neat."

PROMOTING BILITERACY

Although I had a list of chores awaiting me in the classroom, I stood on the corner and watched for nearly 20 minutes. When I greeted my students in line at the start of class a particularly observant little boy asked, "Maestra ¿por qué estás llorando?" (Teacher, why are you crying?) How could I begin to explain the feelings of hope and pride that overwhelmed me as I witnessed some of the early effects of our Two-Way Immersion Program?

Introduction

We became bilingual teachers because we wanted to offer equal educational opportunities to Hispanic students who were failing in English-only classrooms. We knew that bilingual classrooms certainly improved the educational experiences of our Spanish-speaking students. Still we recognized certain program limitations or inherent contradictions that limited the effectiveness of the *transitional bilingual model*. For example, Spanish-speaking students rarely received enough instruction in Spanish to fully develop their primary language. This not only led to low levels of Spanish language proficiency, but also resulted in low levels of English language proficiency. English speakers enrolled in these same programs never had the opportunity to learn to speak, read, or write Spanish fluently.

As dedicated bilingual teachers who have actively participated in the evolution of bilingual education, we are convinced that Two-Way Immersion Education is the bilingual education model of the future. It eliminates the contradictions in bilingual programs by guaranteeing that both language majority and language minority students value and have equal access to both Spanish and English. The Two-Way Immersion Program at Windsor Union School District is in its sixth year. In the upcoming school year we will have 17 Immersion classes, K–6, with 3 classes at most grade levels. It has not been an easy journey to the point where we are today, but we are ensuring a future that will bring dramatic and lasting changes in the quality of education we offer our students.

We have divided this article into two main sections: "What Is Two-Way Immersion?" and "Developing Biliteracy." Although it is impossible to write about everything that we do in the Two-Way setting, we have included all the main instructional strategies we employ and given concrete, practical examples of how we develop bilingualism and biliteracy in the classroom.

What Is Two-Way Immersion?

In Two-Way Immersion classrooms, Spanish is the primary language of instruction for both Spanish-speaking and English-speaking students in the early grades. Our classrooms are made up of approximately 50 percent Spanish-speaking students and 50 percent English-speaking students. This ratio is necessary to maintain an environment of educational and linguistic equity and to promote optimum interactions among speakers of both languages. All students learn to read and write in Spanish first and are later are introduced to these skills in English.

It is important to remember that in the social context of the United States, Spanish is the language at risk for both Spanish- and English-speaking students. Spanish-speaking students are almost certain to choose English as their preferred (and often only) mode of communication within the first few years after entering school. English-speaking students will have no chance to develop full bilingualism unless Spanish is used as the primary language of instruction. Two-Way Immersion Programs elevate the status of the Spanish language and thus offer both groups of students an unmatched opportunity to maintain both languages. Such programs also greatly enhance students' understanding and appreciation of other ethnolinguistic groups while maintaining positive attitudes toward their own cultural group.

In order to understand the differences between the Traditional Bilingual Model and the Two-Way Immersion Model, it is useful to see a side-by-side comparison.

Traditional Bilingual	**Two-Way Immersion**
English and Spanish used on alternate days as language of instruction for class rituals, P.E., art, science, social studies.	Spanish is primary language of instruction. Amount of English instruction increases at each grade level.
Children develop literacy in their dominant language.	All children develop literacy in Spanish initially.
Spanish speakers are transitioned into English.	Both Spanish and English speakers develop and maintain literacy in both languages.
Children are separated into homogeneous language and ability groups for literacy instruction.	Children are grouped heterogeneously for all instruction.
Teachers model both English and Spanish.	Teachers are monolingual role models in either language.

GOALS

The goals of the Two-Way Immersion Program reflect the unique educational, linguistic, and social needs of both minority and majority students. The following are the goals of our Two-Way Immersion Program:

1. fluency in communication and literacy in two languages;

2. academic achievement in all subject areas following state frameworks;

3. appreciation and understanding of other cultures while developing positive attitudes among students, their families, and their communities; and

4. opportunities for students to develop the positive values of self-reliance, initiative, kindness, cooperation, resourcefulness, creativity, responsibility, and love of learning.

PROGRAM DESIGN

The number of minutes of instructional time to be conducted in each language at each grade level was determined by research results from the fields of bilingual and immersion education. Windsor's Two-Way Immersion model uses Spanish for about 75 percent of the *total program* instructional time by beginning with 90 percent of the kindergarten instruction in Spanish and slowly increasing the percentage of time in English until a 50/50 balance is reached in the sixth grade.

PROMOTING BILITERACY

Due to the importance of teachers serving as monolingual role models, students receive Spanish instruction from one teacher and English instruction from another. We accomplish this through a team approach in which program teachers at the same grade-level exchange classes for the English portion of the day. For example, from 12:45 P.M. to 1:10 P.M. the three first-grade teachers take over each other's classes for whole group English language development. The three teachers involved in this team are bilingual since in the early stages of the program students are encouraged to interact in either language and they must be confident that their teacher will understand them. The teachers adhere to their monolingual role very seriously and step outside the classroom if they need to respond to an English-speaking parent. Even in the upper grades we feel it is important that the teacher maintain a monolingual role with students. This ensures that Spanish remains the language of prestige in the classroom and is not slowly undermined by the ever-present influence of English.

The following graph illustrates the percentage of instructional time allocated to each language in Windsor's Two-Way Immersion Program.

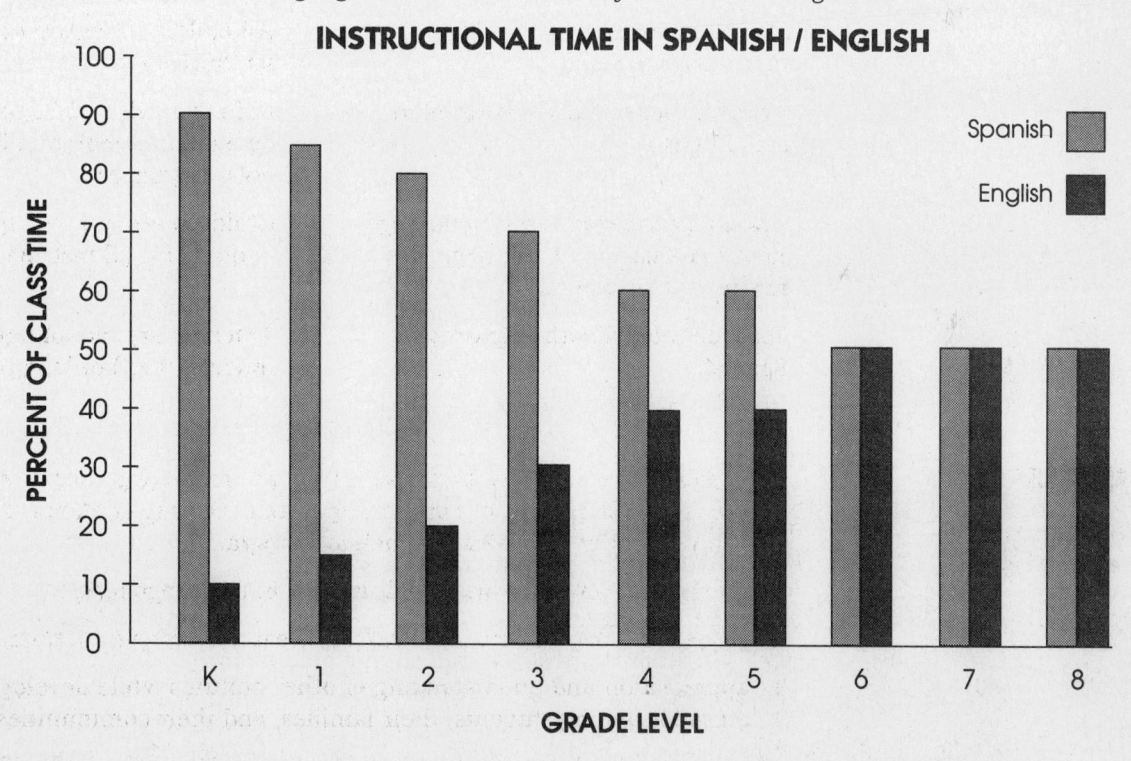

INSTRUCTIONAL TIME IN SPANISH / ENGLISH

Grade Level	Spanish	English
K	90	10
1	85	15
2	80	20
3	70	30
4	60	40
5	60	40
6	50	50
7	50	50
8	50	50

(PERCENT OF CLASS TIME by GRADE LEVEL)

◆ In grades K, 1, and 2 all subject matter is taught in Spanish without translation. The students receive oral English language development for 20-40 minutes daily.

◆ In grade 3 all subject matter is still taught in Spanish. English instruction is increased to 60-90 minutes daily. English literacy is formally introduced while maintaining Spanish literacy.

◆ In grades 4 and 5 Spanish is used for most subject matter. English instruction is increased to 90 minutes daily. Some subject matter is taught in English.

◆ In grades 6, 7, and 8 Spanish is used for half of the instructional time and English the other half. Subjects taught in Spanish one year may be taught in English the following year.

HOW DOES AN IMMERSION CLASSROOM FUNCTION?

Our classrooms are set up in centers revolving around reading, process writing, interactive journal writing, math, language enrichment, art, and science activities. The activities are set up each morning in the centers that correlate to the current thematic unit of study and children rotate to the centers in small groups. Each classroom is also equipped with a special area filled with books, stuffed animals and a comfortable place to read. We are fortunate to have classroom aides, as well as extra help from parent volunteers.

Our interdisciplinary curriculum design provides students a situation similar to the world outside the classroom by not isolating learning into subject areas. This prepares students for independent learning and problem solving in their daily lives. The curriculum is planned around a theme integrating all the traditional subject matter primarily through literature and learning center projects. We systematically integrate language use, development, and complexity of structure into all curricular content. Special effort goes into ensuring that units of study represent a variety of cultures and cultural perspectives. An emphasis is placed on the Hispanic heritage since over 50 percent of our students share that culture. The curriculum is designed to develop children's knowledge and skills in all developmental areas. Integration of physical, emotional, social, and cognitive developmental domains form a base from which teachers prepare the learning environment and plan appropriate curricular activities.

In our classrooms, students are active participants in the learning process. The teacher's primary role is that of facilitator, guiding children through interactive, experiential learning activities in a meaningful context. We subscribe to Cummins's (1985) contention that students must be viewed as "explorers of meaning, as critical and creative thinkers who have contributions to make both in the classroom and in the world beyond" (p. 2). We employ a critical pedogogical model that incorporates instructional factors that promote high levels of first and second language competence, biliteracy, academic achievement in two languages, high self-esteem, and positive cross-cultural attitudes. Each child is recognized as a unique person with an individual pattern and timing of growth, as well as individual personality and family background. Attention is given to the different needs, interests, experiences, and developmental level of all students. Both the curriculum and the teacher's interactions with children are responsive to individual and cultural differences.

We take great care in planning and organizing contacts between minority and majority students so that the achievement of both groups can be maximized. Our classrooms are structured so that students work together in small cooperative teams with each team member contributing to the task at hand.

Both majority and minority students benefit tremendously from cooperative learning. Cooperative learning is an excellent setting for conceptual learning and critical problem solving. It teaches prosocial behavior and takes advantage of academic differences by teaching children to teach each other.

We heterogeneously group our students to ensure that they are never segregated or grouped based on perceived ability or level of language proficiency. The importance of heterogeneous grouping is magnified in the Two-Way Immersion setting where language acquisition is a primary goal. Language development in both languages is accelerated when interactions between native and nonnative speakers are increased. The self-esteem of all students is enhanced because they have the opportunity to be the language model for either English or Spanish.

The language skills of children in our classrooms are developed through sheltered language techniques that make the social and instructional features of classroom language more clear. We accomplish this by simplifying the input through slower speech rate, clear enunciation, repetitive vocabulary, and simplified sentence structure. Another technique we employ is the use of contextual clues such as gestures, facial expressions, dramatization, props, realia, and visuals. Our teachers extend students' speech by putting incomplete verbalizations into complete sentences or thoughts. We engage students in the process of negotiating for meaning by elaborating, checking for comprehension, requesting clarification, rephrasing, and contextualizing.

At the same time, our teachers meld these sheltered language techniques with complex language appropriate for fluent native speakers. One example of how this can be accomplished is by reading traditional language-rich literature to all students, while using gestures, facial expression, and dramatization to make it comprehensible for nonnative speakers. Native speakers are encouraged to assist their teacher by paraphrasing the story and describing the illustrations. The teacher also use various levels of vocabulary and questioning strategies with different students based on their linguistic background.

Developing Biliteracy

Our approach to biliteracy is based on Cummins's theory of a common underlying proficiency (Cummins, 1989), which posits that knowledge learned in one language transfers to the second language once students have acquired the linguistic skill to express that knowledge. For this reason, in kindergarten through second grade we focus on Spanish literacy. Beginning in third grade we formally introduce English literacy to all students. Predictably, many children learn to read simultaneously in both Spanish and English, but this is not a program expectation. It is important to note that we continue Spanish literacy instruction through all the grades.

This section of our article emphasizes the development of Spanish literacy, although most of the same strategies are eventually employed in the development of English literacy. At the end of this section we will give a more detailed description of our English literacy component.

HOLISTIC LANGUAGE AND LITERACY ACQUISITION

In Two-Way Immersion students are provided with authentic language and literacy events in which language acquisition (both oral and written) is a natural process developed through social interaction and need. For language minority students, immersion in their native language provides the necessary linguistic and academic foundation for the later acquisition of English and the further development of proficiency in both languages (Lindholm, 1989). When schools develop and reinforce the native language while introducing the second language, students experience additive bilingualism (Lambert, 1987). Additive bilingualism is an enrichment process through which students acquire a second language with no fear of native language loss or abandonment of their own cultural identity and values. This is associated with high levels of proficiency in both languages and higher levels of scholastic performance.

For the native English-speaking students a second language is best developed through immersion in that language (Genesee, 1985). Children learn a second language similar to the way in which they acquired their first language. In promoting second language acquisition we re-create the conditions that are present in the home, where the children learn their first language. This process necessarily involves trust, language models, interaction, feedback, and a genuine purpose for language use. In a literate, print-rich environment, literacy development occurs naturally for most children. Written language will develop when children have real purposes for reading and writing.

Our literacy program is built around children's literature integrated into the content curriculum through thematic units. Thematic units provide a focal point for inquiry, cultural content, use of language and cognitive development. Students encounter the same vocabulary in a variety of contexts.

Language-rich Environment

In our Two-Way Immersion Program, language is never the focus of learning but rather a tool for learning. Input provided by the teacher is carefully adjusted to guarantee that it is comprehensible to all learners, but at the same time stimulating and enriching for native speakers. A language-rich environment makes use of stories, poetry, songs, games, chants, finger plays, etc., to reinforce and motivate language use. Many of these have been borrowed from folklore, passed down through generations, and are culturally and linguistically rich and engaging for students.

Print-rich Environment

The first thing we accomplish is to surround children with print. One of our first activities at the beginning of the year is to label everything. We often include a statement from a child about a particular object as well as a name label. For instance, the teacher's chair might have two labels: *silla* ("chair") and *La maestra se sienta en esta silla* ("The teacher sits in this chair"). It is a wonderful way to reinforce vocabulary that children are already familiar with, and it also serves as an introduction to new language. New labels are added and old ones are changed throughout the year as we refer to them often in our daily activities. It is not uncommon to see a child using a label to help spell a word or remember the name of a classroom object.

We also start the first day of school with a wall dictionary waiting to be filled with children's favorite words. The first words to be placed on the wall dictionary are the children's and teacher's names. Each day students are asked to choose words from books we are reading or topics we are studying to add to the dictionary. In kindergarten, these wall dictionary cards also have a picture of the object on them so that children can identify the words. Student name cards are adorned with a photograph of the student. It is amazing how quickly and painlessly children develop an awareness of the relationship between letters of the alphabet and their sounds. A frequent comment is something like, "Esa palabra comienza como *Maribel*. Comienza con la *m*." (This word starts like *Maribel*. It starts with an *m*.) Soon children begin to keep dictionaries of their own, entering words that are interesting and important to them. Name cards are not restricted to the wall dictionary but are used in many ways, especially during the first weeks of school. They are worn around children's necks, used to make lists and to label places to sit and work.

As new songs and poems are introduced, the words are put on colorful charts and displayed throughout the room. Once students are familiar with the words, we use the charts to read as we recite or sing. Children are frequently observed using the charts to generate ideas for a journal entry or a new book or to check for the correct spelling of a word. They also enjoy standing in front of the charts and reading the words when they have finished a task early.

In the older grades, the wall dictionary becomes a wall thesaurus. Students are very enthused about finding synonyms in their literature books and in their units of study that they can add to the thesaurus. Poetry and song charts reflecting the current theme fill the room. Other good sources of authentic print include recipes, graphs, lists, jokes, student-authored materials, comic books, magazines, maps, ads, signs, newspapers, etc.

In all the Immersion classrooms a variety of students' work is displayed. Units of study can be easily identified from the process writing books, book reports, projects, etc., that adorn the rooms. The print-rich environment helps children to internalize language structure and new vocabulary. This is equally important for both language minority and language majority students; particularly for those children who have had limited exposure to literacy in the home environment.

READING

Reading to Students

Reading aloud to students is a daily activity; it exposes them to good literature they cannot yet read for themselves. It teaches them structures of language and areas of knowledge they cannot yet acquire through reading independently. Additionally, it familiarizes learners with a variety of moods and styles. This activity continues throughout the grades.

Spanish Literacy in the Early Years

A wide variety of materials are used at the reading center. In kindergarten and first grade, most of our activities center around Big Books and predictable books. Big Books allow children to see the text and join in a choral reading with the teacher until they are gradually able to read the text without the assistance of the teacher. We use smaller copies of the same story for more independent reading. Big Books are read again and again. Detailed teacher-student dialogues take place when children are familiar with a particular story. We also incorporate the Creative Reading Method as proposed by Alma Flor Ada (1986).

As children are able to read the book independently, we talk about the strategies they used to figure out what was coming next or what the text said. We utilize many extension activities such as an oral cloze activity. The next step may be a written cloze task where several words are deleted from the text and must be filled in by children. At first we do this together on the chalkboard, but later children work with individual copies of the text. As they become familiar with the activity, it is fun to try to change the story by adding new words that make sense in the spaces.

Many of the Big Books are predictable in nature as are the majority of the other books we use at the kindergarten and first-grade levels. Predictable books are characterized by rhyme, rhythm, repetition of vocabulary, familiar content and story structure, and cyclical sequencing. We discuss what "helped" them read the book and children readily discover that the repetitive language pattern and picture clues assisted them in reading. They soon begin to match up printed words with their voices and notice letter/sound correspondences.

As we choose words from these books to place in the wall dictionary, students begin to pay more and more attention to the alphabet and its relationship to the reading process. By putting the text on sentence strips to manipulate in the pocket chart, we are able to help children discover the phonetic relationships needed to read that particular text. Although we do not teach phonics in an isolated fashion, children are quick to discover sound/symbol relationships in the context of a motivating story.

Predictable books also provide the setting to study such elements of literature as cause and effect, problem and solution, and lists and sequences. These kinds of discussions are usually not introduced until children are very familiar with a number of different predictable stories. Children never seem to tire of these books because the vocabulary is not controlled for readability as it is in most basal readers, nor is the language stilted. Predictable books encourage a reader's meaning-based interaction with a text from the very first reading experience while the reader begins to generalize about the phonetic similarities between words in a natural and meaningful manner.

After learning to read a predictable story, students often create their own variations of the book based on similar language structures. They also use the books as resources for their own writing—locating words and phrases they need for a particular piece. We make many class books in which each child contributes a page based on the pattern of a familiar book. These books are bound and placed in the classroom library where they are read time and time again.

A very important component of our program is the process of having students make their own books. In the early grades they usually make a copy of most of the books we read at the reading table so that they will have a collection of books in Spanish to be read and enjoyed at home. Both students and their families have enjoyed this aspect of the program. One parent of a kindergarten student reported that every night at bedtime her child insisted on reading a book that she had made in class. Reading her own version of a classroom book to her mother became a nightly ritual that they both looked forward to and enjoyed.

We also create a lot of our own books to be used with children in the early grades when trade books are not available or appropriate for our needs. This is especially true at the kindergarten level. For example, the first kindergarten books focus on skills such as tracing, cutting, pasting, and coloring and on developing students' vocabulary of common nouns, adjectives, and color concepts. The basic sentence structure of the beginning series of books is simple and repetitive so that students become familiar with it quickly and can predict the text easily—*La manzana es roja* ("The apple is red"). Each page of the book involves a number of carefully designed activities that ground the vocabulary and concepts in hands-on, sensory experiences for students. *Manzana* ("apple") becomes part of the child's daily vocabulary when she/he has had the opportunity to taste, touch, and smell it and to use the word in a variety of contexts. At the art table the child has made apple prints in paint. At the math center she/he has made patterns with combinations of green and red apples. At another station she/he has planted an apple seed and learned how apple trees grow. At whole group time she/he has participated with the class in making apple graphs comparing size differences. She/he has been reading stories about apples and apple trees. In this way the curriculum is designed in layers, with each new layer reinforcing and building on previously taught concepts, vocabulary, and skills. For children to experience success in reading, they must be able to predict text and be familiar with the vocabulary on the page.

We have designed many books using the words of songs and rhymes that utilize particular skills (such as memory, number sequencing, color, and number words) or that complement a curricular unit of study. We are also careful to build specific language structures into our books and curriculum so that children can practice them in a natural manner. The possibilities are endless and children are always elated to take their treasured books home after the class has had ample opportunity to enjoy them.

Literature Studies

Beginning in kindergarten, we also choose several titles of quality literature with genuine plots and rich, aesthetic language to complement each unit of study. In the early grades, these books may be too difficult for some children to read independently, but the primary goal of our literature studies is to develop a love of reading and also a love of books. In literature studies we involve students in comparing and contrasting literature to their own experiences. Students live in the author's world by choosing a piece of literature to read independently and later study in small groups. Students analyze and critique components of literature such as style, character, setting, theme, symbolism, and plot. The teacher is a participant, empowering children by valuing their knowledge and opinions. The emphasis is on enjoying literature and examining the author's craft, not on developing isolated reading skills.

At the kindergarten and first-grade levels we find that children love to listen to the stories on headphones and read along in individual copies of the book. They enjoy listening to the same story many times. Children respond to the literature in many ways. They make story maps, rewrite the endings, describe their favorite characters, describe and illustrate their favorite parts, convert the stories into plays or puppet shows, write letters to the author, and relate the stories to events in their own lives.

As children progress through the grade, they choose pieces of literature to read independently and later study in small groups. The selection of titles usually reflects the themes of study in the classroom (i.e., fairy tales, Native American legends, immigration, etc.).

A favorite activity among the older children is to cooperatively decide how they will present their piece to the rest of the class or other classes. Their ideas are endless: plays, puppet shows, television shows, mobiles, dioramas, versions of Big Books, etc. Students create their own scripts and any props needed for the presentation. They cooperatively decide who will take what role and are responsible for putting the presentation together from beginning to end.

For the past several years we have been developing an extensive Spanish core literature list. Our literature selections represent a wide range of reading levels, genres, cultural values, and human values. At each level we may include books written in repetitive, rhythmic language, as well as books with rich, complex language structures. As children get older we include as many works as possible that were originally written in the Spanish language in a wide range of Spanish-speaking countries in addition to the translated classics of children's literature.

WRITING

Children need to be immersed in writing just as they are immersed in reading. Children desire to and think they can write from a very young age. We expect children to write from the very first day of kindergarten. Children are encouraged to spell creatively. The development of the writing process may progress from linear scribbles to combinations of letters, symbols, and numbers, to letters in random order, to experiments with creative spelling, followed by the first standard spellings, and then to standard spellings not represented by speech sounds. Each child progresses at a different pace and may skip some of these stages entirely.

Interactive Journal Writing

Beginning in kindergarten, each child keeps a journal to which the teacher responds on a daily basis. Students record their thoughts, ideas, experiences, and messages and the teacher responds to the content rather than to the structure or form. The journal is a daily interaction between child and teacher, and ultimately very personal thoughts are shared. In the primary grades the entries may begin with one-word entries copied off the walls such as *caballo* accompanied by a picture of a horse. They progress to things like *un cabayo cafe* (un caballo café—a brown horse). Naturally, as they begin to invent their own spellings rather than copy print from the room environment, we see more words misspelled, as this entry by a native Spanish speaker illustrates: "oY FuiAl m A r iNAbE so Lo Nos AviA co mNAdAr." (Yo fui al mar y nadé solo. No sabía como nadar.—I went to the ocean. I swam alone. I didn't know how to swim.) It is not uncommon in these early entries to find entire journals filled with familiar sentence structure such as "A mí me gusta el gato" (I like the cat), "A mí me gusta la naranja" (I like the orange), "A mí me gusta la pelota" (I like the ball), etc.

It pays to be patient because many children rapidly acquire the skills and the confidence to share very meaningful messages. Many children begin to record daily events such as "Hoy fimos a la bibbotka." (Hoy fuimos a la biblioteca.—Today we went to the library.) One disappointed child wrote, "Hoy era el dia de paletas pero yo no gare una paleta porque la mayestra no los dío la nota." (Hoy era el día de paletas pero yo no agarré una paleta porque la maestra no nos dio la nota.—Today was the Popsicle day but I didn't get a Popsicle because the teacher did not give us the notes.)

Even nonnative speakers soon begin to use their journals as a place to share their innermost feeling, as evidenced by this first-grade entry: "Mi mama esta en el hospytal. Le dwele la espalda. Yo voy a la casa de Lauren prque mi mama esta en el hospytal. Yo no ciero ir. Ciero ir con mi mama. Yo y mi papa y mi ermana van a visitar mi mama. No puetho espar." (Mi mamá está en el hospital. Le duele la espalda. Yo voy a la casa de Lauren porque mi mamá está en el hospital. Yo no quiero ir. Quiero ir con mi mamá. Yo y mi papá y mi hermana vamos a visitar a mi mamá. No puedo esperar.—My mother is in the hospital. Her back hurts. I am going to Lauren's house because my mother is in the hospital. I don't want to go. I want to go with my mother. My father and I and my sister are going to visit my mother. I can't wait.)

We find it very helpful to keep class journals to record what we have studied or done in class. This helps children at early stages of writing to grasp the idea of recording thoughts and events. As approximately half of our students are learning to read and write in their second language, it is even more important to keep the focus on meaning, enabling young readers to make sense of the world around them.

Journal Entries

un dia yo fui al zoo. Yo vi un coneJos y un león. yo vi un caballo yo vi un toro. yo vi unamariposa yo vi una aralla. Yo vi un hago. Me gusta mucho el zoo. (Un día yo fui al zoo. Yo vi un conejo y un león. Yo vi un caballo. Yo vi un toro. Yo vi una mariposa. Yo vi una araña. Yo vi un chango. Me gusta mucho el zoo.)

(One day I went to the zoo. I saw a rabbit and a lion. I saw a horse. I saw a bull. I saw a butterfly. I saw a spider. I saw a monkey. I like the zoo.)

Native Spanish Speaker—First Grade

PROMOTING BILITERACY

oY FuiAl m   A r iNAbE so   Lo Nos AviA
co mNAdA r

(Yo fui al mar y nadé solo. No sabía como nadar.)
(I went to the ocean. I swam alone. I didn't know how to swim.)

Native Spanish Speaker—Kindergarten

Yo tiengo una prima y. Ella NO ES MUY BUENA ELlA TIRO
MIS JUGETES Y
ROMPIO MI CAMA

(Yo tengo una prima y ella no es muy buena. Ella tiró mis juguetes y rompió mi cama.)
(I have a cousin and she is not very good. She threw my toys and ripped by bed.)

Native English Speaker—First Grade

Hoy en mi grupo yo vas a ser una corazon y tienes mi nombre en la corazon y tienes que trazar mi nombre con pegadura y luego vaz a poner gliter en mi nombre y luego yo vaz aponer decorazaiones.

(Hoy en mi grupo yo voy a ser un corazón y voy a tener mi nombre en el corazón. Tengo que trazar mi nombre con pegadura y luego voy a poner gliter en mi nombre y luego yo voy a poner decoraciones.)

(Today in my group I am going to be a heart and I will have my name in a heart. I have to trace my name with glue and later I will put glitter on my name and later I will put decorations on it.)

Native English Speaker—First Grade

I like Oregon. Everything is so green and beautiful. The air smells so clean. If you go walking on a trail you will see and hear birds and lots of other animals. If you go to the ocean you will see alot of clear blue water. You will smell salt in the air. That is why I like Oregon.

Native English Speaker—Fourth Grade

Process Writing

Beginning in first grade, we utilize the Process Writing approach advocated by Donald Graves (1983), which allows children to acquire writing skills by engaging in activities that utilize writing as a communicative tool. Our teachers assume the role of facilitator, guiding students through a process where they generate ideas, receive a response to their work, revise and edit successive drafts, and participate in postwriting activities that enable them to share their work with an authentic audience (i.e., publishing a book or report, mailing a letter, etc.). Of course, at the first-grade level the revision and editing process is greatly simplified and the teacher serves as the final editor.

Most of the direct teaching of skills occurs during the revisions of student writing and the editing of final drafts. Children are encouraged to write for content without focusing too much on mechanics in their first drafts. They have learned that things like grammar, spelling, and punctuation will be addressed during the editing stage. Errors are viewed as valuable tools that give teachers insights into where the children are in their development as writers. We look for the logic behind the errors and patterns in the errors that serve as the basis for individual, small group, and/or whole group minilessons. As children progress through the grades, daily minilessons focus on more complex literary elements such as order, detail, lead, voice, point of view, etc. The teachers often use samples of student drafts or journal entries as a starting point for group revision.

The importance of minilessons at the editing stage is intensified in the Immersion classroom. The teacher continually needs to provide guidance and instruction in language forms as well as spelling and punctuation. Classroom peers are wonderful resources when it comes to helping students recognize and correct second language learner errors. As children begin formal literacy in English, they have many questions about the structural differences between Spanish and English that can be addressed during the editing of their own pieces.

We have found that it is important for young writers to publish often. At first we publish every piece a child writes to help develop a sense of the audience, as well as accomplishment. Soon children are able to select their favorite pieces for publication.

Each child's work is kept organized in a writing folder, which has proven to be a valuable tool for the teacher and child alike. It provides the child with a visible collection of his or her best ideas and fosters a strong sense of accomplishment. The writing folder also serves as a valuable record of the child's progress to share with parents. Additionally, it provides the teacher with a record of a year's development from which to discover problems and assess needs.

We are always absolutely astounded by the energy, joy, and determination we witness in our students as they work each day at the writer's workshop. All children are able to participate, sharing a small part of what was important and meaningful to them with each word. Even those at the very beginning stage of invented spelling approach the craft of composing with confidence. English-speaking students often seek help with vocabulary from their Spanish-speaking peers, yet the same children are often able to help others with spelling. In the first-grade Immersion classrooms we see many first drafts full of nonnative speaker errors like "Mi tío pescaste tres peces." (Mi tío pescó tres peces.—My uncle caught three fish.) However, they provide the perfect focal point for a minilesson during conferencing. It is truly amazing how often children help each other correct such errors without any teacher intervention. Children take their role as writers very seriously and create a nurturing atmosphere for others.

Process Writing Samples

Había una vez dos pandas muy enamorados. Uno se llama Janet y el otro se llama Rudy. Un día fueron a la feria y Rudy le pregunta a Janet si se queria casar y Janet te contesto - ¡sí! ¡claro que sí! El siguiente día se casaron y para su luna de miel fueron a Hawie y en Hawie fueron a nadar. Janet traia un biquini muy bonito y Rudy tenia un short muy bonito.

(Once upon a time there were two pandas who were very much in love. One was named Janet and the other was named Rudy. One day they went to the fair and Rudy asked Janet if she wanted to get married and Janet answered him, "yes, definitely I do!" The next day they got married and for their honeymoon they went to Hawaii and in Hawaii they went swimming. Janet brought a very pretty bikini and Rudy had on very nice shorts.)

Native Spanish Speaker—Fourth Grade

Despues que compro un crete que tenia pistola se fue a un planeta que se llama Micka. Se fue cuando luego vio que los dinosaurios eran muy grande muy

muy pero muy grande. El fue porque dijeron que pudia agarar dinero rapido. El choco en el el suerlo y los pedasos de sacate eran gigante. "¿Donde estan los dinosaurios?" Bume "!un temblor"! grito pero solo via un pie. El supio en ella asi pudria ire mas rapido y quesas ver a donde va a ire. Qisase va a vere donde esta y como ira a otro planeta. Otra ves su crete se fue muchuca de los pies del grande gigantesca muy muy pero muy grande asi fue.

(Later he bought a rocket that had a pistol in it and he went to the planet called Micka. He left when later he saw that the dinosaurs were very big very, very but very big. He went because he was told that he could get money quickly. He crashed into the ground and the even the pieces of grass were huge. "Where were the dinosaurs?" Bume yelled "an earthquake!" but it was only a footstep. He climbed back in so that he could go more quickly and perhaps see where it was going to go. Perhaps he would see where he was and how to go to another planet. Again, his rocket went into the feet of a great giant very, very, but very big—that's how it was.)

Native English Speaker—Fifth Grade

DEVELOPING ENGLISH LITERACY

In kindergarten through second grades, we focus on oral language development in English. We do not separate language minority and language majority students for instruction. We have discovered that children acquire a tremendous amount of language through interaction with their peers and are more likely to develop positive cross-cultural relations when they work and learn together.

As with our Spanish instruction, we meld sheltered language techniques with the use of complex language appropriate for native speakers. We choose language goals for our language minority students and then use many interesting mediums to immerse students in comprehensible oral language. We include many books off the district's English core literature list so that children begin to develop story schemata and acquire story language in English. This contributes to an easier transition into English literacy.

In third grade we introduce children to interactive journal writing in English. Sometimes we encounter resistance from a few third-grade students when they are first given a blank journal designated for writing in English.

We do daily editing exercises by lifting excerpts from students' journal entries to revise and edit as a class. This enables us to focus on errors that are universal, as well as individual needs. It provides the perfect setting for minilessons on English spelling, grammar, punctuation rules, and opportunities to work on voice and style. The following journal entry by a native English speaker is a perfect piece to use for a minilesson on capitalization: "This Saturday my friends Bernadette, Alexandria and I are going to 'great America' for my Birhday party. They are going to spend the night friday and in the morning were going to go. My sister is bringing a friend to come too. I have bin to 'great America' before but Alexandria has'nt." This next journal entry by a native Spanish speaker was publicly recognized as a good beginning example of descriptive writing and served to motivate many children to experiment with descriptive writing: "My worst vacation was when we went to México. The time that I spent ther was on my 6th birthday. We went to México D.F.. The air was pouluted. I could smell the smok. The sky looked dark. I cuold fell the hard wind on my face. The sound of cars racing and beping at each other hurt my ears. I could almost tast the dust the cars left behind."

The third graders also participate in literature studies in English. We do not use "watered-down" or simplified texts but rather choose quality pieces of literature that might be found on any third-grade core literature list. Strategies such as choral reading, cooperative learning, and peer partners build confidence and encourage risk taking.

In fourth and fifth grades, children are able to participate in all of the same literacy activities in English that they do in Spanish. Spelling and punctuation are still areas of weakness for children and are emphasized through process writing and other authentic literacy experiences. We have found that it is important not to replicate activities in each language. For example, while students are writing historical biographies in Spanish, we might focus on poetry in English. Children also receive some subject matter instruction in the intermediate grades.

Promoting Literacy in the Home

Dr. Alma Flor Ada has worked with our district in training our teachers in how to implement the "Padres, Niños, y Libros" (Parents, Children, and Books) program. Many of our parents and children have become authors through the influence of this program. Parents are led through the process of reading and discussing a piece of children's literature to help them in working with their children. Parents who cannot read are able to listen to the story and retell it to their children using the illustrations.

Next, parents write a book together around a variety of topics such as "Consejos para nuestros hijos" (Advice for our children), "Nuestros sueños para nuestros hijos y como podemos ayudarles para que se lleven a cabo" (Our dreams for our children and how we help them to realize them), and "Nuestros recuerdos" (Our memories). By putting parents' statements and ideas on chart paper in front of the group and later transcribing it on the computer and publishing it in book form, these parental thoughts are validated and recognized for the golden pieces of wisdom and poetry that they are. Here are the words of one father describing his dreams for his children:

> "Yo deseo que mis hijas prosperen en sus estudios para que ayuden a toda la comunidad. Voy a apoyarlas—tener más atención y escucharlas. También tener cuidado con ellas para que hagan su trabajo en la casa." (I want my girls to prosper in their studies so that they can help the whole community. I am going to support them by giving them more attention and listening to them. Also, I will care for them so that they can do schoolwork at home.)

To encourage parents to continue the process of writing books with their children, we have developed a home learning kit called "La caja de aprendizaje." The home learning kit contains a tape recorder, book/tape sets of children's literature, blank tapes, crayons, scissors, construction paper, writing paper, glue, pencil, eraser, blank books for writing stories, etc. Parents check out the kit and receive training on how to use it with their children. They also receive guidance on a variety of activities that they have the materials to experiment with. We publish, bind, and distribute all of the books that parents and their children write to all of the families who are participating and to each kindergarten through third-grade Immersion classroom. Teachers read the books in the class and put them in their libraries. Children and their families are authors who are recognized and encouraged by their peers.

Padres, Niños, y Libros and the home learning kit component are a vital part of supporting parents in their quest to develop their own and their children's literacy skills. We continually work with families to challenge them to creatively undertake the task of writing books with their children. We motivate parents to record and share their childhood and experiences with their children in this way. Many families ask for multiple copies of their books so that they can send them to their families in Mexico. The history, tradition, and "oro" of the family is preserved and is utilized as a tool to promote literacy in the home and to enrich the classroom.

Parents who have participated in the Parent Education Program have asked us to provide parent literacy training. We hold biweekly ESL classes on the school site and provide child care and transportation so that parents can attend. The child's school becomes the parent's school also. Parents are models for their children of how education is an important part of their lives and the children tell all of their friends that their parents come to school here, too!

Conclusion

> **Never doubt that a small group of thoughtful committed citizens can change the world. Indeed it's the only thing that ever has.**
>
> —Margaret Mead

These words have been an inspiration for the parents and teachers who have worked together in a partnership to develop and implement the Two-Way Immersion Program. Our vision is global:

Un mundo sano donde hay armonía y cada persona se siente que puede alcanzar sus metas y sueños en una sociedad que valore la diversidad cultural y la igualdad.

A healthy, harmonious world where all people are empowered to pursue their dreams and goals in a society that values cultural diversity and equality. Our mission is challenging:

Asegurarnos de que existan oportunidades sin límites en el futuro de nuestros hijos uniendo a los padres y maestros, como socios, para crear un sistema educacional que:

- promueva excelencia académica, igualdad y responsabilidad en la comunidad;
- abra las puertas a la diversidad lingüística y cultural;
- valore el desarrollo personal, la felicidad y la autoestimación;
- inspire a todos a luchar por sus ideales.

To ensure that boundless opportunities exist in our children's future by empowering parents and teachers, as partners, to create an educational system that:

- promotes academic excellence, equality, and community responsibility;
- welcomes cultural and linguistic diversity;
- values personal development, happiness, and self-esteem;
- inspires all individuals to strive for their ideals.

As teachers, we dedicate ourselves to adopting a clear vision of the kind of society and individuals we want to develop. We challenge each of you to empower yourselves and your students by critically examining your curriculum, your interactions with students and their families, and especially the types of interactions your school encourages among students. By committing ourselves to effecting change, we can create an educational system that promotes optimum achievement, the ability to think critically and generate new ideas, and an understanding and appreciation for the diverse peoples of our society in all our students.

We are no longer naive about the commitment or struggle that is involved in fostering this type of program, philosophy, and environment. There are many elements of the system that oppress our children, our teachers, and especially the minority members of our community. We have seen the flag of racism raised high and propelled on the chilling winds of fear and anger. There have been many times when we have had to make tough personal decisions about whether or not it was worth it to keep going. In those moments, we have reaffirmed our vision and taken strength from the words of Albert Einstein, "Great spirits have always encountered violent opposition from mediocre minds." For if our program has nothing else, it has great spirit!

As for our thoughts about the wonders of creating bilingual, biliterate students in our educational system we would like to share this story related by one of our teachers, Ginger Dale. Like most of our Immersion teachers she has her own children enrolled in the program. She was listening one day while her son and two of his Immersion friends were playing a game of superheroes, and each had to decide what power he would possess. One said he would be the strongest in the universe and the rest agreed. One said that he would be able to become invisible and the rest agreed. The last child said that he would be able to speak all the languages of the world. The two others chimed in, **"No, that's not fair. That's too powerful."**

ABOUT THE AUTHORS

Jennifer Martinez and *Julie A. Moore-O'Brien,* Bilingual/Immersion teachers, are cofounders (with Ginger Dale) of the Windsor School District's Two-Way Spanish Immersion Program—recipient of the Jack London Award for Academic Excellence (1989) sponsored by Sonoma State University, California Faculty Association and California Teachers Association/NEA; the Sonoma County Merit for Outstanding Education Practices (1989); the Hispanic Chamber of Commerce Award for Educational Practices Promoting Excellence for Minority Students (1990); and the California Association for Bilingual Education (CABE) Award for Exemplary Practices in Elementary Education (1991). They are coauthors (with Ginger Dale) of the manual and video entitled "How to Plan and Implement a Two-Way Spanish Immersion Program," available through the Foreign Language Department of the California State Department of Education. Jennifer earned her M.A. in Multicultural Education and is currently a first-grade Immersion teacher. Julie is currently the coordinator of the district's Even Start Family Education Program.

REFERENCES

Ada, A. F. (1986, November). Creative education for bilingual teachers. *Harvard Educational Review*, vol. 56, no. 4.

Cummins, J. (1989). *Empowering minority students.* Sacramento: California Association for Bilingual Education.

Cummins, J. (1985). *Special needs in French immersion.* Paper presented at Canadian Parents for French Annual Conference, Whitehorse, Canada.

Dale, G., Moore, J., and Reynolds, J. (1989). *How to plan and implement a two-way Spanish immersion program.* Title II Federal Grant administered by the California Post Secondary Education Commission and the California State Department of Education.

Genesee, F. (1985, Winter). Second language learning through immersion: A review of U.S. programs. *Review of Education Research*, vol. 55, no. 4., pp. 541–61.

Graves, D. (1983). *Writing: Teachers and children at work.* Portsmouth, NH: Heinemann Educational Books.

Lambert, W. E. (1987). The effects of bilingual and bicultural experiences on children's attitudes and social perspectives. In Homel, P., Paliz, M., and Aaronson, D. (Eds.), *Childhood bilingualism: Aspects of linguistics, cognitive and social development.* Hillsdale, NJ: Lawrence Erlbaum Associates, Publishers.

Lindholm, K. J. (1989). *Student progress after two years in a Bilingual Immersion program.* Paper presented at the 1989 14th annual CABE Conference, Anaheim, California.

Supporting and Encouraging Diversity: *Literacy Learning for All*

Diane Lapp, James Flood, and Nancy Farnan
San Diego State University

Teachers do not enter their classrooms at the beginning of the school year with the expectation of educating only a few of their students. On the contrary, they approach each year with the belief that they will be able to create an environment that will support learning for every student. The accomplishment of this goal is becoming increasingly complex since students, as a group, are more linguistically and culturally diverse than ever before in the history of education (García, 1990).

This ever-changing, dynamic, and complex nature of today's schools and school populations requires careful and continuous evaluation if effective curriculum and instruction are to be designed for all students. Educational practices cannot be justified on the basis of tradition. Instead, the changing nature of the school population and the challenges that these changes represent for teachers must be examined thoroughly.

Diversity in the Classroom

You may have twenty-five students, fifteen native-English speakers, the rest non-English speakers. This means that you must meet the needs of many types and levels of students . . . students who can understand the language and keep up with the mandated curriculum, and your ESL students, who may or may not have any English at all, who may or may not know how to read. (Law & Eckes, 1990 p. 1)

The challenge is implicit but clear. Educators must understand the nature of the complexities represented by the diversity in classrooms, specifically linguistic diversity, which cannot be separated from cultural diversity. This linguistic diversity is represented by at least 100 separate language groups in the United States who are acquiring English as a second language. Included are students who:

1. have substantial interaction within a non-English-speaking social environment;

2. function fluently within that environment; and

3. are at the same time expected to function within a predominately English-speaking setting in school (García, 1990).

Another way to think about the diverse nature of classrooms today is to examine the five categories of students in schools throughout the country whose native-language backgrounds are something other than English. While these categories emerged from a study of the 1980 census data (Waggoner, 1984), they appear to be relevant to the study of classrooms of this decade. These categories, which can be described according to the following language characteristics, are useful in that they provide another perspective on the complexity inherent in language minority populations. The five categories are:

1. non-English-speakers who do not speak a second language;

2. non-English speakers who speak their native language in addition to a second language, which is not English (6.9 percent total for categories 1 and 2);

3. children who are non-English-speakers at home but who speak English as a second language (36.7 percent);

4. those who speak some English at home but who also speak a second language (40.5 percent); and

5. those who are from a language minority background but also speak English at home and who do not know the language of their background (15.9 percent).

Figure 1 illustrates the percentages.

Notice on Figure 1 that approximately 44 percent of students described as being from the minority language population (Categories 1–3) speak a language other than English in their home and social environments, while 56 percent speak English (Categories 4 and 5) but are from a language minority background and are identified by formal testing procedures as limited English proficient. These percentages reflect current proportions of students in several states throughout the country.

An additional way to think about the expanse of this linguistic diversity is to examine further the report by Waggoner (1984), which while based on 1980 census data appears to be quite current. She reported that, nationally, one child in every ten was acquiring English as a second language. While this constitutes a significant proportion of the school-aged population, these children were not then or now distributed equally across the country. For example, in New Mexico, students acquiring English represented one third of the school population, with similarly large proportions residing in Arizona, Colorado, California, and Texas.

Based on 1990 statistics from the California Department of Education, out of a total K–12 enrollment of 4,950,474 children in public schools, 54.4 percent, or 2,691,157, were students acquiring English as a second language. To simplify the numbers, let's imagine that in 1990 the total school-child population in California was 100 stu-

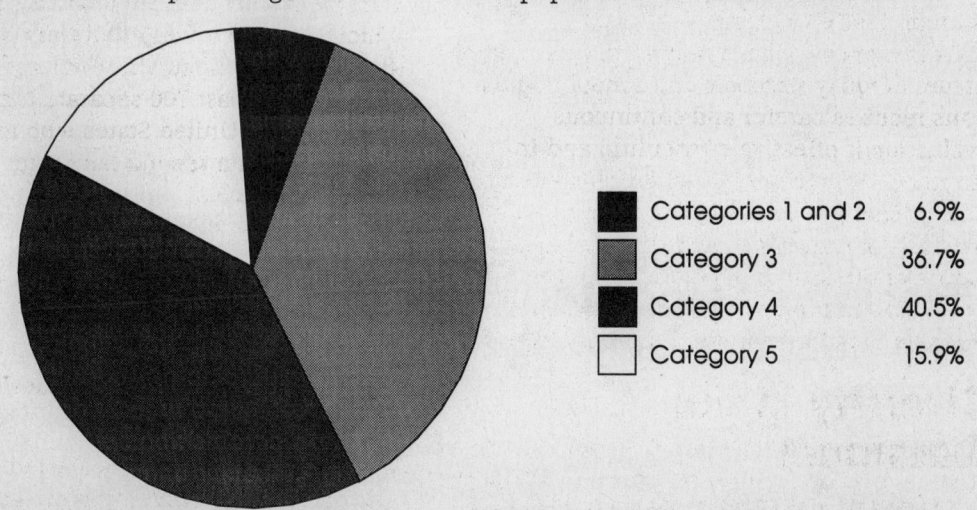

■	Categories 1 and 2	6.9%
▨	Category 3	36.7%
■	Category 4	40.5%
□	Category 5	15.9%

Figure 1 *Categories of Language Backgrounds: Data from 1980 Census*

dents. Out of that 100, approximately 45 would be Caucasian, 34 Hispanic, 9 African American, 8 Asian American, 2 Filipino, 1 American/Alaskan Indian, and 1 Pacific Islander. How many of these children would have the complex task of learning in school settings through a second language they were simultaneously acquiring? Answering this question raises many issues for the development of appropriate curriculum and effective instruction.

The complexity of this linguistic diversity, which is common in many classrooms, can be further examined by looking at the native language backgrounds that are represented among these students. Based on projections for the year 2000, which is almost the present, these languages are as follows (Development Associates, 1984):

Native Language Backgrounds	%
Spanish	77
Southeast Asian (e.g., Cambodian, Vietnamese, Hmong)	8
German, French, and other European languages	5
East Asian (e.g., Korean, Chinese)	5
Other (e.g., Arabic, Navajo)	5

Now almost a decade after these projections were made, they appear to have become a reality.

Of course, understanding the range of diversity is not enough. One must also understand principles of language learning if effective instruction for all students acquiring English proficiency is to be a realistic goal.

Principles Associated with Effective Language Learning

In this section, we explore principles/themes that are critical for learning in the context of the heterogeneity just described.

Although there are multiple ways to talk about basic principles related to language learning, the focus here is only three, which will be discussed in terms of their relevance to each other and to language instruction.

Language is best learned when its use is purposeful and meaningful for the language user.

> Perhaps it is hard to believe that language had to be invented. Words seem to go with human beings, just as barking goes with dogs, and singing goes with birds.
> (F. Folsom, *The Language Book*, New York: Grosset and Dunlap, 1963)

When talking about instruction for students acquiring English (or, for that matter, for all students), the language used is often misleading. Educators refer to *teaching* English as a second language when, in fact, language is not taught. However, it must be *learned*. The distinction here between teaching and learning is not purely philosophical; it is real. As suggested by Folsom, language use is a natural part of the human condition, and it develops as children construct literacy understandings in situations where the language is natural, useful, and meaningful.

A critical concept is embedded in the word "construct." Ferreiro (1990) describes children's construction of literacy concepts in her idea of "interpretation systems," which are essentially theories children form about the nature and function of language. She states that "children's theories are not a pale mirror image of what they have been told. The theories are real constructions which, more often than not, seem very strange to our adult way of thinking" (Ferreiro, 1990, p. 14). For example, the theories often represent overgeneralizations due to lack of experience with a language, such as when the three year old smugly informs his brother that their mother "buyed" some candy only for him. According to Ferreiro's definition, then, these are not theories that teachers can give to students. Rather, they must be constructed by children as they internalize rules and refine their generalizations in the process of using and experimenting with the language.

When the focus is on meaning and when children are in situations where they interact with language users who provide language modeling and motivation for communication, language learners, whether learning in their native language or in a second language, begin to construct theories about the language. These theories represent concepts vital to communication, concepts that center on understanding the relationship between meaning and form.

Language is not learned according to selected skills presented through a prescribed sequence. Rather it is most effectively learned through communication.

> [I]t is language which helps people to cooperate. Language precedes, accompanies, and follows practically all human endeavors. Without this system of communication ninety-nine percent of all activity would cease. (E. Lambert, *The Story of the Words We Use*, New York: Lothrop, Lee & Shepard Co., 1955)

Reflecting on this quote helps one to realize that the primary purpose of language is communication, for as Emily Dickinson so aptly told us in 1872,

> *A Word is dead*
> *When It is said,*
> *Some say.*
>
> *I say it just*
> *Begins to live*
> *That day.*

Problems arise for students acquiring a second language when instructional emphasis is on knowing the structures and forms of language at the expense of language experimentation and communication. In order for a language to be useful, one must be able to understand clues such as those associated with semantics and context that make interpretation, thus language learning, possible. One must know when the language should be used, and where.

When language is used in natural, communicative contexts rather than for focusing primarily on the study of isolated phonemes, spelling lists, and grammatical elements, the learner experiences language in ways that support meaningful communication and language experimentation. For example, although it has been documented that second language learners tend to acquire certain language forms in an identifiable order (e.g., learning the "ing" ending on verbs before other inflectional endings, before the articles "a," "an," and "the," and so forth), the teaching of these forms in order, requiring mastery of one skill before moving on to others, is not the most effective method of instruction (Law & Eckes, 1990; Urzua, 1989).

When this hierarchical skill-based instruction is the primary focus of classroom language experiences, emphasis is on form to the neglect of function, or meaning. The learner is deprived of opportunities for real language use, use upon which such things as making friends, satifying hunger and thirst, and learning new things depend. Language forms can be studied more effectively once use of the language as a means of communication has been mastered.

Learning, whether in a first or second language, takes place most effectively in risk-free environments.

> It took me a long time to learn where he came from. The little prince, who asked so many questions, never seemed to hear the ones I asked him. It was from words dropped by chance that, little by little, everything was revealed to me. (Antoine de Saint-Exupéry, *The Little Prince*)

It is in risk-free environments that children are validated, rather than criticized, for being "close" and where experimentations are treated as evidence of and opportunities for learning. Such an environment allows children to learn language by sharing rather than merely to learn about language. It is through such sharing that their message, like that of the Little Prince, becomes known.

Nearly two decades ago, Rubin (1974) identified the following successful strategies used by second language learners. They still seem very appropriate today.

1. They are motivated to communicate.
2. They practice and monitor their language use and that of others.
3. They are problem solvers, as they attempt to communicate and interpret what has been communicated.

None of these strategies is accomplished without potential risk to the learner, the risk of making an error; and error making is only a problem when errors are viewed as defects or as a lack of learning.

It is instructive that "close" is applauded when individuals work to master other skills. When practicing a landing after a series of giant swings, a gymnast makes certain that the spotter is always ready; and each approximation of a well-executed landing is cause for praise and encouragement, as the gymnast comes closer and closer to "sticking" the landing in precise form. In addition, each landing that gets the gymnast safely on the ground provides its own feedback on the state of the skill development. The same is true in learning to ski, ride a surfboard, write, or master a language.

Practice and feedback are critical elements in language learning, as they are in mastering bicycle riding or windsurfing. The point is not that knowing form and structure of language is unimportant. The issue is that, as Law and Eckes (1990) state, "Communication comes first, then grammatical rules are learned as a part of learning to communicate effectively, not the other way around" (p. 48).

> "Well then," the cat went on, "you see a dog growls when it's angry and wags when it's pleased. Now I growl when I'm pleased and wag my tail when I'm angry. Therefore I'm mad."
>
> "I call it purring, not growling," said Alice.
>
> "Call it what you like," said the cat.
>
> (Lewis Carroll, *Through the Looking Glass*)

Close examination reveals certain themes associated with learning a language. One that is of primary significance when effective curriculum and instructional strategies are designed is that the focus of the situation must be the learner in a natural language setting. Children must be encouraged through experimentation to construct their own theories about using a language. Although teachers can give children insights about effective language structures and the relationship between form and function, effective language use is owned by learners who are encouraged to test what they know and to receive real-life feedback that lets them know whether they are being successful, and if necessary, use opportunities to revise their constructs.

Experimentation without achieving proficiency must not be punished as a fault or attributed to lack of intelligence. In natural and positive communicative contexts, feedback provided by modeling from others proficient in the language (e.g., teacher, peers, other adults, etc.), coupled with the learner's sense of whether the communication worked, highlights the fact that experimenting to acquire communication and language fluency is a learning process. Encouragement, not punishment, must accompany such experimentation.

In the remainder of this article we discuss strategies that will support teachers' endeavors to promote students' literacy development when English is their second language. Specifically, we will examine language-based strategies that support children's literacy and learning.

Literacy and Learning

Reading and writing are both processes in which children construct meaning based on their prior knowledge of language, themselves, and the world. Current research suggests that these processes function similarly for both first- and second-language learning. That is, both rely on prior knowledge for construction of meaning (Anderson and Pearson, 1984; Flood and Lapp,

1987; Pritchard, 1990), and both involve cueing systems to produce, predict, and confirm meaning (Cziko, 1980).

Also, language learning in a first language is not so different from learning in a second language. Almost all of the learner's knowledge about a first language can transfer positively to a second. This knowledge centers on the fact that language is symbolic, that it exists for communicative purposes, and that it adheres to certain rules of phonology, morphology, and syntax (Hakuta, 1985).

Law and Eckes (1990) make the important point that "language learning is a balance between the learner and the language-learning environment, between 'input' and 'intake' " (p. 51). Input involves what learners actually encounter in the environment, most of which is in some way registered as sensory input. Intake, on the other hand, refers to how much learners actually process, understand, and acquire. The focus here, then, is on the learner who must, as we stated earlier, construct meaning in a new language, based on prior knowledge as it relates not only to the content but also as it relates to language itself. Although the focus is on the learner, the teacher is not an insignificant element in the language-learning situation. It is the teacher who can help ensure that the input is comprehensible and thus more accessible for intake. One way to do this is to make certain that students begin to make connections between speech and print. In order to learn a new language, learners must have sufficient vocabulary for the language to be useful.

Developing Language by Using Language

Sounds and symbols mean nothing unless people agree to use them as representations of objects and concepts. The use of language as a symbolic system is more than the manipulation of abstractions. Language is an habitual, even unconscious, response instead of something newly learned for each situation. Language is anchored in a set of shared conventions that must be understood if communication is to occur.

Mastery of language requires complex and sophisticated efforts. Language as communication is the one attribute that sets humans apart from all other creatures and bonds humans together across geographic barriers (Anderson & Lapp, 1987).

Communication is an interesting word. When two or more individuals have a successful communication, they share an understanding or feeling; normally this communication is an exchange of ideas grounded on a common basis of understanding. García spoke to the importance of language as a human attribute requiring explicit sharing when he stated that "the acquisition of language depends on the participation of both the learner and someone who already speaks the language—a friend" (García, 1990, p. 721).

Language is the foremost means of communicating most ideas and feelings. Samuel Taylor Coleridge captured the essence of this in his comment that "Language is the armory of the human mind; and at once contains the trophies of its past, and the weapons of its future conquests."

Creating environments that encourage students who are acquiring English as a second language to test the power of their language through thematically based oral language, reading, and writing experiences is the process used by teachers who encourage literacy learning for all students. Through such literacy experiences, students find that their language is only as limited as their own imaginations. Literacy experiences can occur through shared contexts and/or texts. The primary features of such experiences are:

1. authenticity of the task;

2. engagement of the student;

3. participation by the student; and

4. continuous performance evaluation of all dimensions of the situation by both the teacher and students.

A natural context for language/literacy learning that contains these four features is the environment of the classroom.

Language Learning Within an Environmental Context

One way to help students develop a workable vocabulary in a second language is through labels and classroom displays, which may be topically based. One topic that appropriately combines the language of the home and the school is *Environment*. Whether in elementary or secondary grades, students can make labels for environmental items in the classroom. If all students are acquiring English as a second language, games can be devised to help them remember the labels. For example, cards with words matching the labels can be handed out, and students can match their cards with items in the room. These words, names of common classroom items, become part of a student's sight and spoken vocabulary.

Print found outside the classroom can also be used to expand the second-language learner's environmental vocabulary. Students can regularly bring in a household item with print on it, then share it with the class, reading the print and explaining its meaning. The same sharing time can include advertisements and news articles of items and events that are of interest to them. Students at all grade levels can bring in ads for their favorite movies, the latest clothing, and their favorite cereal. They can also bring in articles about their favorite baseball team, recording group, or author. After sharing their ads and articles with the class, students can display them on a bulletin board or wall for all to read. Students should also be encouraged to copy and bring to class any words or texts from their environment that they would like to have the other students and the teacher help them more fully understand.

Literacy and Content Area Learning

Vocabulary development is especially critical when second-language students are studying specific content area information and concepts. Just as learning common words and phrases such as "Where is the bathroom?" and "When is lunch?" are important for social (and survival) purposes, the understanding of content area vocabulary is crucial for academic learning and successful school endeavors.

Students acquiring English face a tremendous task in mastering the vocabulary presented in content areas of study. It has been estimated that average students in grades three through twelve learn about 3,000 words each year (Nagy & Herman, 1987). As Graves, Slater, and White (1989) suggest, vocabulary learning should not be considered a single task. Rather, it should be considered a series of quite different tasks that vary according to the learner's knowledge of the words and concepts to be taught, the depth and precision of the meaning to be taught, and the extent to which learners are expected to incorporate the taught words into their productive vocabularies.

Learning in a content area requires an understanding of words and related concepts not commonly used in everyday life. For example, when studying transportation systems in third grade, students can brainstorm words that relate to the concept, such as *boats, trains, highways, airplanes, wheels, wagons,* and *taxis,* and relate the experiences they've had with these. As the unit of study progresses, they can add to the list. They can divide the words into categories, cut pictures out of magazines and newspapers to illustrate the words, share personal photographs of themselves using modes of transportation, and use the words to make a book in which they illustrate transportation systems and the effects transportation has had on their lives.

When studying photosynthesis in eighth grade, technical words such as *chlorophyll, sunlight, plants, leaves, cells,* and *carbon dioxide* must become part of the students' vocabularies if students are to have a complete understanding of the concept. One way to promote vocabulary development of this and other content areas is to combine the target words and explanations of concepts during experiments and natural language-based classroom experiences, such as sharing and discussing maps, tables, flow charts, and graphs.

As these examples illustrate, the sharing of personal and natural experiences related to content area topics provides a context that makes learning more meaningful. In addition, one critical resource available to teachers that encourages student engagement is literature, which can serve as the complementary curricular strand to content area learning. Dole and Johnson (1981) suggest that fiction books can be used to motivate students and to provide background for the investigation of science issues. However, Guerra and Payne (1981) caution that this is not their only function. Literary texts can also be used as a primary source if the information presented is conceptually accurate. Schatzberg (1987) expands this notion by illustrating that while works of fiction cannot always thoroughly clarify concepts that are addressed through other means, they can be part of the science curriculum by providing the actual factual and conceptual basis of a science lesson and encouraging the development of reader interests. Literature can be the motivating force that encourages students acquiring English to pursue additional means to clarify unfamiliar scientific concepts (Lapp & Flood, 1992).

Literature and Literacy Development

The challenge is to educate increasing numbers of linguistically and culturally diverse students. At the same time, there is a decline in the proportion of teachers representing the same diverse cultures (Carnegie Forum Report, 1992). Nevertheless, literacy development depends upon making the school environment relevant for all students, that is, making the language and cultural experiences of each child an integral part of the curriculum. One way to do this is to infuse classrooms with literature from many diverse cultures so that linguistically diverse students have opportunities to construct meaning and express their thoughts and ideas using their primary language and life experiences as an integral part of critical thinking and conceptual development.

All children have a need to belong, to be validated, to be recognized as unique while at the same time feeling success as a functioning part of the academic and social milieu. When children see that their cultural and linguistic identities are respected, the educational experience, the center of which is learning, becomes more satisfying.

Cullinan (1989) uses the metaphor of the window and mirror to illustrate the role literature plays in providing the validation, the feelings of belonging as well as feelings of uniqueness. Through the mirror, or the work of literature, children have opportunities to view situations, ways of living, and worlds outside of their immediate experiences. In doing so, they can see similarities as well as differences between themselves and others. As a mirror, a work of literature provides opportunities for children to reflect upon their own lives in the context of the similarities and differences between themselves and others. Through awareness of similarities, children develop a sense of belonging, a sense of their connectedness with other human beings, regardless of linguistic or cultural background. The differences, on the other hand, highlight the uniqueness of individuals and provide opportunities for that uniqueness to be honored.

Storybooks can be introduced in the classroom in multiple languages (Lapp, Flood, Tinajero & Nagel, 1992). For example, the teacher could read *Swimmie* by Leo Lionni, a book about a big fish that scares little fish until they decide to cooperate and swim together in order to create the illusion of size to intimidate the larger fish. The teacher, or perhaps a parent or child, could then read *Nadarín*, the Spanish version of the story. The two versions could be compared, with non-Spanish-speaking children learning English equivalent words and phrases. Both English- and Spanish-speaking children can respond in their journals in either English or Spanish. In one classroom where this experience occurred, a child in response to the question "How did the story make you feel?" replied in Spanish, "Me sentí triste al principio del cuento porque creí que un pez grande se iba a comer a los pecesitos" (I felt sad at the beginning of the story because I thought that a big fish was going to eat the little fish). Another child in English agreed that she felt the same way but it made her happy that the little fish were so smart that they outwitted the large fish. The children giggled in delight when another student commented that he would like to have one of the little fish for his birthday. Through reading, writing, and talking, children are recognized for their individual thoughts and insights, while at the same time they find that they share common thoughts and feelings with their peers.

Gary Soto's book *Baseball in April* is a very good example of a literary work that exemplifies the metaphors of both the window and mirror. It is a collection of short stories about growing up. The characters are streetwise and smart youngsters who happen to be Latino. For example, in "Broken Chain," Alfonso could be any teenager suffering from an inferiority complex over protruding, crooked teeth. He is like any seventh grader who worries about the impression he will make on a girl in his class.

Although Soto writes his stories in English, throughout he sprinkles Spanish words and phrases, which non-Spanish-speaking students delight in learning; and Spanish-speaking students delight in seeing and sharing their home language. For example, Soto writes, "And his father, who was 'puro Mexicano,' would sit in his chair after work sullen as a toad, and call him 'sissy.'" Students who speak Spanish can be in charge of sharing their knowledge of the language, explaining the meanings of the words and the contexts in which they are written.

Nonfiction literature can also help children from diverse cultures make connections with academic learning (Farnan, Flood, & Lapp, 1992). Nonfiction trade books can be motivating as well as fun to read. A fifth-grade student from Samoa may be fascinated with sharks because he knows they are plentiful in waters around the islands of his homeland. He would find Reed's *Sevengill: The Shark and Me,* a book about a diver at a marine park, and Sattler's *Sharks, the Super Fish*, which discusses what is known and raises questions about these fish, to be useful resources and enjoyable reading.

Literature can be combined with non-narrative texts to facilitate the introduction of complex issues (questions) in a manner that causes one to investigate and analyze them in order to understand a scientific phenomena. In addition, this encourages students to evaluate their notions and predictions.

In conclusion, the challenge of promoting the learning of all students is a reality today and will continue to be a reality for the future. If anything, the challenge will escalate as immigration patterns continue to bring non- or limited-English-speaking children into tomorrow's classrooms.

ABOUT THE AUTHORS

Dr. Diane Lapp, Professor of Reading and Language Development in the College of Education at San Diego State University, has taught in elementary and middle schools and has conducted field-based teacher preparation programs. She has served as a consultant, supervisor, and evaluator for public school reading programs throughout the United States and has coauthored with James Flood *Teaching Reading to Every Child* and *Teaching Students to Read*, two texts on reading and language instructional methods. Dr. Lapp has also coauthored a language arts methods text, *Language Skills in Elementary Education*. She is also one of the editors of *The Handbook of Research on Teaching the English Language Arts*, a joint IRA/NCTE venture published by Macmillan.

Dr. James Flood is a professor of Reading and Language Development at San Diego State University. He has taught in preschool, elementary, and secondary schools and has served as a Language Arts/Reading supervisor. He has also been a Fulbright scholar at the University of Lisbon in Portugal. He is currently involved in teacher preparation and research in language arts/reading. His recent publications include *The Handbook of Research on Teaching the English Language Arts*, coedited with Julie Jensen, Diane Lapp, and James Squire, and three textbooks for teachers, *Teaching Students to Read* and *Teaching Reading to Every Child*, both coauthored with Diane Lapp and published by Macmillan, and *Language and the Language Arts*, published by Prentice-Hall.

Nancy Farnan is an associate professor in the School of Teacher Education at San Diego State University who teaches courses in children's literature, English education, reading/language arts, and middle school education. Her work, which appears in such publications as *Journal of Reading, Writing Teacher, Reading and Writing Quarterly, National Reading Conference Yearbook*, and *The Reading Teacher*, includes research in writing and response-based approaches to literature and content area learning. In addition, she is coeditor of *Content Area Reading and Writing: Instructional Strategies* (Prentice-Hall) with James Flood and Diane Lapp.

References

Anderson, P., and Lapp, D. (1988). *Language skills in elementary education*, 4th ed. New York: Macmillan.

Anderson, R., and Pearson, P. D. (1984). A schema-theoretic view of basic processes in reading comprehension. In Pearson, P. D. (Ed.), *Handbook of reading research*, pp. 259–92. White Plains, NY: Longman.

Carnegie Forum Report (1992). *A nation prepared: Teachers for the 21st century*. New York: Carnegie Foundation.

Cullinan, B. (1989). *Literature and the child*. San Diego: Harcourt Brace Jovanovich.

Cziko, G. A. (1980). Language competence and reading strategies: A comparison of first- and second-language oral reading errors. *Language Learning*, vol. 30, pp. 101–16.

Development Associates (1984, December). *Final report: Descriptive study phase of the national longitudinal evaluation of the effectiveness of services for language minority limited English proficient students*. Arlington, VA: Author.

Dole, J., and Johnson, V. R. (1981, April). Beyond the textbook: Science literature for young people. *Journal of Reading*, vol. 24, pp. 578–82.

Farnan, N., Flood, J., and Lapp, D. (1992). Comprehending through reading and writing: Six research-based instructional strategies. In Pritchard, B., and Urbschat, K. (Eds.), *Kids come in all languages: Reading instruction for second language learners*. Newark, DE: International Reading Association.

Ferreiro, E. (1990). Literacy development: Psychogenesis. In Goodman, Y. (Ed.), *How children construct literacy: Piagetian perspectives*. Newark, DE: International Reading Association.

Flood, J., and Lapp, D. (1987). Reading and writing relations: Assumptions and directions. In Squire, J. P. (Ed.), *The dynamics of language learning: National conference on research in English*. Urbana, IL: ERIC Clearinghouse on Reading and Communication.

García, E. E. (1990). Educating teachers for language minority students. In Houston, W. R. (Ed.), *Handbook of research on teacher education*. New York: Macmillan.

Graves, M. F., Slater, W. H., and White, T. G. (1989). Teaching content area vocabulary. In Lapp, D., Flood, J., and Farnan, N. (Eds.), *Content area reading and learning: Instructional strategies*, pp. 214–24. Englewood Cliffs, NJ: Prentice-Hall.

Guerra, C. L., and Payne, D. B. (1981). Using popular books and magazines to interest students in general science. *Journal of Reading*, vol. 24, pp. 583–85.

Hakuta, K. (1985). *Mirror or language: The debate on bilingualism*. New York: Basic Books.

Lapp, D., and Flood, J. (1992). Science and literature: Can they be complementary curricular strands? In Cullinan, B. (Ed.), *Literature across the curriculum: Making it happen*. Newark, DE: International Reading Association.

Lapp, D., Flood, J., Tinajero, J., and Nagel, G. (1992). *Parents and teachers: Partners in developing literacy for multicultural students*. Unpublished manuscript. San Diego State University: School of Teacher Education.

Law, B., and Eckes, M. (1990). *More than just surviving: ESL for every classroom teacher*. Winnipeg, Canada: Peguis Publishers.

Nagy, W. E., and Herman, P. A. (1987). Depth and breadth of vocabulary knowledge: Implications for acquisition and instruction. In McKeown, M. G., and Curtis, M. E. (Eds.), *The nature of vocabulary acquisition*, pp. 19–35. Hillsdale, NJ: Erlbaum.

Pritchard, R. (1990). The effects of cultural schemata in reading processing strategies. *Reading Research Quarterly*, vol. 25, pp. 273–95.

Rubin, J. (1974). What the "good language learner" can teach us. *TESOL Quarterly*, vol. 9, pp. 41–51.

Schatzberg, W. (1987). The relations of literature and science: An annotated bibliography of scholarship, 1880–1980. *Modern Language Association of America*. Report No. ISBN-0-87352-172-2.

Urzua, C. (1989). I grow for a living. In Rigg, P., and Allen, V. G. (Eds.), *When they don't all speak English: Integrating the ESL student into the regular classroom*. Urbana, IL: National Council of Teachers of English.

Waggoner, D. (1984). The need for bilingual education: Estimates from the 1980 census. *NABE Journal*, vol. 8, pp. 1–14.